주한미군지위협정(SOFA)

서명 및 발효 5

주한미군지위협정(SOFA)

서명 및 발효 5

한국학술정보

| 머리말

미국은 오래전부터 우리나라 외교에 있어서 가장 긴밀하고 실질적인 우호 · 협력관계를 맺어 온 나라다. 6 · 25전쟁 정전 협정이 체결된 후 북한의 재침을 막기 위한 대책으로서 1953년 11월 한미 상호방위조약이 체결되었다. 이는 미군이 한국에 주둔하는 법적 근거였고, 그렇게 주둔하게 된 미군의 시설, 구역, 사업, 용역, 출입국, 통관과 관세, 재판권 등 포괄적인 법적 지위를 규정하는 것이 바로 주한미군지위협정(SOFA)이다. 그러나 이와 관련한 협상은 계속된 난항을 겪으며 한미 상호방위조약이 체결로부터 10년이 훌쩍 넘은 1967년이 돼서야 정식 발효에 이를 수 있었다. 그럼에도 당시 미군 범죄에 대한 한국의 재판권은 심한 제약을 받았으며, 1980년대 후반 민주화 운동과 함께 미군 범죄 문제가 사회적 이슈로 떠오르자 협정을 개정해야 한다는 목소리가 커지게 되었다. 이에 1991년 2월 주한미군지위협정 1차 개정이 진행되었고, 이후에도 여러 사건이 발생하며 2001년 4월 2차 개정이 진행되어 현재에 이르고 있다.

본 총서는 외교부에서 작성하여 최근 공개한 주한미군지위협정(SOFA) 관련 자료를 담고 있다. 1953년 한미 상호방위조약 체결 이후부터 1967년 발효가 이뤄지기까지의 자료와 더불어, 이후 한미 합동위원회를 비롯해 민 · 형사재판권, 시설, 노무, 교통 등 각 분과위원회의 회의록과 운영 자료, 한국인 고용인 문제와 관련한 자료, 기타 관련 분쟁 자료 등을 포함해 총 42권으로 구성되었다. 전체 분량은 약 2만 2천여 쪽에 이른다.

2024년 3월

한국학술정보(주)

| 일러두기

· 본 총서에 실린 자료는 2022년 4월과 2023년 4월에 각각 공개한 외교문서 4,827권, 76만 여 쪽 가운데 일부를 발췌한 것이다.

· 각 권의 제목과 순서는 공개된 원본을 최대한 반영하였으나, 주제에 따라 일부는 적절히 변경하였다.

· 원본 자료는 A4 판형에 맞게 축소하거나 원본 비율을 유지한 채 A4 페이지 안에 삽입하였다. 또한 현재 시점에선 공개되지 않아 '공란'이란 표기만 있는 페이지 역시 그대로 실었다.

· 외교부가 공개한 문서 각 권의 첫 페이지에는 '정리 보존 문서 목록'이란 이름으로 기록물 종류, 일자, 명칭, 간단한 내용 등의 정보가 수록되어 있으며, 이를 기준으로 0001번부터 번호가 매겨져 있다. 이는 삭제하지 않고 총서에 그대로 수록하였다.

· 보고서 내용에 관한 더 자세한 정보가 필요하다면, 외교부가 온라인상에 제공하는 『대한민국 외교사료요약집』 1991년과 1992년 자료를 참조할 수 있다.

| 차례

정/리/보/존/문/서/목/록					
기록물종류	문서-일반공문서철	등록번호	914 9587	등록일자	2006-07-27
분류번호	741.12	국가코드	US	주제	
문서철명	한.미국 간의 상호방위조약 제4조에 의한 시설과 구역 및 한국에서의 미국군대의 지위에 관한 협정 (SOFA) 전59권. 1966.7.9 서울에서 서명 : 1967.2.9 발효 (조약 232호) *원본				
생산과	미주과/조약과	생산년도	1952 - 1967	보존기간	영구
담당과(그룹)	조약	조약	서가번호	--	
참조분류					
권차명	V.16 실무교섭회의, 제10-15차, 1963.1-2월				
내용목차	1. 제10차 회의, 1.7 (p.2~41) 2. 제11차 회의, 1.17 (p.42~83) 3. 제12차 회의, 1.24 (p.84~123) 4. 제13차 회의, 2.4 (p.124~152) 5. 제14차 회의, 2.15 (p.153~197) 6. 제15차 회의, 2.25 (p.198~244) * 사진 있음 * 일지 : 1953.8.7 이승만 대통령-Dulles 미국 국무장관 공동성명 - 상호방위조약 발효 후 군대지위협정 교섭 약속 1954.12.2 정부, 주한 UN군의 관세업무협정 체결 제의 1955.1월, 5월 미국, 제의 거절 1955.4.28 정부, 군대지위협정 제의 (한국측 초안 제시) 1957.9.10 Hurter 미국 국무차관 방한 시 각서 수교 (한국측 제의 수락 요구) 1957.11.13, 26 정부, 개별 협정의 단계적 체결 제의 1958.9.18 Dawling 주한미국대사, 형사재판관할권 협정 제외 조건으로 행정협정 체결 의사 전달 1960.3.10 정부, 토지, 시설협정의 우선적 체결 강력 요구 1961.4.10 장면 국무총리-McConaughy 주한미국대사 공동성명으로 교섭 개시 합의 1961.4.15, 4.25 제1, 2차 한.미국 교섭회의 (서울) 1962.3.12 정부, 교섭 재개 촉구 공한 송부 1962.5.14 Burger 주한미국대사, 최규하 장관 면담 시 형사재판관할권 문제 제기 않는 조건으로 교섭 재개 통고 1962.9.6 한.미국 간 공동성명 발표 (9월 중 교섭 재개 합의) 1962.9.20~ 1965.6.7 제1-81차 실무 교섭회의 (서울) 1966.7.8 제82차 실무 교섭회의 (서울) 1966.7.9 서명 1967.2.9 발효 (조약 232호)				

마/이/크/로/필/름/사/항				
촬영연도	*롤 번호	화일 번호	후레임 번호	보관함 번호
2006-11-22	I-06-0068	01	1-244	

0001

1. 제10차 회의, 1.7

0002

정리번호 871

기 안 용 지

자체 통제		기안처	미주과 이경훈	전화번호	근거서류접수일자

과장	수석대표	차관보좌관	차관	장관		
1/7						

관계관 서명	조약과장 기획조정관

기안 년월일	1963.1.7.	시행 년월일		보존 년한		정서 기장
분류 기호		전체 통제		종결		
경유 수신 참조	건 의			발신		
제목	제10차 주둔군 지위협정 체결교섭회의에 임할 우리측 태도.					

1월 7일 개최될 제10차 주둔군 지위협정 체결 한미간 교섭 회의에서는 용어의 정의, 합동위원회, 선박및 항공기의 출입, 항해통제, 그리고 토지및 시설문제를 토의할예정이온바, 이에관련하여 우리측 교섭 실무자는 1월 5일 회합을 갖고 제10차회의에서 취할 우리측 태도를 별첨과 같이 결정하였아오니 재가하여 주시기바랍니다.

별첨: 제 10차 주둔군 지위협정 체결교섭회의에 임할 우리측 태도.

(예고문에 의한 일반문서로 재분류 1966.12.31.)

1966. 12. 31. 예고문에 의거 일반문서로 재분류됨

승인양식 1-1-3 (1112-040-[illegible]) (190mm×260mm16절지)

0003

1964년 9월 30일 미주과 직권으로 일반문서로 재분류

1. 용어의 정의

(1) 군대 구성원에 대한 예외규정

이조항중 " except for those for whom status has otherwise been provided" 라는 구절에 대하여 미국측은 (가) 본구절을 본문에 그대로 두고 (나) 그들이 제시한 합의의사록에서 주한미군사고문단원과 주한미대사관 무관등을 제외한다는 예시적인 규정을 하고 있는데 대하여 우리측은 미국측 제의는 본문과 합의의사록간의 관계가 조문 체제상으로 보아 맞지않어며 미국측 합의의사록에서 규정할 사항은 예시적이 아니라 포괄적이어야 한다는것을 주장하며 (가) 전기 예외규정을 원문에서 삭제하고 (나) 미국측 합의 의사록을 받아주되 동합의의사록의 " has otherwise been provided such as personnel for whom status 라는 구절을 삭제하도록 한다.

(2) 제3국인 군속 문제

"군속"의 정의에 관한 조항에서 미국측은 (가) 우리주장대로 조항원문에 "미국국적 소유자"라는 어구의 삽입을 수락할경우에는 원조문에 한미2중 국적자는 미국인으로 간주한다는 요지의 조항을 첨가하고 (나) 제3국인으로서 한국과 미국으로 부터는 쉽사리 입수할수 없는 기술자와 본협정발효시 군속으로 채용되고 있는 제3국인에 대하여는 "군속"으로 간주하고 (다) 출입국 조항에 있어서 추방에관한 제6항중 " ordinarily resident in "대신 " nationals of "로 논리상 자동적으로 대치하게 될것이라는 미국측제안은 그간 우리측의 주장을 받아 드리고 제3국인에 대한 특례규정을 합의 의사록에서 규제함으로서 한미양국의 요청을 타협한것으로 생각되며 미국측으로서는 이 이상의 양보는 하지않을것으로 보이니 미국측의 이새로운 제안을 받아드리기로 한다. 단 미국측이 제시한 합의 의사록중

0004

"readily" 라는 단어는 일단 삭제토록 제의한다음 미측이 수락을거부한때는 그대로 받아드리도록 한다.

2. 합동위원회

(1) 합동위원회 기능의 예외규정

합동위원회의 기능의 예외규정인 " except where otherwise provided "라는 구절은 토지,시설에 관한 미국측안 B 조2(b)항에 관련한것이라고 사료되는바 이에관한 미측의 설명을 들은후 우리측은 전기 B 조2(b)항에서 규정된 양국정부의 군 통신기관간에 이루어진 협약 (arrangement) 은 합동위원회에서 행하여질 기능보다 우월할것임으로 여사한 예외규정은 사실상 불필요한것이니 이를 삭제토록 한다.

3. 선박 및 항공기의 출입문제

(1) 통보의무에 관한 예외문제

통보의무에 관한 미국측 초안 제3항에서 미국측은 " under normal conditions "라는 단서를 부치고 있는데 이는 미국측이 제의한 합의의사록에서 통고의무가 배제되는 경우에 관한 엄격한 규정을 두고있으므로 본조항을 수락하도록 한다.

4. 항공, 교통 관제문제

(1) 보조시설 설치에 관련된 문제

(가) 미국측 초안 제2항 전단에 미국측은 한국전역 (throughout the Republic of Korea)에 걸처 한공 및 항해보조시설의 설치를 하여 받도록 명백히 규정하고 있는데 이에 대하여 우리측은 "양국정부의 적절한 당국간의 협약을 통하여" (through arrangement between the appropriate authorities of the two Governments 라는 어구를 " territorial water thereof "다음에 삽입토록한다.

(나) 또 후단에서 미국측안은 이들 보조시설이 한국에 기존하는

69-3

체제와 합치함에 있어서 일반적으로만 (generally)
합치하여야 한다고 규정하고 이러한 시설의 설치에 관한
사전통고 의무에 있어서는 가능한 경우에 (where
practicable) 사전통고를 하도록 규정하고 있는데
이는 수락하기로 한다.

5. 토지시설 문제

(1) 토의방법

토지시설문제의 토의는 양측안을 모두 기초로하여 항목별로
토의토록 한다.

(2) 토지시설 사용 허용원측

토지시설사용 허여에 관한 우리측 초안 1항에서 "본협정에
규정된바에 따라" (as provided for in this agreement)라는 구절이 미국측 초안에는 없는데
우리측 초안은 주로 보상을 요구하는 입장에서 작성된 초안임
으로 이것이 필요하고 미국측에서는 보상을 지불하지 않으려는
입장에서 작성한 것이기 때문에 생기는 차이임으로 이에관한
미국측의 입장을 청취한후 우리측 초안을 받아드리도록 요구
한다.

(3) 토지시설 부속물

토지시설의 정의에 관한 미국측 초안 A 조 1 (a)항 후단에서
토지, 시설의 운영에 있어서 사용되는 기존설비, 비품 및
정착물은 "그 위치여하를 막론하고" (wherever located)
토지시설안에 포함된다라고 규정하고 있는데 이는 토지 시설의
범위를 불필요하게 확대시킬 우려도 없지 않으나 일단 미측에
실질적 필요성과 근거의 제시를 요청하고 우리측 입장은 그후에
결정한다.

49-4

0006

(4) 기존 토지시설에 대한 협정적용

기존 토지시설 사용의 법 적근거부여를 위한 규정에 관한 미국측 초안 A 조 1(b)항과 관련하여 우리측 초안에는 "본협정에 의거하여" (under this Agreement) 허용된 토지 시설로 간주한다라고 규정하고 있는데 대하여 미국측 초안에는 "상기 (a)항에 의거하여" (in accordance with sub-paragraph (a) above) 즉 완전 무상허여에 의하여 주어진 토지시설로 간주될수 있는 규정으로 되어 있는데 이는 토지시설 사용허여에 관한 조항에서 우리측이 미국측에 의한 보상을 받도록 하는 원측에 관한 1항에서 규정한 " as provided for in this Agreement "라는 구절을 미국측이 수락하는 한 한미양측의 어느 안을 택하여도 상관없는 것임.

(5) 기존 토지시설의 측정문제

또 우리측 초안 3항 후단에는 기존토지시설에 대하여 합동 위원회를 통한 측정과 결정을 규정하고 있는데 이도 미국측 초안에는 없는것이나 현재 미군이 상용하고 있는 토지시설의 제조사 및 정확한 파악을 통한 소급보상의 책정을 위해 필요한 것임으로 이의 삽입을 요구토록 한다.

(6) 토지시설 반환 및 추가허여 심의

이에관한 미국측 초안 A 조 2항 (우리측 초안 6항) 은 우리측 초안과 실질적인 점에서 차이가 없는것으로 수락하기로 한다.

(7) 토지시설 반환 문제

이에관한 미국측 초안 A 조3항 (우리측 초안 7항)은 우리측 안과 실질적인점에서 차이가 없음으로 미국측안을 수락하도록 한다

49-5

0007

(8) 토지시설의 임시사용 및 일정기간내의 사용문제

이에관한 미국측 초안 A 조 4(a)항 (우리측 초안 8항)과 4(b)항 (우리측 초안 9항)은 우리측 초안과 실질적인 차이점이 없음으로 미국측안을 수락하기로 한다.

(9) 토지시설관리 문제

토지시설내에서의 관리등의 조치에 관한 미국 측 초안 B 조 (1)항 (우리측 초안 10항)에 있어서 미국측 초안은 비상시 (In an emergency....)에는 토지시설 부근에 있어서도 보안조치를 취할수 있도록 규정하고 있는데 이는 본협정의 다른조항에서 비상시에 (전투 행위 발생시) 있어서의 협 정의 운영에관한 규정을 둘것임으로 본조에있어서는 불필요할것으로 생각됨으로 미국측에 보조문에서 말하는 비상시와 앞으로 별도조항에서 취급될 일반적인 비상시에관한 조항간에 관계를 문의하고 우리측 입장을 수락토록 요청한다.

(10) 항해, 항공, 통신문제

(가) 이문제에 관한 미국측 초안 B 조 2(a) 및 (b)항 (우리측 초안 11항)은 우리측 초안과 실질적인 차의점이 없음으로 수락토록 하고,

(나) 미국측 초안 B조 2(c)항은 우리측 초안에는 없으나 미국측 초안에서 "한국의 관계 법률, 규정, 협정의 범위내에서" 한국정부는 미국군대 내의 통신시설에 대한 관계를 피하고 제거할 모든 정당한 조치를 취하도록 규정하고 있음으로 이도 수락하도록 한다.

(11) 공공안전의 존중

이문제에 관한 미국측 초안 B 조 3항 (우리측 초안 12항)은 우리측안과 같음으로 수락토록 한다.

0008

49 6

(12) 원상회복 문제

이문제에 관한 미국측 초안 C조 1항 (우리측 초안 13항) 에 있어서 우리초안은 원칙적으로 미군이 원상회복 의무를 면제하고 단지, 사유재산으로서 미군의 사용으로 막심한 파손을 당한 재산에 대하여 우리정부의 요청에 의하여 미국측이 원상회복 또는 이에 대신하는 보상에관하여 충분한 고려를 하도록 규정하고 있는데 미국측 초안에 있어서는 이에관한 규정을 두고 있지않으니 만일 미측이 우리측의 사유재산에 대한 일반보상에 관한 조항을 수락할 경우에는 과잉보상을 요구하는 결과과 될것임으로 일반보상에 응하는 한 우리측은 본조항에 있어서 미국측에 양보하기로 한다.

(13) 가동설비 소유권 및 처분 문제

미국측 초안 C 조 2항은 우리측 초안에는 규정되어 있지않는 가동설비 (removable facilities)에 대한 미국정부의 소유권과 이들 재산의 반출권에 관한 규정을 두고 있는데 이는 실제문제에 있어서 인정된 사실의 확인이라고 볼수있음으로 받아주도록 한다.

(14) 토지시설 개량에대한 보상의무 면제

우리측 초안 14항은 미국측 초안에서는 규정하고 있지않는 것으로 이는 토지시설의 반환시에 당해시설 및 구역에 가하여진 개량 또는 그곳에 남겨진 건물, 공작물, 공급품 또는 기타의 물자에 대하여 한국정부는 미국측에 보상하지 않는다라는 규정인바 이러한 명시적인 규정은 필요함으로 우리측안의 수락을 요구한다. 본항은 미국측 초안 C조 1항 다음에 2 항으로서 삽입하도록 제의한다. 따라서 미국측 2 항은 3항이되고 3항은 4 항이 될것이다.

48-7

(15) 특수시설 건축에 대한 예외규정

미국측 초안 C 조 3항의 규정은 우리측 초안에는 없으나 기타 특별한 협약은 우리정부가 인정할것임으로 받아드리도록 한다.

(16) 토지시설 유지비

미국측 초안 D 조 1항에 있어서"except those to be borne by the Republic of Korea as provided in paragraph 2" 라는 규정을하고 있는것은 미국측은 보상을 하지 않겠다는 원칙의 입장에서 우리측이 부담하는것을 전제하고 규정한 것이기 때문에 우리측은 이를 삭제토록 요구한다.

(17) 토지시설 보상문제

보상문제에 관한 미국측 초안 D조 2항 (우리측 초안 4항) 에 있어서 양측안은 근본적 차이점을 시현하고 있는데 우리측은 사유재산의 사용에대한 미군측의 보상지불을 요구하고 있는데 대하여 미국측은 이를 한국측이 하도록 규정하고 있는점과 미국측 초안 D 조 2항 후단은 특히 미군이 사용하는 토지 시설에 관련하여 제 3 자 (민간인)에 의하여 야기될지도 모를 청구권으로부터 해를받지 않토록 한국정부가 책임질것을 규정 함으로서 보상문제에 관한 양국측의 근본적인 대립을 보이고있다. 우리측은 우리안의 수락을 요구토록 한다.

관리번호 [struck through]

기 안 용 지

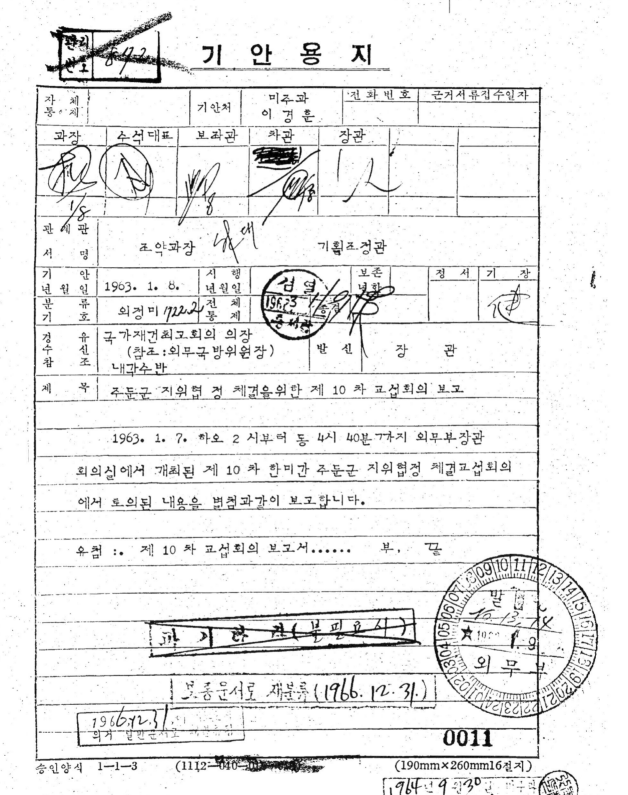

자체통제		기안처	미주과 이경훈	전화번호	근거서류접수일자
과장	수석대표	보좌관	차관	장관	
1/8		1/8	1/8		
관계관 서명	조약과장		기획조정관		
기안년월일	1963. 1. 8.	시행년월일		보존년한	정서 / 기장
분류기호	외정미 722.2	전체통제			
경유 수신 참조	국가재건최고회의 의장 (참조: 외무국방위원장) 내각수반		발신	장관	
제목	주둔군 지위협정 체결을위한 제 10 차 교섭회의 보고				

1963. 1. 7. 하오 2 시부터 동 4시 40분까지 외무부장관 회의실에서 개최된 제 10 차 한미간 주둔군 지위협정 체결교섭회의에서 토의된 내용을 별첨과같이 보고합니다.

유첨 :. 제 10 차 교섭회의 보고서...... 부, 끝

파기한건(불필요시) [struck through]

보통문서로 재분류 (1966. 12. 31.)

1966. 12. 31. 에 예고문에 의거 일반문서로 재분류됨

검열 1966. 1. 9. 발송 외무부

0011

승인양식 1—1—3 (1112—040—01) (190mm×260mm16절지)

1964년 9월 30일 미주국 직권으로 재분류

외 무 부

외정미

수 신 국가재건최고회의 의장

참 조 외무국방위원장

제 목 주둔군 지위협정체결을 위한 제10차 교섭회의 보고

1963. 1. 7. 하오 2시부터 동 4시 40분까지 외무부장관 회의실에서 개최된 제 10 차 한미간 주둔군 지위협정 체결교섭 회의에서 토의된 내용을 별첨과 같이 보고합니다.

유첨 : 제 10 차 교섭회의 보고서 2 부, 끝

외 무 부 장 관 최 덕 신

0012

20-2

외 무 부

외정미

수 신 내각수반

제 목 주둔군 지위협정체결을 위한 제10차 교섭회의 보고

1963. 1. 7. 하오 2시부터 동 4시 40분까지 외무부장관 회의실에서 개최된 제 10 차 한미간 주둔군 지위협정 체결교섭 회의에서 토의된 내용은 별첨과 같이 보고합니다.

유첨 : 제 10 차 교섭회의 보고 1부, 끝

외 무 부 장 관 최 덕 신

0013

20-3

제 10 차

한미간 주둔군지위협정 실무자회의

보 고 서

1. 시 일 : 1963. 1. 7. 하오 2시부터 4시 40분 까지

2. 장 소 : 외무부장관 회의실

3. 참석자 : 한국측 : 진 필 식 (외무부 정무국장, 수석대표)

이 경 호 (법무부 법무국장)

신 관 섭 (재무부 세관국장)

박 근 (외무부 미주과장)

오 윤 용 (외무부 조약과장)

이 남 구 (국방부 군무과장)

이 경 훈 (외무부 2등서기관)

신 정 섭 (")

지 성 구 (외무부 공보관)

강 석 재 (외무부 3등서기관)

미국 측 : 교섭대표단 전원

4. 토의사항 :

(1) 용어의 정의, 합동위원회, 선박 및 항공기의 출입, 항해통제, 그리고 토지 및 시설문제를 순차적으로 토의함.

(2) 용어의 정의에있어서 미국군대 구성원의 정의에 관하여 우리측은 (가) 미국측안에서 규정한 "except for those for whom status has otherwise been provided" 라는 구절을 삭제하고 (나) 미국측이 제시한 합의의사록에서 예시적 규정 (포괄적규정)을 한정적 규정으로 하기위하여 "for whom status has other wise been provided such as personnel" 이라는 어구를 삭제하자고 제의하자

0014

20-4

63-1-1 (3)

88-3(3)

0015

미국측은 (가) 전기 예외규정을 조약의 원문에서 삭제하는데 동의하되 (나) 합의의사록은 미국측안대로 받아줄것을 요구하자 우리측은 다시 (가) 전기예외 규정을 조약원문에 그대로 두어도 좋으니 ~~삭제하되~~ (나) 합의의사록은 우리측이 제시한바와 같은 한정적 규정으로 하자고 주장하여 이문제를 다음회기에 다시 토의키로 함.

(3) 용어의 정의에 있어서 제 3 국인 군속문제에 관하여 우리측 제안인 "미국국적 소유자" 라는 어구를 원문에 삽입할것을 미측이 수락한후 (가) 원조문에 한미 2중국적자는 미국인으로 간주한다라는 조항을 첨가하고 (나) 제 3 국인으로서 한국과 미국으로부터 쉽사리 입수할수 없는 기술자와 본협정 발효시 군속으로 채용되고 있는 제 3 국인에 대하여는 "군속"으로 간주한다는 것을 합의의사록에 규정하고 (다) 출입국 조항에 있어서 추방에관한 제 6 항중 "ordinarily resident in" 은 론리상 "nationals of" 로 대치될것이라는 미국측 타협안은 합의의사록에서 사용된 쉽사리 라는 용어만 미측이 삭제하는데 동의하면 수락 할 용의가 있음을 언명하였음. 이문제는 다음회기에서 다시 토의키로 함.

(4) 합동위원회의 기능의 예외 규정인 "except where otherwise provided" 라는 구절에 관하여 우리측은 본구절은 토지, 시설에 관련된 통신관계 규정에서 말하는 협약 또는 협정과 모순되는것이 아님으로 이의 삭제를 요구한데 대하여 미국측은 동구절의 계속 삽입을 요구하여 합의를 보지못한채로 다시 토의키로 함.

(5) 선박 및 항공기의 기착문제에 있어서 미국측 초안 3 항에서 말하는 "under normal conditions" 라는 구절은 합의의사록에서 통고의무가 배제되는 경우에 관한 엄격한 ~~규정을~~

0016

20-5

13-1-1

미원 88-3

0017

규정을두고 있음으로 우리측은 이를 수락함으로서 선박 및 항공기의 기착에 관한 조항에 완전합의 함.

(6) 항공, 교통관제 문제에 있어서 보조시설 설치에 관한 문제에 관하여 우리측은 "양국정부의 적절한 당국간의 협약을 통하여" 라는 단서를 삽입하여 한국전역에 이의 설치를 허여하도록 하자고 제시한데 대하여 미국측은 이를 고려하겠다고 하고 이문제를 다시 토의키로 함.

(7) 토지시설 문제에 대하여 양국 측은 본문제를 양국측의 안을 대조하여 조항별로 토의하기로 하고 토지시설 사용허여 원측, 토지시설 부속물, 기존 토지시설에 대한 협정적용 및 토지시설의 측정문제등에 관한 쌍방의 해설과 차의점을 비교 지적하였음.

5. 중요합의 사항

(1) 선박 및 항공기의 기착문제에 관한 조항에 완전 합의함.

6. 기타사항

(1) 차기회의 일자 : 1963. 1. 16. 하오 2시

(2) 차기회의 의제 : 차기회의까지 양측 수석대표간에 합의된 사항

보통문서로 재분류(1966. 12. 31.)

63-1-3

1966.12.31.에 예고문에 의거 일반문서로 재분류됨

0018

20-6

/ (3) 미국 88-3(3)

0019

CONFIDENTIAL

TENTETIVE NUMBERING

PREAMBLE	
I	Definitions
II	Facilities and Areas
III	Facilities and Areas
IV	Facilities and Areas
V	Facilities and Areas
VI	Air Traffic Control & Navigational Aids
VII	Joint Committee
VIII	Entry & Exit
IX	Customs
X	Access of Vessels & Aircraft

0020

21-13

CONFIDENTIAL

PREAMBLE	
I	Definitions
II	Facilities and Areas
III	Facilities and Areas
IV	Facilities and Areas
V	Facilities and Areas
VI	Air Traffic Control & Navigational Aids
VII	Joint Committee
VIII	Entry & Exit
IX	Customs
X	Accwss of Vessels & Aircraft

21-14

0021

Definitions Article

1. Mr. Chin opened the meeting by asking whether the U. S. side had any additional comments to make regarding the Definitions Article. Reviewing previous discussion of this article, Mr. Habib noted that the U. S. side had agreed in principle to the inclusion of an Agreed Minute explaining the phrase "those for whom status has otherwise been provided" in subparagraph (a). He reminded the negotiators that the U. S. side had tabled the draft of such an Agreed Minute. He then suggested that the negotiators agree to subparagraph (a) and to the Agreed Minute tabled by the U. S. side.

2. Mr. Chin commented that there were only minor differences in the drafts of the Agreed Minute tabled by the two sides. He suggested that the phrase "except for those for whom status has otherwise been provided" be deleted from subparagraph (a). If this were done, he said the Korean side was prepared to accept the U. S. draft of the Agreed Minute, provided the phrase "for whom status has otherwise been provided such as personnel" were deleted from the draft of the Minute.

3. Mr. Habib replied that elimination of the phrase from both the subparagraph and the Agreed Minute would be too restrictive. He pointed out that the operative phrase in the Agreed Minute is the very phrase which the Korean side wished to eliminate. The question at issue is not whether other personnel are present in Korea; the question is whether or not their status has otherwise been provided for.

0022

2416

4. Mr. Chin inquired whether there were now present in Korea any personnel to whom this provision would apply in addition to the MAAG personnel and the personnel of the Embassy's armed forces attache offices. Mr. Habib replied that there are at present no personnel other than those mentioned for whom status has otherwise been provided.

5. Mr. Chin commented that this provision constituted an exception to the general provisions of the SOFA. In the future, exceptions regarding other personnel, if any, would be provided for in other agreements. He then proposed acceptance of the U. S. draft of subparagraph (a) and the Korean draft of the Agreed Minute. Mr. Habib replied that the U. S. side would consider this proposal.

6. Turning to subparagraph (b), Mr. Chin stated that the Korean side accepted the additional sentence proposed by the U. S. side. He said the draft Agreed Minute tabled by the U. S. side was also acceptable, with the exception of the word "readily" in the second line. He suggested that deletion of the word would not change the substance of the sentence. Mr. Habib replied that the degree of availability of certain skills in the United States or Korea was a practical question. The U. S. side believed that "readily available" was a more honest definition of the existing situation. Assuring the Korean side that the United States authorities had no intention of flooding Korea with third country nationals, Mr. Habib agreed to take the Korean proposal under consideration.

0023

21-17

Entry and Exit

7. Mr. Habib pointed out that sufficient agreement had been reached with regard to subparagraph (b) of the Definitions Article to enable the negotiators to agree on a slight change in paragraph 6 of the Entry and Exit Article. He pointed out that agreement to include the words "of U. S. nationality" after the words "civilian persons" in the first line of subparagraph (b), as well as the additional sentence to which the Korean negotiators had just agreed, made necessary the substitution in paragraph 6 of the Entry and Exit Article of the words "nationals of" for the words "ordinarily resident in". Mr. Chin stated that the Korean side agreed to this change in the Entry and Exit Article, and the final text was confirmed.

Joint Committee

8. Turning to the Joint Committee Article, Mr. Chin recalled that the negotiators had reached general agreement on the U. S. draft, except for the phrase "except where otherwise provided" in the first sentence of Paragraph 1. Mr. Chin said he understood that this phrase referred to special arrangements regarding communications provided for by Paragraph 2(b) of the second Facilities and Areas Article tabled by the U. S. side. Mr. Habib stated that this was correct and pointed out that Paragraph 2(c) also referred to such arrangements. Mr. Chin stated that the Korean side believed that this phrase should be deleted from the Joint Committee Article and that the provisions should be spelled out in the relevant article regarding communications. He said the primacy of the Joint Committee should be fully established by the SOFA and that no exceptions should be made. The Joint Committee should have the power to consider

0024

21-18

any problems connected with the implementation of the SOFA and should also have the authority to delegate its functions to "appropriate authorities".

9. Mr. Habib replied that to establish an exception to the Joint Committee's functions in one part of the SOFA and then not to mention that exception in the article dealing with the Joint Committee's functions would create confusion and misunderstanding. He said the Joint Committee's primacy was fully established by the terms of the SOFA. However, the U. S. side believed that certain matters were not appropriate for discussion by the Joint Committee. The Committee was not, in the opinion of the U. S. side, a suitable forum for the discussion of certain matters which would better be handled elsewhere, such as the communication arrangements provided for in the article dealing with facilities and areas. According to the U. S. drafts, such matters would be handled by joint arrangements agreed upon in mutual discussion by the appropriate authorities of both governments. The U. S. side believed that the pre-eminence of the Joint Committee was fully established.

10. Dr. Pak Kun stated that he wished to re-state the Korean position. He said the Joint Committee should be the central, general, and comprehensive organ for consultation regarding SOFA matters. This principle should be established in the article dealing with the Joint Committee. Naturally, technical matters should be handled by appropriate authorities, as set forth in the Areas and Facilities Article. The Korean side believed that specific provisions should take precedence over general provisions. Therefore, the specific provisions of the Areas and Facilities Article

0025

21-18

would take precedence over the general provisions of the Joint Committee Article. If this principle is clearly understood, Dr. Pak continued, the Joint Committee Article can be left unhampered by exceptions. Mr. Chin added that if agreement were not reached by the appropriate authorities regarding a specific matter under the provisions of the Areas and Facilities Article, the matter should then be referred to the Joint Committee. The point, he said, is to ensure the flexibility of the Joint Committee.

11. Mr. Habib replied that the Korean side appeared willing to make an exception but unwilling to state in the Joint Committee Article that the exception was being made. He stated that the U. S. formula was a much clearer and simpler statement and suggested that perhaps the phrase "except where otherwise provided" was not fully understood. Since both sides had fully stated their positions without reaching agreement, he did not believe further discussion at this meeting would be fruitful.

Access by Vessels and Aircraft

12. Turning to the article concerning access by vessels and aircraft, Mr. Chin stated that the Korean side had already agreed to paragraphs 1 and 2. On the basis of the U. S. side's explanation of Paragraph 3 at the last meeting, he continued, the Korean side accepted the U. S. draft of that paragraph also. This constituted full agreement on this article.

Navigational Aids and Air Traffic Control

13. Taking up the article dealing with navigational aids, Mr. Habib recalled that during the previous discussion of this article, the Korean side had asked the basic question of whether such aids were to be established without consultation or through mutual agreement. The U. S. side wished to make it clear, he said, that navigational aids would be established on a co-

0026

coordinated basis as provided in the relevant article. The only exceptions would be in the case of an emergency when aids were needed immediately or in the case of special combat exercises requiring the establishment of navigational aids on a temporary basis. He pointed out that mutual consultation has been the practice in the past and will continue to be the practice in the future.

14. Mr. Habib remarked that the Korean side had also questioned the meaning of the phrase "shall conform generally" in the U. S. draft. He explained that there are some types of equipment required by the U. S. Armed Forces which are not usable under the navigational aid system now in effect in Korea. This equipment includes the SHORAN system, used primarily for pinpoint bombing and the LORAN system for long-range navigation. In addition, he pointed out, there is the TACAN equipment designed for use by military aircraft in positioning themselves relative to the 38th Parallel. None of these systems is in use by the Korean civilian authorities. In view of constant technological changes, Mr. Habib continued, the U. S. side prefers use of the term "generally".

15. Mr. Chin suggested that the practice of mutual consultation be spelled out in Paragraph 2. Mr. Habib replied that it is spelled out in Paragraph 1 and that Paragraphs 1 and 2 go together. He pointed out that Paragraph 2 of the U. S. draft gives the U. S. Armed Forces the right to establish, construct, and maintain navigational aids. In effect, there is little difference between the two drafts. However, the Korean draft speaks of

areas and territorial waters "adjacent to" established facilities. This is not always practicable in the case of navigational aids. Mr. Chin replied that Mr. Habib's statements had answered the questions raised by the Korean side. He suggested that in Paragraph 2 the following additional phrase be added to the first sentence, following the word "thereof": "through agreement between appropriate authorities of the two governments". Mr. Habib said the U. S. side would consider this proposal.

Facilities and Areas

16. Turning to the drafts of the Facilities and Areas Articles which had been tabled by both sides at the previous meeting, Mr. Chin suggested paragraph by paragraph discussion and asked Mr. Habib to explain the U. S. drafts.

17. Mr. Habib noted that in Paragraph 1(a) of the first U. S. draft article and the corresponding first two paragraphs of the Korean draft article there were certain differences in the use of terms. The U. S. draft spoke of "agreements" rather than "arrangements" because the former term was believed to be more accurately descriptive of what is intended and would include documents. The term "concluded" obviously went with "agreements", just as "arrangements" were "made" in the Korean draft. A more substantive difference was the use in the U. S. draft of the words "wherever located" and "used" instead of the term "necessary" which appeared in the Korean draft. He stated that this particular language had been used as a result of our experience with the operation of the Japanese SOFA. The U. S. side felt that it was an improvement over the

language of the latter Agreement, since experience had shown that furnishings and equipment relating to a facility were not always entirely located within that specific facility. Furthermore, he pointed out, a radio frequencey is a facility and yet cannot be said to be located at any precise location. The word "used" reflects fact, whereas the word "necessary" implies judgement.

18. Mr. Habib continued his analysis by pointing out that Paragraph 1(b) of the U. S. draft and Paragraph 3 of the ROK draft differed to some extent. He asked the Korean side to explain their phrase "for the purpose of this Agreement", which appeared to be redundant. He also requested an explanation of the phrase "surveyed and determined". Pointing out that acquisition documents for all of the areas and facilities presently in use are in existence and will undoubtedly be registered with the Joint Committee, he expressed the opinion that the second sentence of the Korean Paragraph 3 detracted from the previous sentence. He pointed out that Paragraph 1(a) of the U. S. draft provides for agreements regarding these facilities and areas to be concluded by the Joint Committee.

19. In reply, Mr. Chin stated that the Korean side had used the word "arrangements" rather than "agreements" because the former was a broader term, more all-inclusive and more flexible than the latter. He suggested that deletion of the phrase "wherever located" from the U. S. draft would not change the meaning of the paragraph. He said the Korean side would reconsider use of the phrase "for the purpose of this Agreement".

X

0029

Regarding the phrase "surveyed and determined", he said the ~~sole~~ intention of the Korean side was to confirm the existing facilities and areas in use at the time when the Agreement comes into force. There was no other intention, since provision is being made in another paragraph for Joint Committee review of facilities and areas to determine the conditions for their return to the Republic of Korea. ~~He said that the Korean side would~~ attempt to develop alternative language which would make the Korean draft more acceptable to the U. S. side.

20. Regarding Paragraph 2 of the U. S. draft and the corresponding Paragraph 6 of the Korean draft, Mr. Habib stated that the only substantial difference lay in the provision in the U. S. draft for the return of portions of facilities. He expressed the view that this language was preferable. Mr. Chin commented that the antecedent of the word "such" in the U. S. draft should be spelled out.

Next Meeting

21. At this point, the negotiators having been in continuous session for two and one-half hours, it was agreed to adjourn. The next meeting was scheduled for January 16 at 2:00 P.M.

Points of Agreement

22. a. Entry and Exit Article (Text attached)

b. Access by Vessels and Aircraft Article (Text attached)

0030

2/-24

19. In reply, Mr. Chin stated that the Korean side had used the word "arrangements" rather than "agreements" because the former was a broader term, more all-inclusive and more flexible than the latter. Pointing out the phrase in the Korean draft "as provided for in this Agreement" which was not provided in Paragraph 1(a) of ~~the~~ ~~first Article~~ of the ~~of~~ (the U.S. draft), he commented that the Republic of Korea will authorize the use of the areas and facilities not only on the basis of the Mutual Defense Treaty, but also in accordance with relevant provisions of the SOF Agreement. ~~Comparing the words "wherever located" and "used" in the U.S. draft with the words "necessary to the operations" in the Korean draft, he suggested that the words "necessary to the operations" have a broader and flexible meaning and therefore would cover the intended meaning of the words "wherever located" and "used".~~ He suggested that the both sides ~~reconsider this issue~~ give a comparative study to the wording of "used" and "necessary to op." with a view to working out a more acceptable phrase at the next meeting.

In commenting on the U.S. draft he questioned the use of the words "wherever located" and the word "used" as the words "wherever located" is employed in the connection.

He said the Korean side would reconsider the use of the phrases "for the purpose of this Agreement" and "under this Agreement". Regarding the second sentence of Paragraph 2 in the Korean draft, particularly in regard to the words "surveyed and determined", Mr. Chin said that it is not intended to change the status or the scope of the existing facilities and areas which come under the first sentence of the Paragraph. Its intention is to confirm the existing facilities and areas in use by the U.S. armed forces at the time of coming into force of this Agreement. He further said that such matters as the return or the additional provision of the facilities and areas would be appropriately provided for in ~~respective~~ relevant paragraph~~s~~ of the Article.

~~In commenting on the U.S. draft, he questioned the use of the words "wherever located"~~

0031

~~Col. Kenneth Crawford (in place of Col. Miller)~~

Commenting on the U.S. draft, he questioned the use of the words "wherever located" in view of the use of the word "used" in this connection. He suggested that both sides compare and ~~so~~ study the wording of the two drafts in connection with the use of the word "used" in the U.S. draft and the phrase "necessary to the operation of" in the Korean draft with a view to working out a more acceptable phrase at the next meeting.

0032

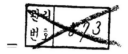

JOINT SUMMARY RECORD OF THE 10TH SESSION
STATUS FORCES NEGOTIATION

관리 번호 23

January 7, 1963

I. Time and Place : 2:00 to 4:40 p.m. January 7, 1963 at the Foreign Minister's Conference Room

II. Attendants:

ROK Side:

Mr. Chin, Pil Shik	Director Bureau of Political Affairs Ministry of Foreign Affairs
Mr. Yi, Kyung Ho	Director Bureau of Legal Affairs Ministry of Justice
Mr. Shin, Kwan Sup	Director Bureau of Costums Duty Ministry of Finance
Mr. Pak, Kun	Chief, America Section Ministry of Foreign Affairs
Mr. O, Won Yong	Chief, Treaty Section Ministry of Foreign Affairs
Col. Lee, Nam Koo	Chief, Military Affairs Section Ministry of National Defense
Mr. Lee, Kyung Hoon	2nd Secretary Ministry of Foreign Affairs
Mr. Shin, Chung Sup	2nd Secretary Ministry of Foreign Affairs
Mr. Chi, Sung Koo	Press Officer Ministry of Foreign Affairs
Mr. Kang, Suk Jae	3rd Secretary Ministry of Foreign Affairs

US Side:

Mr. Philip C. Habib	Counselor of the Embassy for Political Affairs

미주과	담당	과장	국장	특별보좌관	차관	장관

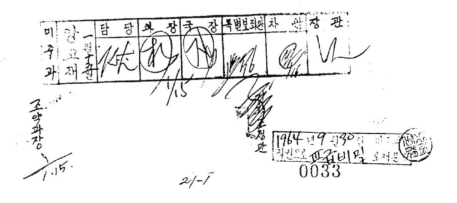

조약과장 1.15.

1964년 9월 30일 직권으로 비밀 재분류

0033

21-1

Brig. Gen J.D. Lawlor	Deputy Chief of Staff 8th Army
Mr. Willian J. Ford	First Secretary of the Embassy
Col. G.G. O'Connor	Deputy Chief of Staff 8th Army
Capt. R.M. Brownlie	Assistant Chief of Staff USN/K
Col. W.A. Solf	Staff Judge Advocate 8th Army
Mr. Benjamin A. Fleck (Rapporteur and Press Officer)	First Secretary of the Embassy
Mr. Robert A. Lewis	Second Secretary and Consul of the Embassy
Lt. Col. R.E. Miller	Staff Officer, JAG 8th Army
Lt. Col. W.A. Burt	J-5
Kenneth Campen	Interpreter

Definitions Article

1. Mr. Chin opened the meeting by asking whether the U.S. side had any additional comments to make regarding the Definitions Article. Reviewing previous discussion of this article, Mr. Habib noted that the U.S. side had agreed in principle to the inclusion of an Agreed Minute explaining the phrase "those for whom status has otherwise been provided" in subparagraph (a). He reminded the negotiators that the U.S. side had tabled the draft of such an Agreed Minute. He then suggested that the negotiators agree to subparagraph (a) and to the Agreed Minute tabled by the U.S. side.

0034

21-2

2. Mr. Chin commented that there were only minor differences in the drafts of the Agreed Minute tabled by the two sides. He suggested that the phrase "except for those for whom status has otherwise been provided" be deleted from subparagraph (a). If this were done, he said the Korean side was prepared to accept the U.S. draft of the Agreed Minute, provided the phrase "for whom status has otherwise been provided such as personnel" were deleted from the draft of the Minute.

3. Mr. Habib replied that elimination of the phrase from both the subparagraph and the Agreed Minute would be too restrictive. He pointed out that the operative phrase in the Agreed Minute is the very phrase which the Korean side wished to eliminate. The question at issue is not whether other personnel are present in Korea; the question is whether or not their status has otherwise been provided for.

4. Mr. Chin inquired whether there were now present in Korea any personnel to whom this provision would apply in addition to the MAAG personnel and the personnel of the Embassy's armed forces attache offices. Mr. Habib replied that there are at present no personnel other than those mentioned for whom status has otherwise been provided.

5. Mr. Chin commented that this provision constituted an exception to the general provisions of the SOFA. In the future, exceptions regarding other personnel, if any, would be provided for in other agreements. He then

0035

21-3

proposed acceptance of the U.S. draft of subparagraph (a) and the Korean draft of the Agreed Minute. Mr. Habib replied that the U.S. side would consider this proposal.

6. Turning to subparagraph (b), Mr. Chin stated that the Korean side accepted the additional sentence proposed by the U.S. side. He said the draft Agreed Minute tabled by the U.S. side was also acceptable, with the exception of the word "readily" in the second line. He suggested that deletion of the word would not change the substance of the sentence. Mr. Habib replied that the degree of availability of certain skills in the United States or Korea was a practical question. The U.S. side believed that "readily available" was a more honest definition of the existing situation. Assuring the Korean side that the United States authorities had no intention of flooding Korea with third country nationals, Mr. Habib agreed to take the Korean proposal under consideration.

Entry and Exit

7. Mr. Habib pointed out that sufficient agreement had been reached with regard to subparagraph (b) of the Definitions Article to enable the negotiators to agree on a slight change in paragraph 6 of the Entry and Exit Article. He pointed out that agreement to include the words "of U.S. nationality" after the words "civilian persons" in the first line of subparagraph (b), as well as the additional sentence to which the Korean negotiators had just agreed, made necessary the substitution in paragraph 6 of the Entry and Exit Article of the words

0036

21-4

"nationals of" for the words "ordinarily resident in". Mr. Chin stated that the Korean side agreed to this change in the Entry and Exit Article, and the final text was confirmed.

Joint Committee

8. Turning to the Joint Committee Article, Mr. Chin recalled that the negotiators had reached general agreement on the U.S. draft, except for the phrase "except where otherwise provided" in the first sentence of Paragraph 1. Mr. Chin said he understood that this phrase referred to special arrangements regarding communications provided for by Paragraph 2(b) of the second Facilities and Areas Article tabled by the U.S. side. Mr. Habib stated that this was correct and pointed out that Paragraph 2(c) also referred to such arrangements. Mr. Chin stated that the Korean side believed that this phrase should be deleted from the Joint Committee Article and that the provisions should be spelled out in the relevant article regarding communications. He said the primacy of the Joint Committee should be fully established by the SOFA and that no exceptions should be made. The Joint Committee should have the power to consider any problems connected with the implementation of the SOFA and should also have the authority to delegate its functions to "appropriate authorities".

9. Mr. Habib replied that ~~the~~ to establish an exception to the Joint Committee's functions in one part of the SOFA and then not to mention that exception in the article

dealing with the Joint Committee's functions would create confusion and misunderstanding. He said the Joint Committee's primacy was fully established by the terms of the SOFA. However, the U.S. side believed that certain matters were not appropriate for discussion by the Joint Committee. The Committee was not, in the opinion of the U.S. side, a suitable forum for the discussion of certain matters which would better be handled elsewhere, such as the communication arrangements provided for in the article dealing with facilities and areas. According to the U.S. drafts, such matters would be handled by joint arrangements agreed upon in mutual discussion by the appropriate authorities of both governments. The U.S. side believed that the pre-eminence of the Joint Committee was fully established.

10. Dr. Pak Kun stated that he wished to re-state the Korean position. He said the Joint Committee should be the central, general, and comprehensive organ for consultation regarding SOFA matters. This principle should be established in the article dealing with the Joint Committee. Naturally, technical matters should be handled by appropriate authorities, as set forth in the Facilities and Areas Article. The Korean side believed that specific provisions should take precedence over general provisions. Therefore, the specific provisions of the Facilities and Areas Article would take precedence over the general provisions of the Joint Committee Article. If this principle is clearly understood, Dr. Pak continued, the Joint Committee Article can be left unhampered by

0038

21-6

exceptions. Mr. Chin added that if agreement were not reached by the appropriate authorities regarding a specific matter under the provisions of the ~~Areas~~ Facilities and ~~Facilities~~ Areas Article, the matter should then be referred to the Joint Committee. The point, he said, is to ensure the flexibility of the Joint Committee.

11. Mr. Habib replied that the Korean side appeared willing to make an exception but unwilling to state in the Joint Committee Article that the exception was being made. He stated that the U.S. formula was a much clearer and simpler statement and suggested that perhaps the phrase "except where otherwise provided" was not fully understood. Since both sides had fully stated their positions without reaching agreement, he did not believe further discussion at this meeting would be fruitful.

Access by Vessels and Aircraft

12. Turning to the article concerning access by vessels and aircraft, Mr. Chin stated that the Korean side had already agreed to paragraphs 1 and 2. On the basis of the U.S. side's explanation of Paragraph 3 at the last meeting, he continued, the Korean side accepted the U.S. draft of that paragraph also. This constituted full agreement on this article.

Navigational Aids and Air Traffic Control

13. Taking up the article dealing with navigational aids, Mr. Habib recalled that during the previous discussion of this article, the Korean side had asked the basic question of whether such aids were to be established

without consultation or through mutual agreement. The U.S. side wished to make it clear, he said, that navigational aids would be established on a coordinated basis as provided in the relevant article. The only exceptions would be in the case of an emergency when aids were needed immediately or in the case of special combat exercises requiring the establishment of navigational aids on a temporary basis. He pointed out that mutual consultation has been the practice in the past and will continue to be the practice in the furture.

14. Mr. Habib remarked that the Korean side had also questioned the meaning of the phrase "shall conform generally" in the U.S. draft. He explained that there are some types of equipment required by the U.S. Armed Forces which are not usable under the navigational aid system now in effect in Korea. This equipment includes the SHORAN system, used primarily for pinpoint bombing and the LORAN system for long-range navigation. In addition, he pointed out, there is the TACAN equipment designed for use by military aircraft in positioning themselves relative to the 38th Parallel. None of these systems is in use by the Korean civilian authorities. In view of constant technological changes, Mr. Habib continued, the U.S. side prefers use of the term "generally".

15. Mr. Chin suggested that the practice of mutual consultation be splled out in Paragraph 2. Mr. Habib replied that it is spelled out in Paragraph 1 and that Paragraphs 1 and 2 go together. He pointed out that Paragraph 2 of the U.S. draft gives the U.S. Armed Forces

0040

21-8

the right to establish, construct, and maintain navigational aids. In effect, there is little difference between the two drafts. However, the Korean draft speaks of areas and territorial waters "adjacent to" established facilities. This is not alwasy practicable in the case of navigational aids. Mr. Chin replied that Mr. Habib's statements had answered the questions raised by the Korean side. He suggested that in Paragraph 2 the following additional phrase be added to the first sentence, following the word "thereof": "through agreement between appropriate authorities of the two governments". Mr. Habib said the U.S. side would consider this proposal.

Facilities and Areas

16. Turhing to the drafts of the Facilities and Areas Articles which had been tabled by both sides at the previous meeting, Mr. Chin suggested paragraph by paragraph discussion and asked Mr. Habib to explain the U.S. drafts.

17. Mr. Habib noted that in Paragraph 1(a) of the first U.S. draft article and the corresponding first two paragraphs of the Korean draft article there were certain differences in the use of terms. The U.S. draft spoke of "agreements" rather than "arrangements" because the former term was believed to be more accurately descriptive of what is intended and would include documents. The term "concluded" obviously went with "agreements", just as "arrangements" were "made" in the Korean draft. A more substantive difference was the use in the U.S. draft of the words "wherever located" and "used" instead of

0041

21-8

the term "necessary" which appeared in the Korean draft. He stated that this particular language had been used as a result of our experience with the operation of the Japanese SOFA. The U.S. side felt that it was an improvement over the language of the latter Agreement, since experience had shown that furnishings and equipment relating to a facility were not always entirely located within that specific facility. Furthermore, he pointed out, a radio frequencey is a facility and yet cannot be said to be located at any precise location. The word "used" reflects fact, whereas the word "necessary" implies judgement.

18. Mr. Habib continued his analysis by pointing out that Paragraph 1(b) of the U.S. draft and Paragraph 3 of the ROK draft differed to some extent. He asked the Korean side to explain their phrase "for the purpose of this Agreement", which appeared to be redundant. He also requested an explanation of the phrase "surveyed and determined". Pointing out that acquisition documents for all of the areas and facilities presently in use are in existence and will undoubtedly be registered with the Joint Committee, he expressed the opinion that the second sentence of the Korean Paragraph 3 detracted from the previous sentence. He pointed out that Paragraph 1(a) of the U.S. draft provides for agreements regarding these facilities and areas to be concluded by the Joint Committee.

19. In reply, Mr. Chin stated that the Korean side had used the word "arrangements" rather than "agreements"

0042

21-10

because the former was a broader term, more all-inclusive and more flexible than the latter. Pointing out the phrase in the Korean draft "as provided for in this Agreement" which was not provided in Paragraph 1(a) of the first Article, the U.S. draft, he commented that the Republic of Korea will authorize the use of the areas and facilities not only on the basis of the Mutual Defense Treaty, but also in accordance with relevant provisions of the SOF Agreement. Commenting on the U.S. draft, he questioned the use of the word "wherever located" in view of the use of the word "used" in this connection. He suggested that both sides compare and study the wording of the two drafts in connection with the use of the word "used" in the U.S. draft and the phrase "necessary to the operation of" in the Korean draft with a view to working out a more acceptable phrase at the next meeting. He said the Korean side would reconsider the use of the phrases "for the purpose of this Agreement" and "under this Agreement". Regarding the second sentence of Paragraph 2 in the Korean draft, particularly in regard to the words "surveyed and determined", Mr. Chin said that it is not intended to change the status or the scope of the existing facilities and areas which come under the first sentence of the Paragraph. Its intention is to confirm the existing facilities and areas in use by the U.S. armed forces at the time of coming into force of this Agreement. He further said that such matters as the return or the additional provision of the facilities and areas would be appropriately provided for in relevant paragraphs of the Article.

20. Regarding Paragraph 2 of the U.S. draft and the corresponding Paragraph 6 of the Korean draft, Mr. Habib stated that the only substantial difference lay in the provision in the U.S. draft for the return of portions of facilities. He expressed the view that this language was preferable. Mr. Chin commented that the antecedent of of the word "such" in the U.S. draft should be spelled out.

Next Meeting

21. At this point, the negotiators having been in continous session for two and one-half hours, it was agreed to adjourn. The next meeting was scheduled for January 16 at 2:00 P.M.

Points of Agreement

22. a. Entry and Exit Article (Text attached)

b. Access by Vessels and Aircraft Article (Text attached)

~~보통문서로 재분류(정정체결시)~~

1966,12,31.에 예고문에 의거 일반문서로 재분류됨

보통문서로 재분류(1966.12.31.)

0044

21-12

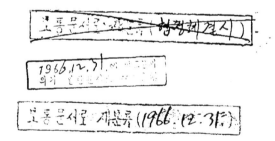

2. 제11차 회의, 1.16

0045

관리 번호 874

기 안 용 지

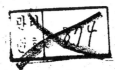

자체 통제		기안처	미주과 이경훈	전화번호	근거서류접수일자
과장	수석대표	보좌관	차관	장관	
1/15			16.		
관계관 서명	조약과장 1.15 기획관리실장				
기안 년월일	1963.1.15	시행 년월일		보존 년한 갑	정서 기장
분류 기호		전체 통제		종결	
경유 수신 참조	건 의		발신		
제목	제11차 주둔군 지위협정 체결 교섭회의에 임할 우리측 태도				

1월 16일에 개최될 제 11차 주둔군 지위협정 체결 한미간 교섭회의에서는 합동위원회, 토지시설, 공익물및 용역사용 그리고 기상 업무 문제에 관하여 토의될 예정이온바, 이에 관련하여 우리측 교섭 실무자는 1월 14일 관계부처 실무자와의 연석회의를 갖고 제 11차회의에서 취할 우리측 태도를 별첨과 같이 결정하였아오니 재가하여 주시기바랍니다.

유첨: 제11차 주둔군 지위협정 체결 교섭회의에 임할 우리측 태도.

보통문서로 재분류(1966.12.31)

1966 에 예고문에 의거 일반문서로 재분류됨

1966년 7월 3일 미주과 직권으로 III 급비밀로 재분류

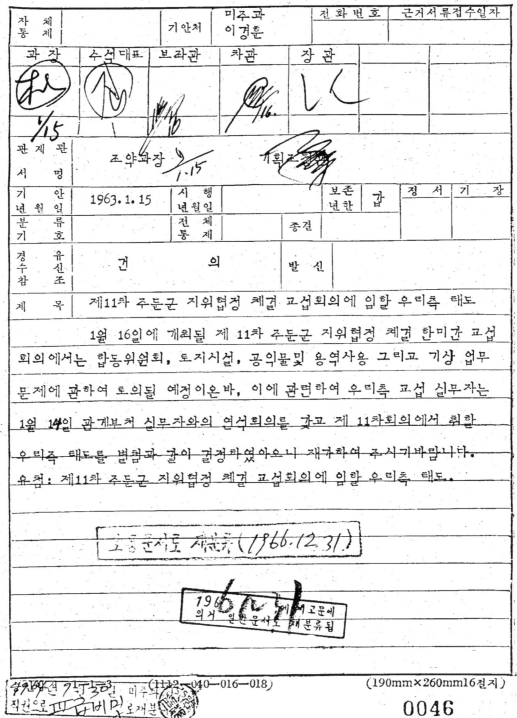

(1112—040—016—018) (190mm×260mm16절지)

0046

11次

1. 합동위원회

(1) 합동위원회 기능의 예외적 규정 (except where otherwise provided) 에 있어서 별도규정에 의한 각종 "한미간의 기관"은 우리정부 관계당국을 포함할것이며 따라서 합동위원회에서 제외되드라도 우리정부 관계당국에서 관여할것임으로 우리측의 견해가 반영될수있을것이고, 또한 미국측으로는 본예외규정을 양보할 기색이 없음으로 이를 수락하기로 한다.

2. 공익물 및 용역의 사용

(1) 공익물 및 용역의사용에 관하여 주한 미군이 어떠한 공익물 및 용역을 사용토록하고 그사용에 있어서는 우리정부 관계부처에 적용되는 것과 동등한 조건에의한 우선권을 부여한다는 원측적인 규정을 한다. (별첨 1.)

(2) 공익물 용역의 사용에 관하여는 1958년 12월 18일자로 서명되고 1957년 7월 1일자로 소급 발효한 "공익물에 관한 청구권 청산을 위한 한미간의 협정"이있고 또 개별적 계약으로서는 수도 사용에 관하여 1957년 7월 3일자로 내무부와 미합중국간에 "수도 공급 계약" 과 전기사용에 관하여는 1957. 7. 3. 자로 경성전기회사와 미국간에 "전기공급 계약" 을 체결한바 있음. 이에 감하여 필요할 경우에는 공익물 및 용역 사용에관한 구체적인 약정은 관계 당사자간에 체결토록 규정하고 전기 한바와 같은 기존 협약 및 약정은 공익물 및 용역사용에 관한 구체적인 약정으로 간주한다는 세부적인 사항을 규정토록 한다. (별첨 2.)

(3) 미국측이 나오는태도를 보고 우리측은 전기 (1)에서 언급한 원측적인 규정만을 제시하든지 또는 전기 (2)에서 언급한 세부적인 규정까지도 제시하든지 결정한다.

50-2

(4) 상공부 전기국장에 의하면 현재 미국측이 사용하고 있는 전기량은 2만5천3백3십 KW (고압)이며 이에대한 월평균 수입액은 15만불이라 함.

3. <u>기상업무</u>

(1) 기상업무에 관하여 한미 양측은 각기 관계당국간의 합의된바에 따라 기상관측, 기상자료 및 지진관측 자료의 상호 제공을 협조한다라고 규정한다. (별첨. 수정초안) (본문제에 관한 최초안은 항해, 항공통제 조항 제시시 이에포함 되어있었음)

(2) 미일 협정 제 8 조에 의하면 일본정부가 일방적으로 미군에게

(가) 육상 또는 해상으로부터의 기상관칙 자료

(나) 기상 관칙소의 일기에관한 정기보고서

(다) 항공기의 안전과 정규운영에 필요한 자료의 전신 전파

(라) 지진관계 자료를 제공하도록 규정되어 있음에 비추어 미국측이 미.일 협정에 따르는 이러한일방적인 제공 의무의 형식으로 기상업무에 관한 초안을 제출할지도 모를것임.

(3) 그러할때는 우리측은 상무적 규정을한 우리측 수정안을 미국측이 수락하도록 요구해보고 미국측이 이를 거부할시는 미국측이 미.일협정과 비등한 안을 제시하는 한 미국측 제안을 받아드리기로 한다.

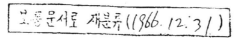

보통문서로 재분류(1966.12.31)

196 . 147 에 예고문에 의거 재분류됨

0048

50-3

별첨 1.

The United States armed forces shall have the use of all public untilities and services belonging to, or controlled or regulated by the Government of the Republic of Korea. In the use of such utilities and services the United States armed forces shall enjoy priorities under conditions no less favorable than those that may be applicable from time to time to the ministries and agencies of the Government of the Republic of Korea.

5-0-4

0049

별첨 2

Specific arrangements as to the use of such public utilities and services by the United States armed forces shall be made between the appropriate authorities of the two Governments or their agencies.

The existing arrangements concerning the use ~~ae~~ of such public utilities and services by the United States armed forces at the effective date of this Agreement shall be regarded as the arrangements made in accordence with the foregoing paragraph.

50-5

0050

별첨 3.

The Governments of the Republic of Korea and the United States shall cooperate in mutually furnishing the relevant authorities of each Government with the following meteorological services in accordance with arrangements between the appropriate authorities of the two Governments:

(a) Meteorological observation,

(b) Climatological information, and

(c) Seismographic data.

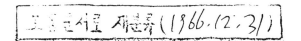

50-6

0051

관리 번호 / 625

기 안 용 지

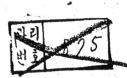

자체 통제		기안처	미주과 이경훈	전화번호	근거서류접수일자
	과장	수석대표	보좌관	차관	장관
관계관 서명	조약과장			기획조정관	
기안 년월일	1963. 1. 17.	시행 년월일		보존 년한	정서 / 기장
분류 기호	외정미 722.2	전체 통제	1962 통제관 종결		
경유 수신 참조	국가재건최고회의 의장 (참조: 외무국방위원장) 내각수반			발신	장관
제목	주둔군지위협정 체결을위한 제11차 교섭회의 보고				

1963. 1. 16. 하오 2시부터 동 4시까지 외무부장관 회의실에서 개최된 제 11 차 한미간 주둔군 지위협정 체결 교섭회의에서 토의된 내용을 별첨과 같이 보고합니다.

유첨 : 제 11 차 교섭회의 보고서 부, 끝

~~예고문에 의거 재분류(1966.12.31)~~

~~파 기 하 다(불 필 요 시)~~

발 1963. 1. 18 외무부

0052

1966.12.31 에 예고문에 의거 일반문서로 재분류됨

1964 년 9 월 30 일 미주과 지휘으로 파기비밀

22-1

승인양식 1-1-3 (1112-040-016-018) (190mm×260mm16절지)

외 무 부

외정미 1963. 1. 18.

수 신 내각수반

제 목 주둔군지위협정 체결을위한 제11차 교섭회의 보고

1963. 1. 16. 하오 2시부터 동 4시까지 외무부장관 회의실에서 개최된 제 11 차 한미간 주둔군 지위협정체결 교섭회의에서 토의된 내용을 별첨과같이 보고합니다.

유첨 : 제 11 차 교섭 회의 보고 1부. 끝

외 무 부 장 관 최 덕 신

0053

22-p

외 무 부

외정미 1963. 1. 18.

수 신 국가재건최고회의 의장

참 조 외무국방위원장

제 목 주둔군지위협정 체결을위한 제11차 교섭회의 보고

1963. 1. 16. 하오 2시부터 동 4시까지 외무부장관 회의실에서 개최된 제11차 한미간 주둔군 지위협정 체결 교섭회의에서 토의된 내용을 별첨과같이 보고합니다.

유첨 : 제 11 차 교섭회의 보고서 2 부. 끝

63-1-18

외 무 부 장 관 최 덕 신

0054

22-8

제 11 차

한미간 주둔군지위 협정체결 실무자회의

보 고 서

1. 시 일 : 1963. 1. 16. 하오 2시부터 4시까지

2. 장 소 : 외무부 장관 회의실

3. 참석자 : 한국측 : 진 필 식 (외무부 정무국장, 수석대표)

박 근 (외무부 미주과장)

오 윤 용 (외무부 조약과장)

이 남 구 (국방부 군무과장)

주 문 기 (법무부 법무과장)

이 경 훈 (외무부 2등서기관)

신 정 섭 (")

지 성 구 (외무부 공보관)

강 석 재 (외무부 3등서기관)

미국측 : O'Cornnor 대령, Brownlie 대령을 제외한 전원 참석 (Miller 중령대신에 Crawford 대령 참석)

4. 토의사항 :

(1) 합동위원회, 토지시설문제를 순차적으로 토의하고 공익물 및 용역사용 문제에 관한 미국측 초안이 제시되었음.

(2) 합동위원회의 기능의 예외적 규정인 "except where otherwise provided" 라는 구절에 관하여 우리측은 본예외 규정을 본문에 남겨두는대신 합의의사록에 이예외규정은 토지시설에 관한 미국측 초안 B 조 2(b), 2(c)항의 규정에 관련한것을 의미한다라고 규제하자고 제의하자 미국측은 이를 고려하겠다고 하였음.

0055

22-21

63-1-2 (30)

外1보 88-2 (30)

0056

(3) 토지, 시설문제에 관하여 쌍방은 지난회의에서 비교 검토된 토지시설 사용 허여 원측, 토지시설 부속물, 기존 토지시설에 대한 협정 적용 및 토지시설의 특정문제에 이어 계속하여 토지시설 반환 및 추가허여에 관한 합의 의무, 토지 시설 반환 조건문제, 토지시설의 임시사용 및 일정기간 내의 사용 문제, 토지시설 관리문제, 항행 항공 통신에관한 협조 문제, 공공안전의 존중, 원상회복 문제, 가동설비 소유권 및 처분 문제, 토지시설 개량에 대한 보상의무 면제, 특수시설 건축에 대한 예외규정, 토지시설 유지비, 그리고 토지시설 보상문제에 관한 쌍방의 해설과 차의점을 비교 지적하면서 검토하였음. 이러한 사항중에서 특히 쌍방간에 근본적 차의점을 나타낸 항은 보상지불 문제인바 이문제에 관하여 미국측은 자국의 초안에 관하여 설명하면서 토지시설의 보상지불은 한국정부가 책임질것을 재차 강조 천명하면서 미국은 ~~또 이미~~ 한미 상호 방위조약의 정신에 입각하여 또 이미 행정협정 체결 교섭회의 개최전 및 교섭초기에 있어서 토지시설의 보상지불을 할수없다고 언명한점을 상기시키면서 이러한 미국의 기본입장에는 하등의 변동이 없다고 말하였음. 이에대하여 우리측은 우리측 초안에 미국측의 보상지불을 규정한것은 어떤 법적 또는 기술적 근거에서 입각한것이라기 보다, 행정협정의 근본 목적의 하나가 양국간의 우호관계의 증진을 위한것이라는 점을 고려하여, 또한 미국측의 입장과 사정도 고려해서 최소한으로 보상을 한정시켜 다만, 사유재산의 사용에 대하여 보상지불을 규정한것이며 미국측에 의한 이러한 보상지불은 실질적으로 한미 양국간의 기존 우호관계의 증진에 크게 기여하게 될것이니 본문제에 대하여 한국측에 유리한 고려가 있기를 바란다고 설명하였음.

0057

22-3

63-1-2

미문 88-2

0058

미국측은 이에대하여 보상문제는 한국정부의 문제이며
본문제에 대하여 ~~고려하지마는~~ 한국측에 유리한 고려는
할수없다고 말하였음.

(4) 용역사용에 관하여 미국측은 자국의 초안을 수교했으며
우리측은 우리안을 준비했으나 미국측안을 검토한후 쌍방
초안에 차이가 있으면 다음회기에서 제시하겠다고 하였음.

5. 기타사항

(1) 차기회의 일자 : 1963. 1. 24. 하오 3 시

(2) 차기회의 의제 : 차기회의까지 양측 수석대표간에 합의된
사항

6. 참고자료 : 미국측이 제의한 협정초안 (용역사용) 별첨참조

0059

22-4

6-1-2

미주 88-2

0060

1. Before beginning substantive discussion, Mr. Habib introduced Colonel Kenneth C. Crawford, of the Staff Judge Advocate's Office, EUSA, who was attending the meeting in place of Lt. Col. R. E. Miller. [redacted] Mr. Habib [redacted] noted the absence of Col. G. G. O'Connor because of illness and Captain R. M. Brownlie, who was also unable to attend the meeting. Mr. Chin noted the absence of Mr. Yi Kyung-ho and Mr. Shin Kwan-sup. He introduced Mr. Chu Mun-ki, Chief of the Legal Affairs Section in the Ministry of Justice, who was attending in place of Mr. Yi, and Major ~~Ah Chung-gun~~ Ahn Seung Keun from the Ministry of Defense.

Joint Committee

2. In opening substantive discussion, Mr. Chin asked whether the U.S. side had any additional remarks to make concerning the Joint Committee article. Mr. Habib replied that at previous negotiating sessions, the negotiators had reached full agreement on the text of the article, except for the phrase [redacted] "except where otherwise provided" at the end of the first sentence of parggraph 1 in the U.S. draft. He reminded the negotiators that this phrase had been inserted in anticipation of certain special communications arrangements as provided for under the provisions of the relevant xx facilities and areas article. Requesting the Korean side to reconsider its opposition to inclusion of the phrase, Mr. Habib pointed out that the Joint Committee article was fundamental to the entire SOFA, inasmuch as it established the mechanism for the smooth coordination and effective implementation of the provisions of the Agreement. He urged acceptance of the U.S. draft in keeping with what the U.S. side understood was the desire of both sides to [redacted] obtain speedy agreement [redacted] with respect to certain key articles.

0061

23-15

63-1-2

73-12

미연 88-2

0062

CONFIDENTIAL

3. Mr. Chin replied that the Korean side had carefully considered this matter. He said it was his understanding that the phrase referred ~~in~~ solely to paragraph 2(b) of the second facilities and areas ~~and~~ draft article tabled by the U.S. side. He inquired whether it also referred to any other draft articles which might be tabled at a later date. Mr. Habib pointed out that the phrase referred to both paragraph 2 (b) and 2 (c) of the relevant facilities and areas article and stated that it was the understanding of the U.S. side, on the basis of their instructions, ~~the information which it had received from Washington,~~ that no ~~other~~ reference to any other portion of the SOFA was intended or planned.

4. Mr. Chin stated that the provisions of paragraph 2(b) were clearly spelled out but that the reference in paragraph 2(c) to the word "agreements" was vague. He requested an explanation of the word "agreements". Mr. Habib replied that the word referred to any agreements entered into with the Korean authorities by the U.S. authorities. In this connection, he mentioned that one such agreement would be one providing for U.S. notification to the International Frequency Registration Board of frequencies used by the U.S. armed forces in Korea.

5. Mr. Chin proposed that the phrase "except where otherwise provided" be retained in the text of the Joint Committee Article and that an Agreed Minute be approved which would explain the [redacted] reference of this phrase to paragraph 2 (b) and 2 (c) of the relevant facilities and areas article. Mr. Habib asked whether the Korean side was prepared to table a [redacted] draft of the Agreed Minute. Mr. Chin suggested that the Agreed Minute read as follows:

> "The exception provided for in the first sentence of paragraph 1 is relevant only to [redacted] paragraph 2, subparagraphs (b) and (c) of Article ____."

0063

6. Mr. Habib suggested that this explanation be written into the ~~mg~~ joint summary record instead of being made an Agreed Minute. However, he agreed to consider the Korean proposal.

23-16

63-1-2

외문 88-2

0064

Facilities and Areas

7. Turning to the drafts of the facilities and areas articles, Mr. Chin noted that at the previous meeting views were exchanged on paragraphs 1 and 2 of the [redacted] U.S. draft article "A" and [redacted] the corresponding paragraphs (1, 2, 3 and 6) of the Korean draft. He suggested that the negotiators proceed with an examination of paragraphs 3 and 4 of the U.S. draft and the corresponding paragraphs 7 and 8 of the Korean draft.

8. Mr. Habib pointed out that the chief difference between [redacted] paragraph 3 of the U.S. draft and paragraph 7 of the Korean draft was the provision in the U.S. draft that facilities are to be returned to the Republic of Korea "under such conditions as may be agreed through the Joint Committee". He reminded the negotiators that the U.S. armed forces continuously review [redacted] the possibility of returning facilities [redacted] no longer needed . Obviously, he said, once the return of a facility is decided upon, it would be returned under whatever provisions the Joint Committee agrees to. He asked whether the Korean side had any other procedure or considerations in mind. He also referred to the use of the word "promptly" in the Korean draft and stated that its use was unnecessary since [redacted] any facility being returned would be returned promptly once the Joint Committee agreed on the conditions of its return. Mr. Chin stated that there was no substantial difference between the two paragraphs. He said the Korean draft did not spell out the details [redacted] concerning the return of facilities because the Joint Committee is the body which will implement [redacted] the provisions of the SOFA. It was agreed that this paragraph presented no problem.

0065 9. Turning to paragraph 4 of the U.S. draft and the corresponding paragraphs 8 and 9 of the Korean draft, Mr. Habib suggested that subparagraph (a) of the U.S. draft was clearer than the Korean paragraph 8. The phrase "and the Government of the Republic of Korea is so advised" is more explicit as to the exact time when the facilities in question would be made available for interim use.

CONFIDENTIAL

63-1-2

0066

The final half of subparagraph (a), he continued, tightens up the procedures and provides a cooperative basis for making the facilities available for interim use. Mr. Habib pointed out that the subparagraph serves two basic purposes: (a) it sets a time schedule, and (b) it provides for cooperation and coordination.

10. Mr. Chin stated that there was no substantive difference between the two drafts; the U.S. draft merely elaborated the subject. Since the Joint Committee will always operate in the spirit indicated in the U.S. draft, the Korean side saw no necessity to elaborate in this article the manner in which the Joint Committee shall perform its functions. He also suggested that the phrase "and the Government of the Republic of Korea is so advised" was unnecessary. Mr. Habib replied that the U.S. side believed the phrase desirable because it would provide the means of avoiding a debate over when any particular facility was to be returned. He said debates at a later date over the meaning of provisions of the Agreement should be avoided whenever possible by making the language of the Agreement as specific as possible. Mr. Chin replied that the two sides were in general agreement. The only disagreement was in how to state the substance of the subparagraph.

11. Mr. Habib noted that paragraph 9 of the Korean draft omitted the words "armed forces" and spoke of a "limited period of time" instead of "limited periods of time". Otherwise, he pointed out that paragraph 9 and subparagraph 4(b) of the U.S. draft are identical.

ARTICLE "B"

12. Mr. Chin noted that there appeared to be little difference between paragraph 1 of the U.S. draft article "B" and the Korean paragraph 10, except for the sentence in the U.S. draft beginning "in an emergency,...". He requested an explanation of this sentence. Mr. Habib replied by stating that this provision was contained in the SOFA with Japan in the form of a separate Agreed Minute. The U.S. side believed

0067

63-1-2 53-18 미문 88.2

0068

XX

it preferable to embody it in the text of the article rather than in an accompanying Agreed Minute. He said that experience has shown that safety measures are necessary in the vicinity of facilities to protect against subversive [redacted] activities during emergency situations. He pointed out that during the present condition of armed truce, security is a paramount consideration. He added that the only other difference between the two texts lay in the U.S. wording [redacted] "United States armed forces" as compared with the Korean wording "Government of the United States". He said that as a practical matter, the armed forces would make any such request on behalf of the United States Government. In addition, he pointed out, both drafts contain the additional requirement of consultation through the Joint Committee. Mr. Chin replied that the Korean side believed that since the request is made to the Government of the Republic of Korea, it should be made by the Government of the United States, thus maintaining a balanced government to government situation. He [redacted] suggested further consideration of this point.

63-1-30

13. Turning to paragraph 2 of the U.S. draft and paragraph 11 of the Korean draft, Mr. Habib pointed out that subparagraph (a) of the U.S. draft [redacted] and the first sentence of the Korean paragraph 11 were identical. The only substantive difference between subparagraph (b) and the second sentence of paragraph [redacted] 11 was the use in the U.S. draft of the phrase "designated military communications authorities" [redacted] in contrast to the phrase "appropriate authorities of the two Governments" in the Korean draft. He said [redacted] that the general subject of paragraph 2 had already been discussed during previous discussions of the Joint Committee Article. However, [redacted] there was in the Korean draft no equivalent to subparagraph (c), which stated an obligation on the Korean government which the U.S. side believed was a corollary to the obligation placed on the U.S. armed forces by the provisions of sucpar[redacted] The U.S. side [redacted] believed that a

0069

23-1P

63-1-2

53-16

비문88-2

0070

[redacted]

mutual obligation existed and should be so stated in the article. With regard to subparagraph (c), Mr. Habib said he wished to remind the negotiators again that one of the agreements envisioned would provide [redacted] for U.S. notification to the International Frequency Registration Board of frequencies used by the U.S. armed forces in Korea.

14. Mr. Habib pointed out that paragraph 3 of the U.S. draft and paragraph 12 of the Korean draft were identical.

15. Mr. Chin stated that the Korean side fully understood the delegation of authority provided in subparagraph (b) of the U.S. draft. However, they had used the word [redacted] "appropriate" in paragraph 11 because of its broad, all-inclusive nature (which encompassed the Joint Committee) and because [redacted] this word had been used elsewhere in the Agreement. Mr. Habib replied that the U.S. side believed a more specific term was desirable in this instance, so as not to involve unnecessarily authotities who [redacted] had no specific interest or competence in these highly technical classified matters. It was agreed to give further consideration to this question.

ARTICLE "C"

16. Mr. Habib pointed out that paragraph 1 of the U.S. draft article "C" was identical with the first sentence of paragraph 13 of the Korean draft. However, the second sentence of paragraph 13 introduced a subject (compensation) which would be discussed in greater detail in connection with U.S. draft article "D". He invited the Korean side to explain their position, if they cared to do so at that juncture. Mr. Chin suggested that discussion of the compensation issue be deferred until the negotiators reached the U.S. draft article "D". Mr. Habib agreed, but pointed out that the point at issue was the provision of facilities and not the source of those facilities. Whether they [redacted]licly owned was irrelevant. 0071

23-20

63-1-2 53-50 外交 88-2

0072

17. In reply to Mr. Chin's request for an explanation of paragraph 2 of the U.S. draft, Mr. Habib replied that to state it in simple terms: "what's ours is ours and we can remove it if we [redacted] wish to do so". Mr. Chin replied that if it were that simple, there was no need to spell it out in the Agreement.

18. Mr. Chin pointed out that paragraph 14 of the Korean draft did not appear in the U.S. draft and could be inserted without difficulty. Mr. Habib replied that the U.S. Government had decided not to request payment of residual value and therefore this provision was omitted from the U.S. draft. He said he agreed in principle to its inclusion but suggested further discussion. However, he indicated the belief of the U.S. side that the words "supply or other materials left thereon" were not relevant and should be omitted. He added that paragraph 3 in the U.S. draft, although it did not appear in the Korean draft, presented no problem and was closely related to paragraph 2.

63-1-32

Article "D"

19. The negotiators then [redacted] proceeded to discussion of the U.S. draft article "D" and the corresponding paragraphs 4 and 5 of the Korean draft. Mr. Habib said there existed a fundamental difference of opinion regarding the payment of compensation for [redacted] the use of facilities and areas. He said the views of the U.S. side were well known. The U.S. draft, he continued, states that the United States Government will pay all expenses incident to the maintenance of the U.S. armed forces in Korea except for those to be paid by the Korean Government as provided in paragraph 2. In contrast, [redacted] paragraph 4 of the Korean draft would place on the U.S. Government the obligation to pay compensation. He reminded the negotiators that early in the negotiations, and also prior to them, [redacted] the U. S. Government had stated [redacted] clearly and explicitly its view that no compensation would be paid. There has been no change since then, he said. The United States does not accept, he continued, any distinction in the origin of the facilities. [redacted] All facilities, he stated, are

0073

23-2

63-1-2

0074

made available to the U.S. armed forces by the Korean Governement. Obviously, however, he continued, the U.S. aremed forces are prepared to cooperate to the maximum extent possible by releasing facilities no longer needed or by accepting alternate facilities offered by the Korean Government. He pointed out that the United States Government has adhered to the principle of no compensation in all of the mutual security negotiations in which it has engaged, on the grounds that the facilities provided are the host country's contribution to the joint effort. There is no reason to deviate from this policy in Korea, he said. He then asked Mr. Chin to state the Korean views.

Rev. + Rewrite

20. Mr. Chin stated that the Korean side was fully aware of the U. S. position. He said the Korean draft [redacted] had no legal or technical basis. One of the objectives of the Status of Forces Agreement, he said, is to further strengthen the friendly relations already existing between the two governments. He said the Korean side was asking for compensation only for privately-owned facilities and areas, as a contribution to that objective. He said if the U. S. Government would agree, it would constitute a great contribution to the Korean Government and to the conclusion of the SOFA. He reiterated that the Korean request was made not on any legal basis but on the basis of strengthening the existing ties of friendship.

21. Mr. Habib replied that he wished to make clear that the question of compensating private owners was not being debated. The U.S. side agreed that there *be* [redacted] a responsibility to compensate them but held that it was not the responsibility of the United States *but of* [redacted] the Government of the Republic of Korea. He said it was well known that the United States Government was already making contributions to the Korean Government. The United States is not prepared, he continued, to increase its present contributions in this manner. *(Mr. Chin requested for favorable consideration of the Korean proposal.* ~~In reply to Mr. Chin's request for favorable consideration of the Korean proposal,~~ *In reply,* Mr. Habib said the U.S. side would give the proposal consideration but not favorable consideration. Mr. Chin stated that this was a difficult matter for both sides and proposed further consideration which might lead to a solution satisfactory to both sides.*)*

Rewrite

0075

23-21

63-1-2

93-91

비문 88.2

0076

CONFIDENTIAL

22. Mr. Habib then tabled paragraphs 3 and 4 of the U.S. draft of article "D", concerning utilities and services. Mr. Chin stated that the Korean side had also prepared corresponding paragraphs but would not table them [redacted], unless [redacted] they differed from the U.S. draft, in which case they would be tabled at the next meeting.

23. Mr. Habib proposed that the [redacted] facilities and areas draft be divided tentatively into separate articles; along the lines of the U.S. draft, in order to make progress possible. [redacted] It was agreed that the chairmen should meet [redacted] and decide how to handle this question.

24. The next meeting was scheduled for January 24 at 3 p.m.

63-1-30

0077

23-21

63-1-2 (30)

53-51

미주. 88-2(30)

0078

Mr. Chin stated that the words "under such conditions as may be agreed through the Joint Committee" ~~was~~ were unnecessary, because it is taken for granted that procedural matters concerning the return of facilities and areas no longer needed would be a matter of mutual consultation at the Joint Committee. He said the Korean draft did not spell correct procedural matters out the details concerning the return of facilities because the Joint Committee is the body which will implement the provisions of the SOFA. He ~~continued to~~ stated, however, that there was no substantial difference between the two paragraphs. It was agreed that this paragraph presented no difficul problem.

0079

20. Mr. Chin stated that the Korean side was not ~~fully~~ un-aware of the U.S. position. But he said he would like to explain the Korean position from a broader view point rather than on a legal or technical basis. ~~He said that the Korean side had prepared its draft with a view to strengthening the friendly relations existing between the two Governments rather than on the basis of any legal or technical considerations.~~ One of the major objectives of the Status of Forces Agreement, he continued, is to further strengthen the friendly relations between the Republic of Korea and the United States. He said that in preparing its draft, the Korean side had fully considered the U.S. position on this matter as well as the objectives of the SOFA, and consequently has limited its ~~was requesting~~ request for compensation only ~~for~~ to the private property as the minimum necessary compensation. He said that if the U.S. would agree to the Korean proposal it would make a great contribution to an early conclusion of the SOFA and to the attainment of the above objective.

196 ,12 ,31 ,에 예고문에 의거 일반문서로 재분류

0080

보통문서로 재분류(1966.12.31.)

Agreed Minutes to Article______

1. It is understood that any change in priority or increase in utility or service rates applicable to the United States armed forces shall be the subject of prior consultation in the Joint Committee.

2. Paragraph 3 of Article____ will not be construed as in any way abrogating the Utilities and Claims Settlement Agreement of December 18, 1958 which continues in full force and effect.

63-1-7

0081

22-7

63-1-2

미문 88-2

0082

Facilities and Areas

Article____

3. (a) The United States armed forces shall have the use of all utilities and services, whether publicly or privately owned, which are controlled or regulated by the Government of the Republic of Korea or political subdivisions thereof. The term "utilities and services" shall include, but not be limited to, transportation and communications facilities and systems, electricity, gas, water, steam, heat, light, power, however produced, and sewage disposal. The use of utilities and services as provided herein shall not prejudice the right of the United States to operate military transportation, communication, power and such other services and facilities deemed necessary for the operations of the United States armed forces.

(b) The use of such utilities and services by the United States shall be in accordance with priorities, conditions, and rates or tariffs no less favorable than those accorded any other user, governmental or private. The Republic of Korea shall insure that, by reason of legislation or otherwise, there shall be no discrimination against the United States

21-1-8

0083

22-5

63-1-2

비문 88-2

0084

armed forces in the procurement of such utilities and services. Should the emergency operating needs of the United States armed forces so require, the Republic of Korea shall, upon notification thereof, take all measures to assure provision of utilities and services necessary to meet these needs.

4. It is agreed that arrangements will be effected between the Governments of the United States and the Republic of Korea for accounting applicable to financial transactions arising out of this Agreement.

63-1-9

0085

22-6

63-1-2

미문 88-2

0086

관리번호 ~~876~~

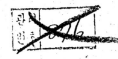

JOINT ~~SUMMARY RECORD OF THE~~ 11TH SESSION
STATUS FORCES NEGOTIATIONS

January 16, 1963

I. Time and Place : 2:00 to 4:00 p.m. January 16, 1963 at the Foreign Minister's Conference Room

II. Attendants:

ROK Side:

Mr. Chin, Pil Shik	Director Bureau of Political Affairs Ministry of Foreign Affairs
Mr. Pak, Kun	Chief, America Section Ministry of Foreign Affairs
Mr. O, Won Yong	Chief, Treaty Section Ministry of Foreign Affairs
Col. Lee, Nam Koo	Chief, Military Affairs Section Ministry of National Defense
Mr. Chu, Mun Ki	Chief, Legal Affairs Section Ministry of Justice
Mr. Lee, Kyung Hoon	2nd Secretary Ministry of Foreign Affairs
Mr. Shin, Chung Sup	2nd Secretary Ministry of Foreign Affairs
Mr. Chi, Sung Koo	Press Officer Ministry of Foreign Affairs
Mr. Kang, Suk Jae	3rd Secretary Ministry of Foreign Affairs

US Side:

Mr. Philip C. Habib	Counselor of the Embassy for Political Affairs
Brig. Gen J.D, Lawlor	Deputy Chief of Staff 8th Army
Mr. William J. Ford	First Secretary of the Embassy
Col. W.A. Solf	Staff Judge Advocate 8th Army

63-1-11

1964 년 9 월 30 일 예고문에 의거 일반문서로 재분류

~~237~~ 22-5 0087

63-1-2   외무 88-2

0088

Mr. Benjamin A. Fleck (Rapporteur and Press Officer)	First Secretary of the Embassy
Mr. Robert A. Lewis	Second Secretary and Consul of the Embassy
Lt. Col. Crawford	Staff Judge Advocate 8th Army
Lt. Col. W.A. Burt	J-5
Kenneth Campen	Interpreter

63-1-12

0089

63-1-2

미분 88-2

0090

1. Before beginning substantive discussion, Mr. Habib introduced Colonel Kenneth C. Crawford, of the Staff Judge Advocate's Office, EUSA, who was attending the meeting in place of Lt. Col. R.E. Miller. Mr. Habib noted the absence of Col. G. G. O'Connor because of illness and of Captain R. M. Brownlie, who was also unable to attend the meeting. Mr. Chin noted the absence of Mr. Yi Kyung-ho and Mr. Shin Kwan-sup. He introduced Mr. Chu Mun-ki, Chief of the Legal Affairs Section in the Ministry of Justice, who was attending in place of Mr. Yi, and Major Ahn Seung Keun from the Ministry of Defense.

Joint Committee

2. In opening substantive discussion, Mr. Chin asked whether the U.S. side had any additional remarks to make concerning the Joint Committee article. Mr. Habib replied that at previous negotiating sessions, the negotiators had reached full agreement on the text of the article, except for the phrase "except where otherwise provided" at the end of the first sentence of paragraph 1 in the U.S. draft. He reminded the negotiators that this phrase had been inserted in anticipation of certain special communications arrangements as provided for under the provisions of the relevant facilities and areas article. Requesting the Korean side to reconsider its opposition to inclusion of the phrase, Mr. Habib pointed out that the Joint Committee article was fundamental to the entire SOFA, inasmuch as it established the mechanism for the

63-1-13

미주과	앙고재	1월 23일	담당	과장	국장	특별보좌관	차관	장관

0091

CONFIDENTIAL

63-1-2

미문 88-2

0092

smooth coordination and effective implementation of the provisions of the Agreement. He urged acceptance of the U.S. draft in keeping with what the U.S. side understood was the desire of both sides to obtain speedy agreement with respect to certain key articles.

3. Mr. Chin replied that the Korean side had carefully considered this matter. He said it was his understanding that the phrase referred solely to paragraph 2(b) of the second facilities and areas draft article tabled by the U.S. side. He inquired whether it also referred to any other draft articles which might be tabled at a later date. Mr. Habib pointed out that the phrase referred to both paragraph 2(b) and 2(c) of the relevant facilities and areas article and stated that it was the understanding of the U.S. side, on the basis of ~~their instuctions,~~ that no reference to any other portion of the SOFA was intended or planned.

4. Mr. Chin stated that the provisions of paragraph 2(b) were clearly spelled out but that the reference in paragraph 2(c) to the word "agreements" was vague. He requested an explanation of the word "agreements". Mr. Habib replied that the word referred to any agreements entered into with the Korean authorities by the U.S. authorities. In this connection, he mentioned that one such agreement would be one providing for U.S. notification to the International Frequency Registration Board of frequencies used by the U.S. armed forces in Korea.

63-1-14

0093

23-4

63-1-2

비문 88-2

0094

5. Mr. Chin proposed that the phrase "except where otherwise provided" be retained in the text of the Joint Committee Article and that an Agreed Minute be approved which would explain the reference of this phrase to paragraph 2(b) and 2(c) of the relevant facilities and areas article. Mr. Habib asked whether the Korean side was prepared to table a draft of the Agreed Minute. Mr. Chin suggested that the Agreed Minute read as follows:

> "The exception provided for in the first sentence of paragraph 1 is relevant only to paragraph 2, subparagraphs (b) and (c) of Article ____."

6. Mr. Habib suggested that this explanation be written into the joint summary record instead of being made an Agreed Minute. However, he agreed to consider the Korean proposal.

Facilities and Areas

7. Turning to the drafts of the facilities and areas articles, Mr. Chin noted that at the previous meeting views were exchanged on paragraphs 1 and 2 of the U.S. draft article "A" and the corresponding paragraphs (1,2,3 and 6) of the Korean draft. He suggested that the negotiators proceed with an examination of paragraphs 3 and 4 of the U.S. draft and the corresponding paragraphs 7 and 8 of the Korean draft.

8. Mr. Habib pointed out that the chief difference between paragraph 3 of the U.S. draft and paragraph 7 of the Korean draft was the provision in the U.S. draft that facilities are to be returned to the Republic of Korea "under such conditions as may be agreed through

63-1-15

0095

23-5

-37-2

미문 88-2

0096

the Joint Committee." He reminded the negotiators that the U.S. armed forces continuously review the possibility of returning facilities no longer needed. Obviously, he said, once the return of a facility is decided upon, it would be returned under whatever provisions the Joint Committee agrees to. He asked whether the Korean side had any other procedure or considerations in mind. He also referred to the use of the word "promptly" in the Korean draft and stated that its use was unnecessary since any facility being returned would be returned promptly once the Joint Committee agreed on the conditions of its return. Mr. Chin stated that the words "under such conditions as may be agreed through the Joint Committee" were unnecessary, because it is taken for granted that procedural matters concerning the return of facilities and areas no longer needed would be a matter of mutual consultation at the Joint Committee. He said the Korean draft did not spell out the details concerning procedural matters connected to the return of facilities because the Joint Committee is the body which will implement the provisions of the SOFA. He stated, however, that there was no substantial difference between the two paragraphs. It was agreed that this paragraph presented no difficult problem.

9. Turning to paragraph 4 of the U.S. draft and the corresponding paragraphs 8 and 9 of the Korean draft, Mr. Habib suggested that subparagrah (a) of the U.S. draft was clearer than the Korean paragraph 8.

63-1-16

0097

23-6

63-1-2

미원 88-2

0098

The phrase "and the Government of the Republic of Korea is so advised" is more explicit as to the exact time when the facilities in question would be made available for interim use. The final half of subparagraph (a), he continued, tightens up the procedures and provides a cooperative basis for making the facilities available for interim use. Mr. Habib pointed out that the subparagraph serves two basic purposes: (a) it sets a time schedule, and (b) it provides for cooperation and coordination.

10. Mr. Chin stated that there was no substantive difference between the two drafts; the U.S. draft merely elaborated the subject. Since the Joint Committee will always operate in the spirit indicated in the U.S. draft, the Korean side saw no necessity to elaborate in this article the manner in which the Joint Committee shall perform its functions. He also suggested that the phrase "and the Government of the Republic of Korea is so advised" was unnecessary. Mr. Habib replied that the U.S. side believed the phrase desirable because it would provide the means of avoiding a debate over when any particular facility was to be returned. He said debates at a later date over the meaning of provisions of the Agreement should be avoided whenever possible by making the language of the Agreement as specific as possible. Mr. Chin replied that the two sides were in general agreement. The only disagreement was in how to state the substance of the subparagraph.

63-1-18

0099

23-7

63-1-2

미문 88-2

0100

11. Mr. Habib noted that paragraph 9 of the Korean draft omitted the words "armed forces" and spoke of a"limited period of time" instead of "limited periods of time". Otherwise, he pointed out that paragraph 9 and subparagraph 4(b) of the U.S. draft are identical.

Article "B"

12. Mr. Chin noted that there appeared to be little difference between paragraph 1 of the U.S. draft article "B" and the Korean paragraph 10, except for the sentence in the U.S. draft beginning "in an emergency,..". He requested an explanation of this sentence. Mr. Habib replied by stating that this provision was contained in the SOFA with Japan in the form of a separate Agreed Minute. The U.S. side believed it preferable to embody it in the text of the article rather than in an accompanying Agreed Minute. He said that experience has shown that safety measures are necessary in the vicinity of facilities to protect against subversive activities during emergency situations. He pointed out that during the present condition of armed truce, security is a paramount consideration. He added that the only other difference between the two texts lay in the U.S. wording "United States armed forces" as compared with the Korean wording "Government of the United States". He said that as a practical matter, the armed forces would make any such request on behalf of the United States Government. In addition, he pointed out, both drafts contain the additional requirement of consultation through the Joint Committee.

63-1-0101

23-8

63-1-2

미문 88.2

0102

Mr. Chin replied that the Korean side believed that since the request is made to the Government of the Republic of Korea, it should be made by the Government of the United States, thus maintaining a balanced government to government situation. He suggested further consideration of this point.

13. Turning to paragraph 2 of the U.S. draft and paragraph 11 of the Korean draft, Mr. Habib pointed out that subparagraph (a) of the U.S. draft and the first sentence of the Korean paragraph 11 were identical. The only substantive difference between subparagraph (b) and the second sentecne of paragraph 11 was the use in the U.S. draft of the phrase "designated military communications authorities" in contrast to the phrase "appropriate authorities of the two Governments" in the Korean draft. He said that the general subject of paragraph 2 had already been discussed during previous discussions of the Joint Committee Article. However, there was in the Korean draft no equivalent to subparagraph (c), which stated an obligation on the Korean government which the U.S. side believed was a corollary to the obligation placed on the U.S. armed forces by the provisions of subparagraph (a). The U.S. side believed that a mutual obligation existed and should be so stated in the article. With regard to subparagraph (d), Mr. Habib said he wished to remind the negotiators again that one of the agreements envisioned would provide for U.S. notification to the International Frequency Registration Board of frequencies used by the U.S. armed forces in Korea.

67-1-70

63-1-2

미문 88-2

0104

14. Mr. Habib pointed out that paragraph 3 of the U.S. draft and paragraph 12 of the Korean draft were identical.

15. Mr. Chin stated that the Korean side fully understood the delegation of authority provided in subparagraph (b) of the U.S. draft. However, they had used the word "appropriate" in paragraph 11 because of its broad, all-inclusive nature (which encompassed the Joint Committee) and because this word had been used elsewhere in the Agreement. Mr. Habib replied that the U.S. side believed a more specific term was desirable in this instance, so as not to involve unnecessarily authorities who had no specific interest or competence in these highly technical classified matters. It was agreed to give further consideration to this question.

Article "C"

16. Mr. Habib pointed out that paragraph 1 of the U.S. draft article "C" was identical with the first sentence of paragraph 13 of the Korean draft. However, the second sentence of paragraph 13 introduced a subject (compensation) which would be discussed in greater detail in connection with U.S. draft article "D". He invited the Korean side to explain their position, if they cared to do so at that juncture. Mr. Chin suggested that discussion of the compensation issue be deferred until the negotiators reached the U.S. draft article "D". Mr. Habib agreed, but pointed out that the point at issue was the provision of

63-1-21

0105

28-10

63-1-2

비문 88-2

0106

facilities and not the source of those facilities. Whether they were originally privately or publicly owned was irrelevant.

17. In reply to Mr. Chin's request for an explanation of paragraph 2 of the U.S. draft, Mr. Habib replied that to state it in simple terms: "what's ours is ours and we can remove it if we wish to do so". Mr. Chin replied that if it were that simple, there was no need to spell it out in the Agreement.

18. Mr Chin pointed out that paragfaph 14 of the Korean draft did not appear in the U.S. draft and could be inserted without difficulty. Mr. Habib replied that the U.S. Government had decided not to request payment of residual value and therefore this provision was omitted from the U.S. draft. He said he agreed in principle to its inclusion but suggested further discussion. However, he indicated the belief of the U.S. side that the words "supply or other materials left thereon" were not relevant and should be omitted. He added that paragraph 3 in the U.S. draft, although it did not appear in the Korean draft, presented no problem and was closely related to paragraph 2.

Article "D"

19. The negotiators then proceeded to discussion of the U.S. draft article "D" and the corresponding paragraphs 4 and 5 of the Korean draft. Mr. Habib said there existed a fundamental difference of opinion regarding the payment of compensation for the use of facilities and areas. He said the views of the U.S.

63-1-22

0107

23-11

63-1-2

미문 88-2

0108

side were well known. The U.S. draft, he continued, states that the United States Government will pay all expenses incident to the maintenance of the U.S. armed forces in Korea except for those to be paid by the Korean Government as provided in paragraph 2. In contrast, paragraph 4 of the Korean draft would place on the U.S. Government the obligation to pay compensation. He reminded the negotiators that early in the negotiations, and also prior to them, the U.S. Government had stated clearly and explicitly its view that no compensation would be paid. There has been no change since then, he said. The United States does not accept, he continued, any distinction in the origin of the facilities. All facilities, he stated, are made available to the U.S. armed forces by the Korean Government. Obviously, however, he continued, the U.S. armed forces are prepared to cooperate to the maximum extent possible by releasing facilities no longer needed or by accepting alternate facilities offered by the Korean Government. He pointed out that the United States Government has adhered to the principle of no compensation in all of the mutual security negotiations in which it has engaged, on the grounds that the facilities provided are the host country's contribution to the joint effort. There is no reason to deviate from this policy in Korea, he said. He then asked Mr. Chin to state the Korean views.

20. Mr. Chin stated that the Korean side was not unaware of the U.S. position. But, he said he would

63-1-23

0109

28-12

63-1-2

미문 88-2

0110

like to explain the Korea position from a broader view point rather than on any legal or technical basis. One of the major objectives of the Status of Forces Agreement, he continued, is to further strengthen the friendly relations between the Republic of Korea and the United States. He said that in preparing its draft, the Korean side had fully considered the U.S. position on this matter as well as the objectives of the SOFA, and consequently has limited its request for compensation only to the private property as the minimum necessary compensation. He said that if the U.S. would agree to the Korean proposal it would make a great contribution to an early conclusion of the SOFA and to the attainment of the above objective.

21. Mr. Habib replied that he wished to make clear that the question of compensating private owners was not being debated. The U.S. side agreed that there may be a responsibility to compensate them but held that it was not the responsibility of the United States but of the Government of the Republic of Korea. He said it was well known that the United States Government was already making contributions to the Korean Government. The United States is not prepared, he continued, to increase its present contributions in this manner. Mr. Chin requested favorable consideration of the Korean proposal. In reply, Mr. Habib said the U.S. side would give the proposal consideration but not favorable consideration. Mr. Chin stated that this was a difficult matter for both sides and proposed

63-1-24

0111

23-13

6ㄱ-1-2

外혼 88-2

0112

further consideration which might lead to a solution satisfactory to both sides.

22. Mr. Habib then tabled paragraphs 3 and 4 of the U.S. draft of article "D", concerning utilities and services. Mr. Chin stated that the Korean side has also prepared corresponding paragraphs but would not table them unless they differed from the U.S. draft, in which case they would be tabled at the next meeting.

23. Mr. Habib proposed that the facilities and areas draft be divided tentatively into separate articles, along the lines of the U.S. draft, in order to make progress possible. It was agreed that the chairman should meet and decide how to handle this question.

24. The next meeting was scheduled for January 24 at 3 p.m.

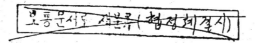

보통문서로 재분류(1966.12.31.)

~~보통문서로 재분류(협정체결시)~~

63-1-25

1966.12.31.에 예고문에 의거 일반문서로 재분류됨

0113

23-14

63-1-2

미문 88-2

0114

~~0089~~

駐屯軍地位協定交涉会議 進度表

第11次会议
(1963. 1. 16. 現在)

題目	次期会議討議予定	條文交換討議開始	合意内容	完全合意	
1 序文					
2 用語의 定義					
3 土地및 施設					
4 航空統制및 航海補助施設問題					34차 1960 (63)
5 合同委員会					
6 出入国管理					
7 関税業務					
8 船舶및 航空機 [illegible] 問題					
9 公益物및 用役問題					45차 ?/16 (64)
10 軍票					✓
11 軍事郵便施設및 郵便行政					40차 ?/24 (64)
12 予備役 訓練問題					
13 美軍人, 家族및 財産의 安全問題					✓
14 気象및 其他 関聯 問題					
15 車輛및 運転免許 問題					
16 貨幣統制問題					
17 非歳出機関活動問題					
18 法規尊重問題					
19 刑事裁判管轄權 問題					
20 請求權 問題					
21 租税問題					✓
22 現地調達 問題					
23 会計節次 問題					34차 [illegible]
24 [illegible] 問題					
25 [illegible] 問題					
26 [illegible]					
27 [illegible]					
28 [illegible]					
保健衛生問題					

0115

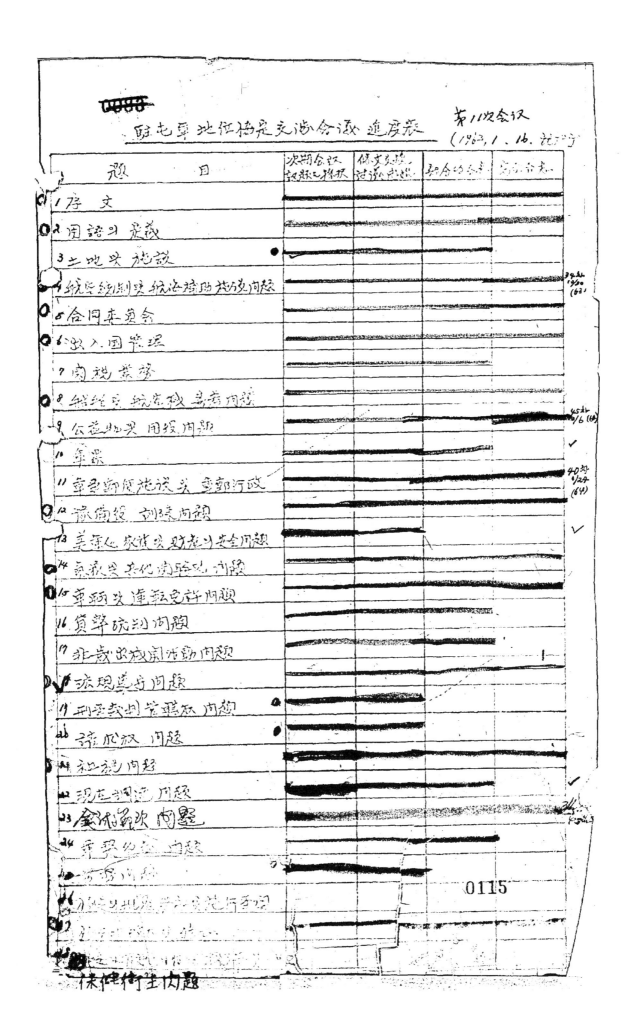

3. 제12차 회의, 1.24

0116

대한해운공사 민성기(사장비서실) ②-1713
P.L.O. (신문회관 2층 212호실) Mr. Won Mr. Lee ②-4056

미주둔군지위협정 체결 교섭관계자 명단

1964. 1. 20.

부처	직위	성명	전화번호
국방부	기획국 정책과장(대령) 국방부차관	김원길	~~[illegible]~~ (302-4116)
		이계훈	④-6208 "
재무부	재무부차관 ~~[illegible]~~	~~신관섭~~	72-4111 ~~72-[illegible]~~
	관세과장	조충훈	72-0011~0019 ~~[illegible]~~
	이재국 외환과장 <과장, 정사무관.	이재설	72-4973
	지도과 (이재선 (정인영)	이재섭	72-4705
	법무차관		2-4085(2-0680)
법무부	법무과장	주문기	2-4072
	검찰과장		~~2-4083~~ 3-6406
	검찰국장 (Yun, Woon Young)	윤 윤영	2-8368
	총무과	윤 검사	3-1461 (3-1462)
노동청	노정국장 노정과장	황 설준 ~~[illegible]~~	3-5437 ②-4295
외무부	구미국장(한국측 수석대표)	장상문	
	미주과장	구충회	4843
	조약과장	오재희	5228
	조약과	이정빈	5229
	~~경제협력과~~	~~조광재~~	~~4850~~
	미주과	~~[illegible]~~	74-3073
	미주과	이근팔	48 K4

숙직실 ~~4844~~ ~~[illegible]~~ 5260

주한미국대사관 관계자

Mr. Philip C. Habib (미국측 수석대표)	Councilor for Political Affairs	2-7111/5 Ext.-210
Mr. Benjamin A. Fleck	First Secretary	Ext.-212 Res.-Y-4123 Compound 102
Mr. Robert A. Lewis	Second Secretary	Ext.-229
Mr. James Sartorius	Second Secretary	Ext.-657

내무부 차관실 2-4880

0117

총무과 인사계 4828-4829

장관비서실 4810 숙직실 5260 (74-1362)

회의실 4814

The United States Negotiators

Lt. Col. ~~Major~~ ~~Robert~~ ~~Peckham~~	~~Mr. James~~ ~~Sarterium~~ Mr. Lamacchia	~~Col. Howard~~ ~~Smigelow~~ Col. Crawford	Brig. ~~Gen.~~ ~~Lawrence~~ J. ~~Fuller~~ Col. Smigelow	Brig.Gen. G.G. O'Connor	(Chief N.) Mr. Philip C. Habib	Mr. Benjamin A. Fleck	Capt. John Wayne	Mr. Rovert A. Lewis	Mr. Robert Kinney
~~Mr. Chung~~ ~~Bin Lee~~ 박정일	~~Mr. Cho~~ ~~Kwang Je~~	Mr. Chung Sup Shin	Mr. Mun Ki Chu	Mr. Shin, Kwan Sup	Mr. Chang, Sang Moon (Chief N.)	Mr. Koo, Choong Whay	Major Lee, Kae Hoon ~~Col. Kim~~ ~~Won Ki~~	~~Mr. Kang,~~ ~~Suk Jae~~	Mr. Lee, Keun Pal

Col. Crawford

Republic of Korea Negotiators

0118

5260

관리 번호 877

기 안 용 지

자 체 통 제		기안처	미주과 이 경 훈	전화번호	근거서류접수일자

	과장	수석대표	보좌관	차관	장관
	1/23		1/23		

관계관 서 명	조약과장 1.23 기획조정관

기 안 년월일	1963. 1. 23.	시 행 년월일		보존 년한		정 서	기 장
분 류 기 호	외정미	전 체 통 제		종결			
경 유 수 신 참 조	건 의			발 신			
제 목	제12차 주둔군 지위협정체결 교섭회의에 임할 우리측 태도						

1월 24일에 개최될 제12차 주둔군지위협정 체결 한미간 교섭회의에서는 관세업무, 공익물 및 용역사용, 기상업무, 접수국국법의 존중, 그리고 예비병의 훈련문제에 관하여 토의될 예정이온바 이에관련하여 우리측 교섭실무자는 1월 22일 관계부처 실무자와의 연석회의를 갖고 제12차 회의에서 취할 우리측 태도를 별첨과같이 결정하였아오니 재가하여 주시기 바랍니다.

유첨: 제12차 주둔군 지위협정 체결 교섭회의에 임할 우리측 태도

보통문서로 재분류(1966.12.31.)

196 에 예고문에 의거 일반문서로 재분류됨

0119

승인양식 1-1-3 (1112-040-016-018) (190mm×260mm16절지)

1964년 9월 30일 미주과 직권으로 [illegible] 재분류

12次

1. 관세업무

(1) 공용순입품의 관세면제 대상에 관한 제 2 항에 관하여 (가) 미국측이 제시한 수정안보다 원안을 수락할것을 제의하되, (나) 원안의 최종문장에 있어서 "other armed forces in Korea" 다음에 "under the Unified Command" 라는 어구를 삽입토록 주장한다.

(2) 개인용수입품의 관세면제 대상에관한 제 3 항에 있어서 동 3 항중 3(b)항에 규정된 차량 및 부속품의 도입에 관하여 우리측은 미국군대 구성원 및 군속이 그들자신 또는 그들의 가족의 사용을 위하여 도입하는 차량에 대하여 그들이 한국에 도착후 3 개월내에 도입할것에 한하여 면세특권을 부여토록 미측에 제의한바 있으나 도입된 차량의 판매를 금지시키고 판매시에는 수입세를 부과하도록 하며는 본특권의 람용을 방지할수 있을것임으로 미국측안을 받아드리기로 한다.

(3) 세관검사 면제대상 규정인 제 5 항에 있어서 우리측은 (가) 계속 단체 (unit)로서 입국하는 자에 한하여 세관검사 면제를 부여토록 주장하고 (만일 미측이 끝끝내 member 에대한 세관검사를 할수없다고 하며는 최종판계에 가서 양보토록한다) (나) 사용우편물에 대하여 세관검사를 실시토록 하고 official mail 에 대하여는 면제하도록 계속 주장하고 (다) 비세출 기관에 송부되는 군용품은 세관검사 면제대상에서 제외하자고 계속 주장하기로 한다.

(4) 한국관세 법규 위반방지를 위한 협조규정인 제 9 항에 있어서 9(c)항 다음에 우리측 초안 7(e)항을 삽입하여 9(d)항으로하고 따라서 미국측안의 9(d)항은 9(e)항으로 하자고 계속 주장한다.

0120

(5) 관세업무 조항에대한 합의의사록에 있어서,

(가) 제 1, 4, 및 5 항을 수락한다.

(나) 제 2 항에 있어서 "free of duty" 다음에 "reasonable quantities of" 라는 구절을 삽입토록 주장한다.

(다) 제 3 항에 있어서 "and their non-appropriated fund organizations provided for in Article__" 을 삭제하고 대신에 "but excluding their non-appropriated fund organizations provided for in Article ____" 를 삽입하도록 주장한다.

(라) 제 6 항에 있어서 "authorized by United States law and service regulations" 의 삭제를 주장한다.

2. 공익물 및 용역사용

(1) 지난회기에서 제출된 미국측안에 대하여 우리측이 준비한 안과 실질적인 면에서는 큰차이가 없으나 표현에 있어서 미국측안이 복잡하고 일방적인 표현이 많음으로 별첨과 같은 우리측 안을 제시키로 한다. (별첨 1. 참조)

3. 기상업무

(1) 기상업무에 관하여 한미 양측은 각기 관계당국 간의 합의된바에 따라 기상관측, 기상자료 및 지진관측 자료의 상호 제공을 협조한다바고 규정한다. (별첨 2. 수정초안) (본문제에 관한 최초안은 항해, 항공통제 조항 제시시 이에포함 되어있었음)

(2) 미일 협정 제8조에 의하면 일본정부가 일방적으로 미군에게

0121

5/-3

(가) 육상 또는 해상으로부터의 기상관측 자료

(나) 기상 관측소의 일계에관한 정기보고서

(다) 항공기의 안전과 정규운영에 필요한 자료의 전신 전파

(라) 지진관계 자료를 제공하도록 규정되어 있음에 비추어 미국측이 미.일 협정에 따르는 이러한 일방적인 제공 의무의 형식으로 기상업무에 관한 초안을 제출할지도 모를것임.

(3) 그러할때는 우리측은 쌍무적 규정을한 우리측 수정안을 미국측이 수락하도록 요구해보고 미국측이 이를 거부할시는 미국측이 미.일협정과 비등한 안을 제시하는 한 미국측 제안을 받아드리기로 한다.

4. 접수국 국법의 존중

(1) 대한민국의 법을 존중하고 주둔군 지위협정의 정신과 어긋나는 활동 특히 대한민국 내에서의 정치활동을 하지않는것은 미국군대 구성원, 군속 및 그들의 가족의 의무라고 규정한 우리측안을 제시키로 한다. (별첨 3. 참조)

(2) 미국측이 제시하는 안이 우리측안과 비등할때는 이를 수락해주기로 한다.

5. 예비병의 훈련

(1) 미국은 대한민국에 거주하고 있는 미국시민을 소집하여 미국군대예비병 훈련기관에서 훈련시킬수 있다고 규정한 우리측 안을 제시한다. (별첨 4. 참조)

(2) 미국측이 제시하는 안이 우리측안과 비등할시에는 이를 수락하기로 한다.

보통문서로 재분류(1966.12.31.)

0122

51-4

196 , , 에 고문에 의거 일반문서로 재분류됨

별첨 1.

1. The United States armed forces shall have the use of all public utilities and services belonging to, or controlled or regulated by the Government of the Republic of Korea. The term "utilities and services "shall include, but not be limited to, transportation and communications facilities and system, electricty, gas, water, steam, heat, light, power, however produced, and sewage disposal. In the use of such utilities and services the United States armed forces shall enjoy priorities under conditions no less favorable than those that may be applicable from time to time to the ministries and agencies of the Government of the Republic of Korea.

2.(a)Specific arrangements as to the use of such public utilities and services by the United States armed forces and the payment therefor shall be made between the appropriate authorities of the two Governments or their agencies.

(b)The existing arrangements concerning the use of such public utilities and services by the United States armed forces at the effective date of this Agreement shall be regarded as the arrangements referred to in the foregoing paragraph.

51-5

0123

별첨 2.

The Governments of the Republic of Korea and the United States shall cooperate in mutually furnishing the relevant authorities of each Government with the following meteorological services in accordance with arrangements between the appropriate authorities of the two Governments:

(a) Meteorological observation,

(b) Climatological information, and

(c) Seismographic data.

51-6

0124

별첨 3.

ARTICLE

It is the duty of the members of the United States armed forces, the civilian component, and their dependents to respect the law of the Republic of Korea, and to abstain from any activity inconsistent with the spirit of the present Agreement, and, in particular, from any political activity in the Republic of Korea.

51-7

0125

별첨 4.

ARTICLE

The United States may enroll and train eligible United States citizens residing in the Republic of Korea in the reserve organizations of the United States armed forces.

보통문서로 재분류(1966.12.31)

1966.12.31에 예고문에 의거 일반문서로 재분류됨

51-8

0126

SOFA NEGOTIATION

Agenda for 12th Session

15:00 January 24,1963

1. Continuation of Discussion on:

    a. Customs Duties

    b. Utilities and Services

2. Discussion on:

    a. Meteorological Services

    b. Respect for Local Law

    c. Enrollment and Training of Reservists

3. Other Business

4. Agenda and Date of Next Meeting

5. Press Release

0127

관리 번호 578

기 안 용 지

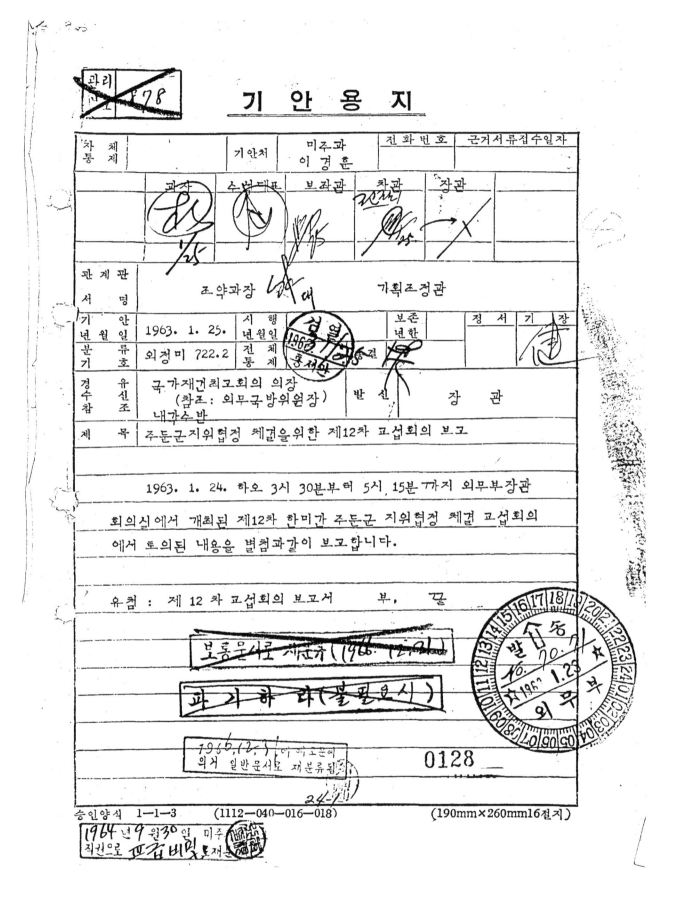

자체 통제		기안처	미주과 이경훈	전화번호	근거서류접수일자
	과장	수석대표	보좌관	차관	장관
관계관 서명	조약과장		기획조정관		
기안 년월일	1963. 1. 25.	시행 년월일	1963. 1. 25	보존 년한	정서 기장
분류 기호	외정미 722.2	전체 통제	총결		
경유 수신 참조	국가재건최고회의 의장 (참조: 외무국방위원장) 내각수반	발신	장관		
제목	주둔군지위협정 체결을위한 제12차 교섭회의 보고				

1963. 1. 24. 하오 3시 30분부터 5시 15분까지 외무부장관 회의실에서 개최된 제12차 한미간 주둔군 지위협정 체결 교섭회의에서 토의된 내용을 별첨과같이 보고합니다.

유첨 : 제 12 차 교섭회의 보고서 부. 끝

~~보통문서로 재분류 (1966. 12. 31)~~

~~파 기 하 라 (불필요시)~~

1966.12.31 에 예고문에 의거 일반문서로 재분류됨

0128

승인양식 1-1-3 (1112-040-016-018) (190mm×260mm16절지)

1964 년 9 월 30 일 미주과 직권으로 비밀 로 재분류

외 무 부

외정미 722.2 (8-3052) 1963. 1. 25.

수 신 국가재건최고회의 의장

참 조 외무국방위원장

제 목 주둔군 지위협정 체결을 위한 제12차 교섭회의 보고

1963. 1. 24. 하오 3시 30분부터 5시 15분 까지 외무부 장관 회의실에서 개최된 제12차 한미간 주둔군 지위협정 체결 교섭 회의에서 토의된 내용을 별첨과 같이 보고합니다.

유첨 : 제 12 차 교섭회의 보고서 2 부. 끝

외 무 부 장 관 최 덕 신

0129

24-6

외 무 부

외정미 722.2 (8-3052) 1963. 1. 25.

수 신 내각수반

제 목 주둔군지위협정 체결을위한 제12차 교섭회의 보고

1963. 1. 24. 하오 3시 30분부터 5시 15분까지 외무부장관 회의실에서 개최된 제12차 한미간 주둔군 지위협정 체결 교섭회의에서 토의된 내용을 별첨과같이 보고합니다.

유첨 : 제 12 차 교섭회의 보고서 1 부. 끝

외 무 부 장 관 최 덕 신

0130

24-5

제 12 차

한미간 주둔군지위협정 체결 실무자회의

보 고 서

1. 시 일 : 1963. 1. 24. 하오 3시 30분부터 5시 15분 까지

2. 장 소 : 외무부장관 회의실

3. 참석자 : 한국측 : 진 필 식 (외무부 정무국장, 수석대표)

신 관 섭 (재무부 세관국장)

박 근 (외무부 미주과장)

오 원 용 (외무부 조약과장)

이 남 구 (국방부 군무과장)

이 경 훈 (외무부 2 등서기관)

신 정 섭 (")

지 성 구 (외무부 공보관)

강 석 재 (외무부 3 등서기관)

미국측 : 대표단전원 ("하비브" 수석대표 불참)

4. 토의사항 :

(1) 관세업무에 있어 공용수입품의 관세면제 대상에관한 제2항 에관하여 우리측은 (가) 미국측이 제시한 원안을 수락하되 (나) 원안의 최종문장에 있어서 "other armed forces in Korea " 다음에 "under the Unified Command" 라는 어구를 삽입토록 주장하자 미국측은 이를 고려해 보겠다고 하였고, 또한 미국측 초안에서 규정된 "non-appropriated fund orginizations"라는 어구는 "non-appropriated fund activities " 로 수정하고, including 이하 구절을 괄호안에 넣을것을 제시하였음. 우리측은 이를 고려해보겠다고 하였음. 63-1-55

0131

24-2

-1-3 (-) 미취원 88-1(6)

0132

(2) 관세업무에 있어서 개인용 수입품으로서 차량 및 부속품의 수입에 일정한 기간을 설치하자고 우리측이 주장하자 미국측은 이러한 기간의 설치를 반대하였으며 여기에대하여 우리측은 한국에 불필요하게 너무 많은 차량이나 부속품이 들어오지 않도록 적절한 제한이 필요하다고 주장함. 본문제는 다음에 다시 토의키로 함.

(3) 세관검사 면제대상에 있어 우리측은 계속하여 (가) 단체 (unit)로서 입국하는자 (나) 공용우편물 (official mail) (다) 군기관 (비세출기관 제외)에 송부된 군용품에 대하여서만 세관검사의 면제를 부여하자고 주장하자 미국측은 이에반대하는 자국측의 입장을 계속 주장하여 이문제는 다음에 다시토의키로 함.

(4) 한국세관 법규위반 방지를 위한 협조규정에 있어서 미국측 초안 9(c)항 다음에 우리측초안 7(e)항을 삽입할것을 주장하자 미국측은 이를 고려하겠다고 하였음.

(5) 공익물 및 용역사용에 관한 우리측 초안이 제시되었음.

(6) 기상업무에 관한 우리측 수정안과 미국측안이 교환되었음.

(7) 접수국 법의 존중문제에 관한 양측초안이 교환되었으며 미국측은 한국측안에 없는 미국측안의 "몇조에 의거하여 대한민국에 현존하는자"에 관한 구절은 앞으로 토의될 조문이라 하였기 우리측은 그러면 이문제는 앞으로 관계 조문이 제시된후에 토의하자고 하였음.

(8) 예비병의 훈련문제에 관하여 양측은 각기초안을 교환한후 쌍방의 안의 차의를 지적하고 이문제를 다음에 다시토의키로 함.

63-1-36

0133

24-3

-1-3

대원 88-1

0134

5. 기타사항 :

(1) 차기회의 일자 : 1963. 2. 5. 하오 2시

(2) 차기회의 의제 : 차기회의까지 양측 수석대표간에 합의된 사항

6. 참고자료 :

미국측이 제의한 협정초안 (기상업무, 접수국법의 존중, 예비병의 훈련) 별첨참조

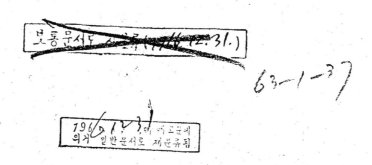

~~보통문서로 재분류(1966.12.31.)~~

63-1-37

1966.12.31 에 예고문에 의거 일반문서로 재분류됨

0135

24-4

63-1-3

0136

~~1. Gen. Lawlor opened the meeting by apologizing for the unavoidable absence of Mr. Habib.~~

Customs

1. In taking up the Customs article for discussion, Mr. Chin noted that at the previous discussion, the Korean side had indicated readiness to accept the [redacted] text of the original paragraph 2 in the U.S. draft, provided a slight modification was [redacted] made in the phrase "other armed forces". Gen. Lawlor replied that Agreed Minutes 4 and 5 in the U.S. draft would provide certain safeguards against abuses of the provisions of paragraph 2. He said the U.S. side still preferred the ~~revision~~ text of paragraph 2 which it had tabled during the previous discussion because the language [redacted] had greater clarity. He said there was no substantive difference between the revision and the original text. Mr. Chin replied that although the U.S. side believed the revision to be more precise, the Korean side [redacted] believed the original text to be clearer and therefore preferred to continue discussion on the basis of the original draft. He then proposed the addition of the words "under the Unified Command" following the phrase "in Korea" in the final sentence of ~~the paragraph~~ original draft. He said the addition would not change the meaning and would include Katusas and any other non-U.S. forces serving as part of the Unified Command.

2. Gen. Lawlor replied that the U.S. side would take this apparently minor change under advisement. He said the U.S. side also wished to make a minor change. He then proposed [redacted] substituting the word "Activities" for the word "organizations" and placing the phrase "including their authorized procurement agencies and their non-appropriated fund activities provided for in Article ___" in parentheses. He indicated that the change should be made twice in paragraph 2, once in paragraph 5, subparagraph (c), and in the Agreed Minute #3, relating to paragraph 5 (c). He ~~[illegible]~~ that the change was not intended to

alter [redacted] the substance of the [redacted] phrase but merely to clarify it. Mr. Chin asked whether the change would broaden the scope of the paragraph. [redacted] Gen. Lawlor replied that it would not. He said the activities under discussion were usually referred to as "activities" and not as "organizations". It was felt that by using the word "activities", these functions were identified more readily as part of the armed forces, [redacted] whereas use of the word "organizations" might give the false implication that they were not part of the armed forces. Mr. Chin stated that the Korean side would study the U.S. proposal.

3. Turning to paragraph 3, subparagraph (b), Mr. Chin stated that during the previous discussion, the Korean side had proposed to limit the period during which importation of vehicles and parts could take ~~place. (Gen. Lawlor said~~ such a limitation would present a serious problem. He pointed out that privately-owned vehicles might have to be replaced, owing to theft, fair wear and tear, or collision, since in many cases these vehicles were the only means which their owners had of [redacted] proceeding to and from their residences and places of duty. Imposition of a customs duty on parts or vehicles brought in as replacements would, he continued, have a serious adverse effect on [redacted] morale. [redacted] He pointed out that the ability of the ROK Government to protect its interests would not be affected, since the disposal of privately-owned vehicles within Korean territory is subject to regulatory and tax regulations. He also reminded the Korean side of other practical difficulties, such as the great distances which these vehicles and parts had to be shipped, the frequent necessity of waiting for the factory to fill an order, and the unexpected delays caused by strikes.

0138

4. Mr. Chin replied that the Korean side had given these matters very careful study. He said ~~they~~ the Korean side did not wish to cause any inconvenience to the personnel of the U.S. armed forces. However, ~~they~~ the Korean side did feel that a time limit was necessary and ~~had changed their original proposal of [illegible] months to three months.~~ Gen. Lawlor asked what the Korean side feared if there were no time limit. Mr. Chin suggested that a certain ~~length of~~ time limit be set.

CONFIDENTIAL

[redacted] reiterated his statement that there was no desire to cause any inconvenience to the U.S. personnel [redacted] and added that a time limit was necessary in order to limit the number of vehicles imported. Gen. Lawlor stated that the U.S. side would [redacted] consider the Korean position [redacted] but reminded the Korean side that Agreed Minute #5 in the U.S. draft should take care of any problem that might arise.

5. Turning to paragraph 5, Mr. Chin stated that the Korean side was still studying subparagraph (a) of the U.S. draft and would comment at a subsequent meeting. He asked for U.S. comments on subparagraph (b). Gen. Lawlor replied that [redacted] the speedy delivery of mail to the troops was also a morale factor. He pointed out that the proposed Agreed Minutes would provide safeguards against abuses. He reminded the ROK side that the U.S. [redacted] authorities were just as interested as the ROK authorities in seeing to it that no abuses occurred. Mr. Chin reminded the negotiators of the Korean side's previous proposal to insert the word "official" before the word "mail". Gen. Lawlor said the U.S. side had considered this proposal but did not favor it. He pointed out that the subject of discussion was the private mail of individuals. Mr. Chin said that the Korean side ~~wished to avoid taking any action which would~~ did not wish to cause any damage to the morale of the troops and reminded the U.S. negotiators of his previous assurance that the ROK Government would do its best to ensure speedy delivery of mails. He said the Korean customs officials would always be cooperative. Gen. Lawlor expressed the appreciation of the U.S. side for the considerate attitude of the Korean side and said that the U.S. side would take the Korean position under advisement.

0139

6. Mr. Chin then pointed out that paragraph [redacted] 3 (c), which had already been agreed to by both sides, provided for the importation of "reasonable quantities" of personal effects and household goods through military post offices, free of customs duties. Therefore, he continued, it would be only logical and proper for the Korean customs officers to be given authority [redacted]

25-14

XXX

under paragraph 5 (b) to check the unofficial mail to insure that only reasonable amounts of these items were being shipped in through the military post offices. The [redacted] provisions of the two paragraphs would then be consistent, he added. Gen. Lawlor stated that the U.S. side would consider this position.

7. With regard to subparagraph (c), Mr. Chin stated that there is a difference between cargo consigned to the U.S. armed forces and cargo [redacted] consigned to non-appropriated fund organizations. He said the sources of funds in [redacted] payment for these two types of cargo [redacted] were different and stated the belief of the Korean side that the goods consigned to the armed forces were more important for military purposes than goods consigned to non-appropriated fund organizations. Gen. Lawlor replied non-appropriated fund activities were considered to be part of the armed forces. He said it would be very difficult to [redacted] assign degrees of importance to the various [redacted] items the U.S. armed forces needed to import into Korea; all such items contribute to the [redacted] operational efficiency of the troops. He pointed out that non-appropriated fund activities have to do with the [redacted] mental attitudes and welfare of the soldier. He added that the authorities of the U.S. armed forces police these activities and that if and when abuses are found, corrective action is taken.

8. Mr. Chin replied that ~~the Korean side~~ he understood the position of the U.S. side. He stated that much of the cargo shipped to the armed forces [redacted] might be of a classified nature. Naturally, he said, the customs officials would not check this cargo. However, the cargo shipped to the non-appropriated fund organizations would not be classified and therefore it would not be inconvenient to the U.S. armed forces to have the Korean customs officials check it. These officials, Chin stated, would do their best to cooperate so as not to cause any unnecessary inconvenience. Gen. Lawlor pointed out that a great deal of the cargo shipped to the armed forces is of an unclassified [redacted] the categorization was not valid.

0140

25-12

9. Mr. Chin suggested that the cargo shipped to non-appropriated fund activities should be deleted from the provisions of subparagraph (c). He pointed out that the U.S. side had already differentiated this type of cargo from other types by making specific reference to it in the draft Agreed Minute #1. Although the Agreed Minute restricts importation of this type of cargo to "reasonable" quantities, how can the ROK Government know whether this provision is being adhered to, he asked, unless the Korean customs officials can check it? He said that there was no question of taxation; this was merely a matter of examination. He again stated that the Korean customs officials would be cooperative.

10. Gen. Lawlor replied that the obligation stated in the Agreed Minute #1 was a unilateral obligation on the U.S. armed forces. Mr. Chin said the Korean side believed the determination of what is a "reasonable" amount should be a mutual determination. In response to Gen. Lawlor's query as to how such a mutual determination could be arrived at, Mr. Chin said that a "reasonable" amount is a reasonable amount and that the Korean customs officials would cooperate. [redacted]

11. Mr. Chin noted that paragraphs 6, 7, and 8 had already been agreed to. He then suggested that the negotiators leave off their discussion of this article, [redacted] in view of the passage of time, and turn their attention to the remaining items on the agenda. At this point, the negotiators exchanged drafts of the articles dealing with meteorological services, respect for local law, and enrollment and training of reservists. The Korean side also tabled the draft of an article dealing with utilities and services.

Respect for Local Law

12. Mr. Chin commented that the drafts of this article were identical

0141

25-13

with the exception of minor differences. He asked whether the reference to "persons [redacted] who are present in the Republic of Korea pursuant to Article ___" referred to persons other than those specified in the Definitions Article as being members of the U.S. armed forces. Gen. Lawlor replied that this reference was to an article which had not yet been tabled. Mr. Chin indicated agreement with the [U.S.] draft article, except for this phrase, which he said the Korean side would take under advisement.

Training of Reservists

13. The differences between the two drafts of this article were noted. Gen. Lawlor pointed out that the U.S. draft [redacted] included persons who might be present in Korea but not necessarily resident in Korea. Mr. Chin stated that the Korean side would study this point.

14. It was then decided to adjourn the meeting. The next meeting was scheduled for February 5 at 2:00 p.m.

0142

25-14

<u>Meteorological Services</u>

Article____

The Government of Korea undertakes to furnish the United States armed forces with the following meteorological services in accordance with arrangements between the appropriate authorities of the two Governments:

(a) Meteorological observations from land and ocean areas including observations from ships;

(b) Climatological information including periodic summaries and historical data wherever available;

(c) Telecommunications service to disseminate meteorological information;

(d) Seismographic data.

63-1-38

0143

24-5

-3-1-3

미윤 88-1

0144

ARTICLE ____

It is the duty of members of the United States Armed Forces, the civilian component, the persons who are present in the Republic of Korea pursuant to Article _____, and their dependents, to respect the law of Korea and to abstain from any activity inconsistent with the spirit of this Agreement, and, in particular, from any political activity in Korea.

63-1-3 P

0145

24-6

63-1-3

미북 88-1

0146

ARTICLE

The United States may enroll in its reserve forces and train, in Korea, eligible United States citizens who are in the Republic of Korea.

63-1-40

~~보통문서로 재분류(1966. 12. 31)~~

1966.12.31 에 예고문에 의거 일반문서로 재분류됨

0147

24-7

63-1-7 (6)

88-1 (6)

0148

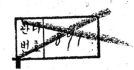

JOINT SUMMARY RECORD OF THE 12TH SESSION
STATUS FORCES NEGOTIATIONS

January 24, 1963

I. Time and Place : 2:00 to 4:00 p.m. January 24, 1963 at the Foreign Minister's Conference Room

II. Attendants:

ROK Side:

Mr. Chin, Pil Shik	Director Bureau of Political Affairs Ministry of Foreign Affairs
Mr. Shin, Kwan Sup	Director Bureau of Costums Duty Ministry of Finance
Mr. Pak, Kun	Chief, America Section Ministry of Foreign Affairs
Mr. O, Won Yong	Chief, Treaty Section Ministry of Foreign Affairs
Col. Lee, Nam Koo	Chief, Military Affairs Section Ministry of National Defense
Mr. Chu, Mun Ki	Chief, Legal Affairs Section Ministry of Justice
Mr. Lee, Kyung Hoon	2nd Secretary Ministry of Foreign Affairs
Mr. Shin, Chung Sup	2nd Secretary Ministry of Foreign Affairs
Mr. Chi, Sung Koo	Press Officer Ministry of Foreign Affairs
Mr. Kang, Suk Jae	3rd Secretary Ministry of Foreign Affairs

US Side:

Brig. Gen J.D. Lawlor	Deputy Chief of Staff 8th Army
Mr. William J. Ford	First Secretary of the Embassy
Col. G.G. O'Connor	Deputy Chief of Staff 8th Army

0149

담당	과장	국장	특별보좌관	차관	장관

Capt. R.M. Brownlie	Assistant Chief of Staff USN/K
Col. W.A. Solf	Staff Judge Advocate 8th Army
Kenneth Campen	Interpreter
Kenneth C. Col. Crawford	Staff Judge Advocate 8th Army
Mr. Benjamin A. Fleck (Rapporteur and Press Officer)	First Secretary of the Embassy
Mr. Robert A. Lewis	Second Secretary and Consul of the Embassy

Customs

1. In taking up the Customs article for discussion, Mr. Chin noted that at the previous discussion, the Korean side had indicated readiness to accept the text of the original paragraph 2 in the U.S. draft, provided a slight modification was made in the phrase "other armed forces". Gen. Lawlor replied that Agreed Minutes 4 and 5 in the U.S. draft would provide certain safeguards against abuses of the provisions of paragraph 2. He said the U.S. side still preferred the revised text of paragraph 2 which it had tabled during the previous discussion because the language had greater clarity. He said there was no substantive difference between the revision and the original text. Mr. Chin replied that although the U.S. side believed the revision to be more precise, the Korean side believed the original text to be clearer and therefore preferred to continue discussion on the basis of the original draft. He then proposed the addition of the words "under the Unified Command" following the phrase "in Korea" in the final sentence of original draft.

0150

25-2

He said the addition would not change the meaning and would include Katusas and any other non-U.S. forces serving as part of the Unified Command.

2. Gen. Lawlor replied that the U.S. side would take this apparently minor change under advisement. He said the U.S. side also wished to make a minor change. He then proposed substituting the word "activities" for the word "organizations" and placing the phrase "including their authorized procurement agencies and their non-appropriated fund activities provided for in Article___" in parentheses. He indicated that the change should be made twice in paragraph 2, once in paragraph 5, ~~subparagraph 5,~~ subparagraph (c), and in the Agreed Minute #3, relating to paragraph 5 (c). He indicated that the change was not intended to alter the substance of the phrase but merely to clarify it. Mr. Chin asked whether the change would broaden the scope of the paragraph. Gen. Lawlor replied that it would not. He said the activities under discussion were usually referred to as "activities" and not as "organizations". It was felt that by using the word "activities", these functions were identified more readily as part of the armed forces, whereas use of the word "organizations" might give the false implication that they were not part of the armed forces. Mr. Chin stated that the Korean side would study the U.S. propsoal.

3. Turning to paragraph 3, subparagraph (b), Mr. Chin stated that during the previous discussion, the Korean side had proposed to limit the period during which importation of vehicles and parts could take place.

0151

25-3

Gen. Lawlor said such a limitation would present a serious problem. He pointed out that privately-owned vehicles might have to be replaced, owing to theft fair wear and tear, or collision, since in many cases these vehicles were the only means which their owners had of proceeding to and from their residences and places of duty. Imposition of a customs duty on parts or vehicles brought in as replacements would, he continued, have a serious adverse effect on morale. He pointed out that the ability of the ROK Government to protect its interests would not be affected, since the disposal of privately-owned vehicles within Korean territory is subject to regulatory and tax regulations. He also reminded the Korean side of other practical difficulties, such as the great distances which these vehicles and parts had to be shipped, the frequent necessity of waiting for the factory to fill an order, and the unexpected delays caused by strikes.

4. Mr. Chin replied that the Korean side had given these matters very careful study. He said the Korean side did not wish to cause any inconvenience to the personnel of the U.S. armed forces. However, the Korean side did feel that a time limit was necessary and suggested that a certain time limit be set. Gen. Lawlor asked what the Korean side feared if there were no time limit. Mr. Chin reiterated his statement that there was no desire to cause any inconvenience to the U.S. personnel and added that a time limit was necessary in order to limit the number of vehicles

0152

25-4

imported. Gen. Lawlor stated that the U.S. side would consider the Korean position but reminded the Korean side that Agreed Minute #5 in the U.S. draft should take care of any problem that might arise.

5. Turning to paragraph 5, Mr. Chin stated that the Korean side was still studying subparagraph (a) of the U.S. draft and would comment at a subsequent meeting. He asked for U.S. coments on subparagraph (b). Gen. Lawlor replied that the speedy delivery of mail to the troops was also a morale factor. He pointed out that the proposed Agreed Minutes would provide safeguards against abuses. He reminded the ROK side that the U.S. authorities were just as interested as the ROK authorities in seeing to it that no abuses occurred. Mr. Chin reminded the negotiators of the Korean side's previous proposal to insert the word "official" before the word "mail". Gen. Lawlor said the U.S. side had considered this proposal but did not favor it. He pointed out that the subject of discussion was the private mail of individuals. Mr Chin said that the Korean side did not wish to cause any damage to the morale of the troops, and reminded the U.S. negotiators of his previous assurance that the ROK Government would do its best to ensure speedy delivery of mails. He said the Korean customs officials would always be cooperative. Gen. Lawlor expressed the appreciation of the U.S. side for the considerate attitude of the Korean side and said that the U.S. side would take the Korean position under advisement.

0153

25-5

6. Mr. Chin then pointed out that paragraph 3(c), which had already been agreed to by both sides, provided for the importation of "reasonable quantities" of personal effects and household goods through military post offices, free of customs duties. Therefore, he continued, it would be only logical and proper for the Korean customs officers to be given authority under paragraph 5 (b) to check the unofficial mail to insure that only reasonable amounts of these items were being shipped in through the military post offices. The provisions of the two paragraphs would then be consistent, he added. Gen. Lawlor stated that the U.S. side would consider this position.

7. With regard to subparagraph (c), Mr. Chin stated that there is a difference between cargo consigned to the U.S. armed forces and cargo consigned to non-appropriated fund organizations. He said the sources of funds in payment for these two types of cargo were different and stated the belief of the Korean side that the goods consigned to the armed forces were more important for militsry purposes than goods consigned to non-appropriated fund organizations. Gen. Lawlor replied non-appropriated fund activities were considered to be part of the armed forces. He said it would be very difficult to assign degrees of importance to the various items the U.S. armed forces needed to import into Korea; all such items contribute to the operational efficiency of the troops. He pointed out that non-appropriated fund activities have to do with the mental attitudes and

0154

welfare of the soldier. He added that the authorities of the U.S. armed forces police these activities and that if and when abuses are found, corrective action is taken.

8. Mr. Chin replied that he understood the position of the U.S. side. He stated that much of the cargo shipped to the armed forces might be of a classified nature. Naturally, he said, the customs officials would not check this cargo. However, the cargo shipped to the non-appropriated fund organizations would not be classified and therefore it would not be inconvenient to the U.S. armed forces to have the Korean customs officials check it. These officials, Chin stated, would do their best to cooperate so as not to cause any unnecessary inconvenience. Gen. Lawlor pointed out that a great deal of the cargo shipped to the armed forces is of an unclassified nature; hence the categorization was not valid.

9. Mr. Chin then suggested that the phrase and their non-appropriated fund organizations provided for in Articles be deleted from subparagraph (c). He pointed out that the U.S. side had already differentiated cargo shipped to these organzation from other types by making specific reference to it in the draft Agreed Minute #1. The Agreed Minute restricts importation of this type of cargo to "reasonable" quantities, and therefore the Korean customs officials should be authorized to examine such cargo to find out if the quantities of cargo are "reasonable".

0155

25-6

He said that there was no question of taxation; this was merely a matter of examination. He again stated that the Korean customs officials would be cooperative.

10. Gen. Lawlor replied that the obligation stated in the Agreed Minute #1 was a unilateral obligation on the U.S. armed forces. Mr. Chin said the Korean side believed that the determination of what is a "reasonable" amount should be a mutual determination. In response to Gen. Lawlor's query as to how such a mutual determination could be arrived at, Mr. Chin said that a "reasonable" amount is a reasonable amount and that the Korean customs officials would cooperate.

11. Mr. Chin noted that paragraphs 6,7, and 8 had already been agreed to. He reminded the negotiators that the Korean side, in the previous discussion, had suggested the insertion of Paragraph 7(e) of the Korean draft between Paragraphs 9(c) and 9(d) of the U.S. draft and that the U.S. side had agreed to consider this proposal. He then suggested that the negotiators leave off their discussion of the Agreed Minutes to the customs and duties Article in view of the passage of time, and turn their attention to the remaining items on the agenda. At this point, the negotiators exchanged drafts of the articles dealing with meteorological sevices, respect for local law, and enrollement and training of reservists. The Korean side also tabled the draft of an article dealing with utilities and services.

0156

25-7

Respect for Local Law

12. Mr. Chin commented that the drafts of this article were identical with the exception of minor differences. He asked whether the reference to "persons who are present in the Republic of Korea pursuant to Article____" referred to persons other than those specified in the Definitions Article as being members of the U.S. armed forces. Gen. Lawlor replied that this reference was to an article which had not yet been tabled. Mr. Chin indicated agreement with the U.S. draft article, except for this phrase, which he said the Korean side would take under advisement.

Training of Reservists

13. The differences between the two drafts of this article were noted. Gen. Lawlor pointed out that the U.S. draft included persons who might be present in Korea but not necessarily resident in Korea. Mr. Chin stated that the Korean side would study this point.

14. It was then decided to adjourn the meeting. The next meeting was scheduled for February 5 at 2:00 p.m.

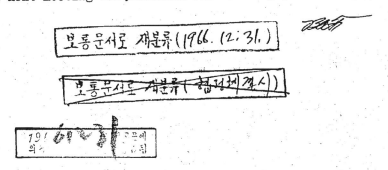

보통문서로 재분류(1966. 12. 31.)

~~보통문서로 재분류(협정체결시)~~

19 ... 의 ...

0157

25-8

협 조 전	응 신 기 일

문서번호 제 목 사진 복사 의뢰

수 신: 문화과장 발 신: 미주과장 년 월 일 63.2.1. 제1의견

별첨 주한미주둔군 지위협정 교섭회의 광경사진을 아래부수와 여히 복사하여 주시기 의뢰합니다.

아 래

회의 광경 (2종) .... 각 6매

미국측 대표사진 5매

한국측 대표사진 7매

계 24매

유첨: 사진 4매 끝

미 주 과 장 무 용 익

미주과	안고재 =월/일	담당	과장	국장	특별보좌관	차관	장관

0158

승인양식 1 — 34 11—13330—01 (195mm×265mm16절지)

0159

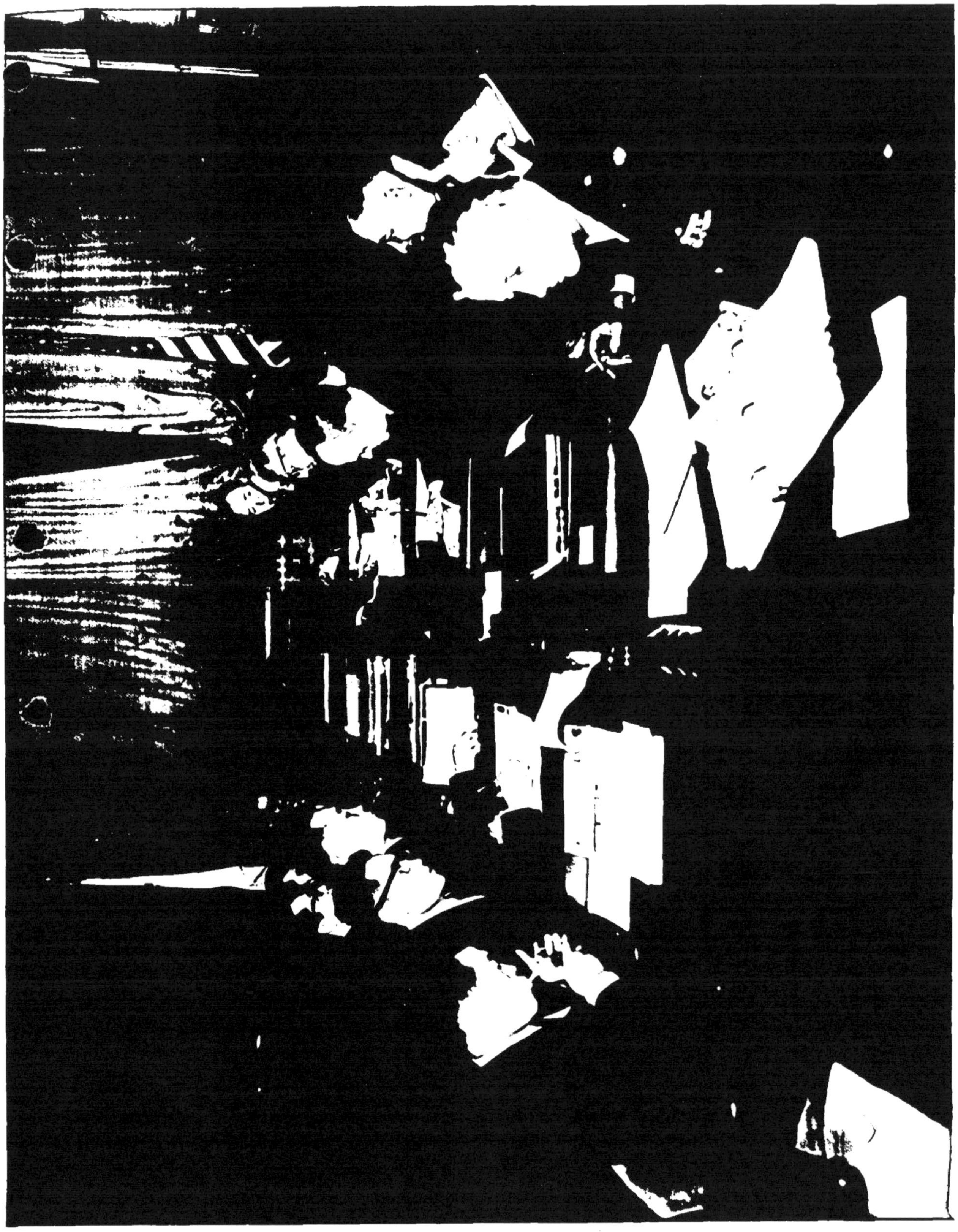

0160

4. 제13차 회의, 2.4

0162

관리 번호 ~~~~

기 안 용 지

자체 통제		기안처	미주과 이경훈	전화번호	근거서류접수일자

	과장	수석대표	보좌관	차관	장관	
				대결		

관계관 서명	조약과장 2.2. 기획조정관

기안 년월일	1963. 2. 2.	시행 년월일		보존 년한		정서 기장
분류 기호		전체 통제		종결		

경유 수신 참조	건의	발신	

제 목 제13차 주둔군지위협정 체결교섭회의에 임할 우리측 태도

2월 5일에 개최될 제13차 주둔군지위협정 체결 한미간 교섭회의에서는 관세업무, 접수국법의 존중 그리고 예비병의 소집 및 훈련 문제에관하여 토의될 예정이온바 이에관련하여 우리측 교섭실무자는 2월 1일 회합을 갖고 제13차 회의에서 취할 우리측태도를 별첨과같이 결정하였아오니 재가하여 주시기 바랍니다.

유첨 : 제 13 차 주둔군지위협정 체결교섭회의에 임할 우리측태도. 끝

보통문서로 재분류 (1966.12.31)

1966.12.31.에 예고문에 의거 일반문서로 재분류됨

0163

4-1

승인양식 1-1-3 (1112-040-016-018) (190mm×260mm16절지)

1966 년9 월30일 미주과 직권으로 Ⅲ급비밀 로재

1. 관세업무

(1) 한국관세 법규위반 방지를 위한 협조규정인 제 9 항에 있어서 9(c)항 다음에 우리측 초안 7(e)항을 삽입하여 9(d)항으로 하고 따라서 미국측 안의 9(d)항은 9(e)항으로 하자고 계속 주장한다.

(2) 관세업무 조항에대한 합의의사록에 있어서,

(가) 제 1, 4 및 5 항을 수락한다.

(나) 제 2 항에 있어서 "free of duty" 다음에 "reasonable quantities of " 라는 구절을 삽입토록 주장한다.

(다) 제 3 항에 있어서 "and their non-appropriated fund organizations provided for in Article___" 을 삭제하고 대신에 "but excluding their non-appropriated fund organizations provided for in Article ____" 를 삽입토록 주장한다.

(라) 제 6 항에 있어서 "authorized by United States law and service regulations" 의 삭제를 주장한다.

2. 접수국법의 존중

(1) 미국측 초안은 우리측 초안에없는 "the persons who are present in the Republic of Korea pursuant to Article___" 이라는 구절을 둠으로서 미국군대 구성원, 군속 및 그들의 가족이외에도 "다른 조에 의거하여 대한민국에 현존하는자"와 이들의 가족도 한국법을 존중할 의무가 있다고 규정하고 있음.

(2) 본조항은 한국법의 존중을 규정한것임으로 존중의 의무를 가진 인적대상이 많을수록 우리측에는 유리하지만

0164

4-2

(가) 미국측 초안에서 말하는 별도 다른 조항이 무엇이며 (이는 미국군대와의 계약체결자[및 고용원]를 말할것임) 그조항에서 말하는 자에대한 특권의 범위가 과대할때에는 오히려 우리측에 불리할지도 모를것이며 또한 (나) 미국측이 접수국법을 존중할 인적대상으로서 미국군대와의 계약체결자를 포함시키는 반면에 접수국의 주둔국 군인, 군속 및 그들의 가족에 대한 안전보장 부여의무 조항에 이를 계약체결자[및 고용원]도 포함시킬때에는 우리측에 불리한점도 있지않겠는가라는 점등을 고려하여야 할것임.

(3) 따라서 본조항에 있어서는 미국측에게 본조항에서 규정한 별도 다른 조항에 의거하여 대한민국에 현존하는자가 무엇인가를 문의하고 별도조항에 관한 쌍방의 초안을 교환하여 검토한후 우리측 태도를 결정하도록 한다.

3. 예비병의 소집 및 훈련

(1) 양측의 초안에 있어서 차의점은 미국이 소집, 훈련시킬수 있는자에 대하여 우리측안은 대한민국에 거주 (residing) 하는 미국시민으로 되어있는데 미국측안은 대한민국에 있는자 (who are in)으로 되어있는 구절임. — 30日以上 [illegible]

(2) 대한민국에 거주하는자라고 할때에는 우리나라의 외국인 출입 등록법관계 조항에 의거하여 그들이 등록을 필요로 하는자라고 할수있으나 대한민국에 있는자라고 할때에는 등록의 의무가없이 잠시 한국에 왔던자도 포함할수 있을것이라고 사료됨.

(3) 따라서 본문제에관하여 우리측은 미국측에대하여 대한민국에 있는자가 무엇을의미하는지 문의한후 우리측태도를 결정토록한다.

보통문서로 재분류(1966.12.31)

0165

1966.12.31.에 예고문에 의거 일반문서로 재분류됨

1966년 9월 30일 미주과장 직권으로 [illegible]

4-3

관리 번호 192

기 안 용 지

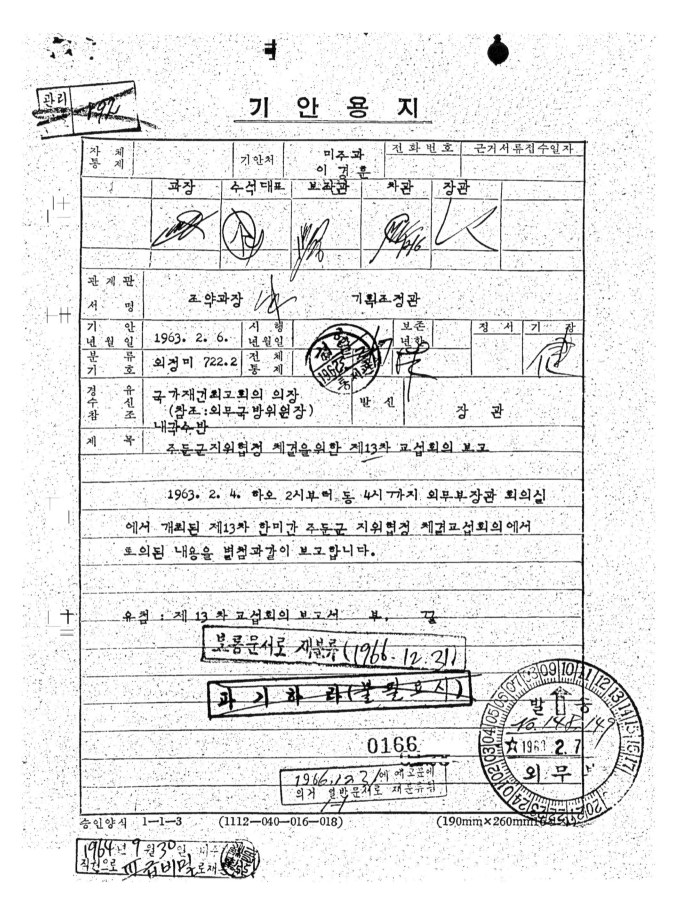

자체 통제		기안처	미주과 이경훈	전화번호	근거서류접수일자
	과장	수석대표	보좌관	차관	장관
관계관 서명	조약과장		기획조정관		
기안 년월일	1963. 2. 6.	시행 년월일		보존 년한	정서기장
분류 기호	외정미 722.2	전체 통제			
경수참 유신조	국가재건최고회의 의장 (참조 : 외무국방위원장) 내각수반	발신	장관		
제목	주둔군지위협정 체결을위한 제13차 교섭회의 보고				

1963. 2. 4. 하오 2시부터 동 4시까지 외무부장관 회의실에서 개최된 제13차 한미간 주둔군 지위협정 체결교섭회의에서 토의된 내용을 별첨과같이 보고합니다.

유첨 : 제 13 차 교섭회의 보고서 부. 끝

보통문서로 재분류 (1966. 12. 31)

파기하라 (불필요시)

발송 16. 148. 149 1963. 2. 7 외무부

0166

1966. 12. 31 에 예고문에 의거 일반문서로 재분류됨

승인양식 1—1—3 (1112—040—016—018) (190mm×260mm16절지)

1964년 9월 30일 에주 직권으로 비밀로 재분류

외 무 부

외정미 722.2　　　　　　　　　　　　　　　　　　1963. 2. 7.

수 신 :　내각수반

제 목 :　주둔군지위협정 체결을위한 제13차 교섭회의 보고

1963. 2. 4. 하오 2시부터 동 4시까지 외무부장관 회의실에서 개최된 제13차 한미간 주둔군 지위협정 체결교섭회의에서 토의된 내용을 별첨과같이 보고합니다.

유첨 : 제 13 차 교섭회의 보고서 1부. 끝

외 무 부 장 관　　　최　　　덕　　　신

0167

1-6

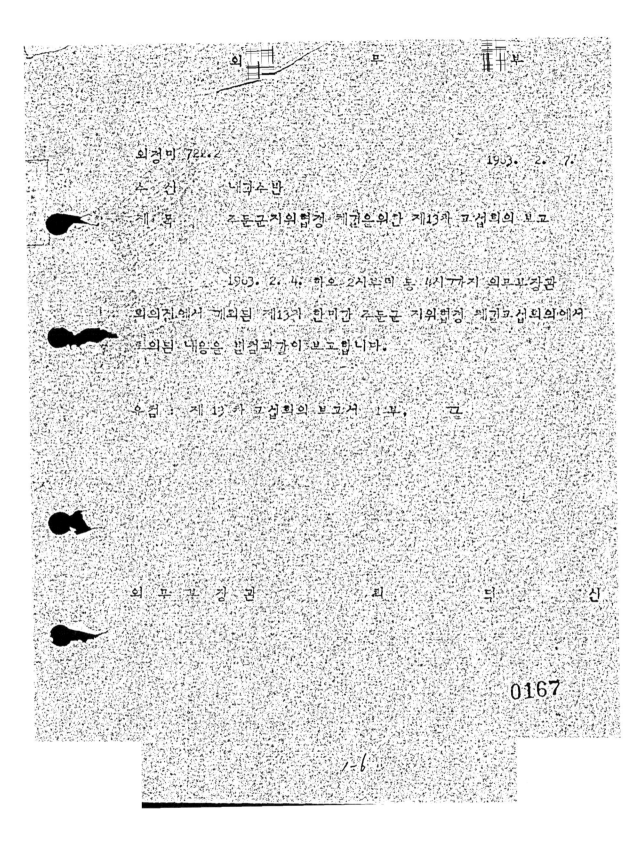

외 무 부

외정미 722.2 1963. 2. 7.

수 신 국가재건최고회의 의장

참 조 외무국방위원장

제 목 주둔군지위협정 체결을위한 제13차 교섭회의 보고

1963. 2. 4. 하오 2시부터 동 4시까지 외무부장관 회의실에서 개최된 제13차 한미간 주둔군지위협정 체결교섭회의에서 토의된 내용을 별첨과같이 보고합니다.

유첨 : 제 13 차 교섭회의 보고서 2 부. 끝

외 무 부 장 관 최 덕 신

0168

1-5

0140

제 13 차

한미간 주둔군지위협정체결 실무자회의

보 고 서

1. 시 일 : 1963. 2. 5. 하오 2시부터 4시까지

2. 장 소 : 외무부장관 회의실

3. 참석자 : 한국측 : 신 관 섭 (재무부 세관국장, 수석대표대리)

박 근 (외무부 1등서기관)

구 충 회 (외무부 미주과장)

오 원 용 (외무부 조약과장)

이 남 구 (국방부 군무과장)

이 경 훈 (외무부 2등서기관)

신 정 섭 (")

강 석 재 (외무부 3등서기관)

이 창 범 (")

미국측 : 대표단 전원

4. 토의사항 :

(1) 접수국법의 존중, 예비병의 소집 및 훈련, 그리고 관세업무 문제를 순차적으로 토의함.

(2) 접수국법의 존중문제에 있어서 미국측은 우리측 초안에는 없고 미국측 초안에만 규정되어있는 "별도조항에 의거하여 대한민국에 현존하는자" 라는 구절은 미국군대와의 계약체결자, 그들의 가족 및 그들에의하여 채용된 고용원을 말하는것이라고 설명하였기 우리측은 그러면 이문제는 미국군대와의 계약체결자에 관한 조항이 교환된후 다시토의하자고 하였음.

63-1-41

0163

1-2

03-1-4(3)

미국안 89-13(3)

0170

(3) 예비병의 소집 및 훈련문제에 있어서 우리측은 양측초안에서 중요한 차의점을 우리측 초안에서는 대한민국에 거주(residing) 하는 미국시민을 미국이 소집, 훈련시킬수 있다고 규정하고 있는데 대하여 미국측안은 대한민국에 현존(who are in) 하는 미국시민으로 규정하고 있는데 이에관한 미국측의 견해를 문의하자 미국측은 미국측 초안은 대한민국에 현존 하는자를 의미하는것이지 합법적 거주자를 의미하는것이 아니라고 하였음. 우리측은 이에대하여 미국측 안대로 대한민국에 일시적으로 현존하는자까지도 미국측이 예비병 소집과 훈련을 시킬수있다면 우리나라 외국인 출입 및 등록법의 운영에 혼돈을 가져올것이라고 말하자 미국측은 이들이 예비병에 소집되어 훈련을 받더라도 대한민국의 법에 복종하여야 할것임으로 별문제가 없을것이라고 말하여, 이문제는 다음에 다시 토의키로 함.

(4) 관세업무에 있어서 우리측은 한국관세 법규위반 방지를위한 협조규정인 제 9 항에 있어서 9(c)항 다음에 우리측 초안 7(e)항을 삽입할것을 제안하자 미국측은 이를 고려하겠다고 하였음.

(5) 관세업무 조항에대한 합의의사록에 있어서

(가) 우리측은 비세출기관이 수입하는 물품의 제한 규정인 1항에 있어서 적절하게 소요되는 범위는 쌍방이 상오 합의하는 적절한 수량으로 양해한다고 제의하자 미국측은 이를 고려해보겠다고 하였음. 63-1-42

(나) 개인용 수입품의 면세범위 규정에대한 세부규정인 2항에 있어서 우리측은 미국군대 구성원, 군속 및 그들의 가족이 수입하는 물품의 관세면제를 적절한

0171

1-3

63-1-4(3) 미문 89-13

0172

수량으로 제한하자고 제의하자 미국측은 이를 고려해 보겠다고 한후 이문제는 다음에 다시 토의키로 함.

(다) 세관검사 규정으로서 군용품에 관한 경의 규정인 3항에 있어서 미국측은 비세출기관에게 운송된 물자도 이에 포함시키자고 한데 대하여 우리측은 이를 제외하자고 한후 이문제를 다음에 다시 토의키로 함.

(라) 한국관세 법규위반 방지를위한 미국군대가 취할 조치 규정인 제 4 항 및 관세규정 남용 및 위반에 대한 한국 세관당국이 취할조치 규정인 제 5 항을 우리측은 수락하여 주었음.

(마) 제6항에 있어서 미국군대가 제공할 모든 지원은 미국 법령에서 허여된 범위에서 적절하고 실질적인 조치라고 미국측은 규정하고 있는데 대하여 우리측은 미국법령에서 허여된 범위를 삭제하자고 주장하고 이문제는 다음에 다시 토의키로 함.

5. 기타사항 :

(1) 차기회의 일자 : 1963. 2. 14. 하오 2시

(2) 차기회의 의제 : 차기회의까지 양측 수석대표간에 합의된사항

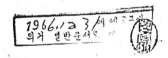

63-1-43

보통문서로 재분류(1966.12.31.)

1966.12.31.에 예고문에 의거 일반문서로

0173

1-4

63-1-4(3)

미국문 89-13(3)

0174

1. Mr. Shin opened the meeting by noting the absence of the Korean Chief Negotiator, Mr. Chin [PIL SHIK] ~~Pil-sik,~~ who was on an official trip abroad. He also noted the absence of Mr. [LEE] ~~Yi~~ Kyung-Hoo. Mr. Shin then announced that Dr. Pak Kun, having received transfer orders to [redacted] the Korean Embassy in Washington, was attending his last negotiating meeting. Mr. Shin introduced Dr. Pak's successor as Chief of the America Section [(MINISTRY OF FOREIGN AFFAIRS)] and as a member of the Korean negotiating team, Mr. [KOO CHOONG WHAY] ~~Ku Chung-hwe.~~ Mr. Shin also announced that Mr. Chi Sung-[KOO] ~~ku~~ had been [appointed as] ~~promoted to the position of~~ Chief of the Southeast Asia Section and, therefore, would no longer participate in the negotiations. Mr. [LEE KYUNG HOON] ~~Yi Kyung-hun~~ will act [for the time being,] as Press Officer for the Korean side in place of Mr. Chi. Mr. Habib expressed [appreciation for the helpful role which] [redacted] [redacted] Dr. Pak [had played in the negotiations and] [redacted] welcomed Mr. [KOO] ~~Ku.~~ [redacted]

Respect for Local Law

2. Turning to substantive matters, Mr. Habib [redacted] announced that regrettably he would have to leave the meeting early. He suggested, therefore, that the draft articles concerning respect for local law and training of reservists be taken up for discussion first. Mr. Shin agreed.

3. Mr. Habib reminded the negotiators that at the previous meeting, the Korean side had questioned the meaning of the phrase "the persons who are present in the Republic of Korea pursuant to Article ____". He said that this phrase had been included in the U.S. draft because the Definitions Article does not include invited contractors. This phrase refers to the draft article dealing with invited contractors. The U.S. draft of the respect for law article, therefore, was more comprehensive than the Korean draft, for it [added] [redacted] invited contractors [redacted] to the list of people called upon to respect Korean law and to refrain from political activity in Korea.

0175

4. Mr. Shin asked whether the phrase included the dependents and the employees of invited contractors. Mr. Habib ~~replied in the affirma~~tive. He said it included all

persons who were in the Republic of Korea pursuant to the invited contractors article. Mr. Shin then stated that the Korean side wished to reserve its position until the invited contractors article was tabled. Mr. Habib replied that this was satisfactory to the U.S. side. He asked whether he was correct in concluding that the respect for local law article was generally acceptable to the Korean side if the terms of the invited contractors article were as he had explained them. Mr. Shin replied that because of the reference to employees of invited contractors, the Korean side wished to discuss this article when the invited contractors article was tabled.

Enrollment and Training of Reservists

5. Discussion of the article dealing with reservists centered around the difference between persons "residing in" Korea in the Korean draft and persons "who are in" Korea in the U.S. draft. Mr. Habib pointed out that there are Americans present in Korea who are not residents of the country. As examples, he mentioned Embassy personnel and civilian employees of the U.S. armed forces. He said that the phraseology of the U.S. draft would permit such people to undertake training here in Korea in order to maintain their reserve status. Mr. Shin replied that under the provisions of the U.S. draft, persons who have not established legal residence in Korea might be called to reserve training. In such case, the Korean immigration authorities might have difficulty keeping track of them. The Korean side, he said, wished ~~some assurance~~ that this provision would not cause any confusion or difficulties for the immigration authorities.

6. Mr. Habib referred the negotiators to the entry and exit article, which provides that members of the civilian component are not eligible for permanent residence. (already agreed to) He said that both the Korean and U.S. drafts of the article under discussion provide for training for residents; the U.S. draft also provides for non-residents. He suggested that this provision would have no effect on the Korean entry and exit pro-

0176

cedures and would not cause any problem with regard to control of alien residents.

7. Dr. Pak said that there would be no confusion regarding the reserve training of members of the civilian component and the Embassy staff. However, the ROK Government might have difficulty enforcing its alien entry, exit and registration laws if temporary visitors or invited guests of the Government were enrolled for such training. Mr. Habib replied that the Korean side was creating a problem where none existed. Such persons who were enrolled for reserve training would still have to comply with Korean law. The Korean side agreed to consider the matter further.

8. Mr. Habib mentioned one additional point of difference between the two drafts. He said that the U.S. draft called for enrollment in "forces" rather than in "reserve organizations". He said this wording was proposed because it reflected the actual situation in Korea, in which reservists were trained in existing units of the armed forces, rather than in separate reserve organizations. Mr. Habib then expressed his regret that another pressing engagement made it necessary for him to leave the meeting at this point.

Customs and Duties

9. Turning to the customs article, Mr. Shin repeated the previous suggestion of the Korean side that paragraph 7(e) of the Korean draft be inserted after subparagraph (c) of Paragraph 9 in the U.S. draft. General Lawlor replied that the U.S. side would consider this proposal. He suggested that the Agreed Minutes of the U.S. draft be discussed. Mr. Ford stated that the word "organizations" in Agreed Minute #1 should be changed to "activities", in line with the changes proposed by the U.S. side at the previous meeting. Mr. Shin replied that the Korean side would discuss this proposed change in conjunction with discussion of the other proposed changes. Mr. Ford asked if the Korean side had any comments ~~regarding Agreed Minute #1~~.

0177

12

10. Mr. Shin replied that, in accordance with their previous comments, the Korean side believed that the meaning of "to the extent reasonably required" should be the subject of mutual determination by both Korean and U.S. authorities. With that understanding, and subject to further discussion of the proposed change of "organizations" to "activities", he said the Korean side agreed to the text of Agreed Minute #1. Mr. Ford replied that the U.S. side was not prepared to agree to mutual determination of what is reasonably required but would consider the Korean position.

11. Turning to Agreed Minute #2, Mr. Shin proposed the insertion of the words "reasonable quantities of" between the words "duty" and the word "their". The second sentence of the Minute would then read as follows: "In this connection, members of the United States armed forces or civilian component and their dependents may import free of duty [redacted] reasonable quantities of their personal and household effects during a period of six months from the date of their first arrival." Mr. Ford replied that the U.S. side would consider this proposal.

12. General Lawlor asked if the Korean side was proposing that "reasonable quantities" were to be mutually determined even for members of the U.S. armed forces. Mr. Shin replied that inasmuch as the Korean side wished to closely define "reasonable quantities" in regard to goods shipped to non-appropriated fund organizations, they also wished to place a similar restriction on personal and household effects. Since such effects will be permitted entry free of duty, he added, it was desired to place a limitation on the amounts permitted to enter.

13. General Lawlor asked how the Korean side proposed to ~~mxkx~~ determine what was a "reasonable" amount. Mr. Shin replied that it was their ~~[illegible]~~ desire to avoid the importation of excessive amounts, over and above those normally required. Mr. Ford pointed out that this Agreed Minute refers to paragraph 3(a) of the article, which had already been agreed to. He said the Minute was intended to deal with the question of the period during which importation could be made. ~~[illegible]~~ He pointed out

0178

that it was not intended to deal with quantitative restrictions.

14. Dr. Pak said he wished to answer General Lawlor's question regarding the determination of what is reasonable. He said the Korean side intended no inconvenience (to the owners) or unreasonable restriction on the amount of such goods to be imported. However, if an individual should import an extraordinarily large amount, the Korean side anticipated no difficulty in reaching agreement that this would be unreasonable. Therefore, the additional language proposed by the Korean side would cause no difficulty or unreasonable restriction.

15. Mr. Ford replied that the article provides for policing of its provisions by both sides. There is also a specific reference to abuses or infringement in Agreed Minute #5. He asserted that these would give all necessary protection to Korean interests and would still provide to the U.S. armed forces sufficient freedom to carry out their mission in Korea.

16. Mr. Shin stated that the provision in paragraph 8 of the article for mutual cooperation is vague and not specifically spelled out. He said that it was necessary to provide in the Agreed Minute standards of what is or is not an abuse of the provisions of the article. General Lawlor replied that the Korean side was unduly worried about abuses. However, the U.S. side would consider the Korean proposal.

17. Mr. Shin agreed with Mr. Ford's remark that the determination of what constitutes a "reasonable quantity" would be handled by the Joint Committee. When Mr. Ford then asked him why it was necessary to put it in the Agreed Minute, Mr. Shin replied that the Joint Committee had to have some standard. Mr. Fleck pointed out that the term "reasonable quantity" was hardly a precise standard and would have to be defined by the Joint Committee any way. Mr. Shin stated that the U.S. side seemed unduly concerned about the insertion of the proposed phrase.

18. General Lawlor stated that the U.S. side is aware of the problems

connected with the importation of these items. He said the armed forces regulations are constantly and stringently enforced. He assured the Korean side that they would continue to be so enforced, without the insertion of the language proposed by the Korean side.

19. Dr. Pak then summarized the Korean position. He said the Korean side appreciated the extreme care and concern shown by the armed forces authorities in dealing with these matters. ~~In practice, he said,~~ Since the U.S side assured that unreasonable quantities of goods were not imported in practice, the insertion of the proposed phrase would not inconvenience anyone, [redacted] it would be only a preventive measure. The question of defining what is "reasonable" is no problem; when the Joint Committee takes it up, sound judgment and common sense will prevail.

20. Turning to Agreed Minute #3, Mr. Shin observed that no agreement had yet been reached on the text of [redacted] paragraph 5(c) to which this Minute refers. He proposed [redacted] that the language be changed to read as follows: "including their authorized procurement agencies but excluding their non-appropriated fund ~~activities~~ organizations provided for in Article ___." He said this change would be consistent with the position previously stated by the Korean side with regard to paragraph 5(c).

21. General Lawlor stated that there had been no change in the U.S. position on this question. He repeated his comment of the previous meeting that the differentiation which the Korean side was attempting to make between goods imported [redacted] for the use of the armed forces and goods imported for the non-appropriated fund activities was not a valid differentiation. He said that many of the items imported for the non-appropriated fund activities were just as important as weapons since they contributed materially to the morale of troops who are thousands of miles from home.

0180

CONFIDENTIAL

22. Mr. Shin replied that Mr. Chin had previously stated specifically that customs examination of such goods was not intended to inconvenience or hurt the morale of the U.S. armed forces. As the representative on the Korean negotiating team of the Korean customs authorities, Mr. Shin [redacted] said he again wished to assure the U.S. side that the Korean customs authorities do not intend to cause the U.S. armed forces any unnecessary inconvenience or hinder the completion of their mission, [redacted]

23. With regard to Agreed Minute #4, Mr. Ford said he wished to make it clear that this Minute was aimed at the importation of harmful substances such as drugs. Mr. Shin acknowledged the clarification and stated that the Korean side agreed to the text of Agreed Minutes #4 and #5 of the U.S. draft.

24. Turning to Agreed Minute #6, Mr. Shin expressed appreciation for the assistance which would be rendered by the U.S. armed forces under the provisions of paragraph 9(b) and this Minute. However, he said, since the U.S. armed forces would in no case act in violation of [redacted] U.S. laws or service regulations, the Korean side proposed the deletion of the phrase "authorized by United States law and service regulations". He said the [redacted] meaning of the Minute would be clear without this phrase. Col. Solf replied that [redacted] the U.S. side had included the phrase because it wished to make clear that the U.S. armed forces would not and could not take any actions in violation of U.S. laws and service regulations.

25. Mr. Shin stated that cooperation between the U.S. armed forces and the Korean authorities had been good to date. However, the Korean side feared a conflict between Korean regulations and U.S. regulations. Including such specific language in the Agreed Minute might cause [redacted] in the future. Col. Solf replied

0181

that [redacted] the U.S. language was drafted with the intention of avoiding the creation of false assumptions by the Korean authorities at some future date. [redacted] As an example, he mentioned the fact that the U.S. armed forces [redacted] cannot try any person over whom [redacted] they do not have jurisdiction. Retaining the present language of the Minute will prevent arguments in the future, he stated. Mr. Shin said that retaining this language might result in less cooperation by the U.S. armed forces than is now being extended. Dr. Pak added that the phrase "within their power" [redacted] was clear enough to the Korean side. General Lawlor brought the discussion to a close by stating that the U.S. side would take the Korean proposal under consideration.

26. It was agreed to hold the next meeting on February 14 at 2:00 p.m.

보통문서로 재분류(1966. 12. 31.)

1966. 12. 31에 예고문에 의거 일반문서로 재분류됨

0182

관리번호

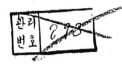

JOINT SUMMARY RECORD OF THE 13TH SESSION
STATUS FORCES NEGOTIATIONS

February 4, 1963

I. Time and Place : 2:00 to 4:00 p.m. February 4, 1963 at the Foreign Minister's Conference Room

II. Attendants:

ROK Side:

Mr. Shin, Kwan Sup	Director Bureau of Costums Duty Ministry of Finance
Mr. Pak, Kun	Counselor of Embassy
Mr. Koo, Choong Whay	Chief, American Section Ministry of Foreign Affairs
Mr. O, Won Yong	Chief, Treaty Section Ministry of Foreign Affairs
Col. Lee, Nam Koo	Chief, Military Affairs Section Ministry of National Defense
~~Mr. Chu, Mun Ki~~	~~Chief, Legal Affairs Section~~ ~~Ministry of Justice~~
Mr. Lee, Kyung Hoon	2nd Secretary Ministry of Foreign Affairs
Mr. Shin, Chung Sup	2nd Secretary Ministry of Foreign Affairs
Mr. Kang, Suk Jae	3rd Secretary Ministry of Foreign Affairs
Mr. Lee, Chang Bum	3rd Secretary Ministry of Foreign Affairs

US Side:

Mr. Philip C. Habib	Counselor of the Embassy for Political Affairs
Brig. Gen. J.D.Lawlor	Deputy Chief of Staff 8th Army

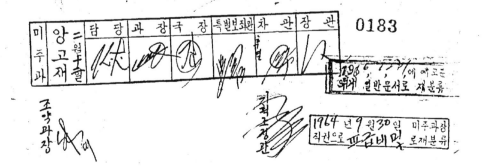

미주과	양고재	담당	과장	국장	특별보좌관	차관	장관

0183

1966 . . . 에 예고문에 의거 일반문서로 재분류

조약과장

기획조정관

1964년 9월 30일 미주과장 직권으로 재분류

Mr. William J. Ford	First Secretary of the Embassy
Col. G.G. O'Connor	Deputy Chief of Staff 8th Army
Capt. R.M. Brownlie	Assistant Chief of Staff USN/K
Col. W.A. Solf	Staff Judge Advocate 8th Army
Mr. Benjamin A. Fleck (Rapporteur and Press Officer)	First Secretary of the Embassy
Mr. Robert A. Lewis	Second Secretary and Consul of the Embassy
Lt. Col. R.E. Miller	Staff Officer, JAG 8th Army
Lt. Col. W.A. Burt	J-5

1. Mr. Shin opened the meeting by noting the absence of the Korean Chief Negotiator, Mr. Chin Pil Shik who was on an official trip abroad. He also noted the absence of Mr. Lee Kyung Ho. Mr. Shin then announced that Dr. Pak Kun, having received transfer orders to the Korean Embassy in Washington, was attending his last negotiating meeting. Mr. Shin introduced Dr. Pak's successor as Chief of the America Section, Ministry of Foreign Affairs, and as a member of the Korean negotiating team, Mr. Koo Choong Whay. Mr. Shin also announced that ~~Mr. Shin also announced that~~ Mr. Chi Sung Koo had been appointed as Chief of the Southeast Asia Section and, therefore, would no longer participate in the negotiations. Mr. Lee Kyong Hoon will act for the time being, as Press Officer for the Korean side in place of Mr. Chi. Mr. Habib expressed appreciation for the helpful role which Dr. Pak had played on the negotiatin and welcomed Mr. Koo.

0184

2-2

Respect for Local Law

2. Turning to substantive matters, Mr. Habib announced that regrettably he would have to leave the meeting early. He suggested, therefore, that the draft articles concerning respect for local law and training of reservists be taken up for discussion first. Mr. Shin agreed.

3. Mr. Habib reminded the negotiators that at the previous meeting, the Korean side had questioned the meaning of the phrase "the persons who are present in the Republic of Korea pursuant to Article ____." He said that this phrase had been included in the U.S. draft because the Definitions Article does not include invited contractors. This phrase refers to the draft article dealing with invited contractors. The U.S. draft of the respect for law article, therefore, was more comprehensive than the Korean draft, for it added invited contractors to the list of people called upon to respect Korean law and to refrain from political activity in Korea.

4. Mr. Shin asked whether the phrase included the dependents and the employees of invited contractors. Mr. Habib replied in the affirmative. He said it included all persons who were in the Republic of Korea pursuant to the invited contractors article. Mr. Shin then stated that the Korean side wished to reserve its position until the invited contractors article was tabled. Mr. Habib replied that this was satisfactory to the U.S. side. He asked whether he was correct in concluding that the respect for local law article was generally accaptable to the Korean side if the terms of the invited contractors

article were as he had explained them. Mr. Shin replied that because of the reference to employees of invited contractors, the Korean side wished to discuss this article when the invited contractors article was tabled.

Enrollment and Training of Reservists

5. Discussion of the article dealing with reservists centered around the difference between persons "residing in" Korea in the Korean draft and persons "who are in" Korea in the U.S. draft. Mr. Habib pointed out that there are Americans present in Korea who are not residents of the country. As examples, he mentioned Embassy personnel and civilian employees of the U.S. armed forces. He said that the phraseology of the U.S. draft would permit such people to undertake training here in Korea in order to maintain their reserve status. Mr. Shin replied that under the provisions of the U.S. draft, persons who have not established legal residence in Korea might be called to reserve training. In such case, the Korean immigration authorities might have difficulty keeping track of them. The Korean side, he said, wished that this provision would not cause any confusion or difficulties for the immigration authorities.

6. Mr. Habib referred the negotiators to the entry and exit article, already agreed to which provides that members of the civilian component are not eligible for permanent residence. He said that both the Korean and U.S. drafts of the article under discussion provide for training for residents; the U.S. draft also provided for non-residents.

0186

2-4

He suggested that this provision would have no effect on the Korean entry and exit procedures and would not cause any problem with regard to control of alien residents,

7. Dr. Pak said that there would be no confusion regarding the reserve training of members of the civilian component and the Embassy staff. However, the ROK Government might have difficulty enforcing its alien entry, exit and registration law if temporary visitors or invited guests of the Government were enrolled for such training. Mr. Habib replied that the Korean side was creating a problem where none existed. Such persons who were enrolled for reserve training would still have to comply with Korean law. The Korean side agreed to consider the matter further.

8. Mr. Habib mentioned one additional point of difference between the two drafts. He said that the U.S. draft called for enrollment in "forces" rather than in "reserve organizations". He said this wording was proposed because it reflected the actual situation in Korea, in which reservists were trained in existing units of the armed forces, rather than in separate reserve organizations. Mr. Habib then expressed his regret that another pressing engagement made it necessary for him to leave the meeting at this point.

Customs and Duties

9. Turning to the customs article, Mr. Shin repeated the previous suggestion of the Korean side that paragraph 7(e) of the Korean draft be inserted after subparagraph (c) of paragraph 9 in the U.S. draft. General Lawlor replied

0187

2-5

that the U.S. side would consider this proposal. He suggested that the Agreed Minutes of the U.S. draft be discussed. Mr. Ford stated that the word "organizations" in Agreed Minute #1 should be changed to "activities", in line with the change proposed by the U.S. side at the previous meeting. Mr. Shin replied that the Korean side would discuss this proposed change in conjunction with discussion of the other proposed changes. Mr. Ford asked if the Korean side had any comments regarding Agreed Minute #1.

10. Mr. Shin replied that, in accordance with their previous comments, the Korean side believed that the meaning of "to the extent reasonably required" should be the subject of mutual determination by both Korean and U.S. authorities. With that understanding, and subject to further discussion of the proposed change of "organizations" to "activities", he said the Korean side agreed to the text of Agreed Minute #1. Mr. Ford replied that the U.S. side was not prepared to agree to mutual determination of what is reasonably required but would consider the Korean position.

11. Turning to Agreed Minute #2, Mr. Shin proposed the insertion of the words "reasonable quantities of" between the word "duty" and the word "their". The second sentence of the Minute would then read as follows: "In this connection, members of the United States armed forces or civilian component and their dependents may import free of duty reasonable quantities of their personal and household effects during a period of six months from the date of their first arrival." Mr. Ford replied that the U.S. side would consider this proposal.

0188

2-6

12. General Lawlor asked if the Korean side was proposing that "reasonable quantities" were to be mutually determined even for members of the U.S. armed forces. Mr. Shin replied that inasmuch as the Korean side wished to closely define "reasonable quantities" in regard to goods shipped to non-appropriated fund organizations, they also wished to place a similar restriction on personal and household effects. Since such effects will be permitted entry free of duty, he added, it was desired to place a limitation on the amounts permitted to enter.

13. General Lawlor asked how the Korean side proposed to determine what was a "reasonable" amount. Mr. Shin replied that it was their desire to avoid the importation of excessive amounts, over and above those normally required. Mr. Ford pointed out that this Agreed Minute refers to paragraph 3(a) of the article, which had already been agreed to. He said the Minute was intended to deal with the question of the period during which importation could be made. He pointed out that it was not intended to deal with quantitative restrictions.

14. Dr. Pak said he wished to answer General Lawlor's question regarding the determination of what is reasonable. He said the Korean side intended no inconvenience to the owners or unreasonable restriction on the amount of such goods to be imported. However, if an individual should import an extraordinarily large amount, the Korean side anticipated no difficulty in reaching agreement that this would be unreasonable. Therefore, the additional language proposed by the Korean side would cause no difficulty or unreasonable restriction.

0189

2-7

15. Mr. Ford replied that the article provides for policing of its provisions by both sides. There is also a specific reference to abuses or infringement in Agreed Minute #5. He asserted that these would give all necessary protection to Korean interests and would still provide to the U.S. armed forces sufficient freedom to carry out their mission in Korea.

16. Mr. Shin stated that the provision in paragraph 8 of the article for mutual cooperation is vague and not specifically spelled out. He said that it was necessary to provide in the Agreed Minute standards of what is or is not an abuse of the provisions of the article. General Lawlor replied that the Korean side was unduly worried about abuses. However, the U.S. side would consider the Korean proposal.

17. Mr. Shin agreed with Mr. Ford's remark that the determination of what constitutes a "reasonable quantity" would be handled by the Joint Committee. When Mr. Ford then asked him why it was necessary to put it in the Agreed Minute, Mr. Shin replied that the Joint Committee had to have some standard. Mr. Fleck pointed out that the term "reasonable quantity" was hardly a precise standard and would have to be defined by the Joint Committee any way. Mr. Shin stated that the U.S. side seemed unduly concerned about the insertion of the proposed phrase.

18. General Lawlor stated that the U.S. side is aware of the problems connected with the importation of these items. He said the armed forces regulations are constantly

0190

2-8

and stringently enforced. He assured the Korean side that they would continue to be so enforced, without the insertion of the language proposed by the Korean side.

19. Dr. Pak then summarized the Korean position. He said the Korean side appreciated the extreme care and concern shown by the armed forces authorities in dealing with these matters. Since the U.S. side assuared that unreasonable quantities of goods were not imported in practice, the insertion of the proposed phrase would not inconvenience anyone. It would be only a preventive measure. The question of defining what is "reasonable" is no problem; when the Joint Committee takes it up, sound judgment and common sense will prevail.

20. Turning to Agreed Minute #3, Mr. Shih observed that no agreement had yet been reached on the text of paragraph 5(c) to which this Minute refers. He proposed that the language be changed to read as follows: "including their authorized procurement agencies but excluding their non-appropriated fund organizations provided for in Article____". He said this change would be consistent with the position previously stated by the Korean side with regard to paragraph 5(a).

21. General Lawlor stated that there had been no change in the U.S. position on this question. He repeated his comment of the previous meeting that the differentiation which the Korean side was attempting to make between goods imported for the use of the armed forces and goods imported for the non-appropriated fund activities was not a valid

0191

2-9

differentiation. He said that many of the items imported for the non-appropriated fund activities were just as important as weapons since they contributed materially to the morale of troops who are thousands of miles from home.

22. Mr. Shin replied that Mr. Chin had previously stated specifically that customs examination of such goods was not intended to inconvenience or hurt the morale of the U.S. armed forces. As the representative on the Korean negotiating team of the Korean customs authorities, Mr. Shin said he again wished to assure the U.S. side that the Korean customs authorities do not intend to cause the U.S. armed forces any unnecessary inconvenience or hinder the completion of their mission.

23. With regard to Agreed Minute #4, Mr. Ford said he wished to make it clear that this Minute was aimed at the importation of harmful substances such as drugs. Mr. Shin acknowledged the clarification and stated that the Korean side agreed to the text of Agreed Minutes #4 and #5 of the U.S. draft.

24. Turning to Agreed Minute #6, Mr. Shin expressed appreciation for the assistance which would be rendered by the U.S. armed forces under the provisions of paragraph 9(b) and this Minute. However, he said, since the U.S. armed forces would in no case act in violation of U.S. laws or service regulations, the Korean side proposed the deletion of the phrase "authorized by United States law and service regulations". He said the meaning of the Minute would be clear without this phrase. Col. Solf replied

0192

2-10

that the U.S. side had included the phrase because it wished to make clear that the U.S. armed forces would not and could not take any actions in violation of U.S. laws and service regulations.

25. Mr. Shin stated that cooperation between the U.S. armed forces and the Korean authorities had been good to date. However, the Korean side feared a conflict between Korean regulations and U.S. regulations. Including such specific language in the Agreed Minute might cause undue arguments in the future. Col. Solf replied that the U.S. language was drafted with the intention of avoiding the creation of false assumptions by the Korean authorities at some future date. As an example, he mentioned the fact that the U.S. armed forces cannot try any person over whom they do not have jurisdiction. Retaining the present language of the Minute will prevent arguments in the future, he stated. Mr. Shin said that retaining this language might result in less cooperation by the U.S. armed forces than is now being extended. Dr. Pak added that the phrase "within their power" was clear enough to the Korean side. General Lawlor brought the discussion to a close by stating that the U.S. side would take the Korean proposal under consideration.

26. It was agreed to hold the next meeting on February 14 at 2:00 p.m.

보통문서로 재분류(1966. 12. 31.)

0193

~~보통문서로 재분류(협정체결시))~~

1966.12.31.에 예고문에 의거 일반문서로 재분류됨

2-11

5. 제 14차 회의 , 2.14

0194

관리 번호 8/1

기 안 용 지

자체 통제		기안처	미주과 이경훈	전화번호	근거서류접수일자
	과장	수석대표	보좌관	차관	장관
	2/13			13.	
관계관 서명	조약과장 2.13		기획조정관		
기안 년월일	1963. 2. 13.	시행 년월일		보존 년한	정서 기장
분류 기호	외정미 7	전체 통제		종결	
경유 수신 참조	건 의		발신		
제목	제14차 주둔군지위협정 체결교섭회의에 임할 우리측 태도				

2월 14일에 개최될 제14차 주둔군지위협정 체결 한미간 교섭회의에서는 공익물 및 용역, 예비병의 소집 및 훈련, 그리고 외환관리 문제에 관하여 토의될 예정이온바 이에관련하여 우리측 교섭실무자는 2월 12일 관계부처 실무자와 연속회합을 갖고 제14차 회의에서 취할 우리측 태도를 별첨과같이 결정하였아오니 재가하여 주시기 바랍니다.

유첨 : 제14차 주둔군지위협정 체결교섭회의에 임할 우리측 태도.

끝

보통문서로 재분류(1966. 12. 31.)

0195

승인양식 1-1-3 (1112-040[redacted] (190mm×260mm16절지)

1964년9월30일 미주과 직권으로 파기 비밀 로재분

13. 공의물 및 용역사용

(1) 공의물 및 용역의 사용허여를 규정한 미국측초안 3(a)항의 전단 (이는 우리측초안 1항의 전단에 해당하는것임)에 있어서 "whether pubblicly or privately owned " 라는 구절은 "controlled or regulated by the Government of the Republic of Korea " 라는 구절과 중복되는것이라고 사료되는바 우리측안에 있는바와같이 "belonging to or controlled or regulated by the Government of the Republic of Korea " 라는 구절을 미측이 받아드리도록 주장한다. "political subdivisions thereof" 라는 구절에 대하여는 미측에 이것이 무엇을 의미하는지 문의한후 불필요한것이니 삭제 하자고 주장한다.

(2) 공의물 및 용역의 정의에관한 미국측초안 3(a)항의 중단 (이는 우리측초안 1항 중단에해당)에있어서 본규정은 공의물 및 용역 그자체의 정의에 관한것이니 만큼 "however produced " 라는 구절은 불필요하니 이의 삭제를 주장한다.

(3) 공의물 및 용역의 운영권리에 관한 미국측초안 3(a)항의 후단(이는 우리측초안에는 없음)에 대하여 미국측에게 설명을 요구한후 사정을 참작하여 다음과같은 수정안중 하나를 제시토록한다.

(가) "The operation by the United States armed forces of the military transportation, Communication, power, and other utilities and services shall be to the extent which ~~are~~ is deemed necessary for the operation of the United States' armed forces and which ~~are~~ is not inconsistent with the operation by the Republic of Korea of such utilities and services."

14次

0196

5-2

(나) "The United States armed forces may operate its owned military transportation, communication power, and other utilities and services deemed necessary for the operations of the United States armed forces."

(4) 공익물 및 용역의 사용 우선순위에 관한 미국측초안 3(b)항의전단 (이는 우리측초안 1항 후단에 해당함)에 있어서 "any other user, governmental or private " 대신에 우리측 규정과같은 "the ministries and agencies of the Government of the Republic of Korea "라는 용어로 대치토록 한다.

(5) 무차별 대우 보증에관한 미국측초안 3(b)항의 중단 및 비상시의 운영에관한 미국측초안 3(b)항의 후단을 우리측 초안에는 없는것으로 이에대하여 우리측은 이러한 규정은 동항 전단의 규정에 비추어보아 불필요할것이니 삭제하자고 주장한다.

(6) 세부규정으로서 협약의 유효성에관한 미국측초안 4항 (이는 우리측초안 2(a)항에 해당)은 우리측안과 실질적 차이가 없으나, 우리측초안이 더 광범함으로 우리측 초안을 받아드리도록 주장한다.

(7) 합의의사록에 있어서 (가) 순위및 사용율의 증가 변경에대한 합동위원회에서의 사전협의에 관한 미국측 초안의 1항은 우리측 초안의 2(a)속에 포함되어 있으니 별도 규정을 둘필요가 없음으로 이의 삭제를 요구한다. (나) 기존협정의 유효성에 관한 2항은 우리측초안 2(b)항에 해당하는 것으로 우리측 초안과 실질적 차이가 없음으로 수락해주기로 한다.

0197

5-3

2. 예비병의 소집 및 훈련

(1) 미국이소집, 훈련 시킬수있는 자에 대하여 우리측안은 대한민국에 거주 (residing)하는 미국시민으로 되어있는데 미국측안은 대한민국에 있는자 (who are in)로되어있는바, 미국측이 주장하는대로 "who are in" 에 해당하는 자가 주한미대사관 직원 및 미국군대 군속을 의미하는것이라면 우리측 안대로 본문에 "residing"으로 규정하고 합의의사록에 "residing" 의 정의를 규정하되 미국측 태도를 참작하여 다음 두개의 안중에서 하나를택하여 제시한다.

(가) "The term "eligible United States citizens residing in the Republic of Korea" includes the staff of the United States Embassy, ~~and~~ the dependents of members of the U.S. armed force and the civilian component ~~of the United States armed forces.~~ and its dependents."

(나) "The term "eligible United States citizens residing in the Republic of Korea" includes those who are present in Korea and obliged to comply with the alien extry, exit and registration law of Korea".

(2) 만일 미국측이 우리측 수정안에 대하여 양보할 기색이 없을 때는 미국측안을 수락하도록 한다.

3. 외환관리

(1) 한국외환관리 복종의무, 외환의 지입 및 지출, 그리고 외환의 지입 및 지출에대한 권리 남용방지를 규정한 우리측 조약원문과 미국군대 및 비세출기관과 미국군인, 군속 그들의 가족과 및 미국군대 계약체결자 간의 외환거래는 한국의 외환관리법에 의거하여야한다는 합의의사록을 제시한다. (별첨참조)

보통문서로 재분류 (   )

0198

5-4

(2) 미국측이 제시하는 안이 우리측의 안과 비등할때에는 이를 수락하기로 한다.

보통문서로 재분류(1966. 12. 31)

1966.12.31.에 예고문에 의거 일반문서로 재분류됨

0199

5-5

Article ____

1. Members of the United States armed forces, the civilian component, and their dependents shall be subject to the foreign exchange controls of the Government of the Republic of Korea.

2. The preceding paragraph shall not be construed to preclude the transmission into or outside of the Republic of Korea of the United States dollars or dollar instruments representing the official funds of the United States or realized as a result of service or employment in connection with this Agreement by members of the United States armed forces and the civilian component, or realized by such persons and their dependents from sources outside of the Republic of Korea.

3. The United States authorities shall take suitable measures to preclude the abuse of the privileges stipulated in the preceding paragraph or circumvention of the Korean foreign exchange controls.

0200

5-6

Agreed Minutes to Article _____

Payment in Korea by the United States armed forces and by those organizations provided in Article ____ to persons other than members of the United States armed forces, civilian component, their dependents and those persons referred to in Article ____ shall be effected in accordance with the Korean Foreign Exchange Control Law and regulations. In these transactions the basic rate of exchange shall be used.

보통문서로 재분류(1966. 12. 31)

1966.12.31에 예고문에 의거 일반문서로 재분류됨

0201

5-7

관리번호

기 안 용 지

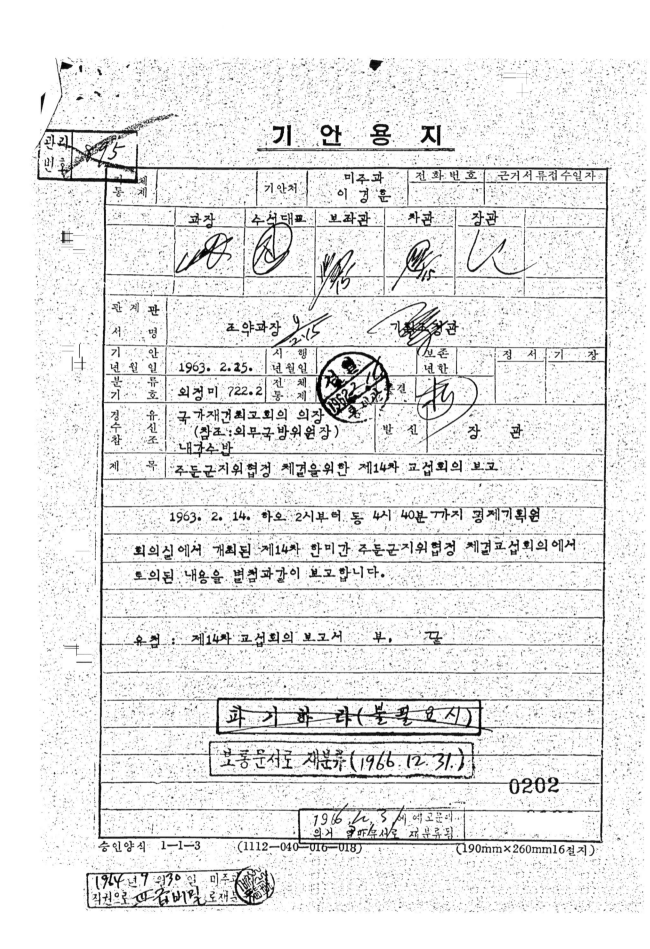

기 통 체 제		기안처	미주과 이 경 훈	전화번호	근거서류접수일자

과장	수석대표	보좌관	차관	장관
			2/15	

관계관 서명	조약과장 2/15 기획조정관				
기안 년월일	1963. 2. 25.	시행 년월일		보존 년한	정 서 기 장
분류 기호	외정미 722.2	전체 통제		종결	
경유 수신 참조	국가재건최고회의 의장 (참조 : 외무국방위원장) 내각수반			발신	장 관
제목	주둔군지위협정 체결을위한 제14차 교섭회의 보고				

1963. 2. 14. 하오 2시부터 동 4시 40분 까지 경제기획원 회의실에서 개최된 제14차 한미간 주둔군지위협정 체결교섭회의에서 토의된 내용을 별첨과같이 보고합니다.

유첨 : 제14차 교섭회의 보고서 부, 끝

~~파 기 하 라 (불 필 요 시)~~

보통문서로 재분류 (1966. 12. 31.)

0202

1966. 12. 31 에 예고문에 의거 일반문서로 재분류됨

승인양식 1—1—3 (1112—040—016—018) (190mm×260mm16절지)

1964 년 9 월 30 일 미주과 직권으로 비밀 로재분류

외 무 부

외정미 722.2 1963. 2. 16.

수 신 내각수반

제 목 주둔군지위협정 체결을위한 제14차 교섭회의 보고

1963. 2. 14. 하오 2시부터 동 4시 40분까지 경제기획원 회의실에서 개최된 제14차 한미간 주둔군지위협정 체결교섭회의에서 토의된 내용을 별첨과같이 보고합니다.

유첨 : 제 14 차 교섭회의 보고서 1 부. 끝

~~과 기 하 라(불필요시)~~

외 무 부 장 관 최 덕 신

0203

3-6

외 무 부

외정미 722.2 1963. 2. 16.

수 신 국가재건최고회의 의장

참 조 외무국방위원장

제 목 주둔군지위협정 체결을위한 제14차 교섭회의 보고

1963. 2. 14. 하오 2시부터 동 4시 40분가지 경제 기획원 회의실에서 개최된 제14차 한미간 주둔군지위협정 체결교섭 회의에서 토의된 내용을 별첨과같이 보고합니다.

유첨 : 제14차 교섭회의 보고서 2부. 끝

~~파 기 하 리(불필요시)~~

외 무 부 장 관 최 덕 신

0204

2-7

제 14 차

한미간 주둔군지위협정체결 실무자회의

보 고 서

1. 시 일 : 1963. 2. 14. 하오 2시부터 4시 40분 까지

2. 장 소 : 경제기획원 회의실

3. 참석자 : 한국측 :

진 필 식	(외무부 정무국장, 수석대표)
신 관 섭	(재무부 세관국장)
구 충 회	(외무부 미주과장)
오 원 용	(외무부 조약과장)
이 남 구	(국방부 군무과장)
주 문 기	(법무부 법무과장)
이 경 훈	(외무부 2등서기관)
신 정 섭	(")
강 석 재	(외무부 3등서기관)
이 창 범	(")

미국측 : 교섭대표단 전원 ("하비브"수석대표 불참)

4. 토의사항 :

63-1 ...

(1) 공익물 및 용역, 예비병의 소집 및 훈련문제를 순차적으로 토의한후 외환관리에 관한 조항안을 교환하였음.

(2) 공익물 및 용역사용 허여에관한 규정에 있어서

(가) 미국측은 자국안에서 규정된 "정치상의 예하기관"이라는 말은 중앙행정관서 이외의 지방또는 기타 정부기관을 말하는 것이라고 말한데대하여 우리측은 이는 대한민국 정부라는 어구에 포함되어 있어 불필요한것이라고 주장하였고,

0205

63-1-5(2)

번호 84-12 (4)

0206

(나) 우리측은 또한 미국측안에서 규정한 "공유이건, 사유이건" 이라는 어구는 불필요한것이니 우리측안대로 "정부에 속한" 이라는 어구를 미측이 수락할것을 주장하였음.

(3) 공익물 및 용역의 정의에있어서 미국측은 "어떻게 생산되든지" 라는 용어의 삽입을 주장한데 대하여 우리측은 정의규정에 있어서 생산과정의 설명은 불필요한것이라고 말하고 이의 삭제를 주장함.

(4) 미국측이 제시한 공익물 및 용역의 운영권에 관한 규정에대하여 우리측은 "미국군대에 의한 군용운수, 통신, 전력 그리고 기타 공익물 및 용역의 운영은 미국군대의 운영에 필요한 정도와 이러한 공익물 및 용역의 대한민국에 의한 운영과 상치하지 않는 정도이어야 한다"라는 수정안을 제시하였음.

(5) 공익물 및 용역의 사용 순위규정에 있어서 미국측은 정부기관이건 개인이건간에 어떠한 사용자에게 부여하는것같은 대우를하여 줄것을 주장한데 대하여 우리측은 정부기관에 대한 대우는 최고의 대우이니 우리측 주장대로 정부기관에 대한것과 같은 대우를하도록 규정하자고 주장함.

(6) 공익물 및 용역의 사용에있어서 미국측이 제시한 무차별대우의 보장규정과 비상시의 조치규정은 불필요한것이니 삭제하자고 우리측은 주장함.

(7) 공익물 및 용역사용에대한 사용료지불에 관한 협약의 유효성 규정에있어서 우리측은 우리측안이 보다 광범하고 포괄적임으로 우리측안의 수락을 주장하였음.

(8) 공익물 및 용역의 사용조항에 대한 합의의사록에 있어서

(가) 미국측이 제시한 기존협정의 유효성에 관한 규정은 우리측 초안과 실질적 차이가없음으로 우리측은 이에대하여는 별의의가 없음을 진술하였고,

0207

3-3

63-1-3

마본 84-12

0208

(나) 미국측이 제시한 우선순위의 변경과 사용료의 변경에 대한 합동위원회에서의 사전협의 규정에 대하여는 우리측은 불필요한것이니 삭제하자고 주장하였음.

(9) 예비병의 소집 및 훈련문제에 있어서 미국측은 대한민국에 현존하는 미국시민을 미국이 소집, 훈련시킬수 있다고 제시한데 대하여 우리측은 보통 관광객은 제외한다는 어구의 삽입을 주장하였음.

(10) 외환관리에 관한 양측초안이 교환되었음.

5. 기타사항 :

(1) 차기회의 일자 : 1963. 2. 25. 하오 2시

(2) 차기회의 의제 : 차기회의까지 양측수석대표간에 합의된사항

6. 참고자료 : 미국측이 제의한 협정초안 (외환관리) 별첨참조

보통문서로 재분류(1966.12.31)

1966 12 31
의거 일반문서로 재분류됨

0209

3-4

63-1-5(4)

외무 84-12

0210

CONFIDENTIAL

ARTICLE

1. Members of the United States armed forces, the civilian component and their dependents, shall be subject to the foreign exchange controls of the Government of the Republic of Korea.

2. The preceding paragraph shall not be construed to preclude the transmission into or out of Korea of United States dollars or dollar instruments representing the official funds of the United States or realized as a result of service or employment in connection with this Agreement by members of the United States armed forces and the civilian component, or realized by such persons and their dependents from sources outside Korea.

3. The United States authorities shall take suitable measures to preclude the abuse of the privileges stipulated in the preceding paragraphs or circumvention of the Korean foreign exchange controls.

63-1-47

CONFIDENTIAL

CONFIDENTIAL

0211

3-5

63-1-5(4)

비밀 89-12(4)

0212

14th mtg.
Feb. 14, 1963

CONFIDENTIAL

Utilities & Services

1. [redacted] ~~Opening the substantive discussion~~, Lt. Col. Miller began the substantive discussion by reminding the negotiators that the U.S. [redacted] side had tabled at the eleventh meeting [redacted] a draft dealing with utilities and services as part of the U.S. draft article "D". At that time, [redacted] Mr. Chin had stated that the Korean side would ~~subsequently~~ table its corresponding draft at a later meeting only if [redacted] there were differences between the two drafts. [redacted] At the twelfth meeting, the Korean side did table its draft. Lt. Col. Miller suggested, therefore, that the Korean side [redacted] give ~~their~~ its views regarding the differences between the two drafts. He also suggested [redacted] subparagraph by subparagraph discussion.

2. [redacted] Pointing out the typographic mistake in the Korean draft, [redacted] Mr. Chin stated ~~that the Korean side wished to amend their draft by deleting from paragraph 1~~ corrected that the phrase "however produced", was to be deleted from paragraph 1 of the Korean draft. [redacted]

3. Turning to a comparison of the U.S. paragraph 3 (a) and the Korean paragraph 1, Mr. Chin requested clarification of the term "political subdivisions thereof" in the U.S. draft. [redacted] Lt. Col. Miller explained [redacted] that this referred to municipal, county, and other subordinate administrative offices, such as the Special Cities of Seoul and Pusan, with which the U.S. armed forces may have dealings from time to time. This language had been included in the U.S. draft in order to insure that the U.S. forces would be able to use utilities controlled or regulated by these subordinate offices. Mr. Chin ~~replied~~ stated that these subordinate administrations were included in the overall term "Government of Korea" and it was unnecessary, therefore, to refer to them specifically. However, if the U.S. side felt that such reference was desirable, they might be mentioned in an Agreed Minute.

0213

4. Lt. Col. Miller pointed out that the U.S. draft makes clear that the U.S. armed forces could use either publicly- or privately-owned utilities. He ~~reminded the negotiators of the desire of the U.S. side to limit the number of Agreed Minutes to the maximum possible extent and stated that an Agreed Minute would [redacted] one more section to the Agreement which would have to be referred to.~~ [handwritten: suggested that an Agreed Minute would unnecessarily complicate this portion of the agreement, inasmuch as the language could be included in the article without complicating or confusing its terms.] [handwritten: He said] The U.S. side [redacted] [handwritten: considered] an Agreed Minute to be unnecessary and preferred to retain this reference in the body of the article. General Lawlor added that the U.S. armed forces [redacted] might have to pay utility bills directly to these [redacted] subordinate administrative offices and therefore this reference should be retained.

5. Mr. Chin stated that there was no substantial difference in content in the two drafts but only in language. Lt. Col. Miller replied that the U.S. side had tried to spell everything out and not leave anything to implication. Mr. Chin ~~agreed~~ [handwritten: stated] that absolutely necessary language must be included but suggested that unnecessary words should be avoided. [redacted] [handwritten: He] pointed out that privately-owned utilities not regulated by the ROKG would not be covered by the phrase "publicly or privately owned" in the U.S. draft. ~~He suggested that the phrase "belonging to, or controlled or regulated by the Government of the Republic of Korea" in the Korean draft was a better formulation.~~ [redacted] ~~Alternatively, he suggested deletion of the phrase~~ [redacted] ~~"whether publicly or privately owned" from the U.S. draft.~~ Lt. Col. Miller stated that [redacted] the U.S. draft is more specific but said the U.S. side would consider the proposal. [redacted]

6. Mr. Chin [redacted] pointed out that the definitions [redacted] of utilities and services was identical in both drafts, except for the phrase "however produced", which remained

0214

[handwritten: Mr. Chin] ~~He~~ expressed the view that the phrase "belonging to, or controlled or regulated by the Government of the Republic of Korea" in the Korean draft was a better formulation. He, further, pointed out that this phrase in the Korean draft would be broad enough to cover the meaning and implication of the phrase "whether publicly or privately owned, which are controlled or regulated by the Government of the Republic of Korea" in the U.S. draft. He, then, suggested that the ~~phraseology used~~ [handwritten: phrase] in the U.S. draft ~~under reference be substituted with the corresponding phraseology appearing~~ [handwritten: be deleted and the corresponding phrase used] in the Korean draft [handwritten: be inserted in its place.]

in the U.S. draft, ~~but had just been deleted from the Korean draft.~~ Lt. Col. Miller pointed out that the [redacted] proposed Agreed Minute #2 of the U.S. draft referred to the existing Utilities and Claims Settlement Agreement and stated that the latter Agreement will remain in full force and effect. Mr. Chin replied that Inasmuch as ~~both~~ the two drafts contained no substantial difference, ~~the~~ smoother ~~provided that utilities and services would not be limited to those specifically mentioned.~~ wording would be better in the formulation. Lt. Col. Miller said the U.S. side recognized this but desired to include a specific reference, in the Agreed Minute, to the fact that the existing utilities agreement would continue [redacted] in force.

7. Mr. Chin [redacted] requested an explanation of the remainder of paragraph 3(a) in the U.S. draft, which was not included in the Korean draft. [redacted] Lt. Col. Miller explained that everything discussed so far had concerned utilities and services provided by the ROKG. However, there were some utilities which the U.S. armed forces themselves had to operate. The nature and extent of these utilities would vary from time to time. The purpose of the language in the U.S. draft is to make clear that the U.S. armed forces have the right to operate such utilities in addition to those which are furnished by the ROKG.

8. Mr. Chin said this would create problems, particularly in the field of transportation, such as the operation of military trains by the U.S. armed forces on the Korean railways system. Lt. Col. Miller replied that the most probable areas were the military communications network, the provision of alternate power sources, and the operation of various types of military transportation facilities. He pointed out that the U.S. armed forces are presently using Korean facilities under the terms of the Utilities and Claims Settlement Agreement. He said the U.S. draft would not permit the expropriation of Korean facilities but would permit the U.S. armed forces to operate their own. Mr. Chin [redacted] again referred to the operation of military [redacted] trains on the Korean railways and inquired whether, in such a case, the U.S. armed forces would consult with the Ministry of Transportation. Lt. Col. Miller

He also emphasized that ~~Article~~ the definition of utilities and services in the draft article was taken from the Utilities and Claims Settlement Agreement which included the term "however produced". He added that use of the Claims Settlement Agreement definition in its entirety was deemed more desirable because it would obviate questions which might later be raised concerning reasons why the SOFA Article definition was different.

0215

replied that this would be necessary and [redacted] that the Joint Committee also would undoubtedly be involved. General Lawlor agreed.

9. Mr. Chin stated that this point was another question of language. He suggested for the consideration of the U.S. side the following alternative language for the third sentence of paragraph 3(a) of the U.S. draft:

> "The operation by the U.S. armed forces of military transportation, communications, power, and other utilities and services shall be to the extent which is deemed necessary for the operations of the U.S. armed forces and which is not inconsistent with operation by the Republic of Korea of such utilities and services."

Mr. Chin emphasized the necessity of ensuring that operation of such utilities by the U.S. armed forces would not interfere with Korean operation of the same utilities. Therefore, the systems and practices of the U.S. armed forces must be consistent with those used by the Korean authorities concerned ~~the Ministry of Transportation. So long as the U.S. armed forces consult with that Ministry, no problems are anticipated.~~

10. General Lawlor stated that under current [redacted] procedures, whenever the U.S. armed forces run military trains, they are operated in a manner consistent with the Korean practices. Lt. Col. Miller pointed out that the U.S. armed forces might also wish to operate other types of utilities which are completely self-contained and unrelated to any existing Korean utilites. General Lawlor [redacted] mentioned that the U.S. armed forces may wish to operate their own bus lines from time to time. ~~the operation of bus lines by the U.S. armed forces,~~ [redacted] Mr. Chin said that vehicles operated by the U.S. armed forces should obey all Korean traffic laws and regulations. General Lawlor agreed. Mr. Chin said if operations are continued on the same basis as at present, there will be no problems.

11. Turning to paragraph 3 (b) of the U.S. draft, Mr. Chin pointed out that the subject of the draft was ~~the priorities~~ conditions under which utilities

0216

furnished by the [redacted] ROKG were to be used by the U.S. armed forces. He said the corresponding Korean draft provided for "conditions no less favorable than those that may be applicable from time to time to the ministries and agencies of the Government of the Republic of Korea". He said the conditions applicable to the Government were the most ~~preferable~~ proper conditions. He then asked the U.S. side to explain their draft.

12. Lt. Col. Miller replied that the U.S. draft differs from the Korean draft in two major respects: (1) it includes mention of rates and tariffs, and (2) it provides that the U.S. armed forces would pay rates equivalent to those paid by the most favored user. He pointed out that this provision would provide additional guidance for the negotiation of utilities agreements under the Utilities and Claims Settlement Agreement. Mr. Chin said the Korean side would have no objection to the inclusion [redacted] of "rates and tariffs" in the article. However, the most ~~favorable~~ reasonable conditions are those which are accorded to the ministries and agencies of the ROKG.

13. Lt. Col. Miller stated that [redacted] U.S. armed forces in other countries have had [redacted] unfortunated experiences in the past by relying on provisions similar to those [redacted] contained in the Korean draft. He said the language of the U.S. draft would avoid misunderstandings such as have arisen elsewhere. Mr. Chin said that it would be reasonable for the U.S. armed forces to receive the same treatment as that accorded ministries and agencies of the ROK Government. He said cases such as those referred to by Lt. Col. Miller were exceptional. General Lawlor [redacted] explained that in some cases in other countries, the U.S. Armed forces have been forced to pay rates higher than those paid by private users because of manipulated "government" rates. Also, there have been cases in which different agencies of the same government have been charged different rates. In such a case, the question arises as to which rate shall be paid by the U.S. armed forces. Mr. Chin replied that such things could never happen in Korea. General Lawlor acknowledged that the U.S. armed forces have

0217

not had that kind of experience in Korea.

14. Mr. Chin explained that according to the existing system, the government pays ~~the lowest~~ a reasonable rate and there is only one rate charged to all government agencies. General Lawlor pointed out that in a mixed economy such as that existing in the Republic of Korea, it is often difficult to distinguish the line between government agencies and private organizations. Lt. Col. Miller added that all the U.S. armed forces were asking for was to be charged the lowest rate, whether that was the rate charged to government agencies or not. Mr. Chin said the U.S. side would understand the Korean side's position if it examined the treatment accorded to agencies of the ROK Government [redacted] to date. General Lawlor replied that no criticism was intended of the treatment which has been given to the U.S. armed forces.

15. Mr. Chin stated that if the rates ~~were raised,~~ [redacted] the matter ~~could~~ might be taken up by the Joint Committee. General Lawlor agreed ~~but pointed~~ out that the U.S. armed forces would be in a poor bargaining position because of their urgent and continuing need for the utilities and services. Mr. Chin ~~suggested~~ stated that any major change in the situation would result in revision of the SOFA itself. [redacted]

16. Moving on to the second sentence of paragraph 3 (b) of the U.S. draft, Mr. Chin said it appeared that the intent of the U.S. draft was to prevent discrimination against the U.S. armed forces. Treatment equal to that accorded the ROK Government is not discrimination, he said. Furthermore, it is taken for granted that the ROK Government will do everything in its power to prevent any such discrimination. He suggested that the language of the U.S. draft was somewhat degrading and proposed deletion of that

15. **Mr. Chin stated that the increase of rates was a very important matter which would affect the interest of the entire population. It was utterly unthinkable that**

U.S. armed forces would be in a poor bargaining position because of their urgent and continuing need for the utilities and services. Mr. Chin suggested that any major change in the situation would result in revision of the SOFA itself. [redacted]

16. Moving on to the second sentence of paragraph 3 (b) of the U.S. draft, Mr. Chin said the intent of the U.S. draft was to prevent discrimination against the U.S. armed forces. Treatment equal to that accorded the ROK Government is not discrimination, he said. Furthermore, it is taken for granted that the ROK Government will do everything in its power to prevent any such discrimination. He suggested that the language of the U.S. draft was somewhat degrading and proposed deletion of that

15. Mr. Chin stated that the increase of rates was a very important matter which would affect the interest of the entire population. It was utterly unthinkable that the Korean authority would manipulate such an important matter of increasing rates, without due regard to the effect on the interest of the entire population but only with the purpose of charging higher rates to the U.S. armed forces. The U.S. side would not but make the representations to the Korean authorities and also refer the matter to the Joint Committee, should such an unthinkable case takes place. General Lawlor agreed but pointed out that the U.S. armed forces would be in a poor bargaining position because of their urgent and continuing need for the utilities and services. Mr. Chin stated that we are discussing the SOFA under the circumstances which are prevailing at present. If the situation be drastically changed after the conclusion of the SOFA, it will bring about the problem on the principle of "change of situation" in international law.

0219

sentence. General Lawlor replied that this sentence also was connected with the position of the U.S. armed forces as customers and it had been included in the draft to ensure that [redacted] the U.S. armed forces [redacted] would be given favorable treatment. He said the U.S. side would consider the position of the Korean side.

17. Regarding the third sentence of paragraph 3(b) of the U.S. draft, Mr. Chin stated that in [redacted] emergency situations, the U.S. and Korean armed forces would receive equal treatment. Lt. Col. Miller pointed out that the SOFA has to be tailored to the needs of specific situations. This sentence constitutes recognition of the fact that the Republic of Korea is a potential combat area. There is thus more chance of an emergency arising here than in many other places. This language is meant to ensure that in such an emergency, the U.S. armed forces would not be limited to the usual or normal arrangements with regard to utilities and services. The exact nature of the emergency cannot be predicted.

18. Mr. Chin replied that the Korean side ~~understood~~ was well aware of Lt. Col. Miller's explanation and had been [redacted] considering the situation. He said that a [redacted] separate article, to be discussed later, would define steps to be taken in the event of the most serious emergency which could arise. He did not think it necessary or desirable to refer to emergency actions in every article of the SOFA. Even if it were not spelled out in this article, he said, the treatment accorded to the U.S. armed forces in the event of emergency would be equivalent to that accorded to the ROK armed forces in such event. He suggested that the sentence be deleted.

19. General Lawlor stated that the point of the sentence was that a commander of military forces must be sure that he is [redacted] able to move, shoot, and communicate in the event of an emergency. That is why the sentence was included in the draft. Lt. Col. Miller added that certain agencies of the Korean Government might ~~need more assistance during~~ an emergency than others and

0220

The purpose of this clause is not to assure that the U.S. armed forces get as many as or mo ~~utilities~~ and ~~services~~ than a ROK government agency but that they have some assurance getting what they require.

CONFIDENTIAL

the U.S. armed forces might need more assistance than any ROK Government agency. [redacted] If such assistance were not forthcoming, the U.S. armed forces might not be able to accomplish their mission.

20. Mr. Chin said the Korean side would study the remarks of the U.S. side concerning this matter. He said apparently there were differences in the ways of thinking of the two sides. He said the Korean side placed ethics and morality [redacted] on a higher plane than the law. He said it was taken for granted, morally and by common sense, that the Korean Government would extend the utmost possible cooperation in time of emergency. He said the Korean side did not disagree with the substance of the U.S. draft but thought inclusion of this sentence was unnecessary. General Lawlor expressed appreciation for Mr. Chin's remarks.

[redacted]

21. Turning to paragraph 4 of the U.S. draft and paragraph 2 (a) of the Korean draft, Mr. Chin expressed the opinion that the Korean draft was more inclusive than the U.S. draft and asked for the comments of the U.S. side. Lt. Col. Miller replied that the U.S. draft was not limited to utilities but refers to accounting arrangements arising out [redacted] of the SOFA as a whole. He pointed out that payments could be made between authorities of the two governments, as provided for in the Korean draft, or between other agencies or [redacted] persons. He said this paragraph must also be considered in conjunction with the proposed Agreed Minute #2 in the U.S. draft, which would continue the existing Utilities and Claims Settlement Agreement in effect. Referring to paragraph 2 (b) of the Korean draft, he pointed out that the existing arrangements are renegotiated from time to time. Therefore, the relevant ~~language~~ must be kept flexible. He asked the Korean side

0221

to clarify their subparagraph (b). Mr. Chin stated that the Korean side would study this point and suggested further discussion at a subsequent meeting. Lt. Col. Miller pointed out that there would be some arrangements which could not be negotiated until the SOFA comes into effect. There are also some existing agreements which may have to be revised. Mr. Chin said the Korean side understood this point and would discuss it at the next meeting.

22. Mr. Chin then asked the U.S. side to explain its proposed Agreed Minute #1. Lt. Col. Miller explained that an increase in utilities rates would mean an increase in the expenditure of appropriated funds and a corresponding decrease in the amount of such funds which could be spent on other activities of the U.S. armed forces in Korea. A change in priorities could similarly affect the military posture of those forces. Therefore, this Agreed Minute is intended to provide the two governments with an opportunity to present their respective views before rates were increased or priorities changed.

23. Mr. Chin commented that the U.S. armed forces are given the same priority as ROK Government agencies. According to the U.S. draft, if the U.S. armed forces' priority were lowered, which would not happen, prior consultation with the armed forces would surely take place. Similarly, prior consultation must take place before any change in rates, in the U.S. draft. He said that if the special rates accorded the U.S. armed forces applied only to those forces, prior consultation would be a simple matter. However, the rates accorded the U.S. armed forces are the same as those accorded generally to agencies of the ROK Government. An increase in the rates would require ~~legislative processes~~ scrupulous deliberation and highly technical actions by the ROK Government. Prior consultation, under these circumstances, would be very difficult. The interests of the entire population would be affected. The ROK Government would try to cooperate with the U.S. Government in order to prevent unnecessary inconvenience but it would be extremely difficult for the ROK Government to commit

0222

itself to prior consultation.

24. General Lawlor pointed out that we were not suggesting a commitment to obtain US Government agreement but only prior ~~discussion~~ consultation. Lt. Col. Miller added that ~~a lot of~~ much advance planning would be required on the part of the U.S. armed forces also. Mr. Chin said the Korean people would not be given the opportunity of prior consultation. In reply, General Lawlor pointed out that the U.S. armed forces were the guests of the ROK Government and would have to do a lot of advance planning if any increase in rates were contemplated.

25. Mr. Chin suggested that the U.S. proposed Agreed Minute #1 be deleted. ~~[redacted] deletion of the phrase [redacted] "or increase in utility or service rates" from the U.S. draft of Agreed Minute #1.~~ General Lawlor observed that a change in rates might be made at a low administrative level. Mr. Chin replied that an increase in rates would be made only after very careful study. General Lawlor observed that the relationship between the U.S. armed forces and the ROK Government was very close. He reminded the negotiators that although a marriage was customarily entered into for [redacted] other than legal reasons, the legal safeguards written into the marriage contract provide a sound basis [redacted] for the smooth functioning of the marriage.

Enrollment and Training of Reservists

26. Turning to the draft article on the enrollment and training of reservists, Col. Solf reminded the negotiators that at the previous meeting the Korean side had expressed certain doubts concerning the U.S. draft. [redacted] Mr. Habib had made certain explanations which the Korean side had agreed to consider, concerning the [redacted] Korean side's fear that the U.S. draft might circumvent the Korean alien registration laws. Col. Solf asked if the Korean side had given further consideration to this question.

27. Mr. Chin ~~asked whether it was~~ the intention of the U.S. armed

~~23~~. Mr. Chin reiterated that since ~~the~~ a change of rates was a matter primarily affecting the interest of the entire population of Korea, such a change would be handled very prudently by the Korean Government. He thus said that, in a word, such a change would generally be taken up as a matter to be dealt with and decided ~~from~~ on the basis of domestic considerations.

forces to draft temporary visitors to Korea for reserve training. Col. Solf replied that it was extremely unlikely that a tourist in Korea ~~for a fifteen day period~~ would be involved in reserve training. He said this was not contemplated under any of the existing reserve procedures. Mr. Chin said the phrase "United States citizens who are in [redacted] the Republic of Korea" includes all U. S. citizens. Col. Solf said that this was possible. However, assuming that a tourist is enrolled for reserve training before the expiration of the 30-day period in which he is required to register with the Korean authorities, the Joint Committee could be expected to work out [redacted] satisfactory procedures to take care of this problem. He pointed out that the only people exempt from the requirement to register were members of the U.S. armed forces on active duty, and other classes enumerated in the definitions article.

28. Mr. Chin said the Korean side had no objection to reserve training for anyone actually residing in Korea. But ~~they~~ the Korean side believed the enrollment of temporary visitors to be unreasonable. Col. Solf pointed out that [redacted] use of the term "resident" had been avoided in the U.S. draft because of the provisions of the Entry and Exit Article, which debarred members of the U.S. armed forces, the civilian component, and their dependents from acquiring [redacted] the status of permanent residents or establishing a domicile.

29. Mr. Chin then suggested the addition to the U.S. draft of the phrase "except for ordinary tourists". Col. Solf said the U.S. side would take this under consideration but assured the Korean side that the enrollment of ordinary tourists for reserve training was an extremely rare occurrence. He [redacted] called the attention of the Korean side to the provisions of the U.S. draft of the Definitions Article, and of paragraphs 2 and 5 of the Entry and Exit Article. He said those provisions should resolve the doubts of the Korean side, inasmuch as reservists not on active duty were in no way exempt from Korean Entry, Exit or registration Laws.

30. At this point, [redacted] drafts were exchanged of the article governing foreign exchange.

0224

31. The next meeting was scheduled for February 25 at 2:00 p.m.

보통문서로 재분류(1966. 12. 31)

1966. 12. 31 에 의거 일반문서로 재분류됨

0225

관리 번호 896

JOINT SUMMARY RECORD OF THE 14TH SESSION
STATUS FORCES NEGOTIATIONS

February 14, 1963

I. Time and Place : 2:00 to 4:40 p.m. February 14, 1963 at the Conference Room of the Economic Planning Board.

II. Attendants:

ROK Side:

Mr. Chin, Pil Shik	Director Bureau of Political Affairs Ministry of Foreign Affairs
Mr. Shin, Kwan Sup	Director Bureau of Costums Duty Ministry of Finance
Mr. Koo, Choong Whay	Chief, America Section Ministry of Foreign Affairs
Mr. O, Won Yong	Chief, Treaty Section Ministry of Foreign Affairs
Col. Lee, Nam Koo	Chief, Military Affairs Section Ministry of National Defense
Mr. Chu, Mun ki	Chief, Legal Affairs Section Ministry of ~~Foreign Affairs~~ Justice
Mr. Lee, Kyung Hoon	2nd Secretary Ministry of Foreign Affairs
Mr. Shin, Chung Sup	2nd Secretary Ministry of Foreign Affairs
Mr. Kang, Suk Jae	3rd Secretary Ministry of Foreign Affairs
Mr. Lee, Chang Bum	3rd Secretary Ministry of Foreign Affairs

US Side:

Brig. Gen. J.D.Lawlor	Deputy Chief of Staff 8th Army
Mr. William J. Ford	First Secretary of the Embassy

0226

기안 주과	과고재	二월二日	담당	과장	국장	특별보좌관	차관	장관

1966.12.31 에 예고문에 의거 일반문서로 재분류됨

1964년 9월 30일 미주과장 지시으로 (비밀)로 재분류

Col. G.G. O'Connor	Deputy Chief of Staff 8th Army
Capt. R.M. Brownlie	Assistant Chief of Staff USN/K
Col. W.A. Solf	Staff Judge Advocate 8th Army
Mr. Benjamin A. Fleck (Rapporteur and Press Officer)	First Secretary of the Embassy
Mr. Robert A. Lewis	Second Secretary and Consul of the Embassy
Lt. Col R.E. Miller	Staff Officer, JAG 8th Army
Lt. Col. W.A. Burt	J-5
Kenneth Campen	Interpreter

Utilities & Services

1. Lt. Col. Miller began the substant discussion by reminding the negotiators that the U.S. side had tabled at the eleventh meeting a draft dealing with utilities and services as part of the U.S. draft article "D". At that time, Mr. Chin had stated that the Korean side would table its corresponding draft at a later meeting only if there were differences between the two drafts. At the twelfth meeting, the Korean side did table its draft. Lt. Col. Miller suggested, therefore, that the Korean side give its views regarding the differences between the two drafts. He also suggested subpargraph by subparagraph discussion.

2. Pointing out typographic mistake in the Korean draft, Mr. Chin stated that the phrase "however produced" was to be deleted from paragraph 1.

0227

3. Turning to a comparison of the U.S. paragraph 3 (a) and the Korean paragraph 1, Mr. Chin requested clarification of the term "political subdivisions thereof" in the U.S. draft. Lt.Col. Miller explained that this referred to municipal, county, and other subordinate administrative offices, such as the Special Cities of Seoul and Pusan, with which the U.S. armed forces may have dealings from time to time. This language had been included in the U.S. draft in order to insure that the U.S. forces would be able to use utilities controlled or regulated by these subordinate offices. Mr. Chin stated that these subordinate administrations were included in the overall term "Government of Korea" and it was unnecessary, therefore, to refer to them specifically. However, if the U.S. side felt that such reference was desirable, they might be mentioned in an Agreed Minute.

4. Lt.Col, Miller pointed out that the U.S. draft makes clear that the U.S. armed forces could use either publicly- or privately-owned utitlities. He suggested that an Agreed Minute would unnecessarily complicate this portion of the Agreement, inasmuch as the language could be included in the Article without complicating or confusing its terms. He said the U.S. side considered an Agreed Minute to be unnecessary and preferred to retain this reference in the body of the article. General Lawlor added that the U.S. armed forces might have to pay utility bills directly to these subordinate administrative offices and therefore this reference should be retained.

0228

4-3

5. Mr. Chin stated that there was no substantial difference in content in the two drafts but only in language. Lt. Col. Miller replied that the U.S. side had tried to spell everything out and not leave anything to implication. Mr. Chin stated that absolutely necessary language must be included but suggested that unnecessary words should be avoided. He pointed out that privately-owned utilities-not regulated by the ROKG would not be covered by the phrase "publicly or privately owned" in the U.S. draft. Mr. Chin expressed the view that the phrase "belonging to, or controlled or regulated by the Government of the Republic of Korea" in the Korean draft was a better formulation. He further pointed out that this phrase in the Korean draft would be broad enough to cover the meaning and implication of the phrase "whether publicly or privately owned, which are controlled or regulated by the Government of the Republic of Korea" in the U.S. draft. He then suggested that the phrase used in the Korean draft be inserted in place of the corresponding phrase in the U.S. draft. Lt. Col. Miller stated that the U.S. draft is more specific but said the U.S. side would consider the proposal.

6. Mr. Chin pointed out that the definition of utilities and services was identical in both drafts, except for the phrase "however produced", which remained in the U.S. draft. Lt. Col. Miller pointed out that the proposed Agreed Minute #2 of the U.S. draft referred

0229

4-4

to the existing Unititlies [redacted] Claims Settlement Agreement and stated that the latter Agreement will remain in full force and effect. He also emphasized that the difinition of utilities and services in the draft article was taken from the Utilities [redacted] Claims Settlement Agreement which included the term "however produced". He added that use of the Claims Settlement Agreement definition in its entirety was deemed more desireable because it would obviate questions which might later be raised concerning reasons why the SOFA Article definition was different. Mr. Chin replied that inasmuch as drafts contain no substantial difference, smoother wording would be better in the formulation. Lt. Col. Miller said the U.S. side recognized this but desired to include a specific reference, in the Agreed Minute, to the fact that the existing utilities agreement would continue in force.

7. Mr. Chin requested an explanation of the remainder of paragraph 3 (a) in the U.S. draft which was not included in the Korean draft. Lt. Col. Miller explained that everything discussed so far had concerned utilities and services provided by the ROKG. However, there were some utilities which the U.S. armed forces themselves had to operate. The nature and extent of these utilities would vary from time to time. The purpose of the language in the U.S. draft is to make clear that the U.S. armed forces have the right to operate such utilities in addition to those which are furnished by the ROKG.

0230

4-5

8. Mr. Chin said this would create problems, particularly in the field of transportation, such as the operation of military trains by the U.S. armed forces on the Korean railways system. Lt. Col. Miller replied that the most probable areas were the military communications network, the provision of alternate power sources, and the operation of various types of military transportation facilities. He pointed out that the U.S. armed forces are presently using Korean facilities under the terms of the Utilities [redacted] Claims Settlement Agreement. He said the U.S. draft would not permit the expropriation of Korean facilities but would permit the U.S. armed forces to operate their own. Mr. Chin again referred to the operation of military trains on the Korean railways and inquired whether, in such a case, the U.S. armed forces would consult with the Ministry of Transportation. Lt. Col. Miller replied that this would be necessary and that the Joint Committee also would undoubtedly be involved. General Lawlor agreed.

9. Mr. Chin stated that this point was another question of language. He suggested for the consideration of the U.S. side the following alternative language for the third sentence of paragraph 3(a) of the U.S. draft:

> "The operation by the U.S. armed forces of military transportation, communications, power, and other utilities and services shall be to the extent which is deemed necessary for the operations of the U.S. armed forces and which is not

0231

4-6

inconsistent with operation by the Republic of Korea of such utilities and services."

Mr. Chin emphasized the necessity of ensuring that operation of such utilities by the U.S. armed forces would not interfere with Korean operation of the same utilities. Therefore, the systems and practices of the U.S. armed forces must be consistent with those used by the Korean authorities concurned.

10. General Lawlor stated that under current procedures, whenever the U.S. armed forces run military trains, they are operated in a manner consistent with the Korean practices. Lt. Col. Miller pointed out that the U.S. armed forces might also wish to operate other types of utilities which are completely self-contained and unrelated to any existing Korean utilities. General Lawlor mentioned that the U.S. armed forces may wish to operate their own bus lines from time to time. Mr. Chin said that vehicles operated by the U.S. armed forces should obey all Korean traffic laws and regulations. General Lawlor agreed. Mr. Chin said if operations are continued on the same basis as at present, there will be no problems.

11. Turning to paragraph 3 (b) of the U.S. draft, Mr. Chin pointed out that the subject of the draft was the priorities and conditions under which utilities furnished by the ROKG were to be used by the U.S. armed forces. He said the corresponding Korean draft provided for "conditions no less favorable than those that may be applicable from time to time to the ministries and

0232

4-7

agencies of the Government of the Republic of Korea". He said the conditions applicable to the Government were the most proper conditions. He then asked the U.S. side to explain their draft.

12. Lt. Col. Miller replied that the U.S. draft differs from the Korean draft in two major respects: (1) it includes mention of rates and tariffs, and (2) it provides that the U.S. armed fordes would pay rates equivalant to those paid by the most favored user. He pointed out that this provision would provided additional guidance for the negotiation of utilities agreements under the Utilities and Claims Settlement Agreement. Mr. Chin said the Korean side would have no objection to the inclusion of "rates and tariffs" in the article. However, the most reasonable conditions are those which are accorded to the ministries and agencies of the ROKG.

13. Lt. Col. Miller stated that U.S. armed forces in other countries have had unfortunated experiences in the past by relying on provisions similar to those contained in the Korean draft. He said the language of the U.S. draft would avoid misunderstandings such as have arisen elsewhere. Mr. Chin said that it would be reasonable for the U.S. armed forces to receive the same treatment as that accorded ministries and agencies of the ROK Government. He said cases such as those referred to by Lt. Col. Miller were exceptional. General Lawlor explained that in some cases in other countries, the U.S. armed forces have been forced to pay rates higher than those paid by ~~private~~ other users because of manipulated

0233

4-8

"government" rates. Also, there have been cases in which different agencies of the same government have been charged different rates. In such a case, the question arises as to which rate shall be paid by the U.S. armed forces. Mr. Chin replied that such things could never happen in Korea. General Lawlor acknowledged that the U.S. armed forces have not had that kind of experience in Korea.

14. Mr. Chin explained that according to the existing system, the government pays a reasonable rate and there is only one rate charged to all government agencies. General Lawlor pointed out that in a mixed economy such as that existing in the Republic of Korea, it is often difficult to distinguish the line between government agencies and private organizations. Lt. Col. Miller added that all the U.S. armed forces were asking for was to be charged the lowest rate, whether that was the rate charged to government agencies or not. Mr. Chin said the U.S. side would understand the Korean side's position if it examined the treatment accorded to agencies of the ROK Government to date. General Lawlor replied that no criticism was intended of the treatment which has been given to the U.S. armed forces.

15. Mr. Chin stated that the increase of rates was a very important matter which would affect the interest of the entire population. It was utterly unthinkable that the Korean authority would manipulate such an important matter of increasing rates, without due regard to the effect on the interest of the entire population but only with the purpose of charging higher

0234

4-9

rates to the U.S. armed forces. The U.S. side would not but make the representations to the Korean authorities and also refer the matter to the Joint Committee, should such an unthinkable case take place. General Lawlor agreed but pointed out that the U.S. armed forces would be in a poor bargaining position because of their urgent and continuing need for the utilities and services. Mr. Chin stated that we are discussing the SOFA under the circumstances which are prevailing at present. If the situation be drastically changed after the conclusion of the SOFA, it will bring about the problem on the principle of "change of situation" in international law.

16. Moving on to the second sentence of paragraph 3 (b) of the U.S. draft, Mr. Chin said it appeared that the intent of the U.S. draft was to prevent discrimination against the U.S. armed forces. Treatment equal to that accorded the ROK Government is not discrimination, he said. Furthermore, it is taken for granted that the ROK Government will do everything in its power to prevent any such discrimination. He suggested that the language of the U.S. draft was somewhat degrading and proposed deletion of that sentence. General Lawlor replied that this sentence also was connected with the position of the U.S. armed forces as customers and it had been included in the draft to ensure that the U.S. armed forces would be given favorable treatment. He said the U.S. side would consider the position of the Korean side.

0235

4-10

17. Regarding the third sentence of paragraph 3(b) of the U.S. draft, Mr. Chin stated that in emergency situations, the U.S. and Korean armed forces would receive equal treatment. Lt. Col. Miller pointed out that the SOFA has to be tailored to the needs of specific situations. This sentence constitutes recognition of the fact that the Republic of Korea is a potential combat area. There is thus more chance of an emergency arising here than in many other places. This language is meant to ensure that in such an emergency, the U.S. armed forces would not be limited to the usual or normal arrangements with regard to utilities and services. The exact nature of the emergency cannot be predicted.

18. Mr. Chin replied that the Korean side was well aware of Lt. Col. Miller's explanation and had been considering the situation. He said that a separate article, to be discussed later, would define steps to be taken in the event of the most serious emergency which could arise. He did not think it necessary or desirable to refer to emergency actions in every article of the SOFA. Even if it were not spelled out in this article, he said, the treatment accorded to the U.S. armed forces in the event of emergency would be equivalent to that accorded to the ROK armed forces in such event. He suggested that the sentence be deleted.

19. General Lawlor stated that the point of the sentence was that a commander of military forces must be sure that he is able to move, shoot, and communicate in the event of an emergency. That is why the sentence

0236

4-4

was included in the draft. Lt Col. Miller added that certain agencies of the Korean Government might need more assistance during an emergency than others and the U.S. armed forces might need more assistance than any ROK Government agency. The purpose of this clause is not to assure that the U.S. aremd forces get as many as or more utilities and services than any ROK Government agency but that they have some assurance of getting what they require. If such assistance were not forthcoming, the U.S. armed forces might not be able to accomplish their mission.

20. Mr. Chin said the Korean side would study the remarks of the U.S. side concerning this matter. He said apparently there were differences in the ways of thinking of the two sides. He said the Korean side placed ethics and morality on a higher plane than the law. He said it was taken for granted, morally and by common sense, that the Korean Government would extend the utmost possible cooperation in time of emergency. He said the Korean side did not disagree with the substance of the U.S. draft but thought inclusion of this sentence was unnecessary. General Lawlor expressed appreciation for Mr. Chin's remarks.

21. Turning to paragraph 4 of the U.S. draft and paragraph 2 (a) of the Korean draft, Mr. Chin expressed the opinion that the Korean draft was more inclusive than the U.S. draft and asked for the comments of the U.S. side. Lt. Col. Miller replied that the U.S. draft

was not limited to utilities but refers to accounting arrangements arising out of the SOFA as a whole. He pointed out that payments could be made between authorities of the two governments, as provided for in the Korean draft, or between other agencies or persons. He said this paragraph must also be considered in conjunction with the proposed Agreed Minute #2 in the U.S. draft, which would continue the existing Utilities [redacted] Claims Settlement Agreement in effect. Referring to paragraph 2 (b) of the Korean draft, he pointed out that the existing arrangements are renegotiated from time to time. Therefore, the relevant language must be kept flexible. He asked the Korean side to clarify their subparagraph (b). Mr. Chin stated that the Korean side would study this point and suggested further discussion at a subsequent meeting. Lt. Col. Miller pointed out that there would be some arrangements which could not be negotiated until the SOFA comes into effect. There are also some existing agreements which may have to be revised. Mr. Chin said the Korea side understood this point and would discuss it at the next meeting.

22. Mr. Chin then asked the U.S. side to explain its proposed Agreed Minute #1. Lt Col, Miller explained that an increase in utitlities rates would mean an increase in the expenditure of appropriated funds and a corresponding decrease in the amount of such funds which could be spent on other activities of the U.S. armed forces in Korea. A change in priorities could

0238

4-13

similarly affect the military posture of those forces. Therefore, this Agreed Minute is intended to provide the two governments with an opportunity to present thier respective views before rates were increased or priorities changed.

23. Mr. Chin commented that the U.S. armed forces are given the same priority as ROK Government agencies. According to the U.S. draft, if the U.S. armed forces priority were lowered, which would not happen, prior consultation with the armed forces would surely take place. Similarly, prior consultation must take place before any change in rates, in the U.S. draft. He said that if the special rates accorded the U.S. armed forces applied only to those forces, prior consultation would be a simple matter. However, the rates accorded the U.S. armed forces are the same as those accorded generally to agencies of the ROK Government. An increase in the rates would require scrupulous deliberation and highly technical actions by the ROK Government. Prior consultation, under these circumstances, would be very difficult. The interests of the entire population would be affected. The ROK Government would try to cooperate with the U.S. Government in order to prevent unnecessary inconvenience but it would be extremely difficult for the ROK Government to commit itself to prior consultation. Mr. Chin reiterated that since a change of rates was a matter primarily affecting the interest of the entire population of Korea, such a change would be handled

0233

4-14

very prudently by the Korean Government. He thus said that, in a word, such a change would generally be taken up as a matter to be dealt with and decided on the base of domestic considerations.

24. General Lawlor pointed out that we were not suggesting a commitment to obtain US Government agreement but only prior consultation. Lt.Col. Miller added that much advance planning would be required on the part of the U.S. armed forces also. Mr. Chin said the Koean people would not be given the opportunity of prior consultation. In reply, General Lawlor pointed out that the U.S. armed forces were the guests of the ROK Government and would have to do a lot of advance planning if any increase in rates were contemplated.

25. Mr. Chin suggested that the U.S. proposed Agreed Minute #1 be deleted. General Lawlor observed that a change in rates might be made at a low administrative level. Mr. Chin replied that an increase in rates would be made only after very careful study. General Lawlor observed that the relationship between the U.S. armed forces and the ROK Government was very close. He reminded the negotiators that although a marriage was customarily entered into for other than legal reasons, the legal safeguards witten into the marriage contract provide a sound basis for the smooth functioning of the marriage.

0240

4-15

Enrollment and Training of Reservists

26. Turning to the draft article on the enrollment and training of reservists, Col. Solf reminded the negotiators that at the previous meeting the Korean side had expressed certain doubts concerning the U.S. draft. Mr. Habib had made certain explanations which the Korean side had agreed to consider, concerning the Korean side's fear that the U.S. draft might circumvent the Korean alien registration laws. Col. Solf asked if the Korean side had given further consideration to this question.

27. Mr. Chin asked whether it was the intention of the U.S. armed forces to draft temporary visitors to Korea for reserve training. Col, Solf replied that it was extremely unlikely that a toutist in Korea would be involved in reserve training. He said this was not contemplated under any of the existing reserve procedures. Mr. Chin said the phrase "United States citizens who are in the Republic of Korea" included all U.S. citizens. Col. Solf said that this was possible. However, assuming that a tourist is enrolled for reserve training before the expiration of the 30-day period in which he is required to register with the Korea authorities, the Joint Committee could be expected to work out satisfactory precedures to take care of this problem. He pointed out that the only people exempt from the requirement to register were members of the U.S. armed forces on active duty, and other classes enumereted in the definitions article.

4-16 0241

28. Mr. Chin said the Korean side had no objection to reserve training for anyone actually residing in Korea. But the Korean side believed the enrollment of temporary visitors to be unreasonable. Col. Solf pointed out that use of the term "resident" had been avoided in the U.S. draft because of the provisions of the Entry and Exit Article, which debarred members of the U.S. armed forces, the civilian component, and their dependents from acquiring the status of permanent residents or establishing a domicile.

29. Mr. Chin then suggested the addition to the U.S. draft of the phrase "except for ordinary tourists". Col. Solf said the U.S. side would take this under consideration but assured the Korean side that the enrollment of ordinary tourists for reserve training was an extremely rare occurence. He called the attention of the Korean side to the provisions of the U.S. draft of the Definitions Article, and of paragraphs 2 and 5 of the Entry and Exit Article. He said those provisions should resolve the doubts of the Korean side, inasmuch as reservists not on active duty were in no way exempt from Korean Entry Exit or registration Laws.

30. At this point, drafts were exchanged of the article govering foreign exchange.

31. The next meeting was scheduled for February 25 at 2:00 p,m.

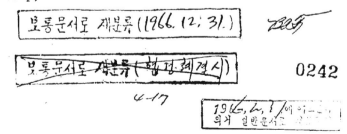

보통문서로 재분류(1966. 12. 31.)

~~보통문서로 재분류(협정 체결시)~~

0242

1966, 6, 7 에 의거 일반문서로

6. 제15차 회의, 2.25

0243

기 안 용 지

자체 통제		기안처	미주과 이 경 훈	전화번호	근거서류접수일자
	과장	국장	보좌관	차관	장관
	(서명)	(서명)	(서명)	(서명)	(서명)
관계관 서명					
기안 년월일	1963. 2. 23.	시행 년월일		보존 년한	정서 기장
분류 기호	외정미	전체 통제		종결	
경유 수신 참조	건 의	발신			
제목	미주둔군 지위협정 교섭대표 추가임명				

정무국장 황 호 을 이사관을 미주둔군 지위협정 체결 교섭 대표단 차석대표로 추가 임명할것을 건의하오니 재가하여 주시기 바라나이다. 끝

0244

6-1

승인양식 1-1-3 (1112-040-016-018) (190mm×260mm16절지)

기 안 용 지

관리번호 ~~84~~

자체통제		기안처	미주과 이경훈	전화번호	근거서류접수일자	
	과장	수석대표	보좌관	차관	장관	
관계관 서명	조약과장			기획조정관		
기안년월일	1963. 2. 23.	시행년월일		보존년한		정서기장
분류기호		전체통제		종결		
경수참 유신조	건 의			발신		
제목	제15차 주둔군지위협정 체결교섭회의에 임할 우리측 태도					

2월 25일에 개최될 제15차 주둔군지위협정 체결 한미간 교섭회의에서는 용어의정의, 합동위원회, 항공 및 교통관제, 예비병의 소집 및 훈련 그리고 외환관리 문제에 관하여 토의될 예정이온바 이에관련하여 우리측 교섭실무자는 2월 22일 회합을갖고 제15차 회의에서 취할 우리측 태도를 별첨과같이 결정하였아오니 재가하여 주시기 바랍니다.

유첨 : 제15차 주둔군지위협정 체결교섭회의에 임할 우리측 태도

~~0244~~ 끝

0245

일반문서로 재분류 (1966.12.31)

~~1966.12.31 예고문에 의거 일반문서로 재분류됨~~

~~보통문서로 재분류 (해정 해제시)~~ 1964. 9.

7-1

승인양식 1—1—3 (1112—040—[illegible]) (190mm×260mm16절지)

1964 년 9 월 30 일 미주과 직권으로 파기비밀 로서분류

4. 1. 용어의 정의

(1) 군대구성원에 관한 규정에 있어서 예외규정인 "except for those for whom status has otherwise been provided"라는 구절을 조약원문에 삽입할것을 받아주되 다음과같은 규정을 합의의사록에 넣도록 주장한다.

The expression "except for those for whom status has otherwise been provided" in Paragraph (a) refers only to personnel on active duty belonging to the United States land, sea or air armed services for whom status is provided in the Military Advisory Group Agreement signed on January 26 1950, and personnel of service attache offices in the Embassy of the United States of America.

(2) 군속에관한 규정에 있어서 미국측이 제시한 합의의사록에서 제3국인으로서 한국과 미국으로부터는 쉽사리 입수할수 없는 기술자는 군속으로 간주한다는 규정에관하여 "쉽사리"라는 단어를 삭제토록 제시한다음 미국측이 이의수락을 거부할 때에는 미측안을 그대로 받아드리기로 한다.

3. 2. 합동위원회

(1) 합동위원회의 기능의 예외규정인 "except where otherwise provided" 라는 구절을 원문에 두는대신에 합의의사록에 "The exception provided for in the first sentence of paragraphs 1 is relevant only to paragraph 2, subparagraphs (b), and (c) of Article ____" 라는 규정을 하자고 제시한 우리측의 입장을 계속 주장한다.

0246

7-2

5. 3. 항공, 교통 관제문제

(1) 보조시설 설치에관한 문제에있어서 미국측 초안 제2항 전단에 미국측은 한국전역 (throughout the Republic of Korea) 에 걸쳐 항공 및 항해보조시설의 설치를하여 받도록 명백히 규정하고 있는데 이에대하여 우리측은 "양국 정부의 적절한 당국간의 협정을 통하여" through agreement between the appropriate authorities of the two governments " 라는 어구를 "territorial water thereof"다음에 삽입토록 계속 주장한다.

(2) 보조시설 설치에관한 미국측 초안 제2항 후단에서 미국측안은 이들 보조시설이 한국에 기존하는 체제와 일반적으로 (generally) 합치하여야 하고 또한 이러한 시설의 설치에관하여는 가능한경우에 (where practicable) 사전통고를 하도록 규정함으로서 이러한 보조시설의 합치 규정 또는 설치에관한 사전 통고 규정에있어서 예외적 경우를 예상한 규정을하고 있는데 이에대하여는 수락해주기로 한다.

2. 4. 예비병의 소집 및 훈련

(1) 미국이 소집 훈련시킬수있는자에 대하여 미국측은 대한민국에 있는자 (who are in)라고 제시한데 대하여 우리측은 미국측 제안의 어미에 "except for ordinary tourists" 라는 구절을 삽입토록 제시한 우리측 입장을 계속 주장한다.

(2) 만일 미국측이 우리측 수정안에 대하여 양보할 기색이없을 때는 미국측안을 수락하도록 한다.

1. 5. 외환관리

(1) 외환관리에 관한 양국측 초안은 그2항에 있어서 우리측의 안에서는 "outside of the Republic of Korea "

0247

7-3

타고 되어있는데 대하여 미국측 안에서는 "out of Korea" 또는 "outside Korea" 타고 규정함으로서 문자상의 차이가 있을뿐 실질적인 차이가 없으므로 미국측안을 받아주기로 한다.

(2) 우리측이 제시한 외환관리 조항에 대한 합의의사록에 있어서 우리측은 동합의의사록을 미국측이 수락하도록 주장한다.

일반문서로 재분류 (1966.12.31.)

1966.12.31.에 예고문에 의거 일반문서로 재분류됨

0248

7-4

LIST OF MEMBERS TO JOIN IN INSPECTION OF U.S. FACILITIES AND AREAS ON MARCH 6, 1963

✓ 1.	Mr. Whang, Ho Eul	Director Bureau of Political Affairs Ministry of Foreign Affairs
✓ 2.	Mr. Shin, Kwan Sup	Director Bureau of Costums Duty Ministry of Finance
✓ 3.	Mr. Koo, Choong Whay	Chief, America Section Ministry of Foreign Affairs
✓ 4.	~~Mr. O, Won Yong~~	Chief, Treaty Section Ministry of Foreign Affairs
✓ 5.	Col. Lee, Nam Koo	Chief, Military Affairs Section Ministry of National Defense
✓ 6.	Mr. Chu, Mun Ki	Chief, Legal Affairs Section Ministry of Foreign Affairs
✓ 7.	Mr. Lee, Kyung Hoon	2nd Secretary Ministry of Foreign Affairs
✓ 8.	Mr. Chai, Eui Sok	2nd Secretary Ministry of Foreign Affairs
✓ 9.	Mr. Kang, Suk Jae	3rd Secretary Ministry of Foreign Affairs
10.	Mr. Lee, Chang Bum (Kim, Yoon Taik)	3rd Sedretary Ministry of Foreign Affairs
✓ 11.	Mr. Jin, Kuan Seop	Assistant to Press Officer Ministry of Foreign Affairs
✓ 12.	Mr. Kang, Yong Joong	Camera man (Still Picture) Ministry of Foreign Affairs
✓ 13.	Mr. Dong, Suk Young	Camera man (Motion Picture) Ministry of Public Information

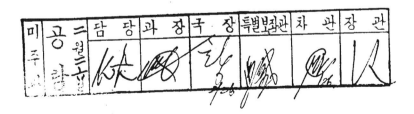

3

미주	공람	담 당	과 장	국 장	특별보좌관	차 관	장 관
		(signature)	(signature)	(signature)	(signature)	(signature)	(signature)

0249

1963.2.25.

CONFIDENTIAL

DEFINITIONS ARTICLE

Agreed Minute:

"The personnel referred to in subparagraph (a) for whom status has otherwise been provided include personnel of the United States armed forces attached to the United States Embassy and personnel for whom status has been provided in the Military Advisory ~~[illegible]~~ Group Agreement of January 26, 1950 as amended."

refers to only

CONFIDENTIAL

0250

CONFIDENTIAL

1963.2.25.

NAVIGATIONAL AIDS ARTICLE

Agreed Minute:

"Installation by the United States Armed Forces of permanent navigational aids for vessels and aircraft outside of areas and facilities in use by the United States Armed Forces will be effected in accordance with the procedures established under paragraph 1 of Article ."

CONFIDENTIAL

0251

CONFIDENTIAL
CONFIDENTIAL

ARTICLE

Non-Appropriated Fund Activities

1. Military exchanges, messes, social clubs, theaters, newspapers and other non-appropriated fund activities authorized and regulated by the United States military authorities may be established by the United States armed forces for the use of members of such forces, the civilian component, and their dependents. Except as otherwise provided in this Agreement, such activities shall not be subject to Korean regulations, licenses, fees, taxes, or similar controls.

2. No Korean tax shall be imposed on sales of merchandise or services by such activities. Purchases within Korea of merchandise and supplies by such activities shall be subject to the Korean taxes to which other purchasers of such merchandise and supplies are subject and at rates no less favorable than those imposed on other purchasers. normal general purchasers ? Except as provided in para 1 (b).

3. Except as such disposal may be permitted by the United States and Korean authorities in accordance with mutually agreed conditions, goods which are sold by such activities shall not be disposed of in Korea to persons not authorized to make purchases from such activities. NEWA paper가 포함되는가? yes.

4. The activities referred to in this Article shall, after consultation between the representatives of the two

CONFIDENTIAL
CONFIDENTIAL

0252

governments in the Joint Committee, provide such information to the Republic of Korea tax authorities as is required by Korean tax legislation.

5. The activities referred to in paragraph 1 may be used by other officers or personnel of the United States Government ordinarily accorded such privileges, by non-Korean persons whose presence in Korea is solely for the purpose of providing contract services financed by the United States Government, by the dependents of the foregoing, by organizations which are present in the Republic of Korea primarily for the benefit and service of the United States armed forces personnel, such as the American Red Cross and the United Service Organizations, and by the non-Korean personnel of such organizations and their dependents.

U.S.O. contractor 7 는 solely for the service of U.S.A.F.

They are subject to same laws and regulations as those who have such privileges and immunities

May 17th 2. P.M.

ARTICLE ____

CONTRACTORS

1. Persons, including corporations, their employees, and the dependents of such persons, present in Korea solely for the purpose of executing contracts with the United States for the benefit of the United States armed forces or other armed forces in Korea under the Unified Command receiving logistical support from the United States armed forces, who are designated by the Government of the United States in accordance with the provisions of paragraph 2 below, shall, except as provided in this Article, be subject to the laws and regulations of Korea. principle 만 協議 not all specific matters

2. The designation referred to in paragraph 1 above shall be made upon consultation with the Government of Korea and shall be restricted to cases where open competitive bidding is not practicable due to security considerations, to the technical qualifications of the contractors involved, to the unavailability of materials or services required by United States standards, or to limitations of United States law. The designation shall be withdrawn by the Government of the United States:

OK'd

(a) Upon completion of contracts with the United States for the United States armed forces or other armed forces in Korea under the Unified Command receiving logistical support from the United States armed forces;

OK'd

(b) Upon proof that such persons are engaged in business activities in Korea other than those pertaining to the United States armed forces or other armed forces in Korea under the Unified Command receiving logistical support from the United States armed forces;

(c) Upon proof that such persons are engaged in practices illegal in Korea.

3. Upon certification by appropriate United States authorities as to their identity, such persons shall be accorded the following benefits of this Agreement:

(a) Rights of accession and movement, as provided for in Article , paragraph 2;

(b) Entry into Korea in accordance with the provisions of Article ;

(c) The exemption from customs duties, and other such charges provided for in Article , paragraph 3, for members of the United States armed forces, the civilian component, and their dependents;

(d) If authorized by the Government of the United States, the right to use the services of the activities provided for in Article ;

(e) Those ~~rights~~ benefits provided in Article , paragraph 2, for members of the United States armed forces, the civilian component, and their dependents;

(f) If authorized by the Government of the United States, the right to use military payment certificates, as provided for in Article ;

(g) The use of postal facilities provided for in Article ;

suggest deletion of sub-para (h)

(h) Those rights accorded the United States armed forces by Article , paragraph 3, relating ~~to utilities and services~~;

(i) Those rights provided to members of the United States armed forces, the civilian component, and their dependents by Article , relating to driving permits and registration of vehicles;

(j) Exemption from the laws and regulations of Korea with respect to terms and conditions of employment, and licensing and registration of businesses and corporations.

4. The arrival, departure, and place of residence in Korea of such persons shall from time to time be notified by the United States armed

no objection

forces to the Korean authorities.

5. Upon certification by an authorized representative of the United States armed forces, depreciable assets, except houses, held, used or transferred by such persons exclusively for the execution of contracts referred to in paragraph 1 shall not be subject to taxes or similar charges of Korea.

6. Upon certification by an authorized representative of the United States armed forces, such persons shall be exempt from taxation in Korea on the holding, use, transfer by death, or transfer to persons or agencies entitled to tax exemption under this Agreement, of movable property, tangible or intangible, the presence of which in Korea is due solely to the temporary presence of these persons in Korea, provided that such exemption shall not apply to property held for the purpose of investment or the conduct of other business in Korea or to any intangible property registered in Korea.

7. The persons referred to in paragraph 1 shall not be liable to pay income or corporation taxes to the Government of Korea or to any other taxing agency in Korea on any income derived under a contract with the Government of the United States in connection with the construction, maintenance or operation of any of the facilities or areas covered by this

Agreement. Persons in Korea in connection with the execution of such a contract with the United States shall not be liable to pay any Korean taxes to the Government of Korea or to any taxing agency in Korea on income derived from sources outside of Korea, nor shall periods during which such persons are in Korea be considered periods of residence or domicile in Korea for the purposes of Korean taxation. The provisions of this paragraph do not exempt such persons from payment of income or corporation taxes on income derived from Korean sources, other than those sources referred to in the first sentence of this paragraph, nor do they exempt such persons who claim Korean residence for United States income tax purposes from payment of Korean taxes on income.

8.

Agreed Minute:

1. The execution of contracts with the United States in addition to those specified in paragraph 1 of Article   shall not exclude the persons provided for in Article   from the application of that Article.

CONFIDENTIAL

ARTICLE

MILITARY POST OFFICES

1. The United States may establish and operate, within the facilities and areas in use by the U.S. armed forces, United States military post offices for the use of members of the United States armed forces, the civilian component, and their dependents, for the transmission of mail between United States military post offices in the Republic of Korea and between such military post offices and other United States post offices.

2. United States military post offices may be used by other officers and personnel of the United States Government, and their dependents, ordinarily accorded such privileges abroad

agreeable to insert in an agreed minutes

CONFIDENTIAL

CONFIDENTIAL

0259

CONFIDENTIAL

ARTICLE

MILITARY PAYMENT CERTIFICATES

1. (a) United States military payment certificates denominated in dollars may be used by persons authorized by the United States for internal transactions. The Government of the United States will take appropriate action to insure that authorized personnel are prohibited from engaging in transactions involving military payment certificates except as authorized by United States regulations. The Government of Korea will take necessary action to prohibit unauthorized persons from engaging in transactions involving military payment certificates and with the aid of United States authorities will undertake to apprehend and punish any person or persons under its jurisdiction involved in the counterfeiting or uttering of counterfeit military payment certificates.

within the facilities and areas in use by the United States forces

(b) It is agreed that the United States authorities will to the extent authorized by United States law, apprehend and punish members of the United States armed forces, the civilian component, or their dependents, who tender military payment certificates to unauthorized persons and that no obligation will be due to such unauthorized persons or to the Government of Korea or its agencies from the United States or any of its agencies as a result of any unauthorized use of military payment certificates within Korea.

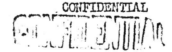

CONFIDENTIAL

CONFIDENTIAL

0260

agreed

2. In order to exercise control of military payment certificates the United States may designate certain American financial institutions to maintain and operate, under United States supervision, facilities for the use of persons authorized by the United States to use military payments certificates. Institutions authorized to maintain military banking facilities will establish and maintain such facilities physically separated from their Korean commercial banking business, with personnel whose sole duty is to maintain and operate such facilities. Such facilities shall be permitted to maintain United States currency bank accounts and to perform all financial transactions in connection therewith including receipt and remission of funds to the extent provided by Article ...... paragraph 2, of this Agreement

CONFIDENTIAL

CONFIDENTIAL

① Joint Committee.

ARTICLE (currency control) adopted (2.25)

1. Members of the United States armed forces, the civilian component and their dependents, shall be subject to the foreign exchange controls of the Government of the Republic of Korea.

2. The preceding paragraph shall not be construed to preclude the transmission into or out of Korea of United States dollars or dollar instruments representing the official funds of the United States or realized as a result of service or employment in connection with this Agreement by members of the United States armed forces and the civilian component, or realized by such persons and their dependents from sources outside Korea.

3. The United States authorities shall take suitable measures to preclude the abuse of the privileges stipulated in the preceding paragraphs or circumvention of the Korean foreign exchange controls.

CONFIDENTIAL

CONFIDENTIAL

0262

CONFIDENTIAL

FOREIGN EXCHANGE CONTROLS

AGREED MINUTE

Payment in Korea by the United States armed forces including those activities provided in Article _____, to persons other than members of the United States armed forces, civilian component, their dependents and those persons referred to in Article _____ shall be effected in accordance with the Korean Foreign Exchange Control Law and regulations. The funds to be used for these transactions shall be convertible into currency of the Republic of Korea at the highest rate in terms of the number of Korean Won per United States dollar which, at the time the conversion is made, is not unlawful in the Republic of Korea.

effective official rate

CONFIDENTIAL

0263

U.S. Draft.

ARTICLE ______ ~~a~~ adopted (2.25)

The United States may enroll in its reserve forces and train, in Korea, eligible United States citizens who are in the Republic of Korea, except for ordinally tourist.

0264

관리 번호 898

기 안 용 지

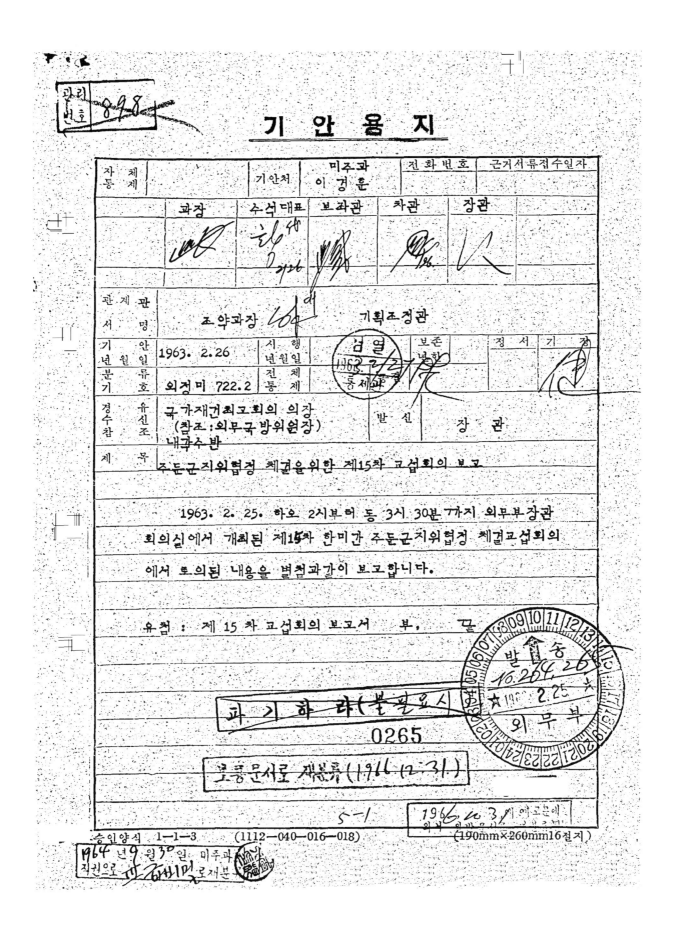

자 체 통 제		기안처	미주과 이 경 훈	전화번호	근거서류접수일자
	과장	수석대표	보좌관	차관	장관
관계관 서명	조약과장		기획조정관		
기안 년월일	1963. 2.26	시행 년월일		보존 년한	정서기장
분류 기호	외정미 722.2	전체 통제			
경유 수신 참조	국가재건최고회의 의장 (참조: 외무국방위원장) 내각수반	발신	장 관		
제목	주둔군지위협정 체결을위한 제15차 교섭회의 보고				

1963. 2. 25. 하오 2시부터 동 3시 30분까지 외무부장관 회의실에서 개최된 제15차 한미간 주둔군지위협정 체결교섭회의에서 토의된 내용을 별첨과같이 보고합니다.

유첨 : 제 15 차 교섭회의 보고서 부, 끝

발송 1963. 2. 25 외무부

파기하라(불필요시)

0265

보통문서로 재분류(1966.12.31.)

5-1

1966. 12. 31 에 예고문에 의거 일반문서로 재분류됨

승인양식 1-1-3 (1112-040-016-018) (190mm×260mm16절지)

1964 년 9 월 30 일 미주과 직권으로 비밀 로 재분류

외 무 부

외정미 722.2 1963. 2. 27.

수 신 국가재건최고회의 의장

참 조 외무국방위원장

제 목 주둔군지위협정 체결을위한 제15차 교섭회의 보고

1963. 2. 25. 하오 2시부터 동 3시 30분 까지 외무부장관 회의실에서 개최된 제15차 한미간 주둔군지위협정 체결 교섭회의에서 토의된 내용을 별첨과같이 보고합니다.

유첨 : 제 15 차 교섭회의 보고서 2 부. 끝

외 무 부 장 관 최 덕 신

0266

5-7

외 무 부

외정미 722.2 1963. 2. 27.

수 신 내각수반

제 목 주둔군지위협정 체결을위한 제15차 교섭회의 보고

1963. 2. 25. 하오 2시부터 동 3시 30분까지 외무부 장관 회의실에서 개최된 제15차 한미간 주둔군지위협정 체결교섭 회의에서 토의된 내용을 별첨과같이 보고합니다.

유첨 : 제 15 차 교섭회의 보고서 1 부. 끝

외 무 부 장 관 최 덕 신

0267

5-8

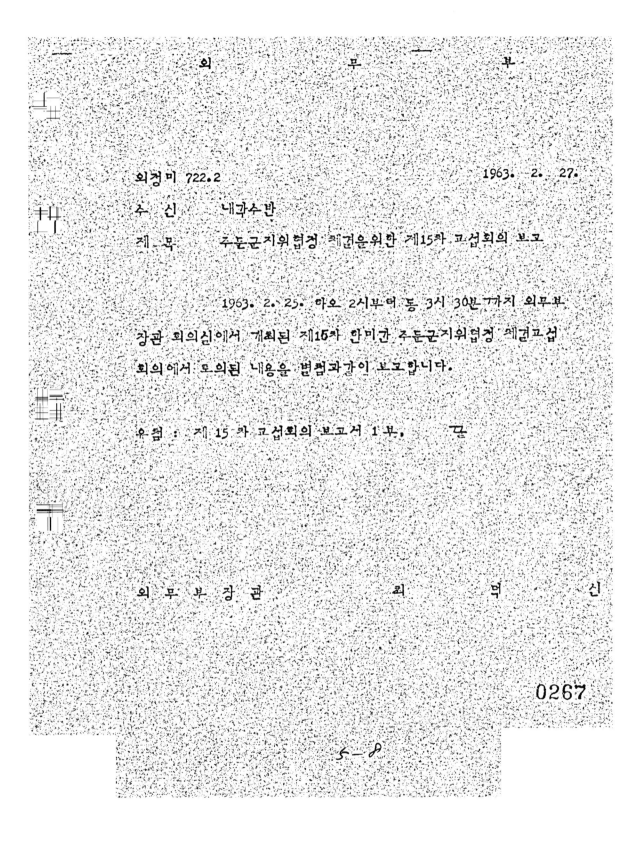

제 15 차

한미간 주둔군지위협정 체결 실무자회의

보 고 서

1. 시 일 : 1963. 2. 25. 하오 2시부터 3시 30분까지

2. 장 소 : 외무부장관 회의실

3. 참석자 : 한국측 :

진 필 식	(외무부 기획조정관, 수석대표)
황 호 을	(외무부 정무국장)
구 충 회	(외무부 미주과장)
이 남 구	(국방부 군무과장)
주 문 기	(법무부 법무과장)
이 경 훈	(외무부 2등서기관)
신 정 섭	(")
강 석 재	(외무부 3등서기관)
이 창 범	(")

미국측 : 교섭대표단 전원 ("토마"장군 불참)

4. 토의사항 :

(1) 외환관리, 예비병의 소집 및 훈련, 합동위원회, 용어의 정의 그리고 항해 및 항공통제 문제를 순차적으로 토의함.

(2) 외환관리문제에 있어서 (가) 조약원문에대한 양국측 초안은 몇개의 용어에있어서 차의가 있을뿐 실질적인 차의가 없음으로 미국측안을 수락해주었으며 (나) 합의의사록은 우리측만이 제시하였음으로 미국측은 다음회기에 합의의사록을 제시하겠다고 하였음.

63-1-48

(3) 예비병의 소집 및 훈련문제에 있어서 미국측은 한국에서 예비병 훈련을위하여 소집된자는 한국의 출입국관리 규정에

5-2

0268

'63-1-6 (5)

明文89-11 (5)

0269

복종하며 보통여행자를 그들의 동의없이 소집할의사는 없으며, 만일 여사한일이 있을때는 출입국관리 관계규정에 따라 신분의 변갱에관하여 한국 당국에 통고할것을 확언하며 동 확언을 한미간 공동회의록에 명백히하겠다고 말하였기 우리측은 미국측의 안을 수락해주었음.

(4) 합동위원회 문제에있어서 우리측은 동위원회 기능의 예외적 규정을 원문에 두는대신에 합의의사록에 이예외적 규정은 토지시설의 둘째번 조항의 2(b), (c)항에만 관련한것 이라라는 규정을 하도록 제의한데 대하여 미국측은 이를 수락하였음.

(5) 용어의 정의 조항중 군속에관한 규정에있어서 우리측은 합의의사록에있은 제3국인으로서 한국과 미국으로부터는 쉽사리 입수할수없는 기술자는 군속으로 간주한다는 규정에있어서 "쉽사리"라는 단어를 삭제하자고 주장한데대하여 미국측은 이의 삭제를수락하되 한미간 공동회의록에는 동용어의 실질적인 의미를 고려하여 실제상 또는 쉽사리 입수할수없는 기술자라고 남기자고 주장하였기 우리측은 이주장을 받아주었음.

(6) 용어의 정의조항중 군대구성원에 관한 규정에있어서 미국측은 별도로 그의 신분이 규정된자라고 하는것은 주한미국대사관 무관과 주한미군사고문단원을 포함한다라고 규정한 수정된 합의의사록을 제시한데 대하여 우리측은 별도로 그의 신분이 규정된자라는 용어는 주한미군사고문단원과 주한미대사관 무관만을 말하는것이다 라고 규정한 수정안을 제시함으로서 이문제는 다음에 다시 토의키로 함. 63-1-4P

(7) 항해 및 항공통제 조항중, 항해보조시설 설치에관한 문제에 있어서 우리측은 "양국정부의 적절한 당국간의 협정을통하여"

0270

5-3

63-1-6

미문 89-11

0271

한국전역에걸쳐 항공, 항해 보조시설을 설치하도록 규정할것을 제의한데 대하여 미국측은 "양국정부의 적절한 당국간의 협정을통하여" 라는 구절대신에 이러한 보조시설의 설치는 토지시설에관한 첫째조항 1항에 의거한 수속절차에 따라서 시행될것이다라는 요지의 합의의사록을 제시하여왔기 이 문제는 다음에 다시 토의키로함.

5. 중요합의사항:

(1) 합동위원회 문제에관한 조항에 완전합의함.

(2) 예비병의 소집 및 훈련문제에 관한 조항에 완전합의함.

6. 기타사항 :

(1) 차기회의 일자 : 1963. 3. 8. 하오 2시

(2) 차기회의 의제 : 차기회의가지 양측수석대표 간에 합의된사항

7. 참고자료 : 미국측이 제의한 합의의사록 초안 (용어의 정의, 항해보조시설) 별첨참조

63-1-80

0272

5-4

63-1-6

비보 89-11

0273

DEFINITIONS ARTICLE

Agreed Minute:

"The personnel referred to in subparagraph (a) for whom status has otherwise been provided include personnel of the United States armed forces attached to the United States Embassy and personnel for whom status has been provided in the Military Advisory Group Agreement of January 26, 1950 as amended."

63-1-51

5-5

0274

63-1-6

미문 89-11

0275

NAVIGATIONAL AIDS ARTICLE

Agreed Minute:

"Installation by the United States Armed Forces of permanent navigational aids for vessels and aircraft outside of areas and facilities in use by the United States Armed Forces will be effected in accordance with the procedures established under paragraph 1 of Article ."

63-1-52

보통문서로 재분류(1966.12.31.)

1966, 12, 31에 예고문에 의거 일반문서로 재분류됨

0276

5-6

63-1-6(5)

대기문 89-11(5)

0277

1. Mr. Chin opened the meeting by introducing Mr. Whang Ho-Eul, Mr. Chin's successor as Director of the Bureau of Political Affairs in the Ministry of Foreign Affairs. Mr. Habib congratulated Mr. Chin and Mr. Whang on their promotions and welcomed Mr. Whang to the SOFA negotiations as an old friend.

Foreign Exchange Controls

2. Beginning the substantive discussion, the negotiators took up the article dealing with foreign exchange controls. Mr. Chin stated that the drafts exchanged at the previous meeting were practically identical. He said the Korean side would accept the U.S. draft of the article if the U.S. side would accept the Korean draft of the Agreed Minute. Mr. Habib replied that the only difference occurred in the final sentence of the Agreed Minute. He asked the Korean side to explain what was meant by the term "basic rate of exchange" in the Korean draft.

3. Mr. Chin replied that the term "basic rate of exchange" referred to the current situation in the Republic of Korea, where there is now in effect a single rate of exchange. Mr. Habib stated that such a definition was not really suitable to an agreement of the kind which was being negotiated, which was intended to endure for a lengthy period and for that reason should include a more precise definition of the exchange rate. Mr. Ford added that even in the present situation, differences of opinion might arise over what constituted the "basic" rate of exchange. He pointed out that the present "basic" rate is 125 won to the dollar. However, there is in addition a certificate rate of 5 won, as well as a service charge of .5 won. The question might therefore be raised whether the basic rate was 125 to 1, 129.5 to 1, or 130 to 1. He explained that the U.S. draft of the Agreed Minute was based on the language of the comprehensive aid agreement of February 8, 1961.

0278

4. Mr. Chin replied that the Korean side had not seen the U.S. draft of the

Agreed Minute. It was then discovered that the text of the Agreed Minute had been omitted inadvertently from the text of the article tabled by the U.S. side at the 14th meeting. Mr. Habib [illegible] expressed the opinion that the Korean draft of the Agreed Minute was not entirely [illegible] suitable. [illegible] He said the U.S. side would submit alternative language at the next meeting. [illegible] Pending agreement on the Agreed Minute, he suggested that both sides agree to the U.S. draft of the article. Mr. Chin agreed.

Enrollment and Training of Reservists

5. Turning to the article on enrollment and training of reservists, Mr. Chin recalled that at the previous meeting, the Korean side had suggested the addition to the U.S. draft of the phrase "except for ordinary tourists". He asked for comment by the U.S. side.

6. Colonel Solf reminded the negotiators that at the previous meeting, the U.S. side had invited the attention of the Korean side to the provisions of other articles of the SOFA as follows:

a. Definitions Article - subparagraph (a):

> "'Members of the United States armed forces" means the personnel on active duty belonging to the land, sea or air armed services of the United States of America when in the territory of the Republic of Korea except for those for whom status has otherwise been provided."

b. Entry & Exit Article - paragraph 2:

> "Members of the United States armed forces shall be exempt from Korean passport and visa laws and regulations. Members of the United States armed forces, the civilian component, and their dependents shall be exempt from Korean laws and regulations on the registration and control of aliens, but shall not be considered as acquiring any right to permanent residence or domicile in the territory of the Republic of Korea."

c. Entry & Exit Article - paragraph 5:

> "If the status of any person brought into the Republic of Korea under paragraph 1 of this Article is altered so that he would no longer be entitled to such admission, the United States authorities shall notify the Korean authorities and shall, if

0279

such person be required by the Korean authorities to leave the Republic of Korea, assure that transportation from the Republic of Korea will be provided within a reasonable time at no cost to the Government of the Republic of Korea."

7. Colonel Solf stated that the U.S. side could again assure the Korean side that a reservist entering Korea who is not on active duty is not exempt from any Korean entry or registration procedures. While in Korea as a reservist not on active duty, he acquires no special privileges or immunities. Colonel Solf added that the U.S. side was also prepared to assure the Korean side that the U.S. armed forces have no intention to order ordinary tourists to active duty without the consent of the tourists. If, under unusual circumstances, a reservist were to enter on active duty from tourist status, Colonel Solf continued, the U.S. armed forces would work out procedures to notify the Korean authorities of the tourist's change of status. Colonel Solf then asked the Korean side if it would agree to the U.S. draft, on the basis of the preceding assurances and explanation. Mr. Habib commented that the problem raised by the Korean side was taken care of by other articles of the SOFA, as just explained by Colonel Solf. Therefore, it would be much simpler to accept the U.S. draft as tabled.

8. Mr. Chin stated that some confusion appeared to have arisen concerning the position of the Korean side. He said the Korean side did not intend to emphasize the question of enforcing Korean entry, exit, and registration regulations. What the Korean side was concerned about, he said, was the possibility of tourists being drafted for reserve training. He expressed concern over the possibility that American students or other American tourists might feel such measures to be unreasonable

9. Mr. Habib replied that there was no intention of drafting tourists for reserve training against their will. He pointed out again that enforcement of the entry and exit regulations was provided for in other articles, and that if the status of a tourist changed, the Korean authorities would be notified. But the fact that an American is a tourist does not change the fact that he is a United States

0280

citizen. The negotiating record, Mr. Habib continued, would include the statement just made by Colonel Solf, which would serve as a guide to the Joint Committee, should the matter ever come up, which he doubted very much. He said the U.S. side greatly [redacted] appreciated the solicitude shown by the Korean side for the rights of U.S. citizens but, in fact, this point would never cause any problem. No such problem has ever arisen in connection with any other SOFA.

10. Mr. Chin then summed up the Korean position by stating that the point at issue was whether tourists who might stay in the country for lengthy periods would be enrolled for reserve training without their consent. He indicated that the use of the term "residing in" had been used in this sense in the Korean draft, rather than in the strictly legal sense of permanent residence. Colonel Solf had previously said that the drafting of tourists for reserve training would be extremely rare, Mr. Chin continued. [redacted] Mr. Chin had then suggested the [redacted] addition of the phrase "except for ordinary tourists". Now Colonel Solf had stated that there was no intention to draft such people for reserve training against their will. On the basis of ~~Colonel Solf's~~ U.S. side's assurances and explanation, Mr. Chin said, the Korean side agreed to the U.S. draft of the article.

11. Mr. Habib pointed out that a tourist~~s~~ can remain in the Republic of Korea as a tourist, for no longer than thirty days. He then suggested that the negotiating record include the statements just made by Colonel Solf and Mr. Chin. Mr. Chin agreed.

Joint Committee

12. Turning to the Joint Committee article, Mr. Chin [redacted] asked if the U.S. side had considered the Agreed Minute proposed by the Korean side at the 11th meeting. Mr. Habib replied that the Korean side had indicated it would accept the text of the U.S. draft of the article, provided the U.S. side accepted [redacted] an Agreed Minute reading as follows:

0281

"The exception provided for in the first sentence of paragraph 1 is relevant only to paragraph 2, subparagraphs (b) and (c) of Article ___."

Mr. Habib stated that the U.S. side accepted the above Agreed Minute. Full agreement was thereupon reached on the Article and Agreed Minute.

Definitions Article

13. Turning to the Definitions Article, Mr. Chin recalled that at previous meetings agreement had been reached on all portions except for Agreed Minutes #1 and #2.

14. With regard to the Korean proposal to delete the word "readily" from the U.S. draft of Agreed Minute #2, Mr. Habib remarked that the word was one of explanation rather than limitation. He said there was no intention that this word provide an occasion for abuse. Without it, the sentence had little meaning, since one could always argue that any skill needed by the U.S. armed forces was "available" in either the United States or Korea. But the practical test was whether such skills were "readily" available or not.

15. Mr. Chin replied that the Korean side fully understood the situation which Mr. Habib had explained. He agreed that "readily" can be interpreted either broadly or narrowly. He suggested the use instead of the phrase "practically not available". Mr. Habib said the proposed phrase did not sound very good in English. He then suggested that the negotiating record show that discussion of this point indicated that the word "available" means available in a practical sense. If this were agreeable to the Korean side, the U.S. side would agree to deletion of the word "readily". Mr. Chin agreed.

16. With regard to Agreed Minute #1, Mr. Habib stated that the U.S. side had considered the draft previously submitted by the Korean side. He said the U.S. side wished to propose alternative language, reflecting the actual situation and the views of the Korean side. A revised draft of Agreed Minute #1 was

thereupon tabled by the U.S. side.

17. After reading the U.S. draft, Mr. Chin suggested that the word "include" be changed to the phrase "refers only to", since the exception actually applies only to those for whom status has already otherwise been provided. Mr. Habib replied that it was for that very reason that the U.S. language should be acceptable to the Korean side. The Korean side had previously objected to the phrase "such as". The U.S. side had now met that criticism. He added that the reference to personnel "attached to" the United States Embassy included both attache personnel and the Marine Guards. He pointed out that the Korean language did not include the Marine
At this point, the Korean side tabled its revised draft of the Agreed Minute #1, and Mr. Chin
Guards. Mr. Chin stated that the Korean side would agree to the U.S. draft of the
preferred its proposed revised draft, but further
Agreed Minute #1, provided the phrase "refers only to" were substituted for the word "include". The U.S. side agreed to take this proposal under consideration. It was agreed that the revised text of the U.S. draft of the article and Agreed Minute #2 was acceptable to both sides.

Navigational Aids

18. Turning to the draft article dealing with air traffic control and navigational aids, Captain Brownlie stated that it was the understanding of the U.S. side that the Korean side had indicated a readiness to accept the U.S. draft, provided the phrase "throughout the Republic of Korea and in the territorial waters thereof" in paragraph 2 were further amplified to provide for mutual consultation prior to the establishment or construction of navigational aids. In order to satisfy the Korean requirements in this regard, he said, the U.S. side wished to table an Agreed Minute as an alternative to the additional language suggested by the Korean side. Having tabled the draft Agreed Minute, Captain Brownlie pointed out that paragraph 1 of the first of four articles on Facilities and Areas previously tabled by the U.S. side, to which this Agreed Minute makes reference, reads, in part, as follows:
stated that the ... would give comparative study to both drafts.

"...Agreements as to specific facilities and areas shall be concluded by the two governments through the Joint Committee."

19. Mr. Chin expressed appreciation to the U.S. side for having taken the previous Korean suggestion under consideration. He said the Korean side would study the proposed Agreed Minute and make known its views at the next meeting.

20. In adjourning the meeting, Mr. Chin noted that the negotiators had made considerable progress that day. The next meeting was scheduled for March 8 at 2:00 p.m.

21. Points of Agreement:

a. U.S. draft of Foreign Exchange Controls Article (Agreed Minute pending)

b. U.S. draft of Enrollment & Training of Reservists Article

c. U.S. draft of Joint Committee Article
Korean draft of Agreed Minute

d. U.S. draft (as revised) of Definitions Article & Agreed Minute #2 (Agreed Minute #1 pending)

보통문서로 재분류(1966. 12. 31.)

1966, 12, 31, 에 예고문에 의거 일반문서로 재분류됨

0284

관리 번호 [struck through]

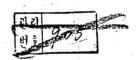

JOINT SUMMARY RECORD OF THE 15TH SESSION
STATUS FORCES NEGOTIATIONS

February 25, 1963

I. Time and Place : 2:00 to 3:30 p.m. February 25, 1963 at the Foreign Minister's Conference Room

II. Attendants:

ROK Side:

Mr. Chin, Pil Shik	Coordinator for Planning and Program
Mr. Whang, Ho Eul	Director Bureau of Political Affairs Ministry of Foreign Affairs
Mr. Koo, Choong Whay	Chief, America Section Ministry of Foreign Affairs
Col, Lee, Nam Koo	Chief, Military Affairs Section Ministry of National Defense
Mr. Chu, Mun Ki	Chief, Legal Affairs Section Ministry of Justice
Mr. Lee, Kyung Hoon	2nd Secretary Ministry of Foreign Affairs
Mr. Shin, Chung Sup	2nd Secretary Ministry of Foreign Affairs
Mr. Kang, Suk Jae	3rd Secretary Ministry of Foreign Affairs
Mr. Lee, Chang Bum	3rd Secretary Ministry of Foreign Affairs

US Side:

Mr. Philip C. Habib	Counselor of the Embassy for Political Affairs
Mr. William J. Ford	First Secretary of the Embassy

미 고	三월 七일	담당	과장	국장	특별보좌관	차관	장관

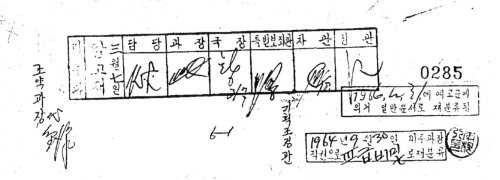

조약과장

0285

1966, 4, 3,에 예고문에 의거 일반문서로 재분류됨

1964년 9월 30일 미주과장 직권으로 비밀 로 재분류

Col. G.G. O'Connor	Deputy Chief of Staff 8th Army
Capt. R.M. Brownlie	Assistant Chief of Staff USN/K
Col. W.A., Solf	Staff Judge Advocate 8th Army
Mr. Benjamin A. Fleck (Rapporteur and Press Officer)	First Secretary of the Embassy
Mr. Robert A. Lewis	Second Secretary and Consul of the Embassy
Lt. Col. R.E. Miller	Staff Officer, JAG 8th Army
Lt. Col. W.A, Burt	J-5

1. Mr. Chin opened the meeting by introducing Mr. Whang Ho Eul, Mr. Chin's successor as Director of the Bureau of Political Affairs in the Ministry of Foreign Affairs. Mr. Habib congratulated Mr. Chin and Mr. Whang on their promotions and welcomed Mr. Whang to the SOFA negotiations as an old friend.

Foreign Exchange Controls

2. Beginning the substantive discussion, the negotiators took up the article dealing with foreign exchange controls. Mr. Chin stated that the drafts exchanged at the previous meeting were practically identical. He said the Korean side would accept the U.S. draft of the article if the U.S. side would accept the Korean draft of the Agreed Minute. Mr. Habib replied that the only difference occurred in the final sentence of the Agreed Minute. He asked the Korean

6-2

0286

side to explain what was meant by the term "basic rate of exchange" in the Korean draft.

3. Mr. Chin replied that the term "basic rate of exchange" referred to the current situation in the Republic of Korea, where there is now in effect a single rate of exchange. Mr. Habib stated that such a definition was not really suitable to an agreement of the kind which was being negotiated, which was intended to endure for a lengthy period and for that reason should include a more precise definition of the exchange rate. Mr. Ford added that even in the present situation, differences of opinion might arise over what constituted the "basic" rate of exchange. He pointed out that the present "basic" rate is 125 won to the dollar. However, there is in addition a certificate rate of 5 won, as well as a service charge of 5 won. The question might therefore be raised whether the basic rate was 125 to 1, 129.5 to 1, or 130 to 1. He explained that the U.S. draft of the Agreed Minute was based on the language of the comprehensive aid agreement of February 8, 1961.

4. Mr. Chin replied that the Korean side had not seen the U.S. draft of the Agreed Minute. It was then discovered that the text of the Agreed Minute had been omitted inadvertently from the text of the article tabled by the U.S. side at the 14th meeting. Mr. Habib expressed the opinion that the Korean draft of the Agreed Minute was not entirely suitable.

6-3

0287

He said the U.S. side would submit alternative language at the next meeting. Pending agreement on the Agreed Minute, he suggested that both dides agree to the U.S. draft of the article. Mr. Chin agreed.

Enrollment and Training of Reservists

5. Turning to the article on enrollment and training of reservists, Mr. Chin recalled that at the previous meeting, the Korean side had suggested the addition to the U.S. draft of the phrase "except for ordinary tourists". He asked for comment by the U.S. side.

6. Colonel Solf reminded the negotiators that at the previous meeting, the U.S. side had invited the attention of the Korean side to the provisions of other articles of the SOFA as follows:

a. Definitions Article - subparagraph (a):

"Members of the United States aremd forces" means the personnel on active duty belonging to the land, sea or air armed services of the United States of America when in the territory of the Republic of Korea except for those for whom status has otherwise been provided."

b. Entry & Exit Article - paragraph 2:

"Members of the United States armed forces shall be exempt from Korean passport and visa laws and regulations. Members of the United States armed forces, the civilian component, and their dependents shall be exempt from Korean laws and regulations on the registration and control of aliens, but shall not be considered as acquiring any right to permanent residence or domicile in the territory of the Republic of Korea."

c. Entry & Exit Article - paragraph 5:

"If the status of any person brought into the Republic of Korea under paragraph 1 of this Article is altered so that he would no longer be entitled to such admission, the United States authorities shall notify the Korean authorities and

6-4

0288

shall, if such person be required by the Korean authorities to leave the Republic of Korea, assure that transportation from the Republic of Korea will be provided within a reasonable time at no cost to the Government of the Republic of Korea."

7. Colonel Solf stated that the U.S. side could again assure the Korean side that a reservist entering Korea who is not on active duty is not exempt from any Korean entry or registration procedures. While in Korea as a reservist not on active duty, he acquires no spcial privileges or immunities. Colonel Solf added that the U.S. side was also prepared to assure the Korean side that the U.S. armed forces have no intention to order ordinary tourists to active duty without the consent of the tourists. If, under unusual circumstances, a reservist were to enter on active duty from tourist status, Colonel Solf continued, the U.S. armed forces would work out procedures to notify the Korean authorities of the tourist's change of status. Colonel Solf then asked the Korean side if it would agree to the U.S. draft, on the basis of the preceding assurances and explanation. Mr. Habib commented that the problem raised by the Korean side was taken care of by other articles of the SOFA, as just explained by Colonel Solf. Therefore, it would be much simpler to accept the U.S. draft as tabled.

8. Mr. Chin stated that some confusion appeared to have arisen concerning the position of the Korean side. He said the Korean side did not intend to emphasize the question of enforcing Korean entry, exit, and registration regulations. What the Korean side was concerned about, he said, was the possibility of tourists being drafted for reserve training. He expressed concern over the

6-5

possibility that American students or other American tourists might feel such measures to be unreasonable.

9. Mr. Habib replied that there was no intention of drafting tourists for reserve training against their will. He pointed out again that enforcement of the entry and exit regulations was provided for in other articles and that if the status of a tourist changed, the Korean authorities would be notified. But the fact that an American is a tourist does not change the fact that he is a United States citizen. The negotiating record, Mr. Habib continued, would include the statement just made by Colonel Solf, which would serve as a guide to the Joint Committee, should the matter ever come up, which he doubted very much. He said the U.S. side greatly appreciated the solicitude shownnby the Korean side for the rights of U.S. citizens but, in fact, this point would never cause any problem. No such problem has ever arisen in connection with any other SOFA.

10. Mr. Chin then summed up the Korean position by stating that the point at issue was whether tourists who might stay in the country for lengthy periods could be enrolled for reserve training without their consent. He indicated that the use of the term "residing in" had been used in this sense in the Korean draft, rather than in the strictly legal sense of permanent residence. Colonel Solf had previously said that the drafting of tourists for reserve training would be extermely rare, Mr. Chin continued. Mr. Chin had then suggested the addition of the phrase "except for ordinary tourists".

6-6

0290

Now Colonel Solf had stated that there was no intention to draft such people for reserve training against their will. On the basis of U.S. side's assurances and explanation, Mr. Chin said, the Korean side agreed to the U.S. draft of the article.

11. Mr. Habib pointed out that a toruist can remain in the Republic of Korea as a tourist for no longer than thirty days. He then suggested that the neogitating record include the statements just made by Colonel Solf and Mr. Chin. Mr. Chin agreed.

Joint Committee

12. Turning to the Joint Committee article, Mr. Chin asked if the U.S. side had considered the Agreed Minute proposed by the Korean side at the 11th meeting. Mr. Habib replied that the Korean side had indicated it would accept the text of the U.S. draft of the article, provided the U.S. side accepted an Agreed Minute ~~regading~~ reading as follows:

> "The exception provided for in the first sentence of paragraph 1 is relevant only to paragraph 2, subparagraphs (b) and (c) of Article ____."

Mr. Habib stated that the U.S. side accepted the above Agreed Minute. Full agreement was thereupon reached on the Article and Agreed Minute.

Definitions Article

13. Turning to the Definitions Article, Mr. Chin recalled that at previous meetings agreement had been reached on all portions except for Agreed Minutes #1 and #2.

6-7

0291

14. With regard to the Korean proposal to delete the word "readily" from the U.S. draft of Agreed Minute #2, Mr. Habib remarked that the word was one of explanation rather than limitation. He said there was no intention that this word provide an occasion for abuse. Without it, the sentence had little meaning, since one could always argue that any skill needed by the U.S. armed forces was "available" in either the United States or Korea. But the practical test was whether such skills were "readily" available or not.

15. Mr. Chin replied that the Korean side fully understood the situation which Mr. Habib had explained. He agreed that "readily" can be interpreted either broadly or narrowly. He suggested instead the use of the phrase "practically not available". Mr. Habib said the proposed phrase did not sound very good in English. He then suggested that the negotiating record show that discussion of this point indicated that the word "available" means available in a practical sense. If this were agreeable to the Korean side, the U.S. side would agree to deletion of the word "readily". Mr. Chin agreed.

16. With regard to Agreed Minute #1, Mr Habib stated that the U.S. side had considered the draft previously submitted by the Korean side. He said the U.S. side wished to propose altermative language, reflecting the actual situation and the views of the Korean side. A regised draft of Agreed Minute #1 was thereupon tabled by the U.S. side.

6-8

0292

17. After reading the U.S. draft, Mr. Chin suggested that the word "include" be changed to the phrase "refers only to", since the exception actually applies only to those for whom status has already otherwise been provided. Mr. Habib replied that it was for that very reason that the U.S. language should be acceptable to the Korean side. The Korean side had previously objected to the phrase "such as". The U.S. side had now met that criticism. He added that the reference to personnel "attached to" the United States Embassy included both attache personnel and the Marine Guards. He pointed out that the Korean language did not include the Marine Guards. At this point, the Korean side tabled its revised draft of the Agreed Minute #1, and Mr. Chin stated that the both sides would give comparative study to both drafts. Mr. Chin stated further that the Korean side preferred its proposed revised draft, but would agree to the U.S. draft of the Agreed Minute #1, provided the phrase "refers only to" were substituted for the word "include". The U.S. side agreed to take this proposal under consideration. It was agreed that the revised text of the U.S. draft of the article and Agreed Minute #2 was acceptable to both sides.

<u>Navigational Aids</u>

18. Turning to the draft article dealing with air traffic control and navigational aids, Captain Brownlie stated that it was the understanding of the U.S. side that the Korean side had indicated a readiness to accept the U.S. draft, provided the phrase "throughout the

6-9 0293

Republic of Korea and in the territorial waters thereof" in paragraph 2 were further amplified to provide for mutual consultation prior to the establishment or construction of navigational aids. In order to satisfy the Korean requirements in this regard, he said, the U.S. side wished to table an Agreed Minute as an alternative to the additional language suggested by the Korean side. Having tabled the draft Agreed Minute, Captain Brownlie pointed out that paragraph 1 of the first of four articles on Facilities and Areas previously tabled by the U.S. side, to which this Agreed Minute makes reference, reads, in part, as follows:

> "../ Agreements as to specific facilities and areas shall be concluded by the two governments through the Joint Committee".

19. Mr. Chin expressed appreciation to the U.S. side for having taken the previous Korean suggestion under consideration. He said the Korean side would study the proposed Agreed Minute and make known its views at the next meeting.

20. In adjourning the meeting, Mr. Chin noted that the negotiators had made considerable progress that day. The next meeting was scheduled for March 8 at 2:00 p.m.

21. <u>Points of Agreement:</u>

a. U.S. draft of Foreign Exchange Controls Article (Agreed Minute pending)

b. U.S. draft of Enrollment & Training of Reservists Article

c. U.S. draft of Joint Committee Article Korean draft of Agreed Minute

d. U.S. draft (as revised) of Definitions Article & Agreed ~~Minute #2~~ (Agreed Minute #1 pending)

보통문서로 재분류(1966.12.31)

~~보통문서로 재분류(협정체결시)~~

0294

1966.12.31에 예고문에 의거 일반문서로 재분류됨

6-10

정/리/보/존/문/서/목/록					
기록물종류	문서-일반공문서철	등록번호	915 9588	등록일자	
분류번호	741.12	국가코드	US	주제	
문서철명	한.미국 간의 상호방위조약 제4조에 의한 시설과 구역 및 한국에서의 미국군대의 지위에 관한 협정 (SOFA) 전59권. 1966.7.9 서울에서 서명 : 1967.2.9 발효 (조약 232호) *원본				
생산과	미주과/조약과	생산년도	1952 - 1967	보존기간	영구
담당과(그룹)	조약	조약		서가번호	--
참조분류					
권차명	V.17 실무교섭회의, 제16-20차, 1963.3-4월				
내용목차	1. 제2차 중간보고 (p.2~35) 2. 제16차 회의, 3.8 (p.36~84) 3. 제17차 회의, 3.19 (p.85~124) 4. 제18차 회의, 3.29 (p.125~162) 5. 제19차 회의, 4.11 (p.163~214) 6. 제20차 회의, 4.24 (p.215~267) * 일지 : 1953.8.7 이승만 대통령-Dulles 미국 국무장관 공동성명 - 상호방위조약 발효 후 군대지위협정 교섭 약속 1954.12.2 정부, 주한 UN군의 관세업무협정 체결 제의 1955.1월, 5월 미국, 제의 거절 1955.4.28 정부, 군대지위협정 제의 (한국측 초안 제시) 1957.9.10 Hurter 미국 국무차관 방한 시 각서 수교 (한국측 제의 수락 요구) 1957.11.13, 26 정부, 개별 협정의 단계적 체결 제의 1958.9.18 Dawling 주한미국대사, 형사재판관할권 협정 제외 조건으로 행정협정 체결 의사 전달 1960.3.10 정부, 토지, 시설협정의 우선적 체결 강력 요구 1961.4.10 장면 국무총리-McConaughy 주한미국대사 공동성명으로 교섭 개시 합의 1961.4.15, 4.25 제1, 2차 한.미국 교섭회의 (서울) 1962.3.12 정부, 교섭 재개 촉구 공한 송부 1962.5.14 Burger 주한미국대사, 최규하 장관 면담 시 형사재판관할권 문제 제기 않는 조건으로 교섭 재개 통고 1962.9.6 한.미국 간 공동성명 발표 (9월 중 교섭 재개 합의) 1962.9.20~ 1965.6.7 제1-81차 실무 교섭회의 (서울) 1966.7.8 제82차 실무 교섭회의 (서울) 1966.7.9 서명 1967.2.9 발효 (조약 232호)				

마/이/크/로/필/름/사/항				
촬영연도	*롤 번호	화일 번호	후레임 번호	보관함 번호
2006-11-22	I-06-0068	02	1-267	

0001

1. 제2차 중간보고

0002

駐韓美國軍隊地位에 関한
協定締結交涉会议第2次中间報告

1. 第1次中间報告 : 1963年 1月

2. 交涉会议経緯 :

(1) 美駐屯軍地位協定締結 韓美间交涉 會议再開을 爲한 交涉은 우리政府에 依하여 美日当局에 対하여 推進되어오던中 1962년 1월에 発生한 坡州나무꾼 被殺事件을 契機로 一層더 強力히 要求되었으며 그結果 韓美両国은 1962年 9月 6日 行政協定締結交涉会议를 再開하고 同協定의 締結은 民政移讓后에 이루어진다는 要旨의 共同声明書를 発表하게 되었다.

(2) 前記共同声明書에 따라 美駐屯軍地位協定締結을 爲한 第1次 韓美间 実務者 交涉会议는 1962年 9月 20日에 開催되었으며, 1963年 2月 25日까지 第15次에 걸친 会议가 開催되었다.

0003

3. 韓美両側代表名單

ROK Side:

Mr. Chin, Pil Shik	Coordinator for Planning and Program
Mr. Whang, Ho Eul	Director Bureau of Political Affairs Ministry of Foreign Affairs
Mr. Yi, Kyung Ho 이 경 호	Director Bureau of Legal Affairs Ministry of Justice 法務部 法務局長
Mr. Shin, Kwan Sup 신 관 섭	Director Bureau of Costums Duty Ministry of Finance 財務部 税関局長
Mr. Koo, Choong Whay	Chief, America Section Ministry of Foreign Affairs
Col. Lee, Nam Koo 이 남 구	Chief, Military Affairs Section 国防部 Ministry of National Defense 軍務課長
Mr. Lee, Kyung Hoon	2nd Secretary Ministry of Foreign Affairs
Mr. Shin, Chung Sup	2nd Secretary Ministry of Foreign Affairs
Mr. Kang, Suk Jae	3rd Secretary Ministry of Foreign Affairs
Mr. Lee, Chang Bum	3rd Secretary Ministry of Foreign Affairs

US Side:

Mr. Philip C. Habib	Counselor of the Embassy for Political Affairs
Brig. Gen. J.D. Lawlor	Deputy Chief of Staff 8th Army
Mr. William J. Ford	First Secretary of the Embassy
Col. G.G. O'Connor	Deputy Chief of Staff 8th Army
Capt. R.M. Brownlie	Assistant Chief of Staff USN/K
Col. W.A. Solf	Staff Judge Advocate 8th Army

0004

8-4

Mr. Benjamin A. Fleck (Rapporteur and Press Officer)	First Secretary of the Embassy
Mr. Robert A. Lewis	Second Secretary and Consul of the Embassy
Lt. Col. R.E. Miller!	Staff Officer, JAG 8th Army
Lt. Col. W.A. Burt	J-5
Kenneth Campen	Interpreter

4. 討議範圍 및 議題 (28個項)

√..... 只今까지 討議된 事項 (13個項)

o..... 完全合意에 到達한 事項 (5個項)

o √ (1) 序文

√ (2) 用語의 定義

√ (3) 土地 및 施設

√ (4) 航空統制 및 航海補助施設

o √ (5) 合同委員會

o √ (6) 出入口管理

√ (7) 關稅業務

0005

8-5

o ✓(8) 船舶및 航空機의 寄着

✓(9) 公益物및 用役

(10) 軍票

(11) 軍事郵便施設및 軍郵行政

o ✓(12) 予備兵의 召集및 訓練

(13) 美軍人家族및 財産의 安全

✓(14) 氣象業務

(15) 車輛및 運転免許問題

✓(16) 外換管理

(17) 非才出機関管理

✓(18) 接受国法의 尊重

(19) 刑事裁判管轄权

(20) 請求权

(21) 租税

(22) 現地調達

(23) 契約上의 紛争

(24) 軍契約者

(25) 労務

0006

8-6

(26) 協定의 批准, 発効 및 施行에 関한 事項

(27) 協定의 改正 및 修正

(28) 協定의 有效期间 및 滿了事項

5. ~~4.~~ 完全合意된 事項의 內容:

(1) 序 文

美國軍隊가 韓国에 駐屯하게된 根據가 國際联合安全保障理事会의 決議와 韓美相互防衛條約 第4條에 있으며 韓美兩國間의 相互利益의 密接한 紐帶를 強化하기 爲하여 土地, 施設 및 駐韓美國軍隊地位에 関한 協定을 締結한다는 것이다.

(2) 出入國管理

出入國管理에 関한 案項은 6個項으로 되어 있으며 各項의 內容은 大略 다음과 같다.

(가) 第1項은 美軍隊構成員, 軍属 및 그들의

0007

8-7

家族은 韓國領域에 出入할수 있으며,
美國当局은 이들의 人員數를 定期的으로
韓國政府에 通告할것을 規定하고 있다.

(나) 第2項은 美軍隊構成員은 韓國의
旅券및 査証에 関한 規定에 따르지
않으며, 美軍隊構成員, 軍属및 그들의
家族은 韓國外國人登録法의 対象에서
除外되나, 永住权을 取得하는것이 아님을
規定하고 있다.

(다) 第3項은 美國軍人이 韓國
領域에 入國時 또는 滯在時 身分証
明書와 旅行命令書를 所持할것을 規定
하고 있다.

(라) 第四項은 軍属및 그家族과 美
軍人家族은 그들의 身分을 確認할수 있는
適切한 文書를 所持할것을 規定하고 있다.

(마) 第5項은 美國은 萬若 規制対象

人員의 身分이 變更될 경우 이를 韓國政府에 通告할것과, 韓國政府가 그러한 人員의 退去를 要求할 境遇 美國側이 이에 應할것을 規定하고 있다.

(바) 第6項은 韓國政府가 美軍隊構成員, 軍属의 退去를 要求하였을 時, 또한 前美軍人, 軍属 및 그들의 家族의 強制退去命令을 내렸을 時, 美國은 이들의 退去에 責任을 질것을 規定하고 있다.

(3) 船舶 및 航空機의 寄着

本問題에 關한 條文은 3個項으로 되어 있으며 各項의 內容은 大略 다음과 같다.

(가) 第1項은 美國所有 또는 美國의 管理下에 運營되는 外國船舶 및 航空機는 韓國港口와 空港에 入港料를 支拂하지 않고 出入할수 있다는것과 이러한 船舶 또는 航空機에 積載된 物品과 人員으로서 本協定의 對象이 되지 않는것은

0009

7

韓國의 法에 따라서 規制된다고 規定하고 있다.

(나) 第2項은 前記 第1項의 船舶 및 航空機와 美國所有車輛이 通行料를 附課받지 않고 韓國에 出入하고 韓國內 土地, 施設間을 往來할것을 規定하고 있다.

(다) 第3項은 船舶의 入港時에는 韓國當局에의 適切한 通告義務를 規定하고 있다.

(4) 合同委員会

本問題에 対한 条文은 3個項으로 되어 있으며 各項의 內容은 大略 다음과 같다

(가) 第1項은 合同委員会는 行政協定의 施行에 関하여 相互協議를 必要로 하는 모든 問題에 対한 韓美間協議体이며 特히 土地, 施設決定을 위한 協議体이라는것을 規定하고 있다.

(나) 第2項은 合同委員会는 韓美間代表로서 構成되며 그의 自身의 節次를 決定하고, 補助機関을 設置할수 있다는 等을 規定하고 있다.

0010

8-10

(다) 第3項은 萬一合同委員会가 어느問題를 解決할수 없을時에는 同委員会는 그러한問題를 適切한 系統을 通하여 各已政府에 廻付한다는 規定을 하고 있다.

(5) 予備兵의 召集및 訓練

이問題에 関한 条文은 第一項으로 되어있으며 그内容은 美国은 大韓民国에 現存하는 該当 美国市民을 韓国에서 美国의 予備軍隊에 召集하고 訓練 시킬수 있다는 것이다.

6 5. 展望:

(1) 現在까지 取扱되었으나 尚今完全合意에 到達치 못한 前記 8個項目; 即 用語의 定義, 関税業務, 航空統制및 航海補助施設, 土地및 施設, 公益物및 用役, 接受国法의 尊重, 外換管理 그리고 氣象業務는 會談의 進捗에 따라 解決되어 完全合意가 될것으로 보임. 但土地및施設問題는 難関임.

(2) 土地및 施設問題에 있어서는, 特히 補償問題에 関하여 韓美両国间에 根本的인 見解의 差異를

0011

되어 있으며, 우리側은 私有財産의 使用에 對하여는 美國이 이의 補償을 負擔할것을 要求하고 있는데 反하여, 美國側은 韓國이 이에 對하여 責任을 져야 하며 第3者(民間人)에 依하여 惹起될지도 모를 請求權으로부터 美國이 害를 받지 않도록 韓國政府가 責任질것을 主張하고 있다.

(3) 土地, 施設問題는 刑事裁判管轄權 및 民事裁判 管轄權問題와 더불어 가장 難問題로 予想되며 特히 土地, 施設 및 刑事裁判管轄權의 2個 問題는 行政協定締結交涉 最終段階까지 論難될것으로 思料된다.

(4) 現在까지 討議에 들어가지 않은 余他問題에 있어서는 刑事 및 民事裁判管轄權問題를 除外하고는 그리 큰 어려운点은 없을것으로 予想된다.

(5) 民政移讓時까지 實務者會議를 끝마치도록 交涉會議를 자주 開催할것이며, 이를 爲하여 外務部는 最大의 努力을 傾注할 것이다.

0012

8-12

美·日 協定에 있어서 合同委員会 構成

日本側 : 代表 外務省 아메리카 局長

代表代理 防衛庁 渉外参事官

調達庁長官

法務省民事局長

外務省 아메리카局 参事官

大蔵省 財務参事官

農林省 農地局長

美國側 : 代表 在日 美軍参謀長

代表代理 在日 美陸海空 各軍 및 在日

美軍司令部 民事部로 부터 各 一名

(在日 美大使館 에서 顧問 一名, 在日

美軍事援助顧問団 에서 옵서버 一名)

보통문서로 재분류(1966.12.31)

1966.12.31 에 예고문에
의거 일반문서로 재분류됨

0013

8-13

관리 번호 906

기 안 용 지

자체 통제		기안처	미주과 강석재	전화번호	근거서류접수일자
	과장	국장	보좌관	차관	장관
관계관 서명					
기안 년월일	63. 3.7	시행 년월일		보존 년한	정서 / 기장
분류 기호	외정미 722.1	전체 통제	검열 1963. 3. 8 통제관		
경유 수신 참조	각의 의장	발신	장관		
제목	주한미국군대 지위에관한 협정체결 교섭회의 제2차 중간보고				

주한 미국군대 지위에관한 협정체결 교섭회의~~에 관한~~ 중간보고를 별첨과 여히 제출하오니 각의에 회부하여 주시기 바랍니다.

별첨 : 주한미국군대 지위에관한 협정체결 교섭회의 제2차 중간보고 .... 35 부. 끝

일반문서로 재분류 (별첨물과 분리시)

발 1963. 3. 8 외무

승인양식 1—1—3 (1112—040—016—018) (190mm×260mm16절지)

8-1 0014

외 무 부

외정미 722.1 1963. 3. 8.

수 신 각의 의장

제 목 주한미국군대 지위에관한 협정체결 교섭회의 제2차 중간보고

주한미국군대 지위에관한 협정체결 교섭회의 중간보고를 별첨과 여히 제출하오니 각의에 회부하여 주시기 바랍니다.

별첨 : 주한미국군대 지위에관한 협정체결 교섭회의 제2차 중간보고 ...... 35 부. 끝

외 무 부 장 관 최 덕 신

40부中
1/40 ~ 35/40 ... 각의에 송부
39/40 ...... 본부 (No. 없음)
40/40 ...... 차관 (")
38/40 ...... 조약과
37/40, 36/40 ...... 미주과

0015

8-14

40

의안번호	제 호	보고사항
상정 년월일	1963. 3. . (제 회)	

주한 미군군대 지위에관한 협정체결 교섭 회의 제 2 차 중간보고

~~일반문서로 재분류 (별도 통고시)~~

제출자	외 무 부 장 관
제출 년월일	1963. 3. .

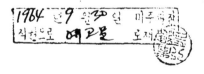

1964 년 9 월 30 일 미주국장 직접으로 예고문 도재분류

0016

8-2

36/40

議案番號	第　號
上程 年月日	1963年 3月　日 (第　回)

報告事項

駐韓 美國軍隊地位에關한 協定締結交涉會議 第2次 中間報告

~~一般文書로 再分類 (別途通告時)~~

提出者	外務部長官
提出年月日	1963年 3月　日

1966.12.31에 예고문에 의거 일반문서로 재분류됨

1966.12.31. 1964.9.30 자신으로 예고문

0017

駐韓美國軍隊地位에關한
協定締結交涉會議第2次中間報告

1. 第1次 中間報告 : 1963年 1月

2. 交涉會議經緯 :

(1) 美駐屯軍地位協定締結韓美間交涉會議再開를爲한 交涉은 우리政府에依하여 美國當局에対하여 推進되어오던中 1962年1月에 發生한 坡州나무꾼 被殺事件을 契機로 一層더 强力히 要求되었으며 그結果 韓美兩國은 1962年 9月6日 行政協定締結交涉會

~1~

0018

議을 再開하고 同協定의 締結은 民政移讓后에 이루어진다는 要旨의 共同聲明書를 發表하게 되었다.

(2) 前記共同声明書에따라 美駐屯軍地位協定締結을 爲한 第1次韓美間 實務者 交涉會議는 1962年 9月 20日에 開催되었으며 1963年 2月 25日까지 15次에 걸친 會議가 開催되었다.

3. 韓美兩側代表名單

韓國側 :

陳弼植	外務部 企劃調整官
黃鎬乙	〃 政務局長
李坰鎬	法務部 法務局長
申寬燮	財務部 稅關局長
具忠會	外務部 美州課長
李南九 大領	國防部 軍務課長
李敬勳	外務部 二等書記官
申貞燮	〃 〃
姜錫在	〃 事務官
李昌範	〃 三等書記官

美國側 :

필립 씨 하비브	駐韓美大使館 參事官

~3~

0020

제이. 디. 로저	准將	駐韓美八軍參謀次長
윌리암. 제이 호드		駐韓美大使館一等書記官
지. 지. 오코나	大領	駐韓美八軍參謀次長
알. 엠. 부룬리	大領	駐韓美海軍參謀部長
다블. 에이. 숄프	大領	駐韓美八軍法務參謀
벤자민 에이 후략		駐韓美大使館一等書記官
로버트 에이. 루이스		駐韓美大使館二等書記官兼領事
알. 이 밀러	中領	駐韓美八軍法務將校
다블 에이. 버트	中領	駐韓美八軍民事參謀
케네즈 켐펜		通譯

4. 討議範圍 및 議題 (28個項)

V ---------- 只今까지 討議된事項 (13個項)

○ ---------- 完全合意에 到達한事項 (5個項)

○ V (1) 序文

V (2) 用語의 定義

V (3) 土地 및 施設

V (4) 航空統制 및 航海補助施設

○ V (5) 合同委員會

○ V (6) 出入國管理

V (7) 關稅業務

○ V (8) 船舶 및 航空機의 寄着

V (9) 公益物 및 用役

(10) 軍票

~5~

0022

(11) 軍事郵便施設 및 軍郵行政

O V (12) 豫備兵의 召集 및 訓練

(13) 美軍人家族 및 財産의 安全

V (14) 氣象業務

(15) 車輛 및 運轉免許問題

✓ (16) 外換管理

(17) 非歲出機關管理

✓ (18) 接受國法의 尊重

(19) 刑事裁判管轄權

(20) 請求權

(21) 租 稅

(22) 現地調達

(23) 契約上의 紛爭

(24) 軍契約者

(25) 労務

(26) 協定의 批准, 発効 및 施行에 関한 事項

(27) 協定의 改正 및 修正

(28) 協定의 有効期間 및 満了事項

5. 完全合意된事項의 内容

(1) 序文

美國軍隊가 韓國에 駐屯하게된 根據가 國際聯合安全保障理事會의 決議와 韓美相互防衛條約第4條에 있으며 韓美兩國間의 相互利益의

~7~

0024

密接한 紐帶를 强化하기 爲하여 土地, 施設및 駐韓美國軍隊地位에 關한 協定을 締結한다는 것이다.

(2) 出入國管理

出入國管理에 關한 條項은 6個項으로 되어있으며 各項의 內容은 大略 다음과 같다.

(가) 第1項은 美軍隊構成員, 軍屬 및 그들의 家族은 韓國領域에 出入할수 있으며, 美國當局은 이들의 人員數를 定期的으로 韓國政府에 通告할것을 規定하고 있다.

(나) 第2項은 美軍隊構成員은 韓國의 旅券및 査證에 關한 規定에따르지 않으며, 美軍隊構成員, 軍屬및 그들의 家族은 韓國外國人登錄法의 対象에서 除外되나, 永住权을 取得하는것이 아님을 規定하고 있다.

(다) 第3項은 美國軍人이 韓國領域에 入國時또는 滞在時 身分證明書와 旅行命令書를 所持할 것을 規定하고있다.

(라) 第4項은 軍屬및 그家族과 美軍人家族은 그들의 身分을

0026

確認할수있는 適切한 文書를
所持할것을 規定하고있다.

(마) 第5項은 美國은 萬若規制対
象人員의 身分이 変更될 경우
이를 韓國政府에 通告할것과
韓國政府가 그러한 人員의 退
去를 要求할 境遇 美國側이
이에 應할것을 規定하고있다.

(바) 第6項은 韓國政府가 美軍隊
構成員, 軍屬의 退去를 要求하
였을時, 또한 前美軍人, 軍屬및
그들의 家族의 強制退去命令을
내렸을時, 美國은 이들의 退去

~10~

0027

에 責任을 질것을 規定하고

있다.

(3) 船舶및 航空機의 寄着

本問題에 關한 條文은 3個項으로 되어있으며 各項의 內容은 大略 다음과 같다.

(가) 第1項은 美國所有 또는 美國의 管理下에 運營되는 外國船舶및 航空機는 韓國港口와 空港에 入港料를 支拂하지 않고 出入할수 있다는것과 이러한 船舶또는 航空機에 積載된 物品과 人員으로서 本協定의 対象

~11~

0028

이 되지않는것은 韓國의 法에 따라서 規制된다고 規定하고 있다.

(나) 第2項은 前記 第1項의 船舶및 航空機와 美國所有車輛이 通行料를 賦課받지않고 韓國에 出入하고 韓國內土地, 施設間을 往來할것을 規定하고있다.

(다) 第3項은 船舶의 入港時에는 韓國當局에의 適切한 通告義務를 規定하고있다.

(4) 合同委員會

本問題에対한 條文은 3個項으로

되어 있으며 各項의 內容은 大略
다음과 같다.

(가) 第1項은 合同委員會는 行政
協定의 施行에 関하여 相互協議
를 必要로 하는 모든 問題에
対한 韓美間協議体이며 特히
土地、施設決定을 為한 協議体
이라는 것을 規定하고 있다.

(나) 第2項은 合同委員會는 韓美
間代表로서 構成되며 그의 自
身의 節次를 決定하고 補助機
関을 設置할 수 있다는 等을 規定
하고 있다.

~13~

0030

(다) 第3項은 萬一合同委員會가 어느問題를 解決할수없을時는 同委員會는 그러한問題를 適切한 系統을 通하여 各己政府에 回附한다는 規定을 하고있다.

(5) 豫備兵의 召集 및 訓練

이問題에 關한 條文은 第1項으로 되어있으며 그 內容은 美國은 大韓民國에 現存하는 該當美國市民을 韓國에서 美國의 豫備軍隊에 召集하고 訓練시킬수 있다는것이다.

~14~

0031

5. 展 望 :

(1) 現在까지 取扱되었으나 尙今 完全合意에 到達치못한 前記 8個目, 即 用語의 定義, 關稅業務, 航空統制및 航空補助施設, 土地및 施設, 公益物및 用役, 接受國法의 尊重, 外換管理 그리고 氣象業務는 会談의 進步에따라 解決되어 完全合意가 될것으로 보임.

但 土地및 施設問題는 難関임.

(2) 土地및 施設問題에 있어서는 特히 補償問題에 関하여 韓美兩國間에 根本的인 見解의 差異를

-15-

0032

보이고 왔으며. 우리側은 私有財產의 使用에 対하여는 美國이 이의 補償을 負担할것을 要求하고있는데 反하여 美國側은 韓國이 이에对하여 責任을 저야하며 第3者(民間人)에 依하여 惹起될지도 모를 請求权으로부터 美國이 害를 받지않도록 韓國政府가 責任질것을 主張하고있다.

(3) 土地. 施設問題는 刑事裁判管轄权및 民事裁判管轄权問題와 더부러 가장 難問題로 豫想되며 特히 土地. 施設및 刑事裁判管轄权

-16-

0033

의 2個問題는 行政協定締結交涉 最終段階까지 論難될것으로 思料된다.

(4) 現在까지 討議에 들어가지않은 其他問題에 있어서는 刑事및 民事裁判管轄权問題를 除外하고는 그리 큰 어려운点은 없을것으로 豫想된다.

(5) 民政移讓時까지 實務者会议를 끝마치도록 交涉会議를 자주 開催할것이며, 이를 爲하여 外務部는 最大의 努力을 傾注할것이다.

~17~

0034

美.日 協定에 있어서 合同委員會 構成

日本側 : 代表　　外務省 아메리카局長

代理代表　防衛庁 涉外參事官

調達庁 長官

法務省 民事局長

外務省 아메리카局參事官

大藏省 財務參事官

農林省 農地局長

美國側 : 代表　　在日美軍參謀長

代表代理　在日美陸海空各軍 및 在日

美軍司令部民事部로부터 各 1名)

(在日 美大使舘에서 顧問 1名, 在日美

軍事援助顧問團에서 옵서버 1名)

~18~

0035

2. 제16차 회의, 3.8

0036

ITINERARY FOR
STATUS OF FORCES
NEGOTIATING TEAM

Wednesday, 6 March 1963:

0930 - 0945	Enroute to I Corps (Group) H-209; met by Brig General R. H. Adams, Chief of Staff, I Corps (Group)
0945 - 1045	Special Staff briefing in I Corps (Group) briefing room
1045 - 1055	Enroute to Hawk Site via helicopter
1055 - 1125	Visit Hawk Site
1125 - 1135	Enroute to A-220, 7th Infantry Division; met by Maj General Chester A. Dahlen, Commanding General, 7th Infantry Division (drive through troop billets and Camp area enroute to Commanding General's Mess)
1135 - 1235	Lunch at Commanding General's Mess hosted by Maj General Dahlen
1235 - 1335	Briefing by Special Staff
1335 - 1350	Enroute to OP 211 via helicopter; met by Maj General Clifton F. von Kann, Commanding General, 1st Cavalry Division and Major Joseph M. Sattin, Civil Affairs Officer, 1st Cavalry Division
1350 - 1420	OP 211 briefing by Lt. Colonel Stanley Y. Kennedy, Commanding Officer, 9th Cavalry
1420 - 1430	Enroute to Munson Middle and Agricultural High School (CS 032822) via helicopter
1430 - 1515	Tour of four AFAK projects (Munson Middle and Agricultural High School, Kunchon Hospital, Paju Girls Middle School and Pongi Chom Primary School, conducted by Major Sattin via bus)
1515 - 1530	Refreshments at Wainwright Hall

0037

Wednesday, 6 March 1963: (Cont'd)

1530 - 1540	Opening remarks by Maj General von Kann
1540 - 1550	Civil Affairs briefing by Major Sattin
1550 - 1605	Provost Marshal briefing by Lt Colonel H. H. Tufts, 1st Cavalry Division Provost Marshal
1605 - 1610	Closing remarks by Maj General von Kann
1610 - 1615	Enroute to H-108 via bus
1615 - 1630	Enroute to Yongsan Helipad via helicopter

0038

관리 비 707

기 안 용 지

자체 통제		기안처	미주과 이경훈	전화번호	근거서류접수일자

과장	수석대표	보좌관	차관	장관

관계관 서명	조약과장 기획조정관
기안 년월일	63. 3. 7.
시행 년월일	
보존 년한	
정서	
기장	
분류 기호	
전체 통제	
종결	
경유 수신 참조	건의
발신	
제목	제16차 주둔군지위협정 체결교섭회의에 임할 우리측 태도

3월 8일에 개최될 제16차 주둔군지위협정 체결 한미간 교섭 회의에서는 항공통제 및 항해 보조시설, 외환관리, 미국군표 그리고 토지시설 문제에 관하여 토의될 예정이온바 이에관련하여 우리측 교섭실무자는 3월 5일 관계부처실무자와 연석 회합을갖고 제16차 회의에서 취할 우리측 태도를 별첨과같이 결정하였아오니 재가하여 주시기 바랍니다.

유첨 : 제16차 주둔군지위협정 체결교섭회의에 임할 우리측 태도. 끝

(1966.12.31.)

~~보통문서로 재분류 (협정체결시)~~ ~~1966. 12. 3~~ 1964. 9. 3

10-1

0039

승인양식 1-1-3 (1112-040-016-018) (190mm×260mm16절지)

1966년 12월 30일 미주과 직권으로 Ⅲ급비밀 로 분류됨

1. 항공통제 및 항해보조시설

(1) 미군측은 항해 항공 보조시설의 설치는 토지시설에 관한 첫재조항 (1)항에 의거한 수속절차에 따라서 시행될 것이라는 요지의 합의의사록을 제시하였는데 동 합의의사록은 (ㄱ) 항해보조시설을 영구시설에 국한시키고 있으며 (ㄴ) 토지시설 첫재조항 제1항은 상금 한미간에 합의되지 않은조항임을 고려하여 우리측은 미국측 안에대한 대안으로 다음과같은 합의의사록 안을 제시토록 한다.

"The establishment and construction of aids to navigation for vessels and aircrafts referred to in Paragraph 2 shall be effected in accordance with arrangements between the two Governments through the Joint Committee provided for in Article ______."

2. 외환관리

(1) 본조항에 대한 우리측이 제시한 합의의사록에 있어서 " basic rate" 라는 용어는 그해석에 있어서 너무 막연함으로 이를 " buying-and-selling rate " 라는 용어로 수정한다. 미측이 이를 수락하지 않을때는 "banking rate" 라는 용어로 다시제시토록한다.

(2) 미국측이 제시하는 안이 우리측안과 비등할때에는 이를 수락하도록 한다.

3. 미국 군표

(1) 군표에관한 우리측 조항에있어서는 크게 나누어 2개항목으로 되어있으며 (가) 첫재항에서는 군표사용의 범위, 허여된 범위내에서의 군표사용 보증을위한 한미양국이 취할조치,

18次

10-2

0040

그리고 불법사용에 대한 처벌 규정등을 규정하고 있으며

(나) 둘째항에 있어서는 군표관리 기관으로서의 미국군사

은행시설의 설치와 이러한 은행기관의 업무한계등을

규정한다. (별첨 참조)

(2) 미국측이 제시하는 안의 우리측안과 비등할때에는 미국측

안을 수락하도록 한다.

4. 토지시설 문제

(1) 토지시설 사용 허여원측에 관한 우리측 초안 1항에서

"본협정에 규정된바에 따라" (as provided for in this

Agreement) 라는 구절이 미국측 초안 A 조 1(a)항

첫째문장에 없는데 우리측 초안은 주로 보상을 요구하는

입장에서 작성된 초안임으로 이것이 필요하고 미국측에서는

보상을 지불하지 않으려는 입장에서 작성한것이기 때문에

생기는 차이임으로 우리측 초안을 받아드리도록 요구한다.

(2) 특정 토지시설에 대한 협정에관하여 미국측은 이를 A 조

1 (a)항 둘째 문장에 규정하고 있는데 이는 우리측 초안

규정과 실질적 차이가 없으므로 수락하기로 한다.

토지시설의 정의에관한 미국측초안 A 조 1(a)항 셋째문장은

우리측 초안 2항에 해당하는것인바 동규정에 있어서 미국측

초안은 토지시설의 운영에있어서 사용되는 기존설비, 비품

및 정착물은 "그위치 여하를 막론하고" (wherever located)

토지시설안에 포함된다라고 규정하고 있는데 대하여 우리측은

토지시설의 운영에 필요한 (necessary) 기존설비, 비품

및 정착물로 규정하고 있는바 우리측안을 받아주도록 미국측

에 요청한후 미국측에서 양보할 기색이 없을때는 미국측안

을 받아주도록 한다.

10-3

(3) 기존토지 시설사용의 법적 근거부여를위한 규정에관한 미국측초안 A 조 1(b)항과 관련하여 우리측 초안에서는 (3항)(가) "본협정에 의거하여" (under this Agreement) 허용된 토지시설로 간주한다고 규정하고 있는데 대하여 미국측 초안에는 "상기 (a)항에 의거하여" (in accordance with such-paragraph (a) above) 즉 완전 무상허여에 의하여 주어진 토지시설로 간주될수 있는 규정으로 되어있는데 이는 토지시설 사용허여에 관한 조항에서 우리측이 미국측에 의한 보상을받도록 하는 원측에관한 1 항에서 규정한"as provided for in this Agreement " 라는 구절을 미국측이 수락하는한 한미 양측의 어느안을 택하여도 상관없는것이며 (나) 우리측 초안에서 "for the purpose of this Agreement" 라는 구절과 "under this Agreeent" 라는 구절은 중복되는것임으로 "for the purpose of this Agreement" 라는 구절은 삭제토록 한다.

(4) 기존 토지시설의 측정문제에 관한 우리측 초안 3항 후단에는 기존토지시설에 대하여 합동위원회를통한 측정과 결정을 규정하고 있는데 이는 미국측 초안에는 없는것이나 현재 미군이 사용하고있는 토지시설의 재조사 및 정확한 파악을통한 소급보상의 책정을 위해 필요한것임으로 이의 삽입을 요구토록 한다.

(5) 토지시설 반환 및 추가 허여심의에 관한 미국측초안 A 조 2항 (우리측초안 6항)은 우리측초안과 실질적인 점에서는 차이가없으나 미국측 초안에서 언급된 "arrangements" 라는 용어는 미국측초안 1 (a)의 "agreements" 라는 용어와 부합되지 않음으로 이를 같은용어로 통일시키고

10-4

0042

" arrangements " 다음에 우리측 초안에서와 같이 "referred to in paragraph 1"이라는 문구를 삽입토록 주장한다.

(6) 토지시설 반환문제에 관한 미국측 초안 A 조 3항 (우리측 초안 7항)은 우리측안과 실질적인 점에서 차이가 없으나 미국측 초안의 " shall be " 다음에 " promptly " 라는 용어를 삽입토록 주장한다.

(7) 토지시설의 임시사용 및 일정기간내의 사용문제에 관한 미국측 초안 A 조 4(a)항 (우리측 초안 8항)과 4(b)항 (우리측 초안 9항)은 우리측 초안과 실질적인 차이점이 없으나 미국측 초안의 " and the Government of the Republic of Korea is so advised " 라는 구절을 삭제토록 주장한다.

(8) 토지시설 관리 등의 조치에관한 미국측 초안 B 조 (1)항 (우리측 초안 10항)에 있어서 미국측 초안은 비상시 (In an emergency .....)에는 토지시설 부근에 있어서도 보안조치를 취할수 있도록 규정하고 있는데 이러한 예외규정은 협정원문에 삽입할 성질이아니다 합의의사록에 규정함이 적당할것임으로 이를 합의의사록에 규정할것을 주장한다.

(9) 항해, 항공,통신문제에 관하여 (가) 이문제에 관한 미국측 초안 B 조 2(a) 및 (b) 항 (우리측 초안 11항)은 우리측 초안과 실질적인 차의점이 없으므로 수락토록 하고, (나) 미국측 초안 B조 2(c)항은 우리측 초안에는 없으나 미국측 초안에서 "한국의 관계법률, 규정, 협정의 범위내에서" 한국정부는 미국군대 내의 통신시설에 대한 관여를 피하고 제거할 모든 정당한 조치를 취하도록 규정하고있으므로 이도 수락토록 한다.

10-5

0043

(3) (10) 공공안전의 존중에관한 미국측 초안 B조 3항 (우리측 초안 12항)은 우리측안과 같음으로 수락토록 한다.

(4) (11) 원상회복문제에 관한 미국측 초안 C조 1항 (우리측 초안 13항)에 있어서 우리초안은원칙적으로 미군이 원상회복 의무를 면제하고 단지 사유재산으로서 미군의 사용으로 막심한 파손을 당한 재산에 대하여 우리정부의 요청에 의하며 미국측이 원상회복 또는 이에 대신하는 보상에관하여 충분한 고려를 하도록 규정하고 있는데 미국측 초안에 있어서는 이에관한 규정을두고 있지않으니 만일 미측이 사유재산에 대한 일반 보상에관한 조항을 수락할 경우에는 과잉보상은 요구하는 결과과될것임으로 일반 보상에 응하는한 우리측은 본조항에 있어서 미국측에 양보하기로 한다.

(5) (12) 가동설비 소유권 및 처분문제에 관한 미국측 초안 C조 2항은 우리측 초안에는 규정되어 있지않는 가동설비 (removable facilities) 에 대한 미국정부의 소유권과 이들 재산의 반출권 에관한 규정을두고 있는데 이는 실재문제에 있어서 인정된 사실의 확인이라고 볼수있음으로 구태어 규정할 필요가 없을 것이니 삭제하자고 주장해본후 미국측에서 양보할 기색이 없을때는 받아드리도록 한다.

(6) (13) 토지시설 개량에대한 보상의무 면제에관한 우리측 초안 14항 은 미국측 초안에서는 규정하고 있지않는것으로 이는 토지 시설의 반환시에 당해시설 및 구역에 가하여진 개량 또는 그곳에 남겨진 건물, 공작물, 공급품 또는 기타의 물자에 대하여 한국정부는 미국측에 보상하지 않는다마는 규정인바 이러한 명시적인 규정은 필요함으로 우리측안의 수락을 요구한다. 본항은 미국측초안 C조 1항 다음에 2항으로서

10-6

0044

삽입토록 제의한다. 따라서 미국측 2항은 3항이되고 3항은 4항이 될것이다.

(7)(14) 특수시설 건축에대한 예외규정에관한 미국측 초안 C조 3항의 규정은 우리측 초안에는 없으나 기타 특별한 협약은 우리정부가 인정할것임으로 받아드리도록 한다.

(8)(15) 토지시설 유지비에 관한 미국측 초안 D조 1항에 있어서 "except those to be borne by the Republic of Korea as provided in Paragraph 2"라는 규정을하고 있는것은 미국측은 보상을 하지않겠다는 원측의 입장에서 우리측이 부담하는것을 전제하고 규정한것이기 때문에 우리측은 이를 삭제토록 요구한다.

(9)(16) 토지시설 보상문제에 관한 미국측 초안D 조 2항 (우리측 초안 4항)에 있어서 양측안은 근본적 차이점을 시현하고 있는데 우리측은 사유재산의 사용에대한 미국측의 보상지불을 요구하고 있는데 대하여 미국측은 이를 한국측이 하도록 규정하고 있는점과 미국측초안 D조 2항 후단은 특히 미군이 사용하는 토지시설에 관련하여 제3자 (민간인)에 의하여 야기될지도 모를 청구권으로부터 해를받지 않도록 한국정부가 책임질것을 규정함으로서 보상문제에 관한 양국측이 근본적인 대립을 보이고 있다. 우리측은 우리안의 수락을 요구토록 한다.

10-7

0045

ARTICLE

1. (a) United States military payment certificates denominated in dollars may be used by persons authorized by the United States for internal transaction within the facilities and areas in use by the United States forces.

(b) The United States Government will take appropriate action to ensure that authorized personnel are prohibited from engaging in transactions involving military payment certificates except as authorized by United States rgulations.

(c) The Government of the Republic of Korea will take necessary action to prohibit unauthorized person from engaging in transactions involving military payment certificates and with the aid of United States authorities will undertake to apprehend and punish any person or persons under its jurisdiction involved in the counterfeiting or uttering of counterfeit military payment certificates.

(d) It is agreed that the United States authorities will apprehend and punish members of the United States forces, the civilian component, or their dependents, who tender military payment certificates to

, o-8

0046

, after the date of coming into force of this Agreement,

unauthorized persons and that no obligation will be due to such unauthorized persons or to the Government of the Republic of Korea or its agencies from the United States or any of its agencies as a result of any unauthorized use of military payment certificates within the Republic of Korea.

2. (a) In order to exercise control of military payment certificates the United States may designate certain American financial institutions to maintain and operate, under United States supervision, facilities for the use of persons authorized by the United States to use military payment certificates.

(b) Institutions authorized to maintain military banking facilities will establish and maintain such facilities physically separated from their Korean commercial banking business, with personnel whose sole duty is to maintain and operate such facilities. Such facilities shall be permitted to maintain United States currency bank accountes and to perform all financial transactions in connection therewith including receipt and remission of funds to the extent provided by Article ___, paragraph 2, of this Agreement.

(c) The United States Government shall take proper measures necessary to ensure the implementation of the foregoing paragraph.

109

0047

Agreed Minute to Article_____

United States military payment certificates under custody of the Government of the Republic of Korea at the time of entry into force of this Agreement shall be disposed in accordance with the agreement between the two governments.

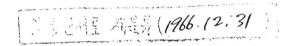

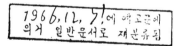

일반문서로 재분류(1966.12.31

1966.12.31에 예고문에 의거 일반문서로 재분류됨

10-10

0048

관리 번호	922

기 안 용 지

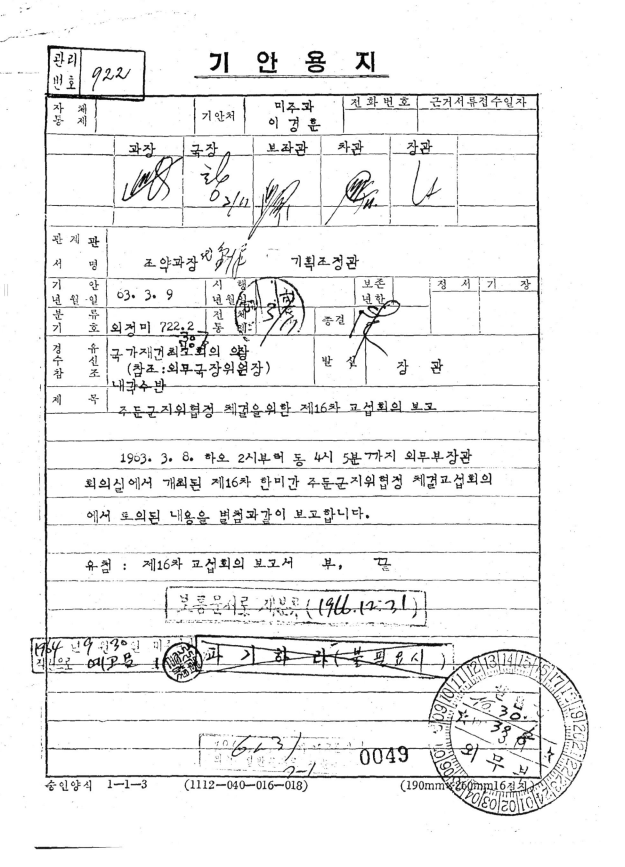

자체 통제		기안처	미주과 이경훈	전화번호	근거서류접수일자

	과장	국장	보좌관	차관	장관
		3/11			

관계관 서명	조약과장 기획조정관
기안 년월일	63. 3. 9
시행 년월일	
보존 년한	
정서 기장	
분류 기호	외정미 722.2
전체 통제	
종결	
경유 수신 참조	국가재건최고회의 의장 (참조: 외무국방위원장) 내각수반
발신	장 관
제목	주둔군지위협정 체결을위한 제16차 교섭회의 보고

1963. 3. 8. 하오 2시부터 동 4시 5분까지 외무부장관 회의실에서 개최된 제16차 한미간 주둔군지위협정 체결교섭회의에서 토의된 내용을 별첨과같이 보고합니다.

유첨 : 제16차 교섭회의 보고서 부, 끝

보통문서로 재분류 (1966.12.31)

1964 년9 월30일 예고문 1
파기하라 (불필요시)

0049

승인양식 1—1—3 (1112—040—016—018) (190mm×260mm16절지)

외 무 부

외정미 722.2 1963. 3. 11.

수 신 내각수반

제 목 주둔군지위협정 체결윤위단 제16차 교섭회의 보고

1963. 3. 8. 하오 2시부터 동 4시 5분까지 외무부 장관 회의실에서 개최된 제16차 한미간 주둔군지위협정 체결교섭 회의에서 토의된 내용을 별첨과같이 보고합니다.

유첨 : 제 16 차 교섭회의 보고서 1 부. 끝

외 무 부 장 관 최 덕 신

0050

17-8

외 무 부

외정미 722.2 1963. 3. 11.

수 신 국가재건최고회의 의장

참 조 외무국방위원장

제 목 주둔군지위협정 체결을위한 제16차 교섭회의 보고

1963. 3. 8. 하오 2시부터 동 4시 5분까지 외무부 장관 회의실에서 개최된 제16차 한미간 주둔군지위협정 체결교섭 회의에서 토의된 내용을 별첨과같이 보고합니다.

유첨 : 제 16 차 교섭회의 보고서 2 부. 끝

외 무 부 장 관 최 덕 신

0051

7-9

제 16 차

한미간 주둔군지위협정 체결 실무자회의

보 고 서

1. 시 일 : 1963. 3. 8. 하오 2시부터 4시5분까지

2. 장 소 : 외무부장관 회의실

3. 참석자 : 한국측 : 황 호 을 (외무부 정무국장)

신 관 섭 (재무부 세관국장)

구 충 회 (외무부 미주과장)

이 남 구 (국방부 군무과장)

주 문 기 (법무부 법무과장)

이 재 설 (재무부 외환과장)

이 경 훈 (외무부 2등서기관)

강 석 재 (외무부 3등서기관)

김 윤 택 (")

미국측 : 교섭대표단 전원

4. 토의사항 :

(1) 항공통제 및 항해 보조시설, 외환관리, 군표, 그리고 토지 및 시설문제를 순차적으로 토의함.

(2) 항해보조시설 설치에관하여 미국측은 항해, 항공 보조시설의 설치를 토지 및 시설의 첫째조항 (1)항에 의거한 수속절차에 따라서 행하자는 요지의 합의 의사록을 지난번 회의에서 제출하였는데 동합의 의사록을 (가) 항해 보조시설을 영구시설에 국한시키고 있으며 (나) 토지시설의 첫째조항 제1항은 상금 한미간에 합의되지 않은 조항임으로 우리측은 항해보조시설의 설치는 합동위원회를 통한 양국 정부간의 협약에의거하여 시행한다는 요지의 합의의사록을 제출함.

7-2 0052

63-1-7 (6)

보존 89-10 (6)

0053

(3) 외환관리 문제에 있어서 우리측은 우리측의 합의의사록안
에서 제시한 기본환율이란 매매율을 말한다고 설명한데
대하여 미국측은 자국측의 합의의사록 안을 제시하면서
동안에서 말하는 최고의 율이라는 용어는 한국측 의도에
부합될것이라고 말하자 우리측은 한국에서는 단일 환율제를
채택하고 있음으로 최고환율이라는 말은 부적당하다고 설명
하여 이문제는 다음에 다시 토의키로 함.

(4) 미국 군표문제에 관한 양측초안을 교환한후, 미국측은 자국측
초안에서 (가) 군표는 "대내적 거래를위하여 사용된다"
라고 규정하고 한국측 초안에있는 "미군이 사용중인 토지시설
내에서" 라는 구절을 삽입하지 않는 이유는 실제 미군이
관광호텔등 토지시설 밖에서도 사용해야하며 또한 "대내적
거래를위하여" 라는 구절로서 족하기때문이며 (나) 군표를
불법사용한 미국군대구성원, 군속 및 그들의 가족에대한 미국
당국의 체포 및 처벌은 "미국법에서 허여된 범위내에서" 라고
규정한것은 미국의 대법원의 관할권과 부합시키기 위한것
이라고 설명하자 우리측은 군표의 불법사용의 결과 미국측
에게 발생될 여하한 부담도 "본협정 효력발생후" 에는 생기지
않는다는 규정은 우리측이 제시한 합의의사록 안에서 본협정
효력 발생시에 한국정부가 보관하고있는 군표는 양국정부간의
협정에따라서 처분된다는 규정과 관련한것이라고 설명
하였음.

(5) (가) 토지시설사용 허여 원측에관하여 우리측은 이러한 허여는
한미 상호방위조약 제4조에 의거하여서 뿐만 아니라 "본협정
에 규정된바에 따라"서 주어져야 한다고 규정한것은
보상을 요구하는 입장에서 필요한것이라고 주장하자 미국측은

0054

7-3

63-1-7

마포 89-10

0055

"본협정에 규정된바에 따라" 라는 문구는 자국측으로서는 보상을 지불할수 없음으로 불필요하다고 주장하였음.

(나) 기존토지시설의 법적근거 부여를위한 규정에서 우리측은 우리측 초안에서 본협정체결시 미군이 사용중인 토지시설은 "본협정의 목적을위하여" 또한 "본협정에 의거하여" 허여된 토지시설로 간주한다고 규정하고 있는데 "본협정의 목적을 위하여" 라는 구절과 "본협정에 의거하여" 라는 구절은 중복되는것임으로 전자를 삭제한다고 함.

(다) 토지시설의 측정문제에 관하여 미국측은 이러한 측정은 이미되어 있는것이니 불필요하다고 주장한데 대하여 우리측은 재확인 및 완전한 정비를 위하여 필요하다고 주장함.

(라) 토지시설 반환 및 추가허여 심의에관한 문제에있어 우리측은 미국측 초안에서 규정한 한미 양국은 특정 토지시설의 허여에관한 "협약"을 심의한다라고 규정하고 있는데 이 "협약"이라는 용어는 특정 토지시설에 관한 협정규정에서 사용된 "협정"이라는 용어와 일치하여야 할것이 아니냐고 제기하자 미국측은 이를 수락하고 "협정"이라는 용어로 통일할것에 합의함.

(마) 토지시설 반환 및 임시사용 및 일정기간 내의 사용문제에 관한 미국측 초안항목은 우리측안과 실질적 차이가 없음으로 수락하였음.

5. 기타사항 :

(1) 차기회의 일자 : 1963. 3. 19. 하오 2시

(2) 차기회의 의제 : 차기회의까지 양측 수석대표간에 합의된사항

6. 참고자료 : 미국측의 제의한 조약문 초안 (군표)및 합의의사록 초안 (외환관리) 별첨참조.

63-1-55

0056

(1966.12.31.)

7-4

1966, , 31,에
의거 일반문서로

8-1-7

대표 89-10

0057

ARTICLE

MINITARY PAYMENT CERTIFICATES

1. (a) United States military payment certificates denominated in dollars may be used by persons authorized by the United States for internal transactions. The Government of the United States will take appropriate action to insure that authorized personnel are prohibited from engaging in transactions involving military payment certificates except as authorized by United States regulations. The Government of Korea will take necessary action to prohibit unauthorized persons from engaging in transactions involving military payment certificates and with the aid of United States authorities will undertake to apprehend and punish any person or persons under its jurisdiction involved in the counterfeiting or uttering of counterfeit military payment certificates.

63-1-56

(b) It is agreed that the United States authorities will, to the extent authorized by United States law, apprehend and punish members of the United States armed forces, the civilian component, or their dependents, who tender military payment certificates to unauthorized persons and that no obligation will be

0058

75

-3-1-7

미문 89-10

0059

due to such unauthorized persons or to the Government of Korea or its agencies from the United States or any of its agencies as a result of any unauthorized use of military payment certificates within Korea.

2. In order to exercise control of military payment certificates the United States may designate certain American financial institutions to maintain and operate, under United States supervision, facilities for the use of persons authorized by the United States (to) use military payments certificates. Institutions authorized to maintain military banking facilities will establish and maintain such facilities physically separated from their Korean commercial banking business, with personnel whose sole duty is to maintain and operate such facilities. Such facilities shall be permitted to maintain United States currency bank accounts and to perform all financial transactions in connection therewith including receipt and remission of funds to the extent provided by Article . . . . . paragraph 2, of this Agreement.

67-1-57

0060

7-6

0061

FOREIGN EXCHANGE CONTROLS

AGREED MINUTE

Payment in Korea by the United States armed forces including those activities provided in Article ____, to persons other than members of the United States armed forces, civilian component, their dependents and those persons referred to in Article___ shall be effected in accordance with the Korean Foreign Exchange Control Law and regulations. The funds to be used for these transactions shall be convertible into currency of the Republic of Korea at the highest rate in terms of the number of Korean Won per United States dollar which, at the time the conversion is made, is not unlawful in the Republic of Korea.

63-1-58

0062

63-1-7 (6)

마이크로 89-10(6)

0063

1. In opening the meeting, Mr. Whang announced that there had been some changes in the personnel of the Korean negotiating team as a result of personnel shifts in the Ministry of Foreign Affairs. He announced that Mr. O Won Young would no longer participate in the negotiations and that Mr. O's successor had not yet been selected. Mr. Lee Chang Bum, having been assigned to an overseas post, ~~would~~ had been replaced by Mr. Kim Yoon Taik, who was present for the first time at this meeting. Mr. Whang also introduced Mr. Lee Jae Sul, Chief of the Foreign Exchange Division, Ministry of Finance, who was attending this meeting for the purpose of participating in discussion of the article on Foreign Exchange Controls and the article on Military Payment Certificates.

~~4.~~ Mr. Habib replied by welcoming Mr. Whang to the negotiating table as Chief Negotiator for the Korean side. He also welcomed Mr. Kim and Mr. Lee.

2. Mr. Whang then ~~expressed the gratitude of the Korean side for the most interesting and~~ stated that the enlightening trip which the entire group had made on March 6 to certain of the areas and facilities occupied by the U.S. armed forces had been very useful in understanding actual situation and some of the problems encountered by U.S. armed forces in Korea. Mr. Habib stated that he hoped that there would be additional such trips in the future, to other facilities and areas.

Navigational Aids

3. Substantive discussion began with consideration of the Agreed Minute, proposed by the U.S. side at the previous meeting, to the article dealing with air traffic control and navigational aids. Mr. Whang stated that the Korean side had considered the U.S. proposal. He pointed out that it referred to one of the articles dealing with facilities and areas, which had not yet been agreed to. Therefore, the Korean side wished to propose an alternative Agreed Minute which did not refer to the facilities and areas article. Mr. Whang thereupon tabled the Korean Agreed Minute, stating that there was no ~~substantial~~ great difference in substance between the two drafts.

0064

4. Mr. Habib replied that there was a substantial difference. While the U.S.

draft refers to the facilities and areas article, the Korean draft refers to the Joint Committee article. He pointed out that reference to paragraph 1(a) of the draft article "A" on facilities and areas was much more relevant than reference to the Joint Committee, since the subject of the Agreed Minute was the provision of facilities. He pointed out that paragraph 1(a), Article "A", refers to the Joint Committee but provides a focal point in the SOFA for provisions regarding facilities.

5. Recapitulating the previous discussion of the navigational aids article, Mr. Habib said that the Korean side had originally agreed with the language of the U.S. draft, except for requesting that the article should explicitly provide for mutual ~~state the manner~~ consultation with regard to the ~~in which~~ installations of new facilities, ~~should be arranged, particularly~~ specifically new facilities established outside existing areas and facilities. In an effort to satisfy the request of the Korean side, the U.S. side had drafted and tabled an Agreed Minute which provides for the establishment of new navigational aids outside of existing areas and facilities under the provisions of the pertinent article relating to facilities and areas which itself refers to the Joint Committee. He said that the U.S. draft thus provides a satisfactory answer to the question previously raised by the Korean side, while the Korean draft Agreed Minute goes beyond the position previously taken by the Korean side. He expressed the hope that the Korean side would reconsider the matter and accept the U.S. draft.

6. Mr. Whang asked whether the word "permanent" in the U.S. draft is meant to exclude arrangements between the two governments through the Joint Committee on ~~the~~ construction of temporary navigational aids from the provisions regarding of the article. Mr. Habib replied that under operational or exercise conditions, temporary aids might be needed. He pointed out, however, that the problem raised by the Korean side to which this Agreed Minute addresses itself is that of the establishment of permanent aids outside of existing facilities and areas. Mr. Whang stated that the installation of permanent aids would benefit not only the U.S. armed forces but also the ROK nationals ~~forces and~~ those of third countries. However,

0065

It appeared that temporary aids were not covered by the Agreed Minute. Mr. Habib pointed out that they were covered by the article itself, particularly by the last two sentences of paragraph 2. The Agreed Minute had been drafted to cover the specific problem raised by the Korean side.

7. Mr. Whang stated that the Korean side would take the matter under further consideration. He again pointed out that the article on facilities and areas to which the U.S. draft Agreed Minute refers has not yet been agreed upon. He suggested that further discussion of this matter be deferred until agreement has been reached on the relevant paragraph of the facilities and areas article. Mr. Habib replied that if the Korean side so desired, the U.S. side had no objection. However, the U.S. side did not think it necessary to delay approval of the navigational aids article until agreement was reached on the facilities and areas article.

Foreign Exchange Controls

8. Turning to the article dealing with foreign exchange controls, Mr. Whang stated that Mr. Lee of the Ministry of Finance would present the position of the Korean side. Mr. Habib stated that Mr. Ford would explain the position of the U.S. side.

9. Mr. Ford tabled the U.S. draft of an Agreed Minute. He stated that the most pertinent point in the Agreed Minute was that the final sentence incorporated language taken directly from the comprehensive aid agreement between the United States and the Republic of Korea, which had been signed on February 8, 1961 and had gone into effect on February 28, 1961. He pointed out that this agreement determines the rate at which aid funds are converted from dollars to won. He said that the two governments had been operating under this agreement for two years and there had been no difficulties whatsoever in its administration. He said the language of this agreement was more specific and much tighter than the corresponding language in the Korean draft.

10. Mr. Whang replied that the Korean side's explanation at the previous

0066

meeting of the term "basic rate of exchange" might have been misunderstood. He said that the term "basic rate" actually means the buying and selling rate. He asked the U.S. side to consider the Korean draft in that light. Mr. Ford replied that Mr. Whang's explanation illustrated the difficulty which lay in the Korean draft. He pointed out that the buying rate and the selling rate are two different rates and that one is higher than the other. He then asked which was the basic rate?

11. Mr. Lee replied that, as Mr. Ford had pointed out, the buying and selling rates are different. When the buying rate is 129.50, the selling rate is 130.50, but the basic rate is 130 to the dollar. Mr. Habib stated that the point at issue was not the mechanics of buying and selling; what the negotiators were interested in were the terms on which any transaction takes place, whether it is a purchase or a sale. He pointed out that the language of the U.S. draft was clear - it provided for the highest rate, either buying or selling, which was not unlawful. These are the terms under which other U.S. Government agencies do business in Korea and the U.S. side is unable to see why the U.S. armed forces should not operate under the same terms. The U.S. draft, Mr. Habib continued, is more relevant to the types of transactions which will be conducted under the SOFA. He said the U.S. side was prepared to hear any further comments which the Korean side might wish to make, but since the U.S. draft had just been tabled, the Korean side might desire to have time in which to consider it.

12. Mr. Lee pointed out that Korean law provides for a unitary rate of exchange. Mr. Habib replied that the U.S. draft took that into account and referred specifically to the "highest rate which is not unlawful". Mr. Whang said the Korean side would consider the U.S. draft [redacted] for further discussion at a later date.

Military Payment Certificates

13. Each side tabled a draft of an article dealing with military payment certificates (MPC) and a few minutes were devoted to study of the drafts. Mr. Habib

then explained the U.S. draft. He pointed out that the first sentence specifies that MPC may be used by authorized personnel for "internal transactions". He said that no limitation of these transactions within facilities and areas, such as had been included in the Korean draft, had been put in the U.S. draft because during field exercises and maneuvers outside the designated facilities and areas, it may be desirable to set up mobile and temporary post exchanges. Furthermore, it might also prove desirable to establish such facilities in tourist hotels or similar establishments. In any event, he pointed out, inclusion of the term "internal" limits the transactions to the extent desired by both sides.

14. Mr. Habib continued his explanation of the U.S. draft by pointing out that in paragraph 1(b) there is contained the phrase "to the extent authorized by U.S. law" which does not appear in the Korean draft. It was ~~inserted~~ included in the U.S. draft, he explained, because of U.S. Supreme Court decisions which affected the jurisdiction of the U.S. armed forces over civilians. In effect, he said, the U.S. draft stated that the U.S. authorities will exercise the authority which they possess. He then asked the Korean side to explain its draft, including the Agreed Minute.

15. Mr. Lee stated that the Agreed Minute had been included in order to provide for a way in which to dispose of the MPC in custody of the ROK Government at the time the SOFA comes into force. Mr. Habib remarked that disposition of MPC held by the ROK Government had been the subject of discussions between the two governments in the past. He pointed out that there was a very simple way in which the Korean Government could solve its problem. That was to pack up the MPC in a bundle and return it to the U.S. authorities the next day. Mr. Habib then asked if the same motive lay behind the inclusion in paragraph 1(d) of the Korean draft of the phrase "after the date of coming into force of this Agreement". Mr. Lee replied in the affirmative. Mr. Habib suggested that the points just discussed appeared to be the only points of difference in the two drafts. He

0068

suggested that the drafts be studied by both sides and discussed at the next meeting. The Korean side agreed.

Facilities and Areas

16. Turning to the drafts of the facilities and areas articles, Mr. Whang stated that the phrase "as provided for in this Agreement" had been included in paragraph 1 of the Korean draft because of the Korean desire to have the Agreement provide for compensation for use of privately-owned facilities and areas. He said that the positions of both sides on the question of compensation had previously been made clear and that the Korean side felt the retention of this phrase to be necessary. He also pointed to the use of the phrase "wherever located" in the U.S. draft in contrast to the use of the phrase "necessary to" in the Korean draft. Since there was no intention on the part of the Korean side to limit the extent of the furnishings, equipment and fixtures, he believed that the phrase "necessary to" really meant the same thing as "wherever located".

17. In reply, Mr. Habib stated that in regard to Mr. Whang's first point, the U.S. side desired exclusion of the phrase "as provided for in this Agreement" for the same reason that the Korean side desired its inclusion. The U.S. side has made clear, he continued, that payment of compensation is not envisaged in the U.S. draft of the Agreement. In previous discussion of this point, Mr. Chin had stated that the Korean side was well aware of the U.S. position. Mr. Chin had pointed out that the Korean position was based not on legality but on the desire of the Korean Government for strengthening the friendly ties existing with the United States Government.

18. Mr. Habib stated that a Status of Forces Agreement has one major purpose: that is to set out the conditions under which the armed forces of one nation are permitted to be on the territory of another nation. It sets out the respective rights, duties, obligations, privileges and immunities and other

0069

guarantees and undertakings of the respective governments and the personnel involved. It is devoted to the subject of stationing of forces. It has been the consistent policy of the U.S. Government, he continued, that facilities and areas made available to U.S. forces for mutual defense should be furnished to the United States without cost. The U.S. Government has adhered to this policy in all of its mutual defense negotiations on the agreed assumption that areas and facilities made available for use by U.S. forces constitute one of the host country's contributions to mutual secutity. The U.S. side continues to hold that view, Mr. Habib concluded.

11th Record

19. Mr. Whang replied that the Korean side was fully aware of the U.S. position. Mr. Chin had said that the request for compensation was based more on the desire for promotion of friendly ties than legality. Mr. Whang reiterated that there had been no change in the Korean position.

20. Mr. Habib asked how the payment of compensation would fulfill the function of promoting friendly ties in any way that all the other existing U.S. programs in Korea do not. He said the SOFA is not intended to be a vehicle for making financial contributions. It has a specific purpose and we should concentrate on that purpose. In all previous discussion of this point, he continued, the U.S. side has made it clear, and will continue to make it clear, that payment of compensation is outside the scope of this SOFA. It was then agreed to defer any further discussion of this subject until consideration was again given to draft article "B".

21. Turning to paragraph 3 of the Korean draft, Mr. Whang recalled that the U.S. side had expressed the opinion that the phrase "for the purpose of this Agreement" was redundant since it is followed by the phrase "under this Agreement". He said the Korean side agreed and that the phrase "for the purpose of this Agreement" may be stricken from the Korean draft while retaining the phrase "under this Agreement". He asked for any further comment by the U.S. side. Mr. Habib stated that the language of the corresponding paragraph in the U.S. draft (paragraph 1(b)) was more specific in its reference to the pre-

0070

ceding paragraph. He also questioned the necessity for the phrase "shall be surveyed and determined" in the Korean draft. He pointed out that survey documents are already in existence and will be used by the Joint Committee. Furthermore, an extensive joint survey was carried out with the Ministry of National Defense in 1962. He expressed the opinion that the language of this paragraph should establish the principle set forth in the first sentence of BOTH drafts; namely that the facilities and areas granted to the United States under the SOFA should be those in use at the time of entry into force of the Agreement. He suggested that once having established the principle, the negotiators should leave the bookkeeping to the Joint Committee.

22. Continuing the discussion of Paragraph 3 of the Korean draft, Mr. Whang replied that the Korean side wished to make a clear record of all facilities and areas in use. In some cases, he said, no survey had been made when the facility was originally made available. The survey could be made by the Joint Committee but the purpose of this language was to give guidance to the Joint Committee. Mr. Habib replied that this was taken care of by the next paragraph. He then stated that the U.S. side wished to ~~[illegible]~~ substitute the word "agreements" for the word "arrangements" in paragraph 2 of the U.S. draft. He expressed the opinion that the wording of the U.S. paragraph was preferable to that of the comparable paragraph in the Korean draft (paragraph 6). He pointed out that this paragraph sets out the guidelines for the Joint Committee. The Joint Committee article itself says clearly that the Joint Committee shall be the means for consultation between the two governments. Obviously, he said, this had special reference to the entire question of facilities and areas. He reminded the Korean side that the U.S. side had deleted even more specific language from the draft of the Joint Committee article at the request of the Korean side. He said the Joint Committee may decide that it is not necessary to survey all of the facilities and areas.

설명을 요구

0071

However, the U.S. side is prepared to [redacted] have the Joint Committee review all of the facilities in order to determine the necessity for such a survey.

23. Mr. Whang stated that the [redacted] Korean side would consider the position set forth by the U.S. side. Mr. Habib remarked that the two sides appeared to agree on the substance but not on the wording of this paragraph. Mr. Whang suggested that in addition to changing "arrangements" to "agreements" the phrase "referred to in paragraph [redacted] 1" be added. Mr. Habib pointed out that the additional phrase was unnecessary because the phrase "such agreements" referred to the agreements mentioned in the previous paragraph. [redacted] He added that the phrase [redacted] "or portions thereof" in the U.S. draft was intended to facilitate the return of portions of a facility [redacted] if the return of the entire facility was not feasible or possible. The U.S. side believed this phrase to be a useful addition to the paragraph. Mr. Whang agreed to this addition of the phrase. ~~and accepted the text of the U.S. draft of paragraph 2.~~

24. Turning to paragraph 3 of the U.S. draft and paragraph 7 of the Korean draft, Mr. Whang referred to the use of the word "promptly" in the Korean draft and said that since the U.S. forces were prepared to return facilities promptly, the U.S. side should not object to the inclusion of this word in the text of the article. Mr. Habib replied that the U.S. draft took care of this, inasmuch as the phrase "under such conditions as may be agreed through the Joint Committee" was all-inclusive. He pointed out that the phraseology of the U.S. draft was responsive to the requirements of the ROK Government. He said that "promptly" [redacted] requires interpretation and judgment, whereas the U.S. language was very specific and not subject to varying interpretation. Mr. Whang replied that with the understanding that ~~the~~ language of the U.S. draft was all-inclusive, the Korean side accepted the [redacted] text of paragraph 3 of the U.S. draft.

0072

25. Turning to paragraph 4 of the U.S. draft and paragraph 8 of the Korean draft, Mr. Whang asked for clarification of the meaning of the phrase "and the Government of the Republic of Korea is so advised" in the U.S. draft. Mr. Habib replied that quite simply the phrase was intended to avoid debate on the question of the exact timing of making facilities available to the ROK Government. He said it was intended to be a facilitating phrase and had no other meaning. It placed on the U.S. Government an obligation to establish a precise date for making the facilities available.

26. Mr. Whang said he understood the explanation and then asked what the implication was of the word "harmful". Mr. Habib replied that ~~the xxxxxx xxxxxxxxxx~~ "harmful" was ~~xxxxxxx~~ intended to mean the temporary use of a facility by Korean nationals ~~xxxxxxxxxx~~ in such a manner as to damage the facility or render it unusable at a later date by the U.S. armed forces. ~~xxxxxxx~~ For instance, he said, if the temporary Korean users ~~tore~~ down buildings ~~at~~ of a facility which were needed for later use by the U.S. armed forces, that would be "harmful" use of the facility and would be prohibited by the terms of this paragraph. Mr. Whang agreed and stated that the Korean side accepted the text of paragraph 4 (a) and (b) of the U.S. draft.

27. At this point, it was decided to adjourn the meeting. The next meeting was scheduled for March 19 at 2:00 p.m.

28. Points of agreements:
Facilities and Areas, Article A, Par. 2, 3 and 4.

0073

7. Mr. Whang reminded the negotiators that the Korean side had originally suggested the insertion of the phrase "through agreement between the appropriate authorities of the two Governments" at the end of the first sentence of paragraph 2. As a compromise to this suggestion, he continued, the U.S. side tabled its draft of the Agreed Minute providing inter alia that installation of navigational aids would be effected in accordance with "the procedures established under paragraph 1 of Article " instead of "arrangements between through the appropriate authorities of the two Governments." Since the U.S. side made it clear that the "Article" referred to in its draft of the Agreed Minute meant the first Article dealing with the facilities and areas, and the phrase "the procedures established under paragraph 1 of Article " was considered to indicate that the installation of navigational aids would be effected in accordance with the agreements between the two Governments through the Joint Committee, the Korean side proposed, in its draft of the Agreed Minute, to use the phrase "arrangements between the two Governments through the Joint Committee."

0074

관리 923

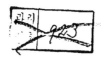

JOINT SUMMARY RECORD OF THE 16TH SESSION
STATUS FORCES NEGOTIATIONS

March 8, 1963

I. Time and Place : 2:00 to 4:50 p.m. March 8, 1963 at the Foreign Minister's Conference Room

II. Attendants:

ROK Side:

Mr. Whang, Ho Eul	Director Bureau of Political Affairs Ministry of Foreign Affairs
Mr. Shin Kwan Sup	Director Bureau of Customs Duty Ministry of Finance
Mr. Koo, Choong Whay	Chief, America Section Ministry of Foreign Affairs
Col. Lee, Nam Koo	Chief, Military Affairs Section Ministry of National Defense
Mr. Chu, Mun Ki	Chief, Legal Affairs Section Ministry of Justice
Mr. Lee, Jae Sul	Chief of the Foreign Exchange Division, Ministry of Finance
Mr. Lee, Kyung Hoon	2nd Secretary Ministry of Foreign Affairs
Mr. Kang, Suk Jae	3rd Secretary Ministry of Foreign Affairs
Mr. Kim, Yoon Taik	3rd Secretary Ministry of Foreign Affairs

US Side:

Mr. Philip C. Habib	Counselor of the Embassy for Political Affairs
Brig. Gen. J.D. Lawlor	Deputy Chief of Staff 8th Army
Mr. William J. Ford	First Secretary of the Embassy

미주과	안고재	三월十일	담당	과장	국장	특별보좌관	차관	장관
					3/18			3/18

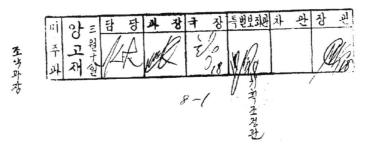

조약과장

8-1

기획조정관

0075

Col. G.G. O'Connor	Deputy Chief of Staff 8th Army
Capt. R,M. Brownlie	Assistant Chief of Staff USN/K
Col. W.A. Solf	Staff Judge Advocate 8th Army
Mr. Benjamin A. Fleck (Rapporteur and Press Officer)	First Secretary of the Embassy
Mr. Robert A. Lewis	Second Secretary and Consul of the Embassy
Lt. Col. R.E. Miller	Staff Officer, JAG 8th Army
Lt. Col. W.A. Burt	J-5
Kenneth Campen	Interpreter

1. In opening the meeting, Mr. Whan announced that there had been some changes in the personnel of the Korean negotiating team as a result of personnel shifts in the Ministry of Foreign Affairs. He announced that Mr. O Won Young would no longer participate in the negotiations and that Mr. O's successor had not yet been selected. Mr. Lee Chang Bum, having been assigned to an overseas post, had been replaced by Mr. Kim Yoon Taik, who was present for the first time at this meeting. Mr. Whang also introduced Mr. Lee Jae Sul, Chief of the Foreign Exchange Division, Ministry of Finance, who was attending this meeting for the purpose of participating in discussion of the article on Foreign Exchange Controls and the article on Military Payment Certificates.
Mr. Habib replied by welcoming Mr. Whang to the negotiating table as Chief Negotiator for the Korean side. He also welcomed Mr. Kim and Mr. Lee.

0076

2. Mr. Whang then stated that the trip which the entire group had made on March 6 to certain of the areas and facilities occupied by the U.S. armed forces had been very useful ~~and enlightening~~ in understanding the actual situation and some of the problems encountered by U.S. armed forces in Korea. Mr. Habib stated that he hoped that there would be additional such trips in the future, to other facilities and areas.

Navigational Aids

3. Substantive discussion began with consideration of the Agreed Minute, proposed by the U.S. side at the previous meeting, to the article dealing with air traffic control and navigational aids. Mr. Whang stated that the Korean side had considered the U.S. proposal. He pointed out that it referred to one of the article dealing with facilities and areas, which had not yet been agreed to. Therefore, the Korean side wished to propose an alternative Agreed Minute which did not refer to the facilities and areas article. Mr. Whang thereupon tabled the Korean Agreed Minute, stating that there was no great ~~substantial~~ difference in substance between the two drafts.

4. Mr. Habib replied that there was a substantial difference. While the U.S. draft refers to the facilities and areas article, the Korean draft refers to the Joint Committee article. He pointed out that reference to paragraph 1(a) of the draft article "A" on facilities and areas was much more relevant than reference to the

8-3

0077

Joint Committee, since the subject of the Agreed Minute was the provision of facilities. He pointed out that paragraph 1(a), Article "A", refers to the Joint Committee but provided a focal point in the SOFA for provisions regarding facilties.

5. Recapitualating the previous discussion of the navigational aids article, Mr. Habib said that the Korean side had originally agreed with the language of the U.S. draft, except for requesting that the article should explicitly provide for mutual consultation with regard to the installation of new facilities, spacifically new facilities established outside existing areas and facilities. In an effort to satisfy the request of the Korean side, the U.S. side had drafted and tabled an Agreed Minute which provides for the establishment of new navigational aids outside of existing areas and facilities under the provisions of the pertinent article relating to facilities and areas which itself refers to the Joint Committee. He said that the U.S. draft thus provides a satisfactory answer to the question previously raised by the Korean side, while the Korean draft Agreed Minute goes beyond the position previously taken by the Korean side. He expressed the hope that the Korean side would reconsider the matter and accept the U.S. draft.

6. Mr. Whang asked whether the word "permanent" in the U.S. draft is meant to exclude arrangements between the two governments through the Joint Committee regarding the construction of temporary navigational aids from the

4-4

0078

provisions of the article. Mr. Habib replied that under operational or exercise conditions, temporary aids might be needed. He pointed out, however, that the problem raised by the Korean side to which this Agreed Minute addresses itself is that of the establishment of permanent aids outside of existing facilities and areas. Mr. Whang stated that the installation of permanent aids would benefit not only the U.S. armed forces but also the ROK nationals and those of third countries. However, it appeared that temporary aids were not covered by the Agreed Minute. Mr. Habib pointed out that they were covered by the article itself, particularly by the last two sentences of paragraph 2. The Agreed Minute had been drafted to cover the specific problem raised by the Korean side.

7. Mr. Whang reminded the negotiators that the Korean side had originally suggested the insertinn of the phrase "through agreement between the appropriate authorities of the two Governments" at the end of the first sentence of paragraph 2. As a compromise to this suggestion, he continued, the U.S. side tabled its draft of the Agreed Minute providing inter alia that installation of navigational aids would be effected in accordance with "the procedures established under paragraph 1 of Article___" instead of through "agreement between the appropriate authorities of the two Governments." Since the U.S. side made it clear that the "Artidle" referred to in its draft of the Agreed Minute meant the first Article dealing with the facilities and areas, and

the phrase "the procedures established under paragraph 1 of Article____" was considered to indicate that the installation of navigational aids would be effected in accordance with the agreements between the two Governments through the Joint Committee, the Korean side proposed, in its draft of the Agreed Minute, to use the phrase "arrangements between the two Governments through the Joint Committee". Mr. Whang stated that the Korean side would take the matter under further consideration. He again pointed out that the article on facilities and areas to which the U.S. draft Agreed Minute refers has not yet been agreed upon. He suggested that further discussion of this matter be deferred until agreement has been reached on the relevant paragraph of the facilities and areas article. Mr. Habib replied that if the Korean side so desired, the U,S. side had no objection. However, the U.S. side did not think it necessary to delay approval of the navigational aids article until agreement was reached on the facilities and areas article.

Foreign Exchange Controls

8. Turning to the article dealing with foreign exchange controls, Mr. Whang stated that Mr. Lee of the Ministry of Finance would present the position of the Korean side. Mr. Habib stated that Mr. Ford would explain the position of the U.S. side.

9. Mr. Ford tabled the U.S. draft of an Agreed Minute. He stated that the most pertinent point in

in the Agreed Minute was that the final sentence incorporated language taken directly from the comprehensive aid agreement between the United States and the Republic of Korea, which had been signed on February 8, 1961 and had gone into effect on February 28, 1961. He pointed out that this agreement determines the rate at which aid funds are converted from dollars to won. He said that the two governments had been operating under this agreement for two years and there had been no difficulties whatsoever in its administration. He said the language of this agreement was more specific and much tighter than the corresponding language in the Korean draft.

10. Mr. Whang replied that the Korean side's explanation at the previous meeting of the term "basic rate of exchange" might have been misunderstood. He said that the term "basic rate" actually means the buying and selling rate. He asked the U.S. side to consider the Korean draft in that light. Mr. Ford replied that Mr. Whang's explanation illustrated the difficulty which lay in the Korean draft. He pointed out that the buying rate and the selling rate are two different rates and that one is higher than the other. He then asked which was the basic rate?

11. Mr. Lee replied that, as Mr. Ford had pointed out, the buying and selling rates are different. When the buying rate is 129.50, the selling rate is 130.50, but the basic rate is 130 to the dollar. Mr. Habib stated that the point at issue was not the mechanics of buying and selling foreign exchange ; what the negotiators were interested in were the terms on which

any transaction takes place, regardless of whether it is a purchase or a sale. He pointed out that the language of the U.S. draft was clear - it provided for the highest rate, either buying or selling, which was not unlawful. These are the terms under which other U.S. Government agencies do business in Korea and the U.S. side is unable to see why the U.S. armed forces should not operate under the same terms. The U.S. draft, Mr. Habib continued, is more relevant to the types of transactions which will be conducted under the SOFA. He said the U.S. side was prepared to hear any further comments which the Korean side might wish to make, but since the U.S. draft had just been tabled, the Korean side might desire to have time in which to consider it.

12. Mr. Lee pointed out that since Korean law provides for a unitary rate of exchange, the use of the term "highest rate" was not adequate. Mr. Habib replied that the U.S. draft took that into account by referring specifically to the "highest rate which is not unlawful". Mr. Whang said the Korean side would consider the U.S. draft for further discussion at a later date.

Military Payment Certificates

13. Each side tabled a draft of an article dealing with military payment certificates (MPC) and a few minutes were devoted to study of the drafts. Mr. Habib then explained the U.S. draft. He pointed out that the first sentence specifies that MPC may be used by

8-8

0082

authorized personnel for "internal transactions". He said that no limitation of these transactions within facilities and areas, such as had been included in the Korean draft, had been put in the U.S. draft because during field exercises and maneuvers outside the designated facilities and areas, it may be desirable to set up mobile and temporary post exchanges. Furthermore, it might also prove desirable to establish such facilities in tourist hotels or similar establishments. In any event, he pointed out, inclusion of the term "internal" limits the transactions to the extent desired by both sides.

14. Mr. Habib continued his explanation of the U.S. draft by pointing out that in paragraph 1(b) there is contained the phrase "to the extent authorized by U.S. law" which does not appear in the Korean draft. It was included in the U.S. draft, he explained, because of the U.S. Supreme Court decisions which affected the jurisdiction of the U.S. armed forces over civilians. In effect, he said, the U.S. draft stated that the U.S. authorities will exercise the authority which they possess. He then asked the Korean side to explain its draft, including the Agreed Minute.

15. Mr. Lee stated that the Agreed Minute had been included in order to provide for a way in which to dispose of the MPC in custody of the ROK Government at the time the SOFA comes into force. Mr. Habib remarked that disposition of MPC held by the ROK Government had been the subject of discussions between the two governments

8-9

0083

in the past. He pointed out that there was a very simple
the Korean could solve its problem. That was to pick up the MPC in a bundle and
way in which return it to the U.S. authorities the next day. Mr. Habib then asked if the same motive lay behind the inclusion in paragraph 1(d) of the Korean draft of the phrase "after the date of coming into force of this Agreement". Mr. Lee replied in the affirmative. Mr. Habib suggested that the points just discussed appeared to be the only points of difference in the two drafts. He suggested that the drafts be studied by both sides and discussed at the next meeting. The Korean side agreed.

Facilities and Areas

16. Turning to the drafts of the facilities and areas articles, Mr. Whang stated that the phrase "as provided for in this Agreement" had been included in paragraph 1 of the Korean draft because of the Korean desire to have the Agreement provide for compensation for use of privately-owned facilities and areas. He said that the positions of both sides on the question of compensation had previously been made clear and that the Korean side felt the retention of this phrase to be necessary. He also pointed to the use of the phrase "wherever located" in the U.S. draft in contrast to the use of the phrase "necessary to" in the Korean draft. Since there was no intention on the part of the Korean side to limit the extent of the furnishings, equipment and fixtures, he believed that the phrase "necessary to" really meant the same thing as "wherever located".

8-10

0084

17. In reply, Mr. Habib stated that in regard to Mr. Whang's first point, the U.S. side desired exclusion of the phrase "as provided for in this Agreement" for the same reason that the Korean side desired its inclusion. The U.S. side has made clear, he continued, that payment of compensation is not envisaged in the U.S. draft of the Agreement. In previous discussion of this point, Mr. Chin had stated that the Korean side was well aware of the U.S. position. Mr. Chin had pointed out that the Korean position was based not on legality but on the desire of the Korean Government for strengthening the friendly ties existing with the United States Government.

18. Mr. Habib stated that a Status of Force Agreement has one major purpose: that is to set out the conditions under which the armed forces of one nation are permitted to be on the territory of another nation. It sets out the respective rights, duties, obligations, privileges and immunities and other guarantees and undertakings of the respective governments and the personnel involved. It is devoted to the subject of stationing of forces. It has been the consistent policy of the U.S. Government, he continued, that facilities and areas made available to U.S. forces for mutual defense should be furnished to the United States without cost. The U.S. Government has adhered to this policy in all of its mutual defense negotiations on the agreed assumption that areas and facilities made available for use by

U.S. forces constitute one of the host country's constributions to mutual security. The U.S. side continues to hold that view, Mr. Habib concluded.

19. Mr. Whang replied that the Korean side was fully aware of the U.S. position. Mr. Chin had said that the request for compensation was based more on the desire for promotion of friendly ties than on legality, Mr. Whang reiterated that there had been no change in the Korean position.

20. Mr. Habib asked how the payment of compensation would fulfill the function of promoting friendly ties in any way that all the other existing U.S. programs in Korea do not. He said the SOFA is not intended to be a vehicle for making financial contributions. It has a specific purpose and we should concentrate on that purpose. In all previous discussion of this point, he continued, the U.S. side had made it clear, and will continue to make it clear, that payment of compensation is outside the scope of this SOFA. It was then agreed to defer any further discussion of this subject until consideration was again given to draft article "B".

21. Turning to paragraph 3 of the Korean draft, Mr. Whang recalled that the U,S. side had expressed the opinion that the phrase "for the purpose of this Agreement" was redundant since it is followed by the phrase "under this Agreement". He said the Korean side agreed and that the phrase "for the purpose of this Agreement" may be stricken from the Korean draft while retaining the phrase "under this Agreement". He asked for any further comment

8-12

0086

by the U.S. side. Mr. Habib stated that the language of the corresponding paragraph in the U.S. draft (paragraph 1(b)) was more specific in its reference to the preceding paragraph. He also questioned the necessity for the phrase "shall be surveyed and determined" in the Korean draft. He pointed out that survey documents are already in existence and will be used by the Joint Committee. Furthermore, an extensive joint survey was carried out with the Ministry of National Defense in 1962. He expressed the opinion that the language of this paragraph should establish the principle set forth in the first sentence of both drafts, namely that the facilities and areas granted to the United States under the SOFA should be those in use at the time of entry into force of the Agreement. He suggested that once having established the principle, the negotiators should leave the bookkeeping to the Joint Committee.

22. Continuing the discussion of Paragraph 3 of the Korea draft, Mr. Whang replied that the Korea side wished to make a clear record of all facilities and areas in use. In some cases, he said, no survey had been made when the facility was originally made available . The survey could be made by the Joint Committee but the purpose of this language was to give guidance to the Joint Committee. Mr.Habib replied that this was taken care of by the next paragraph. He then stated that the U.S. side wished to substitute the word "agreements" for the word "arrangements" in paragraph 2 of the U.S. draft. He expressed the opinion that the wording of the U.S. paragraph

8-13

0087

was preferable to that of the comparable paragraph in the Korean draft (paragraph 6.). He pointed out that paragraph sets out the guidelines for the Joint Committee. The Joint Committee article itself says clearly that the Joint Committee shall be the means for consultation between the two governments. Obviously, he said, this had special reference to the entire question of facilities and areas. He reminded the Korean side that the U.S. side had deleted even more specific language from the draft of the Joint Committee article at the request of the Korean side. He said the Joint Committee may decide that it is not necessary to survey all of the facilities and areas. However, the U.S. side is prepared to have the Joint Committee review all of the facilities in order to determine the necessity for such a survey.

23. Mr. Whang stated that the Korean side would consider the position set forth by the U.S. side. Mr. Habib remarked that the two sides appeared to agree on the substance but not on the wording of this paragraph. Mr. Whang suggested that in addition to changing "arrangements" to "agreements" the phrase "referred to in paragraph 1" be added. Mr. Habib pointed out that the additional phrase was unnecessary because the phrase "such agreements" referred to the agreements mentioned in the previous paragraph. He added that the phrase "or portions thereof" in the U.S. draft was intended to facilitate the return of portions of a facility if the return of the entire facility was not feasible or possible. The U.S. side believed this phrase to be a useful addition to the paragraph. Mr. Whang agreed to this addition of the phrase

0088

8-14

and accepted the text of the U.S. draft of paragraph 2.

24. Turning to paragraph 3 of the U.S. draft and paragraph 7 of the Korean draft, Mr. Whang referred to the use of the word "promptly" in the Korean draft and said that since the U.S. forces were prepared to return facilities promptly, the U.S. side should not object to the inclusion of this word in the text of the article. Mr. Habib replied that the U.S. draft took care of this, inasmuch as the phrase "under such conditions as may be agreed through the Joint Committee" was all-inclusive. He pointed out that the phraseology of the U.S. draft was responsive to the requirements of the ROK Government. He said that "promptly" requires interpretation and judgment, whereas the U.S. language was very specific and not subject to varying interpretation. Mr. Whang replied that with the understanding that the language of the U.S. draft was all-inclusive, the Korean side accepted the text of paragraph 3 of the U.S. draft.

25. Turning to paragraph 4 of the U.S. draft and paragraph 8 of the Korean draft, Mr. Whang asked for clarification of the meaning of the phrase "and the Government of the Republic of Korea is so advised" in the U.S. draft. Mr.Habib replied that quite simply the phrase was intended to avoid debate on the question of the exact timing of making facilities available to the ROK Government. He said it was intended to be a facilitating phrase and had no other meaning. It placed on the U.S. Government an obligation to establish a precise date for making the facilities available.

0089

8-15

26. Mr. Whang said he understood the explanation and then asked what the implication was of the word "harmful". Mr. Habib replied that "harmful" was intended to mean the temporary use of a facility by Korean nationals in such a manner as to damage the facility or render it unusable at a later date by the U.S. armed forces. For instance, he said, if the temporary Korean users of a facility tore down buildings which were needed for later use by the U.S. armed forces, that would be "harmful" use of the facility and would be prohibited by the terms of this paragraph. Mr. Whang agreed and stated that the Korean side accepted the text of paragraph 4(a) and (b) of the U.S. draft.

27. At this point, it was decided to adjourn the meeting. The next meeting was scheduled for March 19 at 2:00 p,m..

28. Points of Agreements:
Facilities and Areas Article A. Par. 2, 3 and 4.

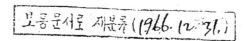

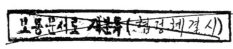

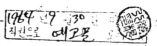

3. 제17차 회의, 3.19

0091

관리번호 ~~905~~

기 안 용 지

자체통제		기안처	미주과 이경훈	전화번호	근거서류접수일자

과장	국장	보좌관	차관	장관		
(서명)	(서명) 18	(서명) 18		(서명) 18.		

관계관 서명	조약과장 (서명) 기획조정관

기안년월일	63. 3. 18.	시행년월일		보존년한		정서	기장
분류기호		전체통제		종결			

경유 수신 참조	건의	발신	

제목	제 17차 주둔군 지위협정 체결 교섭 회의에 임할 우리측 태도

3월 19일에 개최될 제 17차 주둔군 지위협정 체결 한미간 교섭 회의에서는 외환관리, 미국 군표, 용어의 정의 그리고 토지 및 시설 문제에 관하여 토의될 예정이온바, 이에 관련하여 우리측 교섭 실무자는 3월 15일 관계 부처 실무자와 연석 회합을 갖고 제 17차 회의에서 취할 우리측 태도를 별첨과 같이 결정하였아오니 재가하여 주시기 바랍니다.

유첨 : 제 17차 주둔군지위협정 체결 교섭회의에 임할 우리측 태도

끝.

1966.12.31.에 예고문에 의거 일반문서로 재분류됨

~~보통문서로 재분류 (협정체결시)~~

~~일반문서로 재분류 (1966. 12. 31.)~~ 13-1

1964년 9월 30일 미주과장 직권으로 예고문 폐지분

승인양식 1—1—3 (1112—040—016—018) (190mm×260mm16절지)

0092

1. 외환 관리

(1) 본 조항에 대한 합의 의사록 전단에 있어서 우리측 초안은 " and by those organizations " 으로 되어 있는데 미국측 초안은 " including those activities " 로 되어 있는바, 미국측이 주장하고 있는 " activities " 라는 용어는 본 조항에 있어서 뿐만 아니라 다른 조항, 특히 관세업무 조항에도 규정되어 있음으로 " organizations " 으로 할것이냐 또는 " activities " 로 할것이냐에 대한 문제는 일괄적으로 해결한다는 조건하에 본 전단을 수락한다.

(2) 합의 의사록 후단에 있어서 미국측이 제시한 안에서 사용된 " at the highest rate " 라는 용어는 현재 우리 나라가 단일환율제를 채택하고 있으므로 부적당하며 따라서 우리측안의 " basic rate " 라는 용어 대신에 " official rate " 라는 용어로 수정하고 우리측 안을 받아 주도록 요구한다.

2. 미국 군표

(1) 군표의 사용 허여에 관한 미국측 초안 1. (a) 항 첫째 문장 (이는 우리측 초안 1 (a) 항에 해당함) 에는 우리측 초안에 있는 구절 " within the facilities and areas in use by the United States forces " 라는 구절이 없는바, 이 문제에 관하여 우리측은 토지 시설 밖에서 취급될 군표 업무를 위한 설비를 미국측이 어떻게 취할 것이냐는 점을 문의한후 미군측이 이러한 설비 제공에 관하여 한국 정부에 협력 한다는 조건하에 미국측 안을 수락하기로 한다.

13-2

0093

(2) 미국측 초안 1 (a) 둘째 문장 및 셋째 문장은 우리측 초안 1 (b) 및 (c) 와 사실상 같으므로 미국측 안을 수락한다.

(3) 미국측 초안 1 (b) 첫째 문장은 우리측 초안 1 (d) 항에 해당되는바 이에 있어서 (가) 미국측 초안에는 우리측 초안에 없는 " to the extent authorized by United States law" 라는 구절이 있는바, 동 구절이 구체적으로 무엇을 의미하는지 미국측에 문의한후 우리측 태도를 결정하고, (나) 또한 우리측 초안에는 미국측 초안에 없는 " after the date of coming into force of this Agreement " 라는 구절이 있는바, 이는 우리측 합의 의사록에서 행정 협정 체결당시 한국 정부가 보관하고 있는 군표는 양 정부간에 합의된바에 따라 처분한다는 규정과 부합시키기 위한 것으로 우리측 안을 수락토록 요구한다.

(4) 미국측 초안 2항은 우리측 초안 2 (a) (b) 항과 꼭 같으므로 미국측 안을 수락토록 한다.

(5) 우리측 초안 2 (c) 항은 미국측 안에 없는바 이를 받아주도록 요구한다.

(6) 우리측 합의 의사록은 미국측에는 없는바, 우리측 안을 수락토록 요구한다.

3. <u>용어의 정의</u>

(1) 군대 구성원에 관한 규정에 있어서 예외규정인 " except for those for whom status has otherwise been provided " 라는 구절을 조약원문에 삽입한 대신에 미국측에서 이를 설명하는 합의 의사록을 제시한바 우리측은 동 합의 의사록에서 사용된 " include " 라는 용어 대신에 " refer only to " 라는 용어로 수정하거나 또는 우리측이 제시한 합의 의사록

13-3

0094

안을 받아 줄것을 요구한바 있는데 만일 미국측에서 우리측 안과 비등한 제의를 할때에는 이를 수락하기로 하며 여전히 미국측이 " include " 란 용어의 사용을 주장한다면 우리측은 동 용어가 " refer only to " 를 의미한다는 것을 회의록에 명백히 기록하고 미국측 안을 수락한다.

4. 토지 및 시설

(1) 토지 시설 관리 등의 조치에 관한 미국측 초안 (B) 조 (1) 항 (우리측 초안 10항) 에 있어서 미국측 초안은 비상시 (In an emergency ....) 에는 토지 시설 부근에 있어서도 보안 조치를 취할수 있도록 규정하고 있는데 이에 대하여 우리측은 동문장 말미에 " within the extent that the Korean nationals and their properties are not unduly impaired " 라는 구절을 삽입토록 주장한다.

(2) 항해, 항공, 통신 문제에 관하여 (가) 이 문제에 관한 미국측 초안 B 조 2(a) 및 (b) 항 (우리측 초안 11항) 은 우리측 초안과 실질적인 차이점이 없으므로 수락토록 하고, (나) 미국측 초안 B 조 2 (c) 항은 우리측 초안에는 없으나 미국측 초안에서 "한국의 관계법률, 규정, 협정의 범위내에서" 한국정부는 미국 군대내의 통신 시설에 대한 관여를 피하고 제거할 모든 정당한 조치를 취하도록 규정하고 있으므로 이도 수락토록 한다.

(3) 공공안전의 존중에 관한 미국측 초안 B 조 3항 (우리측 초안 12항) 은 우리측 초안과 같음으로 수락토록 한다.

(4) 원상회복 문제에 관한 미국측 초안 C 조 1항 (우리측 초안 13항) 에 있어서 우리 초안은 원측적으로 미군이 원상회복 의무를

3-4

0095

면제하고 단지 사유 재산으로서 미군의 사용으로 막심한 파손을 당한 재산에 대하여 우리 정부의 요청에 의하여 미국측이 원상 회복 또는 이에 대신하는 보상에 관하여 충분한 고려를 하도록 규정하고 있는데 미국측 초안에 있어서는 이에 관한 규정을두고 있지 않으니 만일 미측이 사유 재산에 대한 일반 보상에 관한 조항을 수락할 경우에는 과잉 보상을 요구하는 결과가 될것임으로 일반 보상에 응하는한 우리측은 본 조항에 있어서 미국측에 양보하기로 한다.

(5) 가동 설비 소유권 및 처분 문제에 관한 미국측 초안 C 조 2항은 우리측 초안에는 규정되어 있지 않는 가동설비 (removable facilities) 에 대한 미국 정부의 소유권과 이들 재산의 반출권에 관한 규정을 두고 있는데 이는 실제 문제에 있어서 안정된 사실의 확인이라고 볼수 있음으로 구태여 규정할 필요가 없을 것이니 삭제하자고 주장해 본후 미국측에서 양보할 기색이 없을때는 받아 드리도록 한다.

(6) 토지 시설 개량에 대한 보상 의무 면제에 관한 우리측 초안 14항은 미국측 초안에서는 규정하고 있지 않는 것으로 이는 토지 시설의 반환시에 당해 시설 및 구역에 과하여진 개량 또는 그곳에 남겨진 건물, 공작물, 공급품 또는 기타의 물자에 대하여 한국 정부는 미국측에 보상하지 않는다 라는 규정인바, 이러한 명시적인 규정은 필요함으로 우리측 안의 수락 을 요구 한다. 본항은 미국측 초안 C 조 1항 다음에 2항으로서 삽입 토록 제의한다. 따라서 미국측 2항은 3항이 되모 3항은 4항이 될것이다.

(7) 특수시설 건축에 대한 예외규정에 관한 미국측 초안 C 조 3항의

13-5

0096

규정은 우리측 초안에는 없으나 기타 특별한 협약은 우리 정부가 인정할것임으로 받아 드리도록 한다.

(8) 토지 시설 유지비에 관한 미국측 초안 D 조 1항에 있어서 " except those to be borne by the Republic of Korea as provided in paragraph 2 " 라는 규정을 하고 있는 것은 미국측은 보상을 하지 않겠다는 원측의 입장에서 우리측이 부담하는 것을 전제하고 규정한것이기 때문에 우리측은 이를 삭제토록 요구한다.

(9) 토지 시설 보상 문제에 관한 미국측 초안D 조 2항 (우리측 초안 4항) 에 있어서 양측안은 근본적 차이점을 시현하고있는데 우리측은 사유재산의 사용에 대한 미국측의 보상 지불을 요구하고 있는데 대하여 미국측은 이를 한국측이 하도록 규정하고 있는 점과 미국측 초안 D 조 2항 후단은 특히 미군이 사용하는 토지 시설에 관련하여 제 3자 (민간인) 에 의하여 야기될지도 모를 청구권으로 부터 해를 받지 않도록 한국정부가 책임질것을 규정함으로 보상 문제에 관한 양국측이 근본적인 대립을 보이고 있다. 우리측은 우리안의 수락을 요구토록 한다.

보통문서로 재분류 (1966. 12. 31)

196 . . . 에 예고문에 의거 일반문서로 재분류됨

13-6

0097

기 안 용 지

자 체 통 제		기안처	미주과 이 경 훈	전화번호	근거서류접수일자
	과 장	국 장	보좌관	차관	장관
	3/20	20	20		20
관계관 서 명	조약과장 기획조정관				
기 안 년월일	63. 3. 20	시 행 년월일		보존 년한	정 서 / 기 장
분 류 기 호	외정미 722.2 -364	전 체 통 제		종결	
경 유 수 신 참 조	국가재건최고회의 의장 (참조: 외무국방위원장) 내각수반		발 신	장 관	
제 목	주둔군지위협정 체결을위한 제17차 교섭회의 보고				

1963. 3. 19. 하오 2시부터 동 4시 35분까지 외무부장관 회의실에서 개최된 제17차 한미간 주둔군지위협정 체결교섭회의에서토의된 내용을 별첨과같이 보고합니다.

유첨 : 제17차 교섭회의 보고서 부, 끝

보통문서로 재분류(1966. 12. 31.)

~~파 기 하 라 (불필요시)~~

1964년 9월 30일 예고문에 의거 일반문서로 재분류

9-1

승인양식 1—1—3 (1112—040—016—018) (190mm×260mm16절지)

발송 1963 3 외무부

0098

외　　　　무　　　　부

외정미 722.2 (8-3052)　　　　　　　　　　1963. 3. 21.

수　신　　국가재건최고회의 의장

참　조　　외무국방위원장

제　목　　주둔군지위협정 체결을위한 제17차 교섭회의 보고

1963. 3. 19. 하오 2시부터 동 4시 35분까지 외무부장관 회의실에서 개최된 제17차 한미간 주둔군지위협정 체결교섭회의에서 토의된 내용을 별첨과같이 보고합니다.

유첨 : 제17차 교섭회의 보고서 2부, 끝

외 무 부 장 관　　　　김　　　용　　　식

0093

9-5

외 무 부

외정미 722.2 (8-3052) 1963. 3. 21.

수 신 내각수반

제 목 주둔군지위협정 체결을위한 제17차 교섭회의 보고

1963. 3. 19. 하오 2시부터 동 4시 35분까지 외무부장관 회의실에서 개최된 제17차 한미간 주둔군지위협정 체결 교섭회의에서 토의된 내용을 별첨과같이 보고합니다.

유첨 : 제17차 교섭회의 보고서 1 부. 끝

외 무 부 장 관 김 용 식

9-6

0100

제 17 차

한미간 주둔군지위협정 체결 실무자회의

보 고 서

1. 시 일 : 1963. 3. 19. 하오 2시부터 4시 35분 까지

2. 장 소 : 외무부장관 회의실

3. 참석자 : 한국측 : 황 호 을 (외무부 정무국장)

신 관 섭 (재무부 세관국장)

구 충 회 (외무부 미주과장)

이 남 구 (국방부 군무과장)

이 재 설 (재무부 외환과장)

이 경 훈 (외무부 2등서기관)

강 석 재 (외무부 3등서기관)

김 윤 택 (")

미국측 : "하비브"참사관 및 "토마" 장군을 제외한 교섭대표단 전원

63-1-62

4. 토의사항 :

(1) 외환관리, 군표 그리고 용어의정의 문제를 순차적으로 토의함.

(2) 외환관리 문제에대한 합의의사록 전단에 있어서 우리측 초안은 미국군대 및 "비세출기관"과 미국군대 구성원, 군속, 그들의 가족 및 계약체결자간의 외환거래는 한국외환관리법에 의거하여 유효하다라고 규정한데 대하여 미국측 초안은 "비세출활동을 포함한" 미국군대와 미국군대 구성원, 군속, 그들의 가족 및 계약체결자간의 외환거래는 한국 외환관리법에 의거하여 유효하다라고 규정하고 있는고로 우리측은 "비세출 기관"이라는 ~~이라는~~ 용어를 사용할것인지 "비세출활동"이라는 용어를 사용

9-2

0101

63-1-9(3)

마이크로 89-9(3)

0102

할것인지에 관하여는 다른조항 특히 관세업무의 조항에도 규정되어 있음으로 이문제는 일괄적으로 해결한다는 조건하에 본항 전단을 수락한다고 말하자 미국측은 이에 동의하였음.

(3) 외환관리 문제에대한 합의의사록 후단에있어서 우리측은 한국에는 단일 환율제가 채택되어 있음으로 외환거래는 "공정환율"로 하자고 주장한데 대하여 미국측은 1961년 2월 8일자 한미간 경제, 기술원조 협정에서 사용된바와 같은 "최고의 환율"이라는 용어를 사용하자고 주장하여 다음에 다시 토의키로 함.

(4) 군표사용 허여에관한 문제에있어서 미국측은 군표는 토지, 시설밖에서도 사용케하여야 한다고 주장한데 대하여 우리측은 토지시설 밖에서 사용할시에는 미국측에서 시설설치에관한 조처가있어야 할것이니 이계획에 대한 설명을 요구하자 미국측은 이는 장차 성안될 문제이라고하여 본문제에 대하여는 다음에 다시 토의키로 함.

(5) 미국측은 군표를 불법사용한 미국군대 구성원, 군속 및 그들의 가족에대한 미국당국의 체포 및 처벌은 "미국법에서 허여된 범위내에서" 행하도록 하자고 주장한데 대하여 우리측은 여기서 말하는 "미국법에서 허여된 범위내에서" 라는 구절의 구체적 설명을 요구하자 미국측은 한국에 주둔하고있는 미국 군법은 평시에 민간인에 대하여는 재판권이 없고 다만 그들에게 부여된 특권을 박탈하고 특정직에서 해고 시키는 등의 행정적 조치를 취할수만 있다고하여 이문제는 다음에 다시 토의키로 함.

63-1-63

(6) 군표의 불법사용의 결과 미국측에서 발생될 여하한 부담도 "본협정 효력 발생후에는" 생기지 않는다는 규정은 우리측이 제시한 합의의사록안에서 본협정 효력 발생시에 한국정부가 보관하고있는 군표는 양국정부간의 협정에 따라서 처분된다는

0103

9-3

63-1-9

마문 89-9

0104

규정과 관련한것이라고 하면서 우리측은 우리측안의 수락을 요구하자 미국측은 이러한 문제는 행정협정 밖의 문제라고 하여 이는 다음에 다시 토의키로 함.

(7) 미국군대 은행시설에 관한 항목에있어서 우리측안과 미국측안은 우리측안에서 미국군대 은행기관이 취할 적절한 조치 규정을 한것을 제외하고는 양측안이 같으며 또한 이러한 조치규정은 사실상 불필요함으로 이를 철회하고 미국측안을 수락하였음.

(8) 용어의 정의조항중 군대 구성원에 관한 규정에 있어서 이의 예외규정으로서 "미국대사관 소속 미국군대 구성원 및 개정된 1950년 1월 26일자 군사고문단 협정에서 그의 신분이 규정된 자는 제외" 한다라는 구절을 조약원문에 삽입할것을 요구하는 타협안을 미국측이 제시한데 대하여 동안은 우리측의 주장과 부합되는 것임으로 우리측은 이를 수락하였음.

5. 중요합의사항 :

(1) 용어의 정의에관한 조항에 완전 합의함

6. 기타사항 :

(1) 차기회의 일자 : 1963. 3. 29. 하오 2시

(2) 차기회의 의제 : 차기회의가지 양측 수석대표간에 합의된 사항

63-1-64

보통문서로 재분류(1966. 12. 31.)

0105

9-4

63-1-9(3)

비국문 89-9(3)

0106

CONFIDENTIAL

Joint Summary
17th Meeting
March 19, 1963

Foreign Exchange Controls

1. Mr. Whang opened the meeting by reminding the negotiators that discussion had been completed on the text of the article dealing with foreign exchange controls. He stated that there were still two unresolved points in regard to the Agreed Minute, however. The first of these was the difference between the wording "including those activities provided in Article ___" in the U.S. draft and the wording "by those organizations provided in Article ___" in the Korean draft. The second was the difference between "the highest rate in terms of the number of Korean Won per United States Dollar which, at the time the conversion is made, is not unlawful in the Republic of Korea" in the U.S. draft and "the basic rate of exchange" in the Korean draft.

2. With regard to the first point, Mr. Whang stated that no agreement had yet been reached with regard to the use of "activities", as proposed by the U.S. side, or "organizations" as proposed by the Korean side. He said this point would be settled when final agreement was reached on the text of the customs article. He suggested, therefore, that the negotiators ~~tentatively agree on the word "activities" in the U.S. draft, pending final agreement on the customs article~~ withhold the discussion on this matter until that time. Mr. Ford agreed and pointed out that the reference to "activities provided in Article ___" was a reference to the non-appropriated fund activities article, which had not yet been tabled.

3. Mr. Whang said Mr. Lee Chae Sul would explain the position of the Korean side in regard to the second point. Mr. Lee said that he wished to point out that the Korean Foreign Exchange Law was first passed on November 30, 1961. At the previous meeting, he recalled, Mr. Ford had said the U.S. side would like to have the rate spelled out in language similar to that of Article 6 (c) of the Comprehensive Aid Agreement (The Agreement on Economic Cooperation, signed at Seoul on February 8, 1961). However, he said, the situation has changed since the Aid Agreement was entered into. The Republic of Korea now has a unitary rate of exchange. The Korean side suggested amendment of its draft to read "effective official rate of

0107

exchange."

4. Mr. Ford replied that the unitary exchange rate had ~~gone into effect~~ been adopted by the ROK government on February 1, 1961. ~~A prior move toward the unitary rate had taken place~~ On January 1, 1961, the official rate ~~was raised~~ moved from 650 hwan (65 Won) to the dollar to 1000 hwan (100 Won) to the dollar. When the unitary rate ~~adopted on February 1 and~~ became effective on February 2, the rate was set at 1300 hwan (130 Won) to the dollar. This was part of a package designed to stabilize the Korean Economy. Another element of the stabilization program was the conclusion of the Agreement on Economic Cooperation, commonly known as the Comprehensive Aid Agreement. This was a government to government agreement, signed by the Foreign Minister and the Ambassador. One element of the agreement was the rate at which United States dollars would be convertible into hwan. The wording of this provision had been given very careful attention by both sides and had been agreed upon. It is clear, unambiguous, and not subject to misinterpretation. There can be no dispute regarding its meaning. This provision, Mr. Ford continued, has worked very well in the context of the unitary rate system. It is difficult to understand why it should now be changed. Not a single question regarding it has been raised in over two years. If the language is changed now, he pointed out, a situation might arise in which one agency of the U.S. Government would be purchasing won at one rate while another agency would be purchasing won at a different rate. If the language had proved unsatisfactory to the ROKG, Mr. Ford suggested, the first step ~~should be~~ would have been to seek an amendment to the aid agreement, rather than to put revised language into the SOFA. The U.S. side, he continued, does not understand the reason why the language should be changed. He asked the Korean side to reconsider its position, so that both the aid agreement and the SOFA might contain standard language.

5. In reply, Mr. Lee Chae Sul stated that it was true that the unitary exchange rate had been adopted in February, 1961 and set at 1300 hwan (130 Won) to the dollar.

0108

He pointed out that at the time the Comprehensive Aid Agreement was signed there had been no foreign exchange regulation ~~s regarding~~ setting the unitary rate, which at that time was decided through mutual consultation. Such a regulation was adopted on December 30, 1961. Therefore, the situation was now different, because of the existence of the regulation. Mr. Ford had asked why the wording of the aid agreement should be changed. ~~Mr. Lee continued, and had mentioned the possibility of the existence of different rates.~~ The wording of the U.S. draft, Mr. Lee stated, would create the misunderstanding among the Korean people that there is more than one rate. If there had been an exchange regulation in existence at the time the aid agreement was negotiated, the language of the aid agreement would have been different, he said. He then suggested adoption of the phrase "effective official exchange rate". He asked the U.S. side to reconsider its position so as not to confuse the Korean people.

6. Mr. Ford pointed out that the fact that the ROKG was adopting a unitary rate was well known at the time the Comprehensive Aid Agreement was negotiated. Mr. Ford said that although Mr. Lee had said that the exchange regulations came into effect in December, 1961, it must be assumed that these regulations were written to be in conformity with the inter-governmental agreement which the ROKG had entered into only a few months previously. This assumption is strengthened by the fact that there has been no complaint during the ~~over~~ more than two years in which the aid agreement has been in effect. There thus appears to be no conflict between the aid agreement and the ROKG regulations. Mr. Ford stated that ~~[illegible]~~ Mr. Lee had alleged that there might be misunderstanding regarding the language of the U.S. draft Agreed Minute. It is clear, Mr. Ford said, that there has been no such misunderstanding during the past two years. The language ~~is tried and true~~ has stood the test of time, Mr. Ford continued, and this is ~~no time~~ not the point at which to ~~to~~ shift to new wording. The wording proposed by Mr. Lee ~~were~~ was open ~~[illegible]~~ to misunderstanding because the word "effective" in the phrase "effective official exchange rate" implies the existence of more than one rate.

7. Mr. Lee replied that it appeared that misunderstanding would arise

0109

if the original Korean wording ~~were accepted~~ or ~~if~~ the original U.S. wording were accepted. ~~(As Mr. Ford had pointed out, the comprehensive aid agreement had been signed on February 28, 1961 and the Currency Exchange Law had gone into effect on December 30, 1961. The Law had not been drafted with the aid agreement in mind.)~~ The ROK proposal of "effective official exchange rate" was intended to mean the legal rate. There could, therefore, be no misunderstanding regarding the language.

8. Mr. Ford reiterated that there has been no misunderstanding regarding the meaning of the language of the Comprehensive Aid Agreement. In the light of two years of experience with this language, it would be a mistake to abandon it now. Mr. Ford pointed out that an intolerable situation would arise if one U.S. Government agency should buy at one rate while another agency was buying at a different rate. Standard language in both the aid agreement and the SOFA would avoid the possibility of such a situation developing. ~~Mr. Lee had stated that the aid agreement was not taken into consideration, Mr. Ford continued, when the currency exchange regulations were drafted.~~ Mr. Ford said he knew of no conflict between the two, but ~~assuming~~ if such conflict did exist, he assumed that it would be resolved in favor of the treaty. However, the fact that there has been no disagreement in two years indicates that no conflict, in fact, exists.

9. Mr. Whang said that Mr. Ford was assuming that one agency could convert at one rate and another agency at a different rate. However, he said, there is a foreign exchange law and a unitary rate in effect. Therefore, the situation envisioned by Mr. Ford could not arise. Mr. Whang expressed the opinion that the substance of both sides' drafts was the same; only the language differed. Both drafts referred to the rate ~~of~~ which is now 130 won to the dollar. The Korean language was intended to avoid any misunderstanding that there was a multiple rate. He suggested that inasmuch as the foregoing discussion would appear in the summary record, there could be no misunderstanding of the positions of the two sides. He urged

0110

the U.S. side to consider and accept the Korean proposal.

10. Mr. Ford replied that the Comprehensive Aid Agreement had taken fully into account the existance of a unitary rate of exchange. He said if the Korean proposal were adopted, we would have a situation of two agreements (made) within two years of each other, containing differing language. He asked the negotiators to consider the possibility of future difficulties arising out of such a situation. He said the language of the aid agreement had served well and the U.S. side urged that it be used in the SOFA also. Mr.Whang remarked that discussion of this article had consumed too much time. He suggested that Mr. Ford and Mr. Lee discuss this questioh privately and report at the next meeting. ~~It was so agreed.~~

Military Payment Certificates

11. Turning to the draft article regarding military payment certificates, Mr. Whang stated that the Korean side assumed that "persons authorized by the United States" to use MPC are persons authorized to do so by U.S. law. He asked for identification of such persons. Mr. Ford replied that these are persons authorized to use MPC by U.S. armed forces regulations. Mr. Whang asked if there were any persons included in addition to members of the armed forces, the civilian component, and their dependents. Mr. Ford replied that in addition to the types of persons listed by Mr. Whang there were U.S. Government officials, invited contractors and the dependents of both. These were merely illustrative examples, he said, and not all-inclusive.

12. Mr. Lee Chae Sul pointed out that the phrase "within the facilities and areas in use by the United States forces" in the Korean draft was not included in the U.S. draft. He expressed the opinion that if this phrase were omitted, both sides would be confronted by difficulties, since the scope of MPC transactions would not be defined. On the other hand, if such a restriction were established, the U.S. personnel would be inconvenienced. The Korean side believed that the

use of MPC must be made available ~~in~~ during exercises and maneuvers and also in hotels and tourist attractions. Therefore, he continued, it is desirable to find some way in which to authorize the use of MPC in certain areas outside established areas and facilities through mutual agreement. Since the phrase in question had been omitted from the U.S. draft, the U.S. side must have given prior consideration to this problem. The Korean side, he said, would like to hear the views of the U.S. side.

13. Mr. Ford replied that the governing phrase in the U.S. draft is the phrase "for internal transactions". As Mr. Habib had pointed out during a previous meeting, the temporary use of MPC outside of areas and facilities was desirable as a factor in maintaining the morale of the troops. In regard to preventing abuse, Mr. Ford referred to the second sentence of paragraph 1 (a) of the U.S. draft, which provides that "The Government of the United States will take appropriate action to insure that authorized personnel are prohibited from engaging in transactions involving military payment certificates except as authorized by United States regulations". He also referred to the next sentence, which lays certain obligations upon the ROK Government. The U.S. side, he concluded, believes that the controls provided for in these two sentences are sufficient to prevent any significant abuse of MPC utilization outside of established areas and facilities. When special problems arise, he added, they can be discussed by the Joint Committee.

14. Mr. Lee replied ~~that~~ However, even now, before agreement on the use of MPC, ~~the U.S.~~ authorities have placed limitations on the amount of Won sold to MPC holders ~~restrictions on such use. He pointed out also~~ that Korean law also prohibits unauthorized use of MPC by Koreans. Furthermore, there are quite a few existing facilities where there is no provision for the ~~use of MPC~~ official sale of Won to authorized holders of MPC. The Korean side, he said, feared that the continued existence of such restrictions ~~might~~ would cause difficulties. Although the U.S. draft provides for appropriate action to prevent abuse, the Korean side desired clarification of how such abuse was to be prevented, at the same time providing for convenient facilities for the exchange of Won.

15. In reply, Colonel Solf stated that the U.S. armed forces would continue to take ~~all~~ appropriate administrative, disciplinary, and penal measures against those persons under their control and jurisdiction to prevent the illegal use of MPC. He added that the U.S. side expected the ROK Government to do the same. Mr. Whang stated that the Korean side did not wish to inconvenience the U.S. armed forces by limiting use of MPC to existing areas and facilities. However, the Korean side believed that some agreed procedures should be worked out for establishing MPC facilities at places such as tourist hotels so that the troops would not be inconvenienced.. ~~Colonel Solf replied that at the present time~~, the U.S. armed forces had no specific proposals ~~of this sort in mind. The U.S. side agreed,~~ of course, that any procedures of the kind proposed by the Korean side would have to be mutually ~~agreeable.~~ acceptable. ~~In concluding discussion of paragraph 1 (a), Mr. Whang stated that the provisions of this subparagraph could be implemented by the Joint Committee.~~

(margin note: in other paper in version)

16. Turning to paragraph 1(b) of the U.S. draft, Mr. Whang asked for clarification of the remarks made by Mr. Habib at a previous meeting regarding the phrase "to the extent authorized by United States law". Colonel Solf explained that, in a series of decisions affecting the jurisdiction of courts-martial, the United States Supreme Court had held that in time of peace civilians [redacted] accused of crimes against the United States are [redacted] liable solely to the jurisdiction of United States civil courts.

~~17. Mr. Whang pointed out that the provisions of paragraph 1(b) apparently did not apply to invited contractors or third-country nationals. He~~ Mr. Whang asked what court had jurisdiction over such categories of persons as invited contractors or third-country nationals. In reply, Colonel Solf stated that U.S. citizens could be tried in U.S. civil courts. He pointed out that while the U.S. armed forces might not have court-martial jurisdiction over such persons, they still retained all administrative ~~powers,~~ jurisdiction, including discharge, deprivation of access to facilities, and deprivation of privileges. Mr. Whang asked specifically if invited contractors would be subject to ~~trial by~~ court-martial. ~~Colonel~~ Solf replied that if

0113

they are civilians, they are not subject to trial by court-martial during time of peace. Mr. Whang ~~replied~~ stated that it appeared that there would be people authorized to use MPC who would not be liable to trial or punishment if they abused this privilege. Colonel Solf replied that the administrative sanctions at the disposal of the U.S. armed forces were quite effective in dealing with such abuses. He pointed out that the U.S. armed forces would retain administrative control over all such persons.

18. Mr. Whang then referred to the phrase in paragraph 1 (d) of the Korean draft which would state that no obligation will be due to the Government of the Republic of Korea "after the date of coming into force of this agreement". He said that this phrase had been inserted in the Korean draft ~~in an attempt to clarify the desire of the ROK Government~~ in order to obtain payment for the ~~large~~ amount of MPC currently in ~~its~~ the custody of the ROK Government.

19. Mr. Ford replied that ~~this~~ the redemption of this MPC would be impossible. He stated that there is no way in which the ROK Government can receive payment for MPC held by it. He pointed out that ~~the SOFA would say~~ the wording of Paragraph 1 (d) of the ROK draft provides specifically that there would be no obligation to the ROK Government after the SOFA goes into effect; why then should there be any obligation before it goes into effect? Mr. Lee Chae Sul replied that a different situation ~~existed~~ exists in Korea than in any other country. He pointed out that the U.S. armed forces have been present in Korea since 1945 and that during this period a huge amount of MPC had been accumulated by the ROK Government. He said the ROK Government was anxious to dispose of this accumulation but that it felt a moral obligation to the Korean people who had earned it through sales or services to Americans. The thousands of Koreans who had turned in the MPC should be reimbursed; otherwise they would be placed in the position of having rendered goods and services to the U.S. armed forces without compensation.

0114

20. At this point, Mr. Ford read into the record the following statement:

"a. Military Payment Certificates are issued by the United States Government solely for internal use in United States military areas and facilities and such other places as may be agreed. MPC are issued for the use of persons authorized by the United States and such use is subject to the specific regulations of the United States Government.

"b. MPC are the property of the United States Government. MPC are not a currency of the United States and do not constitute a valid claim against the United States Government for redemption when in the possession of unauthorized holders.

"c. MPC are not convertible into dollars or dollar instruments, except by authorized holders in circumstances specified in United States Government regulations.

"d. MPC may be held temporarily in the possession of unauthorized persons or agencies in the following cases:

"1. Pending the return to an authorized person who was illegally deprived of possession of the MPC through loss or theft;

"2. During the time necessary for a law enforcement agency to hold the MPC in its possession for use in judicial proceedings;

"3. During the time necessary for a law enforcement agency to process seized MPC for return to the appropriate United States authority.

"e. Authorized holders of MPC may use them only in internal transactions to purchase approved goods and services from U.S. authorized sources, and such authorized holders may not use them for the purchase of goods and services except as I have indicated.

"f. Since MPC are issued by the United States Government for use by authorized persons for specific purposes, the use of MPC by unauthorized persons or for unauthorized purposes is not recognized by the United States Government.

"g. The MPC in the possession of any Korean Government agency should therefore be returned to the appropriate United States authorities. The Embassy has for some time been requesting the Korean Government to return the MPC confiscated by Korean law-enforcement agencies.

"h. In view of the special character of MPC and the fact that these requests have been made for their return, we do not consider this matter a ~~subject for discussion~~ in the context of these negotiations.

0115

21. Turning to paragraph 2 of both drafts, Mr. Whang stated that since there did not appear to be any difference in language, the Korean side accepted the text of paragraph 2 of the U.S. draft. He pointed out that in the Korean draft, there appeared an additional sentence (as subparagraph (c)), which referred to the preceding sentences. Mr. Ford voiced the opinion that the sentence was unnecessary, inasmuch as mutual obligations on both governments appear in the text of paragraph 1. Mr. Whang replied that the sentence had been intended to refer only to paragraph 2. Mr. Ford said that the U.S. side believed such a reference to be unnecessary, since it was implicit in the text of paragraph 2 that the U.S. Government would take whatever measures were necessary to ensure the implementation of the provisions of the paragraph. Mr. Whang stated that with that understanding, the Korean side withdrew the proposed subparagraph (c).

22. Mr. Ford said that he wished to state for the record that nothing in the Foreign Exchange Controls Article or in the Military Payment Certificate Article is intended to preclude future discussions between the ROK and U.S. Governments concerning the possibility of the future substitution of U.S. coins or currency for MPC, should it appear desirable and feasible. Mr. Ford said he wished to make it clear, however, that no such discussions are presently contemplated.

23. Mr. Whang reminded the negotiators that the ROK side had proposed an Agreed Minute to the MPC Article, providing for disposal of MPC in the custody of the ROK Government at the time of entry into force of the SOFA, in accordance with mutually agreed upon procedures. Mr. Ford said the U.S. side thought that it had been agreed during the discussion just held that inasmuch as this matter was currently being handled in other channels it was outside the scope of the SOFA negotiations. Mr. Whang suggested that the both sides discuss further this matter at the next meeting.

0116

Definitions

24. Turning to the Definitions Article, Mr. Ford reminded the negotiators that they were very close to final agreement. With regard to the ~~Korean proposal~~ language of the proposed Agreed Minute #1 referring to ~~subparagraph~~ subparagraph (a), Mr. Ford ~~pointed~~ stated that the U.S. side was prepared to agree to the latest Korean proposal. However, the U.S. side now questioned the need for the Agreed Minute and proposed that the language of the subparagraph itself be changed instead. Mr. Ford proposed that the Agreed Minute be deleted and that ~~subpara the language of~~ subparagraph (a)be altered by ~~dropping~~ deleting the language following the words "except for" and inserting in its place the following language: "personnel of the U.S. Armed forces attached to the U.S. Embassy and personnel for whom status has been provided in the Military Advisory Group Agreement of January 26, 1950, as amended". ~~The Korean side~~ Mr. Whang said the Korean side agreed to this change ~~[illegible]~~ and noted that full agreement had been reached on the text of the Definitions Article.

25. It was agreed to hold the next meeting on March 29 at 2 p.m.

26. Points of agreement:

Definitions Article (as revised).

보통문서로 재분류(1966.12.31)

6.12.31 일반문서로 재분류

0117

관리 번호 927

JOINT SUMMARY RECORD OF THE 17TH SESSION
STATUS FORCES NEGOTIATIONS

March 19, 1963

I. Time and Place : 2:00 to 4:35 p.m. March 19, 1963 at the Foreign Minister's Conference Room

II. Attendants:

ROK Side:

Mr. Whang, Ho Eul	Director Bureau of Political Affairs Ministry of Foreign Affairs
Mr. Shin Kwan Sup	Director Bureau of Costums Duty Ministry of Finance
Mr. Koo, Choong Whay	Chief, America Section Ministry of Foreign Affairs
Col. Lee, Nam Koo	Chief, Military Affairs Section Ministry of National Defense
Mr. Lee, Jae Sul	Chief of the Foreign Exchange Division, Ministry of Finance
Mr. Lee, Kyung Hoon	2nd Secretary Ministry of Foreign Affairs
Mr. Kang, Suk Jae	3rd Secretary Ministry of Foreign Affairs
Mr. Kim, Yoon Taik	3rd Secretary Ministry of Foreign Affairs

US Side:

Mr. William J. Ford	First Secretary of the Embassy
Col. G.G. O'Connor	Deputy Chief of Staff 8th Army
Capt. R.M. Brownlie	Assistant Chief of Staff USN/K

기안	고재	四월 소일	담당	과장	국장	특별보좌관	차관	장관
			(signed)	(signed)	(signed)	(signed)	(signed)	

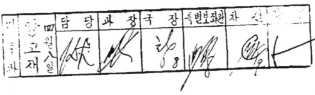

조약과장

0118

1966 . 12 . 31 에 예고 일반문서로 재분류

10-1

Col. W.A. Solf	Staff Judge Advocate 8th Army
Mr. Benjamin A. Fleck (Rapporteur and Press Officer)	First Secretary of the Embassy
Mr. Robert A. Lewis	Second Secretary and Consul of the Embassy
Lt. Col. R,E. Miller	Staff Officer, JAG 8th Army
Lt. Col. W.A. Burt	J-5
Kenneth Campen	Interpreter

Foreign Exchange Controls

1. Mr. Whang opened the meeting by reminding the negotiators that discussion had been completed on the text of the article dealing with foreign exchange controls. He stated that there were still two unresolved points in regard to the Agreed Minute, however. The first of these was the difference between the wording "including those activities provided in Article ___" in the U.S. draft and the wording "by those organizations provided in Article ___" in the Korean draft. The second was the difference between "the highest rate in terms of the number of Korean Won per United States Dollar which, at the time the conversion is made, is not unlawful in the Republic of Korea" in the U.S. draft and "the basic rate of exchange" in the Korean draft.

2. With regard to the first point, Mr. Whang stated that no agreement had yet been reached with regard to the use of "activities", as proposed by the U.S. side, or "organizations" as proposed by the Korean side.

0119

rp-2

He said this point would be settled when final agreement was reached on the text of the customs article. He suggested, therefore, that the negotiators withhold discussion on this matter until that time. Mr. Ford agreed and pointed out that the reference to "activities provided in Article ____" was a reference to the non-appropriated fund activities article, which had not yet been tabled.

3. Mr. Whang said Mr. Lee Chae Sul would explain the position of the Korean side in regard to the second point. Mr. Lee said that he wished to point out that the Korean Foreign Exchange Law was first passed on November 30, 1961. At the previous meeting, he recalled, Mr. Ford had said the U.S. side would like to have the rate spelled out in language similar to that of Article 6 (c) of the Comprehensive Aid Agreement (The Agreement on Economic Cooperation, signed at Seoul on February 8, 1961). However, he said, the situation has changed since the Aid Agreement was entered into. The Republic of Korea now has a unitary rate of exchange. The Korean side suggested amendment of its draft to read "effective official rate of exchange".

4. Mr. Ford replied that the unitary exchange rate had been adopted by the ROK Government on February 1, 1961. On January 1, 1961, the official rate moved from 650 hwan (650 Won) to the dollar to 1000 hwan (100 won) to the dollar. When the unitary rate became effective on February 2, the rate was set at 1300 hwan (130 won) to the dollar. This was part of a package

0120

10-3

designed to stabilize the Korean economy. Another element of the stabilization program was the conclusion of the Agreement on Economic Cooperation, commonly known as the Comprehensive Aid Agreement. This was a government to government agreement, signed by the Foreign Minister and the Ambassador. One element of the agreement was the rate at which United States dollars would be convertible into hwan. The wording of this provision had been given very careful attention by both sides and had been agreed upon. It is clear, unambiguous, and not subject to misinterpretation. There can be no dispute regarding its meaning. This provision, Mr. Ford continued, has worked very well in the context of the unitary rate system. It is difficult to understand why it should now be changed. Not a single question regarding it has been raised in over two years. If the language is changed now, he pointed out, a situation might arise in which one agency of the U.S. Government would be purchasing won at one rate while another agency would be purchasing won at a different rate. If the language had proved unsatisfactory to the ROKG, Mr. Ford suggested, the first step would have been to seek an amendment to the aid agreement rather than to put revised language into the SOFA. The U.S. side, he continued, does not understand the reason why the language should be changed. He asked the Korean side to reconsider its position, so that both the aid agreement and the SOFA might contain standard language.

0121

10-4

5. In reply, Mr. Lee Chae Sul stated that it was true that the unitary exchange rate had been adopted in February, 1961 and set at 1300 hwan (130 won) to the dollar. He pointed out that at the time the Comprehensive Aid Agreement was signed there had been no foreign exchanges regulations setting the unitary rate, which at that time was decided through mutual consultation. Such a regulation was adopted on December 30, 1961. Therefore, the situation was now different, because of the existence of the regulation. Mr. Ford had asked why the wording of the aid agreement should be changed. The wording of the U.S. draft, Mr. Lee stated, would create the misunderstanding among the Korean people that there is more than one rate. If there had been an exchange regulation in existence at the time the aid agreement was negotiated, the language of the aid agreement would have been different, he said. He then suggested adoption of the phrase "effective official exchange rate". He asked the U.S. side to reconsider its position so as not to confuse the Korean people.

6. Mr. Ford pointed out that the fact that the ROKG was adopting a unitary rate was well known at the time the Comprehensive Aid Agreement was negotiated. Mr. Ford said that although Mr. Lee had said that the exchange regulations came into effect in December, 1961, it must be assumed that these regulations were written to be in conformity with the inter-governmental agreement which the ROKG had entered into only a few months previously. This assumption is strengthened by the fact

10-5

0122

that there has been no complaint during the more than two years in which the aid agreement has been in effect. There thus appears to be no conflict between the aid agreement and the ROKG regulations. Mr. Ford stated that Mr. Lee had alleged that there might be misunderstanding regarding the language of the U.S. draft Agreed Minute. It is clear, Mr. Ford said, that there has been no such misunderstanding during the past two years. The language has stood the test of time, Mr. Ford continued, and this is not the point at which to shift to new wording. The wording proposed by Mr. Lee was open to misunderstanding because the word "effective" in the phrase "effective official exchange rate" implies the existence of more than one rate.

Mr. Lee replied that it appeared that misunderstanding would arise if either the original Korean wording or the original U.S. wording were accepted. The ROK proposal of "effective official exchange rate" was intended to mean the legal rate. There could, therefore, be no misunderstanding regarding the language.

8. Mr. Ford reiterated that there has been no misunderstanding regarding the meaning of the language of the Comprehensive Aid Agreement. In the light of two years of experience with this language, it would be a mistake to abandon it now. Mr. Ford pointed out that an intolerable situation would arise if one U.S. Government agency should buy at one rate while another agency was buying at a different rate. Standard language in both the aid agreement and the SOFA would avoid the possibility

of such a situation developing. Mr. Ford said he knew of no conflict between the two, but if such conflict did exist, he assumed that it would be resolved in favor of the treaty. However, the fact that there has been no disagreement in two years indicates that no conflict, in fact, exists.

9. Mr. Whang said that Mr. Ford was assuming that one agency could convert at one rate and another agency at a different rate. However, he said, there is a foreign exchange law and a unitary rate in effect. Therefore, the situation envisioned by Mr. Ford could not arise. Mr. Whang expressed the opinion that the substance of both sides' drafts was the same; only the language differed. Both drafts referred to the rate which is now 130 won to the dollar. The Korean language was intended to avoid any misunderstanding that there was a multiple rate. He suggested that inasmuch as the foregoing disucssion would appear in the summary record, there could be no misunderstanding of the positions of two sides. He urged the U.S. side to consider and accept the Korean proposal.

10. Mr. Ford replied that the Comprehensive Aid Agreemment had taken fully into account the existance of a unitary rate of exchange. He said if the Korean proposal were adopted, we would have a situation of two agreements made within two years of each other, containing differing language. He asked the negotiators to consider the possibility of future difficulties arising out of such a situation. He said the language of the

0124

107

aid agreement had served well and the U.S. side urged that it be used in the SOFA also. Mr. Whang remarked that discussion of this article and consumed too much time. He suggested that Mr. Ford and Mr. Lee discuss this question privately and report at the next meeting.

Military Payment Certificates

11. Turning to the draft article regarding military payment certificates, Mr. Whang stated that the Korean side assumed that "persons authorized by the United States" to use MPC are persons authorized to do so by U.S. law. He asked for identification of such persons. Mr. Ford replied that these are persons authorized to use MPC by U.S. armed forces regulations. Mr. Whang asked if there were any persons included in addition to members of the armed forces, the civilian component, and their dependents. Mr. Ford replied that in addition to the types of persons listed by Mr. Whang there were U.S. Government officials, invited contractors and the dependents of both. These were merely illustrative examples, he said, and not all-inclusive.

12. Mr. Lee Chae Sul pointed out that the phrase "within the facilities and areas in use by the United States forces" in the Korean draft was not included in the U.S. draft. He expressed the opinion that if this phrase were omitted, both sides would be confronted by difficulties, since the scope of MPC transactions would not be defined. On the other hand, if such a restriction were established, the U.S. personnel would be inconvenienced. The Korean side believed that the

0125

10-8

use of MPC must be made available during exercises and meneuvers and also in hotels and tourist attractions. Therefore, he continued, it is desirable to find some way in which to authorize the use of MPC in certain areas outside established areas and facilities through mutual agreement. Since the phrase in question had been omitted from the U.S. draft, the U.S. side must have given prior consideration to this problem. The Korean side, he said, would like to hear the views of the U.S. side.

13. Mr. Ford replied that the governing phrase in the U.S. draft is the phrase "for internal transactions". As Mr. Habib had pointed out during a previous meeting, the temporary use of MPC outside of areas and facilities was desirable as a factor in maintaining the morale of the troops, In regard to preventing abuse, Mr. Ford referred to the second sentence of paragraph 1 (a) of the U.S. draft, which provides that "The Government of the United States will take appropriate action to insure that authorized personnel are prohibited from engaging in transactions involving military payment certificates except as authorized by United States regulations". He also referred to the next sentence, which lays certain obligations upon the ROK Government. The U.S. side, he concluded, believes that the controls provided for in these two sentences are sufficient to prevent any significant abuse of MPC utilization outside of established areas and facilities. When special problems arise, he added, they can be discussed by the Joint Committee.

0126

10-9

14. Mr. Lee replied that Korean law also prohibits unauthorized use of MPC by Koreans. However, even now, before agreement on the use of MPC, the U.S. authorities have placed limitations on the amount of Won Sold to MPC holders. Furthermore, there are quite a few existing facilities where there is no provision for the official sale of won to authorized holders of MPC. The Korean side, he said, feared that the continued existence of such restrictions would cause difficulties. Although the U.S. draft provides for appropriate action to prevent abuse, the Korean side desired clarification of how such abuse was to be prevented, at the same time providing for convenient facilities for the exchange of Won.

15. In reply, Colonel Solf stated that the U.S. armed forces would continue to take all appropriate administrative, disciplinary, and penal measures against those persons under their control and jurisdiction to prevent the illegal use of MPC. He added that the U.S. side expected the ROK Government to do the same. Mr. Whang stated that the Korean side did not wish to inconvenience the U.S. armed forces by limiting use of MPC to existing areas and facilities. However, the Korean side believed that some agreed procedures should be worked out for establishing MPC facilities at places such as tourist hotels so that the troops would not be inconvenienced. In this respect, he asked whether the U.S. side had any specific plans as to when and where such MPC facilities are to be established. Colonel Solf replied that the U.S. armed forces had no specific proposals in mind at this time. It is recognized, however,

0127

10-10

that at some future time it may be considered to be mutually advantageous to establish such facilities at locations to be mutually agreed to. The U.S. language is intended to provide the necessary flexibility for making such arrangements. The U.S. side agreed, of course, that any procedures of the kind proposed by the Korean side would have to be mutually acceptable.

16. Turning to paragraph 1(b) of the U.S. draft, Mr. Whang asked for clarification of the remarks made by Mr. Habib at a previous meeting regarding the phrase "to the extent authorized by United States law". Colonel Solf explained that, in a series of decisions affecting the jurisdiction of courst-martial, the United States Supreme Court had held that in time of peace civilians accused of crimes against the United States are liable solely to the jurisdiction of United States civil courts.

17. Mr. Whang asked what court had jurisdiction over such categories of persons as invited contractors or third-country nationals. In reply, Colonel Solf stated that U.S. citizens could be tried in U.S. civil courts. He pointed out that while the U.S. armed forces might not have court-martial jurisdiction over such persons, they still retained all administrative jurisdiction, including discharge, deprivation of access to facilities, and deprivation of privileges. Mr. Whang asked specifically if invited contractors would be subject to trial by court-martial. Colonel Solf replied that if they are civilians, they are not subject to trial by court-martial during time of peace. Mr. Whang stated that it

10-11

0128

appeared that there would be people authorized to use MPC who would not be liable to trial or punishment if they abused this privilege. Colonel Solf replied that the administrative sanctions at the disposal of the U.S. armed forces were quite effective in dealing with such abuses. He poihted out that the U.S. armed forces would retain administrative control over all such persons.

18. Mr. Whang then referred to the phrase in paragraph 1 (d) of the Korean draft which would state no obligation will be due to the Government of the Republic of Korea "after the date of coming into force of this agreement". He said that this phrase had been inserted in the Korean draft in order to obtain payment for the amount of MPC currently in the custody of the ROK Govarnment.

19. Mr. Ford replied that the redemption of this MPC impossible. He stated that there is no way in which the ROK Government can receive payment for MPC held by it. He pointed out that the wording of Paragraph 1(d) of the ROK draft provides specifically that there would be no obligation to the ROK Govarnment after the SOFA goes into effect; why then should there be any obligation before it goes into effect? Mr. Lee Chae Sul replied that a different situation exists in Korea than in any other country. He pointed out that the U.S. armed forces have been present in Korea since 1945 and that during this period a huge amount of MPC had been accumulated by the ROK Government. He said the ROK Government was anxious to dispose of this accumulation but that it felt a moral obligation to the Korean people who had

0123

10-12

earned it through sales or services to Americans. The thousands of Korean who had turned in the MPC should be reimbursed; otherwise they would be placed in the position of having rendered goods and services to the U.S. armed forces without compensation.

20. At this point, Mr. Ford read into the record the following statement:

"a. Military Payment Certificates are issued by the United States Government solely for internal use in United States military areas and facilities and such other places as may be agreed. MPC are issued for the use of persons authorized by the United States and such use is subject to the specific regulations of the United States Government.

"b. MPC are the property of the United States Government. MPC are not a currency of the United States and do not constitute a valid claim against the United States Government for redemption when in the possession of unauthorized holders.

"c. MPC are not convertible into dollars or dollar instruments, except by authorized holders in circumstances specified in United States Government regulations.

"d. MPC may be held temporarily in the possession of unauthorized persons or agencies in the following cases:

"1. Pending the return to an authorized person who was illegally deprived of possession of the MPC through loss or theft;

"2. During the time necessary for a law enforcement agency to hold the MPC in its possession for use in judicial proceedings;

"3. During the time necessary for a law enforcement agency to process seized MPC for return to the appropriate United States authority.

"e. Authorized holders of MPC may use them only in internal transactions to purchase approved goods and services from U.S. authorized sources, and such authorized holders may not use them for the purchase of goods and services except as I have indicated.

"f. Since MPC are issued by the United States Government for use by authorized persons for specific purposes, the use of MPC by unauthorized persons or for unauthorized purposes is not recognized by the United States Government.

"f. The MPC in the possession of any Korean Government agency should therefore be returned to the appropriate United States authorities. The Embassy has for some time been requesting the Korean Government to return the MPC confiscated by Korean law-enforcement agencies.

"h. In view of the special character of MPC and the fact that these requests have been made for their return, we do not consider this matter a subject for discussion in the context of these negotiations.

21. Turning to paragraph 2 of both drafts, Mr. Whang stated that since there did not appear to be any difference in language, the Korean side accepted the text of paragraph 2 of the U.S. draft. He pointed out that in the Korean draft, there appeared an additional sentence (as subparagraph (c)), which referred to the preceding sentences. Mr. Ford voiced the opinion that the sentence was unnecessary, inasmuch as mutual obligations on both governments appear in the text of paragraph 1. Mr. Whang replied that the sentence had been intended to refer only to paragraph 2. Mr. Ford said that the U.S. Side believed such a reference to be unnecessary, since it was implicit in the text of paragraph 2 that the U.S. Government would take whatever measures were necessary to ensure the implementation of the provisions of the pragraph. Mr. Whang stated that with that understanding, the Korean side withdrew the proposed subparagraph (c).

0131

10-14

22. Mr. Ford said that he wished to state for the record that nothing in the Foreign Exchange Controls Article or in the Military Payment Certificate Article is intended to preclude future discussions between the ROK and U.S. Governments concerning the possibility of the future substitution of U.S. coins or currency for MPC, should it appear desirable and feasible. Mr. Ford said he wished to make it clear, however, that no such discussions are presently contemplated.

23. Mr. Whang reminded the negotiators that the ROK side had proposed an Agreed Minute to the MPC Article, providing for disposal of MPC in the custody of the ROK Government at the time of entry into force of the SOFA, in accordance with mutually agreed upon procedures. Mr. Ford said the U.S. side thought that it had been agreed during the discussion just held that inasmuch as matter was currently being handled in other channels it was outside the scope of the SOFA negotiations. Mr. Whang suggested that the both sides discuss further this matter at the next meeting.

Definitions

24. Turning to the Definitions Article, Mr. Ford reminded the negotiators that they were very close to final agreement. With regard to the language of the proposed Agreement Minute #1 referring to subparagraph (a), Mr. Ford stated that the U.S. side was prepared to agree to the latest Korean proposal. However, the U.S. side now questioned the need for the Agreed Minute and proposed that the language of the subparagraph itself

be changed instead. Mr. Ford proposed that the Agreed Minute be deleted and that subparagraph (a) be altered by deleting the language following the words "except for" and inserting in its place the following language: "personnel of the U.S. armed forces attached to the U.S. Embassy and personnel for whom status has been provided in the Military Advisory Group Agreement of January 26, 1950, as amended". Mr. Whang said the Korean side agreed to this change and noted that full agreement had been reached on the text of the Definitions Article.

25. It was agreed to hold the next meeting on March 29, at 2 p.m.

26. Points of agreement: (U.S. draft Article I, as modified)
b Definitions Article (as revised).
a paragraph 2, MPC Article (U.S. draft Article XIX)

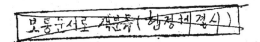

~~보통문서로 재분류(협정체결시)~~

보통문서로 재분류(1966. 12. 31.)

1964년 9월 30일 미주과장
직권으로 예고문 으로 재분류

4. 제18차 회의, 3. 29

0134

관리 번호 [crossed out]

기 안 용 지

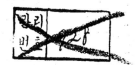

자체 통제		기안처	미주과 이경훈	전화번호	근거서류접수일자
	과장	국장	보좌관	차관	장관
관계관 서명	조약과장			기획조정관	
기안 년월일	63. 3. 28	시행 년월일		보존 년한	정서 기장
분류 기호	외정미	전체 통제		종결	
경유 수신 참조	건 의			발신	
제목	제18차 주둔군지위협정 체결교섭회의에 임할 우리측 ~~태도~~ 입장				

3월 29일에 개최될 제 18 차 주둔군 지위협정 체결 한미간 교섭 회의에서는 토지 및 시설, 군사우편 문제에 관하여 토의될 예정이온바, 이에관련하여 우리측 교섭실무자는 3월 27일 관계부처 실무자와 연석회합을 갖고 제 18 차회의에서 취할 우리측 태도를 별첨과같이 결정하였아오니 재가하여 주시기 바랍니다.

유첨 : 제18차 주둔군지위협정 체결 교섭회의에 임할 우리측태도,

끝

~~보통문서로 재분류 (협정체결시)~~

19 에 예고문에 의거 일반문서로 재분류됨 1966. 12. 31.

1964 년 9 월 30 일 미주과 직권으로 예고문 토지

승인양식 1-1-3 (1112-040-016-018) (190mm×260mm16절지)

0135

1. 토지 및 시설

(1) 토지 시설 관리등의 조치에관한 미국측 초안 (B)조 (1)항 (우리측 초안 10항)에 있어서 미국측 초안은 비상시 (In an emergency ......)에는 토지 시설 부근에 있어서도 보안 조치를 취할수 있도록 규정하고 있는데 이에대하여 우리측은 동문장 말미에 " within the extent that the Korean nationals and their properties are not unduly impaired " 라는 구절을 삽입토록 주장한다.

(2) 항해, 항공, 통신문제에 관하여 (가) 이문제에 관한 미국측 초안 B조 2(a) 및 (b)항은 우리측 초안 11항에 해당하는바 양측초안은 실질적인 큰차이가 없음으로 미국측 초안을 수락해주되 다만 2(b)항에 있는 "designated military communications authorities"라는 구절에 대하여는 현재 미 8군과의 체신관계의 주요연락사무는 우리나라 체신부에서 행하고 있으며 또한 미군에게 부여한 주파수등에 대하여는 우리정부가 국제 주파수 등록위원회에 통고하도록 되어있는 점등을 고려하여 미국측안과 같이 군당국으로 제한할것이 아니라 보다 포괄적인 용어로서 "appropriate authorities" 나, "designated communications authorities" 로 하든지 그렇지않으면 "designated military and other communications authorities"로 규정할것을 제시하고 (나) 미국측 초안 B조 2(c)항은우리측 초안에는 없으나 미국측 초안에서 "한국의 관계법률, 규정, 협정의 범위내에서" 한국정부는 미국 군대내의통신 시설에 대한 관여를 피하고 제거할 모든 정당한 조치를 취하도록 규정하고 있으므로 이도 수락토록 한다.

0136

14-2

(3) 공공안전의 존중에 관한 미국측 초안 B조 3항 (우리측 초안 12항)은 우리측 초안과 같음으로 수락토록 한다.

(4) 원상회복 문제에관한 미국측 초안 C 조 1항 (우리측 초안 13항)에 있어서 우리초안은 원측적으로 미군이 원상회복 의무를 면제하고 단지 사유재산으로서 미군의 사용으로 막심한 파손을 당한 재산에 대하여 우리정부의 요청에 의하여 미국측이 원상회복 또는 이에 대신하는 보상에 관하여 충분한 고려를 하도록 규정하고 있는데 미국측 초안에 있어서는 이에 관한 규정을두고 있지않으니 만일 미측이 사유 재산에 대한 일반 보상에관한 조항을 수락할 경우에는 과잉 보상을 요구하는 결과가 될것임으로 일반 보상에 응하는한 우리측은 본 조항에 있어서 미국측에 양보하기로 한다.

(5) 가동설비 소유권 및 처분문제에 관한 미국측 초안 C조 2항은 우리측 초안에는 규정되어있지 않는바 이는 실제문제에 있어서 인정될 사실의 확인이라고도 볼수있으나 동항에 있어서 "will remain the property of the United States Government"라는 구절은 토지시설 개량에대한 보상 의무 면제에관한 우리측 초안 14항 특히 "supply or any other materials left thereon" 이라는 구절과 모순되는것이니 "will remain the property of the United States Government and" 라는 구절은 삭제하고 미국측 초안 C조 2항을 수락하도록 한다.

(6) 토지시설 개량에대한 보상의무 면제에관한 우리측 초안 14항은 미국측 초안에서는 규정하고 있지 않는것으로 이는 토지시설의 반환시에 당해 시설 및 구역에 과하여진 개량 또는 그곳에

16-3

0137

남겨진 건물, 공작물, 공급품 또는 기타의 물자에 대하여 한국 정부는 미국측에 보상하지 않는다라는 규정인바, 이러한 명시적인 규정은 필요함으로 우리측 안의 수락을 요구한다. 본항은 미국측 초안 C조 1항 다음에 2항으로서 삽입 토록 제의한다. 따라서 미국측 2항은 3항이되고 3항은 4항이 될것이다.

(7) 특수시설 건축에 대한 예외규정에 관한 미국측 초안 C 조 3항의 규정은 우리측 초안에는 없으나 기타 특별한 협약은 우리 정부가 인정할것임으로 받아 드리도록 한다.

(8) 토지 시설 유지비에관한 미국측 초안 D 조 1항에 있어서 "except those to be borne by the Republic of Korea as provided in paragraph 2 " 라는 규정을 하고 있는것은 미국측은 보상을 하지않겠다는 원측의 입장에서 우리측이 부담하는 것을 전제하고 규정한것이기 때문에 우리측은 이를 삭제토록 요구한다.

(9) 토지 시설 보상문제에 관한 미국측 초안 D 조 2항 (우리측 초안 4항)에 있어서 양측안은 근본적 차이점을 시현하고 있는데 우리측은 사유재산의 사용에대한 미국측의 보상지불을 요구하고 있는데 대하여 미국측은 이를 한국측이 하도록 규정하고 있는점과 미국측 초안D 조 2항 후단은 특히 미군이 사용하는 토지 시설에 관련하여 제 3 자 (민간인)에 의하여 야기될지도모를 청구권으로부터 해를 받지않도록 한국정부가 책임질것을 규정함으로 보상문제에관한 양국측이 근본적인 대립을 보이고 있다. 우리측은 우리안의 수락을 요구토록 한다.

14-4

0138

2. 군사 우편

(1) 미국은 미국군대 구성원, 군속 및 그들의 가족의 사용을위하여 미국군사 우편국을 대한민국내 미국 군사우편국간 및 이러한 군사 우편국과 기타 미국 우편국간의 우편물의 송달을 위하여 미국군대가 사용하고 있는 시설 및 토지내에 설치하고 운영할수있다라는 요지의 우리측 초안을 제시토록 한다. (별첨참조)

(2) 미국측이 제시하는 안이 우리측초안과 비등할때에는 이를 수락토록 한다.

14-5

0139

ARTICLE ___

The United States may establish and operate, within the facilities and areas in use by the United States armed forces, United States military post offices for the use of members of the United States armed forces, the civilian component, and their dependents, for the transmission of mail betwen United States military post offices in the Republic of Korea and between such military post offices and other United States post offices.

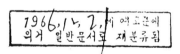

1966. 12. 31.

1966, 12. 31. 에 예고문에 의거 일반문서로 재분류됨

16-6

0140

관리 번호	929

기 안 용 지

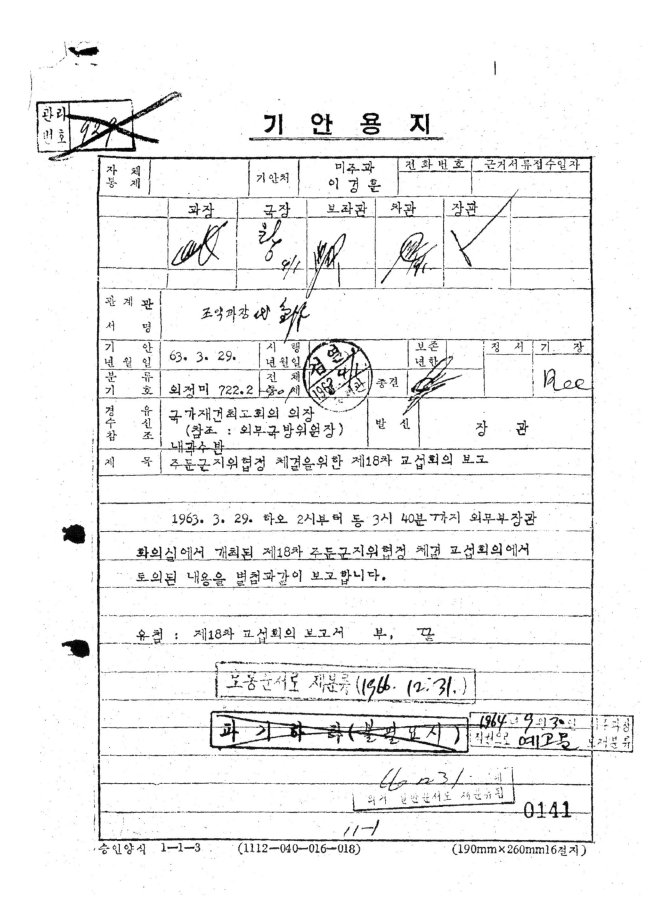

자 체 통 제		기안처	미주과 이경훈	전화번호	근거서류접수일자
	과장	국장	보좌관	차관	장관
관계관 서명	조약과장				
기안 년월일	63. 3. 29.	시행 년월일		보존 년한	정서 / 기장
분류 기호	외정미 722.2	전체 통제		종결	
경유 수신 참조	국가재건최고회의 의장 (참조 : 외무국방위원장) 내각수반		발신	장관	
제목	주둔군지위협정 체결을위한 제18차 교섭회의 보고				

1963. 3. 29. 하오 2시부터 동 3시 40분까지 외무부장관 회의실에서 개최된 제18차 주둔군지위협정 체결 교섭회의에서 토의된 내용을 별첨과같이 보고합니다.

유첨 : 제18차 교섭회의 보고서 부, 끝

보통문서로 재분류(1966. 12. 31.)

~~파기하라(불필요시)~~

1964년 9월 30일 미주과장 직권으로 예고문 보기분류

66. 12. 31. 에 외거 일반문서로 재분류됨

0141

11-1

승인양식 1-1-3 (1112-040-016-018) (190mm×260mm16절지)

외 무 부

외정미 722.2 1963. 4. 1.

수 신 국가재건최고회의 의장

참 조 외무국방위원장

제 목 주둔군지위협정 체결을위한 제18차 교섭회의 보고

1963. 3. 29. 하오 2시부터 동 3시 40분까지 외무부 장관 회의실에서 개최된 제18차 주둔군지위협정 체결 교섭회의에서 토의된 내용을 별첨과같이 보고합니다.

유첨 : 제18차 교섭회의 보고서 2부. 끝

외 무 부 장 관 김 용 식

0142

11-7

외 무 부

외정미 722.2 1963. 4. 1.

수 신 내각수반

제 목 주둔군지위협정 체결을위한 제18차 교섭회의 보고

1963. 3. 29. 하오 2시부터 동 3시 40분까지 외무부장관 회의실에서 개최된 제18차 주둔군지위협정 체결 교섭회의에서 토의된 내용을 별첨과같이 보고합니다.

유첨 : 제18차 교섭회의 보고서 1부, 끝

외 무 부 장 관 김 용 식

0143

11-8

제 18 차

한미간 주둔군지위협정 체결 실무자회의

보 고 서

1. 시 일 : 1963. 3. 29. 하오 2시부터 3시 40분까지

2. 장 소 : 외무부장관 회의실

3. 참석자 : 한국측 : 황호을 (외무부 정무국장)

구충회 (외무부 미주과장)

이남구 (국방부 군무과장)

주문기 (법무부 법무과장)

박봉진 (재무부 관세과장)

이경훈 (외무부 2등서기관)

강석재 (외무부 3등서기관)

김윤택 (")

미국측 : "하비브" 참사관 및 "오코나" 대령을 제외한 교섭대표단 전원

4. 토의사항 : 63-1-65

(1) 군사우편 그리고 토지 및 시설문제를 순차적으로 토의함.

(2) 한미 양측은 군사우편문제에 관한 조문을 교환한후 우리측은 양측초안에 있어서의 차이점을 지적하면서 우리측 초안에 없는 미국측 초안의 규정 즉 "미국 군사우편국은 통상 해외에서 그러한 특권이 부여되고 있는 미국정부의 기타관리 및 직원과 그들의 가족에 의하여 사용될수 있다" 라는 추가적 항에 대하여 "미국정부의 기타관리 및 직원" 이란 무엇을 의미하는가라고 문의하자, 미국측은 이는 광범한것으로 미국의 각부처 또는 독립기관의 직원, 퇴역군인으로서 미국

0144

11-2

63-1-10 (

대국89-8 (5)

0144-1

기관에 종사하는 자, 군해상 수송의 선원, 미국 적십자사 요원 및 그들의 가족등을 말한다고 답변하였음.

이에대하여 우리측은 주한봉사단체도 이에 포함되느냐 라고 문의하자 미국측은 이들은 포함되지 않으며 따라서 행정협정 발효후에는 군사우편의 사용이 불가능하다고 말하였음.

(3) 토지시설 관리등의 조치에관한 규정에 있어서 미국측은 그의 초안에서 비상시에는 토지 시설부근에 있어서도 보안조치를 취할수있도록 규정하고 있는데 이에대하여 우리측은 이러한 비상시의 보안조치는 "한국국민과 그들의 재산이 부당하게 해를받지 않는 범위내에서" 취할수 있도록 하자는 추가적 구절을 제의하자 미국측은 이를 고려하겠다고 하여 이문제는 다음에 다시 토의키로 합.

63-1-66

(4) 항해, 항공, 통신문제에 관한 미국측 초안 B 조 2항은 우리측 초안 11항에 해당하는바 동항에 있어서 우리측은 미국측 초안에서 원거리 통신에 관한 모든문제는 양국정부의 "지정된 군사통신 당국" 간의 협약에 의하여 해결한다라는 요지의 규정을 한데대하여 우리측은 주한 미국당국과 통신문제에 관한 협력사무는 우리나라체신부가 주로 취급하고 있으므로 "지정된 군사통신 당국" 이라는 용어는 너무나 제한적이라고 말하자 미국측은 그러면 "군사"라는 용어를 삭제하고 "지정된 통신 당국"으로 변경하면 한국측 요구에 충당할것이 아니냐고 제의하였기 우리측은 이를 수락하여 항해, 항공, 통신문제에 관한 미국측 초안 2항에 대하여 쌍방간에 합의에 도달함.

(5) 공용안전의 존중에관한 미국측 초안 B 조 3항은 우리측 초안 12항과 같음으로 이조항에 대하여도 합의에 도달함.

0145

11-3

미원 89-8

0145-1

(6) 원상회복 문제에관한 규정에 있어서 우리측 초안은 원칙적으로 미군이 원상회복 의무를 면제하고 단지 사유재산으로서 미군의 사용으로 막심한 파손을 당한 재산에 대하여 우리정부의 요청에 의하여미국측이 원상회복 또는 이에대신하는 보상에관하여 충분한 고려를하도록 규정하고 있는데 미국측 초안에는 이에관한 규정을 두고있지 않아 이문제는 다음에 다시토의키로 함.

(7) 미국측 초안에서만 규정하고있는 가동설비 소유권 및 처분 문제는 다음에 다시토의키로 하고 또한 토지시설 개량에대한 보상의무 면제에관한 규정은 우리측 초안에만 규정되어 있었는데 이에관하여 미국측은 우리측안에 대한 수정안을 제시하였기 이문제도 또한 다음에 다시 토의키로 함.

(8) 한미간의 특별협약에 의거하여 설치된 건물은 원상회복, 가동설비 처분 및 토지시설 개량에대한 보상의무 면제 등의 규정에 적용을 받지않는다 라는 미국측 초안 C 조 3항은 합의에 도달함.

5. 기타 사항 :

(1) 차기회의 일자 : 1963. 4.11. 하오 2시

(2) 차기회의 의제 : 차기회의까지 양측수석 대표간에 합의된 사항

6. 참고자료 : 미국측이 제의한 조약문 초안 (군사우편 및 토지시설 반환에관한 미국측 대안)

63-1-67

보통문서로 재분류(1966. 12.31.)

1966.4.3 0에 예고문에 의거 일반문서로 재분류됨

0146

11-4

63-1-10

外務 84-8

0146-1

ARTICLE

MILITARY POST OFFICES

1. The United States may establish and operate, within the facilities and areas in use by the U.S. armed forces, United States military post offices for the use of members of the United States armed forces, the civilian component, and their dependents, for the transmission of mail between United States military post offices in Korea and between such military post offices and other United States post offices.

2. United States military post offices may be used by other officers and personnel of the United States Government, and their dependents, ordinarily accorded such privileges abroad.

63-1-68

0147

CONFIDENTIAL

11-5

63-1-10

미용 89-8

0148

0120

AREAS AND FACILITIES ARTICLE

PROPOSED ADDITIONAL PARAGRAPH TO AREAS AND FACILITIES ARTICLE PERTAINING TO RETURN OF FACILITIES AND AREAS

The Republic of Korea is not obligated to compensate the United States for improvements made in United States facilities and areas or for the buildings or structures remaining thereon upon the return of the facilities and areas.

63-1-61

0143

63-1-10

0150

Military Post Offices

1. Mr. Lewis began the substantive discussion by tabling the U.S. draft of the article dealing with Military Post Offices. He stated that a military post office is numerically designated as a branch of a United States Post Office and is activated, manned, and operated by military authorities to provide postal services to authorized organizations and personnel. He pointed out that the U.S. draft article provides for the establishment and operation of military post offices in Korea, for the transmission of mail between these facilities and other U.S. post offices, and for the furnishing of related financial services. Following Mr. Lewis' opening remarks, the Korean side tabled its draft of this article.

2. After a period of comparison of the two drafts, Mr. Whang stated that paragraph 1 in both drafts was identical, except for the use of the word "Korea" in the U.S. draft and the term "Republic of Korea" in the Korean draft. He urged the U.S. side to agree to the latter wording. Mr. Lewis replied that this created a small technical problem for the U.S. side in that approval for the change would have to be sought from Washington. He agreed that the U.S. side would take the Korean language under consideration.

3. Mr. Whang asked for clarification of the scope of paragraph 2 of the U.S. draft. He said the Korean side would like to know who was included in the term "other officers and personnel of the United States Government, and their dependents, ordinarily accorded such privileges abroad." Mr. Lewis replied that this term included such persons as U.S. Embassy personnel, retired military personnel, civilian crews of Military Sea Transport Service ships bringing supplies to the U.S. armed forces in Korea, American Red Cross personnel (who are members of the civilian component), and the dependents of these persons. He said this was an illustrative listing and should not be considered to be exhaustive or all-inclusive.

0151

4. Mr. Whang asked whether relief organizations, such as KAVA and CARE, or religious organizations would be included. Mr. Lewis replied that personnel of such organizations would not be authorized the use of MPO facilities when the SOFA came into force.

5. Mr. Whang stated that the SOFA was intended to provide solely for members of the armed forces, the civilian component, and their dependents. However, from Mr. Lewis' remarks, it appeared that many other persons would be authorized to use the MPO facilities. Therefore, he said, the Korean side would study the U.S. draft and consult with other agencies of the ROK Government before expressing any views.

6. Mr. Lewis called the attention of the Korean side to the fact that language similar to that in the U.S. draft was a commonly-accepted provision in other Status of Forces Agreements. He urged the Korean side to study ~~some of the~~ Status of Forces Agreements now in force, particularly that between the U.S. Government and the Government of Japan, in which this provision appears as an Agreed Minute. Mr. Whang replied that the Korean side understood and wished to study the matter further in order to ascertain whether the proposed language was in conflict with any current Korean laws or regulations, in which case either the proposed language or the laws and regulations might have to be ~~amended~~ changed.

Facilities and Areas

7. Turning to the draft articles relating to facilities and areas, Lt. Col. Miller reminded the negotiators that at a previous meeting they had already discussed the U.S. draft article "A". He suggested that discussion ~~proceed with regard to~~ begin on draft article "B", corresponding to paragraphs 10, 11, and 12 of the Korean draft article.

8. Mr. Whang stated that there were two points of difference between paragraph 1 of the U.S. draft and paragraph 10 of the Korean draft. The first

0152

was the second sentence of the U.S. draft, reading "In an emergency, measures necessary for their safeguarding and control may also be taken in the vicinity thereof". The second was the use in the [third sentence of the] U.S. draft of the phrase "United States armed forces" whereas the phrase used in the Korean draft was "Government of the United States". With regard to the first point, [he said,] the Korean side would prefer to cover the question of emergency measures in an Agreed Minute. ~~He continued that~~ [However, the Korean side would not object to retaining] ~~if the U.S. side wished to retain~~ the sentence in the text of the Agreement. [Then he] ~~The Korean side~~ proposed the addition of the following words to the second sentence of paragraph 1 of the U.S. draft: "within the extent that Korean nationals and their property are not unduly impaired". With regard to the second point of difference, Mr. Whang said any request based on this provision would be made to the Government of the ROK. Therefore, for the sake of balance, the party making the request should be identified in the language of the Agreement as the Government of the United States. He said the Korean side understood that the request would be made, in actual fact, by the U.S. armed forces but the language proposed by the Korean side would be preferable in the Agreement.

9. Replying [first] to the second point made by Mr. Whang, Lt. Col. Miller [pointed out] that the term "Government of the United States" appeared three times in paragraph 10 of the Korean draft. He said the nature of the government to government relationship was well spelled out in the Joint Committee Article, which establishes the Joint Committee as the focal point of consultation between the two governments. He called [the] attention of the negotiators to the sentence in the Joint Committee Article which reads "In particular, the Joint Committee shall serve as the means for consultation in determining the facilities and areas in the Republic of Korea which are required for the use of the United States in carrying out the purposes of this Agreement". He said this made it clear that relations on a government to government basis were to be conducted through the Joint Committee. In actual practice, any request would probably originate with the U.S. armed forces [and] be

0153

passed by them to the U.S. component of the Joint Committee, which in turn would take it up with the Korean component. The request would then become a government to government matter. Lt. Col. Miller said the language of the U.S. draft makes this process clear and avoids repetition of the term "Government of the United States". However, the U.S. side would take under consideration the position of the Korean side.

10. General Lawlor asked the Korean side to whom it referred when it used the term "Government of the United States", if not to the U.S. armed forces. Mr. Whang replied that the SOFA would be concluded between the two governments. The United States, as one of the parties to the Agreement, obviously would be represented primarily by the U.S. armed forces. But the Korean side believed that the text of the Agreement in this instance should reflect the government to government relationship. In response to General Lawlor's further inquiry, Mr. Whang stated that the term "Government of the United States" in this context was not intended by the Korean side to be limited to the U.S. Embassy or any other US Government agency. He confirmed that the difference between the two drafts was one of language rather than substance.

11. Reverting to Mr. Whang's first point, Lt. Col. Miller said that the U.S. side preferred to have language regarding emergency actions incorporated in the body of the text rather than in an Agreed Minute. He pointed out that the situation in Korea was unique in that the armed forces are constantly in a state of readiness against the resumption of hostilities. With regard to an emergency, no one knows in advance what measures might be necessary. One of the principal problems, however, would be subversive activities and attempts to infiltrate. He assured the Korean side that if the U.S. armed forces were obliged to take emergency measures, they would hold property damage to an absolute minimum. He said the additional language suggested by the Korean side was implicit in the U.S. language. However, the U.S. side would take the Korean proposal under consideration.

12. Mr. Whang stated that the Korean side was

sure that in the event of an emergency the U.S. armed forces would take all measures necessary to safeguard Korean property. This being the case, the Korean side did not see why the U.S. side should object to the proposed additional language. Lt. Colonel Miller replied that the U.S. draft called for all measures "necessary". This would include everything covered by the language proposed by the Korean side. He pointed out that the word "necessary" placed limits on the actions which could be taken by the U.S. armed forces, since they would be authorized to take only those actions which are actually necessary and not all actions which they might think desirable.

13. Turning to paragraph 2, Mr. Whang stated that inasmuch as there was no substantive difference between subparagraph (a) of the U.S. draft and the first sentence of paragraph 11 of the Korean draft, the Korean side accepted the text of subparagraph (a) of the U.S. draft, with the proviso that the difference between "United States" and "Government of the United States" be resolved at a later date.

14. With regard to subparagraph (b), Mr. Whang stated that the Korean side agreed with the U.S. draft, except for the phrase "designated military communications authorities". He pointed out that the relevant competent authority of the ROK Government was the Ministry of Communications, not the Korean military establishment. Lt. Colonel Miller replied that the U.S. side was willing to delete the word "military". The phrase "designated communications authorities" would more accurately describe the actual situation, he said. Mr. Whang said that because of the highly classified and technical nature of the subject, the Korean side was willing to accept the text of subparagraph (b) of the U.S. draft, with the word "military" deleted.

15. Mr. Whang recalled that at the 11th meeting, Mr. Habib, with reference to subparagraph (c) of the U.S. draft, had stated that one of the agreements envisioned under the terms of this subparagraph would provide for notification by

0155

~~by~~ the [redacted] United States to the International Frequency Registration Board of frequencies used in Korea by the U.S. armed forces. ~~He~~ Mr. Whang said that according to Resolution No. 5 ~~the fifth resolution~~ adopted by the Administrative Radio Conference ~~held~~ of the ITU held ~~International Telecommunication Union~~ at ~~its~~ Geneva in 1959 ~~1959 conference in Genoa~~, the host country should notify the IFRB. Lt. Colonel Miller stated that [redacted] the U.S. side was referring only to frequencies used by the U.S. armed forces. He said [redacted] the U.S. forces were currently notifying the IFRB of these frequencies and what the U.S. side had in mind was merely a continuation of the present practice, which apparently is acceptable to the IFRB. Mr. Whang replied that the ROK Government is a member of the ITU and the ITU had adopted the resolution to which he had referred. Therefore, it was appropriate that the ROK Government do the notifying from now on.

16. The U.S. side agreed to look into this matter further. Lt. Colonel Miller stated that the question of who should notify the IFRB of frequencies in use did not affect the agreement of both sides on the language of subparagraph (b) of the U.S. draft. Mr. Whang said that was correct and stated that the Korean side had agreed to subparagraphs (a) and (b) of paragraph 2 of the U.S. draft.

17. Turning to subparagraph (c) of the U.S. draft, Mr. Whang pointed out that no similar paragraph appeared in the Korean draft. He said the Korean side had no objection in principle to the subparagraph but wished to hear any further comment which the U.S. side might wish to make. Lt. Colonel Miller replied that the U.S. side believed that both [redacted] parties to the SOFA would have obligations under the provisions of this article. Subparagraph (c) had been inserted in the U.S. draft as a counterbalance to subparagraph (a). The latter subparagraph spells out the obligations of the United States Government and subparagraph (c) would spell out the obligations of the ROK Government. Mr. Whang stated that inasmuch as both sides were already cooperating "in the utmost spirit of coordination and cooperation", as stated in subparagraph (b), the Korean side agreed to the text of subparagraph (c) of paragraph 2 of the U.S. draft.

0156

18. Mr. Whang stated that since paragraph 3 of the U.S. draft and paragraph 12 of the Korean draft were identical, the Korean side agreed to the text of the U.S. draft.

Article "C"

19. Turning to Article "C" of the U.S. draft, Mr. Whang noted that paragraph 1 was practically identical with the first sentence of paragraph 13 of the Korean draft, the only difference being the use of "United States" in one and "Government of the United States" in the other. With the proviso that this conflict of language be resolved at a later date, he said the Korean side agreed to the text of paragraph 1 of the U.S. draft.

20. Mr. Whang suggested that discussion on the remainder of paragraph 13 of the Korean draft be deferred until a later date. He said that the views of both sides on this subject had already been fully exchanged and it was unlikely that agreement could be reached on the working level.

21. With regard to paragraph 14 of the Korean draft, Mr. Whang recalled that the U.S. side had stated that the phrase "supply or other materials left thereon" was unnecessary. He pointed out that this paragraph correlated with paragraph 2 of the U.S. draft. In explanation of the phrase in question, he said that there was no ~~xxxxxxxxxxxxxxxx~~ question ~~but~~ about the fact that equipment brought into Korea by the U.S. armed forces is the property of the U.S. armed forces and can be removed from Korea by those forces. However, the Korean side wished to point out that after a particular facility has been returned to the ROK Government by the U.S. armed forces, the ROK Government must not be held responsible for the protection of any U.S.-owned supplies or materials temporarily left at the facility.

22. In reply, Lt. Colonel Miller stated that a Property Disposal Agreement already exists, which provides for disposition of equipment, supplies, or materials which the U.S. forces do not wish to remove from Korea. He suggested that this question

0157

be discussed elsewhere since the U.S. side did not believe it relevant to the facilities and areas articles.

23. Turning to paragraph 3 of the U.S. draft, Mr. Whang asked for an explanation of the special arrangements referred to therein. Lt. Colonel Miller explained that this paragraph provides the authority for construction outside the terms of paragraphs 1 and 2. He said this authority would be utilized only in the case of a special situation in which both governments agreed that the provisions of paragaraphs 1 and 2 would not apply. In response to a query by Mr. Whang, he said that no such construction is contemplated at the present time. In the future, any such construction could be carried out only by mutual agreement. Mr. Whang stated that since the terms of the paragraph would apply only after mutual agreement of the two governments, the Korean side agreed to the text of paragraph 3 of the U.S. draft.

24. Mr. Whang stated that the Korean side proposed that paragraph 14 of the Korean draft be inserted between the present paragraphs 1 and 2 of the U.S. draft. Lt. Colonel Miller then stated that the U.S. side wished to suggest alternative language to paragraph 14. He tabled the following proposed paragraph:

> "The Republic of Korea is not obligated to compensate the United States for improvements made in United States facilities and areas or for the buildings or structures remaining thereon upon the return of the facilities and areas."

Mr. Whang stated that the Korean side would take this proposal under consideration.

25. Before adjourning the meeting, Mr. Whang introduced Mr. Park Bong Hin, Chief of the Customs Duties Section of the Ministry of Finance, who attended the meeting on behalf of Mr. Shin Kwan Sup.

26. It was agreed to hold the next meeting on April 11 at 2 p.m.

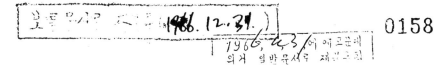

관리 번호 932

JOINT SUMMARY RECORD OF THE 18TH SESSION
STATUS FORCES NEGOTIATIONS

March 29, 1963

I. Time and Place : 2:00 to 3:40 p.m. March 29, 1963 at the Foreign Minister's Conference Room

II. Attendants:

ROK Side:

Mr. Whang, Ho Eul	Director Bureau of Political Affairs Ministry of Foreign Affairs
Mr. Koo, Choong Whay	Chief, America Section Ministry of Foreign Affairs
Col. Lee, Nam Koo	Chief, Military Affairs Section Ministry of National Defense
Mr. Chu, Mun Ki	Chief, Legal Affairs Section Ministry of Justice
Mr. Park, Bong Jin	Chief of the Customs Section Ministry of Finance
Mr. Lee, Kyung Hoon	2nd Secretary Ministry of Foreign Affairs
Mr. Kang, Suk Jae	3rd Secretary Ministry of Foreign Affairs
Mr. Kim, Yoon Taik	3rd Secretary Ministry of Foreign Affairs

U.S. Side:

Brig. Gen. J.D. Lawlor	Deputy Chief of Staff 8th Army
Mr. William J. Ford	First Secretary of the Embassy
Capt. R.M. Brownlie	Assistant Chief of Staff USN/K

미주과	안 고 재	담 당	과 장	국 장	특별보좌관	차 관	장 관

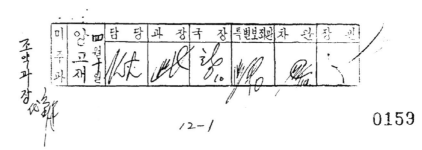

조약과장

12-1

0159

Col. W.A. Solf	Staff Judge Advocate 8th Army
Mr. Benjamin A. Fleck (Rapporteur and Press Officer)	First Secretary of the Embassy
Mr. Robert A. Lewis	Second Secretary and Consul of the Embassy
Lt. Col. R.E. Miller	Staff Officer, JAG 8th Army
Lt. Col. W.A. Burt	J-5

Military Post Offices

1. Mr. Lewis began the substantive discussion by tabling the U.S. draft of the article dealing with Military Post Offices. He stated that a military post office is numerically designated as a branch of a United States Post Office and is activated, manned, and operated by military authorities to provide postal services to authorized organizations and personnel. He pointed out that the U.S. draft article provides for the establishment and operation of military post offices in Korea, for the transmission of mail between these facilities and other U.S. post offices, and for the furnishing of related financial services. Following Mr. Lewis' opening remarks, the Korean side tabled its draft of this article.

2. After a period of comparison of the two drafts, Mr. Whang stated that paragraph 1 in both drafts was identical, except for the use of the word "Korea" in the U.S. draft and the term "Republic of Korea" in the Korean draft. He urged the U.S. side to agree to the

0160

12-2

latter wording. Mr. Lewis replied that this created a small technical problem for the U.S. side in that approval for the change would have to be sought from Washington. He agreed that the U.S. side would take the Korean language under consideration.

3. Mr. Whang asked for clarification of the scope of paragraph 2 of the U.S. draft. He said the Korean side would like to know who was included in the term "other officers and personnel of the United States Government, and their dependents, ordinarily accorded such privileges abroad". Mr. Lewis replied that this term included such persons as U.S. Embassy personnel, retired military personnel, civilian crews of Military Sea Transport Service ships bringing supplies to the U.S. armed forces in Korea, American Red Cross personnel (who are members of the civilian component), and the dependents of these persons. He said this was an illustrative listing and should not be considered to be exhaustive or all-in-clusive.

4. Mr. Whang asked whether relief organizations, such as KAVA and CARE, or religious organizations would be included. Mr. Lewis replied that personnel of such organizations would not be authorized the use of MPO facilities when the SOFA came into force.

5. Mr. Whang stated that the SOFA was intended to provide solely for members of the armed forces, the civilian component, and their dependents. However, from Mr. Lewis' remarks, it appeared that many other persons would be authorized to use the

0161

12-3

MPO facilities. Therefore, he said, the Korean side would study the U.S. draft and consult with other agencies of the ROK Government before expressing any views.

6. Mr. Lewis called the attention of the Korean side to the fact that language similar to that in the U.S. draft was a commenly-accepted provision in other Status of Forces Agreements. He urged the Korean side to study some of the Status of Forces Agreements now in force, particularly that between the U.S. Government and the Government of Japan, in which this provision appears as an Agreed Minute. Mr. Whang replied that the Korean side understood and wished to study the matter further in order to ascertain whether the proposed language was in conflict with any current Korean laws or regulations, in which case either the proposed language or the laws and regulations might have to be changed.

Facilities and Areas

7. Turning to the draft articles relating to facilities and areas, Lt. Col. Miller reminded the negotiators that at a previous meeting they had already discussed the U.S. draft article "A". He suggested that discussion begin on draft article "B", corresponding to paragraphs 10, 11, and 12 of the Korean draft article.

0162

12-4

8. Mr. Whang stated that there were two points of difference between paragraph 1 of the U.S. draft and paragraph 10 of the Korean draft. The first was the second sentence of the U.S. draft, reading "In an emergency, measures necessary for their safeguarding and control may also be taken in the vicinity thereof". The second was the use in the third sentence of the U.S. draft of the phrase "United States armed forces" whereas the phrase used in the Korean draft was "Government of the United States". With regard to the first point, he said the Korean side would prefer to cover the question of emergency measures in an Agreed Minute. However, the Korean side would not object to retaining the sentence in the text of the Agreement. Then he proposed the addition of the following words to the second sentence of paragraph 1 of the U.S. draft: "within the extent that Korean nationals and their property are not unduly impaired". With regard to the second point of difference, Mr. Whang said any request based on this provision would be made to the Government of the ROK. Therefore, for the sake of balance, the party making the request should be identified in the language of the Agreement as the Government of the United States. He said the Korean side understood that the request would be made, in actual fact, by the U.S. armed forces but the language proposed by the Korean side would be preferable in the Agreement.

9. Replying first to the second point made by Mr. Whang, Lt. Col. Miller pointed out that the term "Government of the United States" appeared three

0163

12-5

times in paragraph 10 of the Korean draft. He said the nature of the government to government relationship was well spelled out in the Joint Committee Article, which established the Joint Committee as the focal point of consultation between the two governments. He called the attention of the negotiators to the sentence in the Joint Committee Article which reads "In particular, the Joint Committee shall serve as the means for consultation in determining the facilities and areas in the Republic of Korea which are required for the use of the United States in carrying out the purposes of this Agreement". He said this made it clear that relations on a government to government basis were to be conducted through the Joint Committee. In actual practice, any request would probably originate with the U.S. armed forces and be passed by them to the U.S. component of the Joint Committee, which in turn would take it up with the Korean component. The request would then become a government to government matter. Lt. Col, Miller said the language of the U.S. draft makes this process clear and avoids repetition of the term "Government of the United States". However, the U.S. side would take under consideration the position of the Korean side.

10. General Lawlor asked the Korean side to whom it referred when it used the term "Government of the United States", if not to the U.S. armed forces.

Mr. Whang replied that the SOFA would be concluded between the two governments. The United States, as one of the parties to the Agreement, obviously would be represented primarily by the U.S. armed forces. But the Korean side believed that the text of the Agreement in this instance should reflect the government to government relationship. In response to General Lawlor's further inquiry, Mr. Whang stated that the term "Government of the United States" in this context was not intended by the Korean side to be limitted to the U.S. Embassy or any other US Government agency. He confirmed that the difference between the two drafts was one of language rather than substance.

11. Reverting to Mr. Whang's first point, Lt. Col. Miller said that the U.S. side preferred to have language regarding emergency actions incorporated in the body of the text rather than in an Agreed Minute. He pointed out that the situation in Korea was unique in that the armed forces are constantly in a state of readiness against the resumption of hostilities. With regard to an emergency, no one knows in advance what measures might be necessary. One of the principal problems, however, would be subversive activities and attempts to infiltrate. He assured the Korean side that if the U.S. armed forces were obliged to take emergency measures, they would hold property damage to an absolute minimum. He said the additional language suggested by the Korean side was implicit in the U.S. language. However, the U.S. side would take the Korean proposal under consideration.

0165

12-7

12. Mr. Whang stated that the Korean side was sure that in the event of an emergency the U.S. armed forces would take all measures necessary to safeguard Korean property. This being the case, the Korean side did not see why the U.S. side should object to the proposed additional language. Lt. Colonel Miller replied that the U.S. draft called for all measures "necessary". This would include everything covered by the language proposed by the Korean side. He pointed out that the word "necessary" placed limits on the actions which could be taken by the U.S. armed forces, since they would be authorized to take only those actions which are actually necessary and not all actions which they might think desirable.

13. Turning to paragraph 2, Mr. Whang stated that inasmuch as there was no substantive difference between subparagraph (a) of the U.S. draft and the first sentence of paragraph 11 of the Korean draft, the Korean side accepted the text of subparagraph (a) of the U.S. draft, with the proviso that the difference between "United States" and "Government of the United States" be resolved at a later date.

14. With regard to subparagraph (b), Mr. Whang stated that the Korean side agreed with the U.S. draft, except for the phrase "designated military communications authorities". He pointed out that the relevant competent authority of the ROK Government was the Ministry of Communications, not the Korean military establishment.

0166

12-8

Lt. Colonel Miller replied that the U.S. side was willing to delete the word "military". The phrase "designated communications authorities" would more accurately describe the actual situation, he said. Mr. Whang said that because of the highly classified and technical nature of the subject, the Korean side was willing to accept the text of subparagraph (b) of the U.S. draft, with the word "military" deleted.

15. Mr. Whang recalled that at the 11th meeting, Mr. Habib, with reference to subparagraph (c) of the U.S. draft, had stated that one of the agreement envisioned under the terms of this subparagraph would provide for notification by the United States to the
frequencies used in Korea by the U.S. armed forces. Mr. Whang said that according to
International Frequency Registration Board of Resolution No. 5 adopted by the Administrative Radio Conference of the ITU held at Geneva in 1959, the host country shoult notify the IFRB. Lt. Colonel Miller stated that the U.S. side was referring only to frequencies used by the U.S. armed forces. He said the U.S. forces were currently notifying the IFRB of these frequencies and what the U.S. side had in mind was merely a continuation of the present practice, which apparently is acceptable to the IFRB. Mr. Whang replied that the ROK Government is a member of the ITU and the ITU had adopted the resolution to which he had referred. Therefore, it was appropriate that the ROK Government do the notifying from now on.

0167

12-9

16. The U.S. side agreed to look into this matter further. Lt. Colonel Miller stated that the question of who should notify the IFRB of frequencies in use did not affect the agreement of both sides on the language of subparagraph (b) of the U.S. draft. Mr. Whang said that was correct and stated that the Korean side had agreed to subparagraph (a) and (b) of paragraph 2 of the U.S. draft.

17. Turning to subparagraph (c) of the U.S. draft, Mr. Whang pointed out that no similar paragraph appeared in the Korean draft. He said the Korean side had no objection in principle to the subparagraph but wished to hear any further comment which the U.S. side might wish to make. Lt. Colonel Miller replied that the U.S. side believed that both parties to the SOFA would have obligations under the provisions of this article. Subparagraph (c) had been inserted in the U.S. draft as a counterbalance to subparagraph (a). The latter subparagraph spells out the obligations of the United States Government and subparagraph (c) would spell out the obligations of the ROK Government. Mr. Whang stated that inasmuch as both sides were already cooperating "in the utmost spirit of coordination and cooperation", as stated in subparagraph (b), the Korean side agreed to the text of subparagraph (c) of paragraph 2 of the U.S. draft.

18. Mr. Whang stated that since paragraph 3 of the U.S. draft and paragraph 12 of the Korean draft were identical, the Korean side agreed to the text of the U.S. draft.

0168

12-10

Article "C"

19. Turning to Article "C" of the U.S. draft, Mr. Whang noted that paragraph 1 was practically identical with the first sentence of paragraph 13 of the Korean draft, the only difference being the use of "United States" in one and "Government of the United States" in the other. With the proviso that this conflict of language be resolved at a later date, he said the Korean side agreed to the text of paragraph 1 of the U.S. draft.

20. Mr. Whang suggested that discussion on the remainder of paragraph 13 of the Korean draft be deferred until a later date. He said that the views of both sides on this subject had already been fully exchanged and it was unlikely that agreement could be reached on the workihg level.

21. With regard to paragraph 14 of the Korean draft, Mr. Whang recalled that the U.S. side had stated that the phrase "supply or other materials left thereon" was unnecessary. He pointed out that this pragraph correlated with paragraph 2 of the U.S. draft. In explanation of the phrase in question, he said that there was no question about the fact that equipment brought into Korea by the U.S. armed forces is the property of the U.S. armed forces and can be removed from Korea by those forces. However, the Korean side, wished to point out that after a particular facility has been returned to the ROK Government by the U.S. armed forces, the

0169

12-11

ROK Government must not be held responsible for the protection of any U.S. owned supplies or materials temporarily left at the facility.

22. In reply, Lt. Colonel Miller stated that a Property Disposal Agreement already exists, which provides for disposition of equipment, supplies, or materials which the U.S. forces do not wish to remove from Korea. He suggested that this question be discussed elsewhere since the U.S. side did not believe it relevant to the facilities and areas articles.

23. Turning to paragraph 3 of the U.S. draft, Mr. Whang asked for an explanation of the special arrangements referred to therein. Lt. Colonel Miller explained that this paragraph provides the authority for construction outside the terms of paragraph 1 and 2. He said this authority would be utilized only in the case of a special situation in which both governments agreed that the provisions of paragraphs 1 and 2 would not apply. In response to query by Mr. Whang, he said that no such construction is contemplated at the present time. In the future, any such construction could be carried out only by mutual agreement. Mr. Whang stated that since the terms of the paragraph would apply only after mutual agreement of the two governments, the Korean side agreed to the text of paragraph 3 of the U.S. draft.

24. Mr. Whang stated that the Korean side proposed that paragraph 14 of the Korean draft be inserted between the present paragraphs 1 and 2 of the U.S. draft.

0170

12-12

Lt. Colonel Miller then stated that the U.S. side wished to suggest alternative language to paragraph 14. He tabled the following proposed paragraph:

"The Republic of Korea is not obligated to compensate the United States for improvements made in United States facilities and areas or for the buildings or structures remaining thereon upon the return of the facilities and areas".

Mr. Whang stated that the Korean side would take this proposal under consideration.

25. Before adjourning the meeting, Mr. Whang introduced Mr. Park Bong Jin, Chief of the Customs Duties Section of the Ministry of Finance, who attended the meeting on behalf of Mr. Shin Kwan Sup.

26. It was agreed to hold the next meeting on April 11 at 2 p.m.

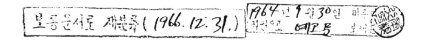

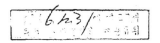

1. 주한미국 군대지위에 관한 협정
체결 교섭 회의

가. 주한미국군대 지위에관한 협정체결을위한 제1차 한미간 실무자 교섭회의는 1962. 9. 20.에 개최되었으며, 1963. 3. 29.까지 제18차에 걸친 회의가 개최되었음.

나. 18차에 걸쳐서 한미 양국간에 취급된 사항은 다음과 같음.

*(1) 서문

*(2) 용어의 정의

*(3) 출입국 관리

*(4) 합동위원회

*(5) 선박 및 항공기의 기착

*(6) 예비병의 소집 및 훈련

(7) 토지 및 시설

(8) 항공통제 및 항해보조 시설

(9) 관세 업무

(10) 공익물 및 용역

(11) 군표

(12) 기상업무

(13) 외환관리

(14) 접수국법의 존중 (* 는 한미간에 완전합의에 도달한 조항임)

(15) 군사우편

다. 되도록 조속히 실무자회의를 끝마치도록 노력할것이다.

0172

17-14

라. 기자들로부터 1962년 9월 6일자로 발표된 미주둔군지위 협정 교섭재개에 관한 한미간 공동성명서에서는 "한국에 불원간 있을 헌법개정에 감하여 주둔군지위협정의 체결은 민정이양을 기다려 이루어지게 될것으로 이해하는 바이다" 라고 선언하고 있는데 만일 민정이양 시기가 연장될경우에는 행정협정의 체결이 어떻게 될것인가라는 질문을 받을경우에는 아직 언급할 시기가 아니다 라고 답변한다.

0173

17-15

5. 제19차 회의, 4.11

0174

대 한 민 국 외 무 부 (본)

착신전보

O RD
종 별

번 호: DW-0413
일 시: 021700

수 신 인: 장관

1. 한·미간행정협정체결교섭미측대표의 한사람인 COL. SOLF 의 후임으로 COL. LAWRENCE JOSEPH FULLER가 4월중순경 서울로 향발예정임을 보고하오며 한편 COL. FULLER 는 국무성이 마련한 비공식오찬석상에서 한국법원의 독립성에관하여 관심을 표명하였음으로 이에관하여 충분한 설명을 하여주었음을 참고로 보고함. (주미정)

주미대사

0175

수신시간: 1963 APR 3 PM 3 58

검 인

외신과

한국법학원 ([illegible]) ②-1236
[illegible] 김규성
P.L.O. (신문회관 2층 212호실) Mr. Won, Mr. Lee ②-4056

주둔군지위협정 체결 교섭관계자 명단

부처	직위 및 성명		전화번호
국방부	차관		4-2022
	정책과장 대령	김원길	4-6208
	정책과 대외정책연구관 소령	이계훈	"
재무부	차관		72-4111
재무부	세관국 관세과장	조충훈	72-0011-0019
	이재국장서리	이재설	72-4973
법무부	차관		2-4055
	검찰국장	윤운영	2-8568
	검찰과장	허형구	3-6406
	검찰과 검사	이명희	"
	법무과장	주문기	2-4072
내무부	차관		2-4880
노동청	노정국장	허성준	3-5437
	직업안정국장	심강섭	3-5085
	노정과장	김대청	2-4295

U.S. Embassy 2-7111/5

Mr. Philip C. Habib (Chief U.S. Negotiator)
Councelor for Political Affairs Ext. 210

Mr. Benjamin A. Fleck
First Secretary Ext. 212
Res. Ext. 696
Compound 102

8th U.S. Army

Mr. Robert A. Kinney J-5 Office Y-2374
Resid. 72-8305

0176

기 안 용 지

자체 통제		기안처	미주과 강석재	전화번호	근거서류접수일자

	과장	국장	보좌관	차관	장관
	(서명)	(서명) 12	(서명) 12	(서명) 13.	(서명)

관계관 서명	통상국장 (서명)					
기안 년월일	1963. 4. 10	시행 년월일		보존 년한		정서기 장
분류 기호		전체 통제		종결		
경유 수신 참조	건의		발신			
제목	미주둔군 지위협정 교섭대표 추가					

미주둔군지위 협정 교섭대표의 이동과 또한 통상관계 실무자를 참석케 함이 좋다고 사료되어 아래 직원을 한국측 교섭대표로 추가코저 건의하오니 재가하여 주시기 바랍니다.

아 래

1. 소 속: 통상국 경제협력과
2. 직 위: 2등 서기관
3. 성 명: 조 광 제 끝
   — 1등서기관 윤하정

16-1

0177

승인양식 1-1-3 (1112-040-016-018) (190mm×260mm16절지)

기 안 용 지

관리 번호 137

자체 통제		기안처	미주과 이경훈	전화번호	근거서류접수일자	
	과장	국장	보좌관	차관	장관	
		10		10		
관계관 서명	조약과장 10			기획조정관		
기안 년월일	63. 4. 10.	시행 년월일		보존 년한		정서 기장
분류 기호		전체 통제		종결		
경유 수신 참조	건의		발신			
제목	제19차 주둔군지위협정 체결교섭회의에 임할 우리측 입장					

4. 11일에 개최될 제19차 주둔군지위협정 체결 한미간 교섭 회의에서는 군사우편, 토지 및 시설 그리고 관세업무 문제에관하여 토의될 예정이온바 이에관련하여 우리측 교섭실무자는 4월 9일 관계부처 실무자와 연석회합을 갖고 제19차 회의에서 취할 우리측 태도를 별첨과같이 결정하였아오니 재가하여 주시기 바랍니다.

유첨 : 제19차 주둔군 지위협정체결 교섭회의에 임할 우리측태도,

끝

1966, 12, 31 에 예고문에 의거 일반문서로 재분류

~~보통문서로 재분류 (협정체결시)~~

1964년 9월 30일 재분류 예고문

(보통문서로 재분류 (1966. 12. 31.))

16-1

승인양식 1-1-3 (1112-040-016-018) (190mm×260mm16절지)

0178

1. 군사우편

(1) 미국측이 제시한 조문초안의 2항은 우리측안에는 없는것으로 동항은 미국정부의 기타관리, 직원 및 그들의 가족도 미국 군사우편국을 사용할수 있다는요지의 규정인바 이러한 규정은 미국측 초안 1항에서 규정되어 있는 군사우편국의 사용에대한 인적범위가 주한미국군대 구성원, 군속 및 그들의 가족으로 되어있는 점에 비추어 ~~제2항은~~ 군사우편 사용에대한 예외적 규정이라고 볼수있으며 따라서 미국측 초안 2항은 조약원문에 규정할것이 아니라 합의의사록에 규정함이 적당할것이므로 동 미국측 조문초안 2항을 합의의사록에 규정도록 제시하되 이규정은 또한 관세업무 조항중 세관검사 면제 규정의 제 5(b)항과 밀접한 관련이 있으므로 관세조항의 5 (b)항이 한미간에 완전합의에 도달할것을 기다려 최종적인 결정을 하도록 한다.

2. 토지 및 시설

(1) 토지시설 사용 허여원측에관한 우리측초안 1항에서 "본협정에 규정된바에 따라" (as provided for in this Agreement)라는 구절이미국측 초안 A조 1(a)항 첫째문장에없는데 우리측 초안은 주로 보상을 요구하는 입장에서 작성된 초안임으로 이것이 필요하고 미국측에서는 보상을 지불하지 않으려는 입장에서 작성한것이기 때문에 생기는 차이임으로 우리측 초안을 받아드리도록 요구한다.

(2) 특정 토지시설에 대한 협정에관하여 미국측은 이를 A조 1 (a)항 둘째 문장에 규정하고있는데 이는 우리측 초안 규정과 실질적 차이가 없으므로 수락하기도 한다.

16-2

0179

토지시설의 정의에관한 미국측 초안 A조 1(a)항 셋째문장은 우리측 초안 2항에 해당하는것인바 동규정에 있어서 미국측 초안은 토지시설의 운영에있어서 사용되는 기존설비, 비품 및 정착물은 "그위치 여하를 막론하고" (wherever located) 토지시설안에 포함된다라고 규정하고 있는데대하여 우리측은 토지시설의 운영에 필요한 (necessary) 기존설비, 비품 및 정착물로 규정하고 있는바 우리측안을 받아주도록 미국측에 요청한후 미국측에서 양보할 기색이 없을때는 미국측안을 받아주도록 한다.

(3) 기존토지 시설사용의 법적 근거부여를 위한 규정에 관한 미국측 초안 A 조 1 (b)항과 관련하여 우리측 초안에서는 허용된 토지시설로 간주한다고 규정하고 있는데 대하여 미국측 초안에는 "상기 (a)항에 의거하여" (in accordance with sub-paragraph (a) above) 즉 완전 무상허여에 의하여 주어진 토지시설로 간주될수 있는 규정으로 되어있는데 이는 토지시설 사용허여에 관한 조항에서 우리측이 미국측에 의한 보상을 받도록하는 원측에관한 1항에서 규정한 "as provided for in this Agreement" 라는 구절을 미국측이 수락하는한 한미 양측의 어느안을 택하여도 상관없는 것임.

(4) 기존 토지시설의 측정문제에관한 우리측 초안 3항 후단에는 기존토지시설에 대하여 합동위원회를 통한 측정과 결정을 규정하고 있는데 이는 미국측 초안에는 없는것이나 현재 미군이 사용하고있는 토지시설의 재조사 및 정확한 파악을통한 소급보상의 책정을 위해 필요한것임으로 이의 삽입을 요구토록한다.

0180

16-3

(5) 토지시설 관리등의 조치에관한 미국측 초안 (B)조 (1)항 (우리측 초안 10항)에 있어서 미국측 초안은 비상시 (In an emergency ....)에는 토지 시설부근에 있어서도 보안 조치를 취할수 있도록 규정하고 있는데 이에대하여 우리측은 동문장 말미에 "within the extent that the Korean nationals and their properties are not unduly impaired "라는 구절을 삽입토록 계속 주장한다.

(6) 원상회복 문제에관한 미국측 초안 C 조 1항 (우리측 초안 13항)에 있어서 우리초안은 원측적으로 미군이 원상회복 의무를 면제하고 단지 사유재산으로서 미군의 사용으로 막심한 파손을당한 재산에 대하여 우리정부의 요청에 의하여 미국측이 원상회복 또는 이에 대신하는 보상에관하여 충분한 고려를 하도록 규정하고 있는데 미국측 초안에 있어서는 이에관한 규정을두고 있지않으니 만일 미측이사유 재산에 대한 일반 보상에관한 조항을 수락할 경우에는 광이보상을 요구하는 결과가 될것임으로 일반 보상에응하는 한 우리측은 본조항에 있어서 미국측에 양보하기로 한다.

(7) 가동설비 소유권 및 처분문제에 관한 미국측 초안 C 조 2항은 우리측초안에는 규정되어있지 않는바 이는 실제문제에 있어서 인정된 사실의 확인이라고도 볼수있으나 동항에 있어서 "will remain the property of the United States Government" 라는 구절은 토지시설 개량에대한 보상의무 면제에관한 우리측초안 14항 (이는 미국측이 제시한 추가조항안에 해당함) 중 "supply or any other materials left thereon" 이라는 구절과 모순되는것이니 "will remain the property of the United States Government and "

16-4

0181

라는 구절은 삭제하고 미국측 초안 C 조 2항을 수락하도록 한다.

(8) 토지시설 개량에대한 보상의무 면제에관한 미국측이 제시한 추가조항안 (이는 우리측초안 14항에 해당함) 은 받아주되 미국측 초안에 있어서의 " for the buildings or structures" 대신에 "for the buildings, structures, supply or any other materi-als" 라는 구절을 삽입토록 주장한다.

(9) 특수시설 건축에대한 예외규정에 관한 미국측 초안 C 조 3항의 규정은 우리측 초안에는 없으나 기타 특별한 협약은 우리정부가 인정할것임으로 받아드리도록 한다.

(10) 토지시설 유지비에관한 미국측 초안 D 조 1항에 있어서 "except those to be borne by the Republic of Korea as provided in paragraph 2" 라는 규정을하고 있는것은 미국측은 보상을 하지않겠다는 원측의 입장에서 우리측이 부담하는 것을 전제하고 규정한것이기 때문에 우리측은 이를 삭제토록 요구한다.

(11) 토지시설 보상문제에 관한 미국측 초안 D조 2항 (우리측 초안 4항)에 있어서 양측은 근본적 차이점을 시현하고있는데 우리측은 사유재산의 사용에대한 미국측의 보상지불을 요구하고 있는데 대하여 미국측은 이를 한국측이 하도록 규정하고 있는 점과 미국측 초안 D조 2항 후단은 특히 미군이 사용하는 토지시설에 관련하여 제3자 (민간인)에 의하여 야기될지도 모를 청구권으로부터 해를 받지않도록 한국정부가 책임질것을 규정함으로 보상문제에 관한 양국측이 근본적인 대립을 보이고있다. 우리측은 우리안의 수락을 요구토록 한다.

0182

16-5

3. 관세업무

(1) 공용수입품의 관세면제 대상에관한 제 2 항에 관하여

(가) 미국측이 제시한 수정안보다 원안을 수락할것을 제의하되

(나) 원안의 최종문장에 있어서 "other armed forces in Korea " 다음에 "under the Unified Command " 라는 어구를 삽입토록 계속 주장한다.

(2) 개인용 수입품의 관세면제 대상에관한 제3항에 있어서 동 3항중 3(b)항에 규정된 차량 및 부속품의 도입에 관하여 우리측은 미국군대 구성원 및 군속이 그들자신 또는 그들의 가족의 사용을위하여 도입하는 차량에 대하여 그들이 한국에 도착후 3개월내에 도입할것에 한하여 면세특권을 부여토록 미측에 제의한바 있으나 계속 이입장을 주장하되 6개월까지도 미측이 원한다면 6개월내에 도입할것에 대하여 면세특권을 부여토록 한다.

(3) 세관검사 면제대상 규정인 제5항에 있어서 우리측은 (가) 계속단체 (unit) 로서 입국하는 자에 한하여 세관검사 면제를 부여토록 주장하고 (만일 미측이 끝끝내 member 에대한 세관검사를 할수없다고 하며는 최종단계에 가서 양보토록한다) (나) 사용우편물에 대하여 세관검사를 실시토록 하고 official mail 에 대하여는 면제하도록 계속 주장하고 (다) 비세출 기관에 송부되는 군용품은 세관검사 면제대상에서 제외하자고 계속 주장하기로 한다.

(4) 한국관세 법규 위반방지를 위한 협조규정인 제9항에 있어서 9(c)항 다음에 우리측 초안 7(e)항을 삽입하여 9(d)항으로 하고 따라서 미국측안의 9(d)항은 9(e)항으로 하자고 계속 주장한다.

16-6

0183

(5) 관세업무 조항에 대한 합의의사록에 있어서,

(가) 제2항에 있어서 "free of duty" 다음에 "reasonable quantities of " 라는 구절을 삽입토록 계속 주장한다.

(나) 제3항에 있어서 "and their non-appropriated fund organizations provided for in Article ____" 을 삭제하고 대신에 "but excluding their non-appropriated fund organizations provided for in Article ____" 를 삽입토록 주장한다.

(다) 제6항에 있어서 "authorized by United States law and service regulations " 의 삭제를 계속 주장한다.

일반문서로 재분류 (1966. 12. 31.)

1966, 12, 31, 에 예고문에 의거 일반문서로 재분류됨

관리 번호 ~~134~~

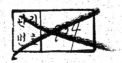

한미 행정협정에 있어서의 우리의 태도 (토지 및 시설, 형사 및 민사재판관할권)

1963. 4. 11.

1. 토지 및 시설

(1) 토지 및 시설문제에 관한 조항은 한미간에 이미 교환되어 상당히 토의되었으며 동문제에 있어서의 우리측 입장은 대개 다음과 같음.

(2) 토지 및 시설에관한 조항은 4개조문으로 되어있으며 첫째 조문은 토지 및 시설의 제공에관하여 규정하고 있으며 둘째 조문은 토지 및 시설의 관리등의 조치에관한 사항을 규정하고 있으며 셋째조항은 토지 및 시설의 원상회복 및 개량에대한 보상문제에 관련한 사항을 규정하고있으며 마지막으로 네째 조항은 토지 및 시설의 보상문제에 관하여 규정하고 있음.

(3) 첫째조항은 다시 4개항목으로 구성되어 있으며 제1항은 토지 시설사용 허여원칙에관한 규정인바 우리측은 보상을 요구하는 입장에 있으므로 미군에의한 토지시설 사용허여를 한미간 상호 방위조약 제4조에 의거하여서뿐만 아니라 토지시설에대한 보상을 규정한 주둔군지위협정의 규정에도 의거하여 부여한다 라는 입장을취하고 있음. 제1항에는 또한 토지시설 부속물 그리고 기존토지시설에대한 협정적용문제등도 규정되어있으나 이문제에 대하여는 한미간에 실질적인 차의가 없음.

0185

1

17-5

제2항은 토지시설반환 및 추가에 대한 심의에관하여 규정하고 있으며 제3항은 토지시설 반환문제를 규정하고 있으며 제4항은 토지시설의 임시사용 및 일정기간내의 사용문제를 규정하고 있으나 이러한 문제는 한미간에 실질적 차의가 없으므로 이미 합의되었으며 다만 기존토지 시설의 측정문제에 관한 한국측 제안만이 미결로 되어있음.

(4) 토지시설의 관리등의 조치문제에 관한 둘째조항은 3개항으로 구성되어 있으며 첫째항은 토지시설 관리문제를 규정하고 있는바 동항에서는 비상시의 토지시설 부근에 있어서 취할 조치에관련하여 한미간에 약간의 의견의 대립을 보이고있으나 이문제는 큰차이가 아니므로곧 해결된것이며 제2항은 항해, 항공 통신문제에 관하여 규정되어 있으며 제3항은 공공안전의 존중문제를 규정하고 있는바 제2항과 제3항은 한미 양측간에 실질적 차이가 없으므로 이미 합의에 도달하였음.

(5) 토지 및 시설의 원상회복 및 개량에대한 보상면제에 관한 셋째조항은 4개항으로 되어있으며 제1항은 원상회복 문제에 관한 규정을하고 있는바 이에있어서 우리측은 원칙적으로 미군이 토지시설에 대한 원상회복 의무를 면제하나 단지 사유재산으로서 미군의 사용으로 말미암아 막심한 피손을당한

0186

17-6

재산에대하여는 우리정부의 요청에의하여 미국측이 원상회복 또는 이에대신하는 보상에관하여 충분한 고려를 하도록 규정하고있는데 미국측은 이러한 규정을 두는것에 반대하여 아직까지 해결을 보지못하고 있음.

제2항은 토지시설의 개량에대한 대한민국측에 의한 보상의무 면제에관한 규정으로서 우리측은 토지시설의 반환시에 당해시설 및 구역에과하여진 개량 또는 그것에 남겨진 건물, 공작물, 공급품 또는 기타의 물자에대하여 한국정부는 미국측에 보상하지 않는다라고 주장하고 있는데 반하여 미국측은 공급품 또는 기타의 물자는 동 조항에서 삭제하자고 주장하여 이문제도 아직 해결되지 못하고 있음.

제3항은 가동설비 소유권 및 처분문제에 관한 규정인바 이문제도 상금 완전한 합의를 보지못하고 있음.

제4항은 특수시설 건축에대한 예외규정에 관한것인바 본항에 대하여는 한미간에 합의에 도달하였음.

(6) 끝으로 최종 조문인 넷째조항은 보상문제에 관한 규정으로서 동조항은 2개항으로서 구성되어 있으며 제1항은 토지시설 유지비에 관한 규정을하고 있으며 제2항은 토지시설 보상문제에 관하여 규정하고 있는바 한미 양국측은 이문제들에 관하여

0187

아직 합의를 보지못하고 있음. 특히 보상 지불문제에 관하여서는 우리측은 사유재산의 사용에대한 미국측의 보상 지불을 요구하고 있는데 대하여 미국측은 이를 한국측이 부담하도록 주장하고 있을뿐단 아니라 미국이 사용하는 모지시설에 관련하여 제3자 (민간인)에 의하여 야기되지도 모르는 청구권으로부터 해를받지 않도록 한국정부가 책임질것을 주장함으로서 보상문제에 관한 양국측이 근본적인 견해의 대립을 보이고있음.

2. 형사재판 관할권

(1) 형사재판 관할권 문제에관한 조항은 아직 한미 양국측에서 초안을 교환하지 않았으나 우리측이 제시하고저 하는 초안의 주요내용은 다음과 같음.

(2) 본조항은 10개 항목으로 구성되어 있으며 제1항은 한국당국과 주한미국 당국의 미국군대 구성원, 군속 및 그들의 가족에대한 일반적인 재판관할권의 원칙을 규정한것임. 즉, 미군당국은 미국 군법에 따르는 모든자에 대하여 미국법률이 부여한 모든 형사상 및 징계상의 관할권을 한국내에서 행사할 권한을 가진다는 것임에 대하여 한국측은 한국 영역내에서 행한 범죄로서 한국법률에의하여 처벌할수 있는것에 대하여 미국군대 구성원, 군속 및 그들의 가족에대한 관할권을 갖는다는 것이다.

0188

(3) 제2항은 한국측 및 미군측의 전속적 관활권을 규정하고 있는데 이는 3항에서 규정하고 있는 관활권의 경합에 관한 규정과 더부터 제1항에서 규정한 일반적 재판관환권의 원칙에 제약을 주는규정임. 제2항은 전속적 관활권을 규정하고 있으므로 본항에서 규정한 사항은 상대방의 관활권을 완전히 배제하게 되는것이다. 즉, 미군당국은 미국의 안전에대한 범죄를 포함하여 미국법률에 의하여서는 처벌할수 있으나 한국법률에 의하여서는 처벌할수 없는 범죄에 관하여 미국군법에 복종하는 자에 대하여 전속적 관활권을 행사할 권한을 인정한것이며 이에대하여 한국측은 반대로 한국의 안전에 관한 죄를 포함하는 한국법률에 의하여서만 처벌할수 있는 범죄에관하여 미국군대 구성원, 군속 및 그들의 가족에대하여 전속적 관활권을 행사한다는것임.

(4) 제3항은 제1항에서 규정한 일반적 관활권의 원칙에 의하여 양국법률이 모두 처벌할수 있는 범죄에대하여 양당상국의 관활권이 경합하는 경우에 있어서 관활권에 우선 순위를 규정한 것임. 즉, 미군당국은 미국의 재산 및 안전에대한 범죄 및 다른 미국군대 구성원, 군속 및 그들의 가족의 신체 또는 재산에대한 범죄와 공무중의 작위, 부작위로인한 범죄에관하여 미국군대 구성원 및 군속에대하여 제일차적인 관활권은 ~~갖는다는~~

17-9 0189

갖는다는 것이다. 따라서 미국군인 또는 군속의 가족들은 미국측이 전속적 관할권에 속하는 범죄를 제외하고는 미군 당국의 제1차적 관할권에서 배제되며 한국측의 제1차적 관할권에 복속하게 되는것임. 또한 본항에서는 공무중의 범죄와 관련하여 그범죄가 공무중에 행하여졌느냐에 문제는 한국의 관계지방 검사가 재정권을 갖도록 규정하고 있음.

(5) 제4항은 미군당국의 일반적 또는 전속적 관할권이 어떠한 경우에 있어서도 한국국민 또는 통상적인 거류민에 대하여서는 미치지 않는다는 원칙을 규정하고 있으며 제5항은 미국군대 구성원, 군속 및 그들의 가족을 체포 또는 인도하는데관한 양국간의 협조와 한국당국이 이들을 체포한경우의 미군당국에 대한 통고 및 이들의 관리에관한 것을 규정하고 있으며 제6항은 범죄의 수사 및 증거물의 수집, 제출에관하여 한미 양당사국이 상호 협조하여야 하며 또한 관할권이 경합하는 모든사건의 처리에관하여 상대방에 통고해줄 의무를 규정하고 있으며 제7항은 한국의 법률이 동일한 범죄에대하여 사형을 규정하지 않는한 미군당국이 한국내에서 사형을 집행함을 금지하고 있으며 또한 한국 당국은 한국 영역내에서 본규정에

0190

17-18

의하여 미군당국이 선언한 자유영의 집행에관하여 미국측의 요구가 있을때에는 이에대하여 호의적인 고려를 하여야함을 규정하고 있으며 제8항은 일사부재리의 원칙을 규정하고있으며 제9항은 한국의관할권하에 소취된 피고인의 재판 절차상의 모든권리를 규정하고 있으며 끝으로 제10항은 미군당국이 사용하는 토지 시설내에서의 경찰권을 인정한것임.

3. 민사재판 관할권

(1) 민사관할권에 관한 조항은 아직 한미 양국간에 교환되지 않았으나 우리측이 제시하고저 하는 초안의 주요내용은 다음과 같음.

(2) 본조항은 13개 항으로 구성되어 있으며 제1항은 주둔군의 민사관할권에 관한 일반적인 원칙적 규정을하고 있음. 즉, 주한미국군대의 구성원, 고용원은 원칙적으로 한국의 민사재판으로부터의 면제를 향유하지 못한다는것임. 다시말하면, 주둔군은 민사 청구권 조문에서 별도 규정에없는한 접수국의 재산관할권에 따라야 한다는 것임. 다만 공무집행중의 행위로부터 야기된 불법행위로 인하여 한국인의 생명 및 재산에 손해를 입힌경우 그 가해자 개인에 대하여서는 민사재판권을 행사할수 없는것임. 이는 미국군대의 공무집행중의 불법행위에 대하여는 주둔군에 대하여 치외법권을 인정하고 있는것임.

0191

(7-1)

(3) 제2항은 청구권에 대한 일반적 규정으로서 양국정부 소유의 재산으로서 군대가 사용하는 재산에대한 손해에 대하여서는 그것이 공무집행중에 발생하는 한 이에대한 청구권은 서로 포기한다는 것이다. 제3항은 일방국이 소유하는 다른재산이 제1 및 2항과 같은 사정하에서 즉, 공무집행중에 훼손된경우에 타방국의 보상책임을 규정하고 있으며 제4항은 제2항 및 3항에서 규정한 일방국가 정부가 소유하는 선박의 정의를 규정하고 있으며 제5항은 한국군대나 미국군대의 구성원이 공무집행중에 부상을당하거나 사망을 한경우에는 서로 청구권이 포기됨을 규정하고 있으며 제6항은 미국군대 구성원이나 고용원이 공무집행중에 작위, 부작위에 의한 불법행위로 인하여 또는 미국군대가 법적책임을지는 불법행위로 인하여 한국정부 이외의 제3자에게 손해를 가한 경우에 보상청구는 한국측이 관할할 권리가있음을 규정하고 있으며 제7항은 상기 제항과는 관계없이 작위 또는 부작위로인한 불법행위에 대한 보상청구권을 규정하고있으며 제8항은 미국군용 차량을 허가없이 사용함으로서 기인한 손해에대한 보상청구는 비공무중의 불법행위에대한 보상방법을 규정한 제7항을 준용한다는것을 규정하고 있으며

0192

17-1-2

제9항은 미국군대가 사용하는 토지 및 시설내에 한국 법률에 의하여 강제집행을 행하여야 할 사유동산 (미국군대가 사용하는 동산은 제외) 이 있을때에는 미군당국이 한국법원의 요청에 기하여 그의 재산을 압수하며 인도하여야 한다는것을 규정하고 있으며 제10항은 양당사국은 본조에서 규정한 청구권의 처리와 공정한 민사재판을 위한 증거수집에 있어 상호 협조한다는 규정이며 제11항은 미국군대의 구성원 또는 고용원의 작위 또는 부작위에 의한 불법행위가 공무중에 행하여진것인가 비공무중에 행하여진것인가 혹은 미국군대 차량이 허가없이 사용되었는가의 여부에대하여는 당사자간에 분쟁이 생긴경우 이문제를 제3항에서 규정한 중재인에게 제출하여 결정을 받도록하며 그의결정은 최종적이며 재심을 불허한다는 것이며 제12항은 미국군대가 물자나 용역의 구입 및 공급에관하여 계약에서 발생하는 분쟁은 계약 당사자간에 해결을 보지못한 경우에는 합동위원회에그 해결을 위촉할수 있음을 규정하고있으며 끝으로 제13항은 3항 및 6항의 규정이 오직 비전투 행위에 기인하는 청구권에 대하여서만 적용될수 있음을 규정한것임.

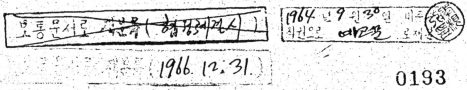

기 안 용 지

관리 번호 232

자체 통제		기안처	미주과 이경훈	전화번호	근거서류접수일자

	과장	국장	보좌관	차관	장관
		4/12		4/12	후열

관계관 서명	조약과장

기안 년월일	63. 4. 12	시행 년월일		보존 년한		정서	기장
분류 기호	외정미 722.2 441	전체 통제		종결			
경유 수신 참조	국가재건최고회의 의장 (참조: 외무국방위원장) 내각수반			발신	장관		
제목	주둔군지위협정 체결을위한 제19차 교섭회의 보고						

1963. 4. 11. 하오 2시부터 동 4시 20분 까지 외무부장관 회의실에서 개최된 제19차 주둔군지위협정 체결 교섭회의에서 토의된 내용을 별첨과같이 보고합니다.

유첨 : 제19차 교섭회의 보고서 부, 끝

~~보통문서로 재분류 (1966. 12. 31.)~~

~~파 기 하 라 (분 된 보 시)~~

1967년 9월 30일 직권으로

0194

1966. 12. 31. 에 예고문에 ...

승인양식 1—1—3 (1112—040—016—018) (190mm×260mm16절지)

외 무 부

외정미 722.2 1963. 4. 13.

수 신 국가재건최고회의 의장

참 조 외무국방위원장

제 목 주둔군지위협정 체결을위한 제19차 교섭회의 보고

1963. 4. 11. 하오 2시부터 동 4시 20분까지 외무부 장관 회의실에서 개최된 제19차 주둔군지위협정 체결 교섭회의에서 토의된 내용을 별첨과같이 보고합니다.

유첨 : 제19차 교섭회의 보고서 2부. 끝

외 무 부 장 관 김 용 식

0195

13-6

외 무 부

외정미 722.2 1963. 4. 13.

수 신 내각수반

제 목 주둔군지위협정 체결을위한 제19차 교섭회의보고

1963. 4. 11. 하오 2시부터 동 4시 20분까지 외무부 장관 회의실에서 개최된 제19차 주둔군지위협정 체결 교섭회의에서 토의된 내용을 별첨과같이 보고합니다.

유첨 : 제19차 교섭회의 보고서 1 부, 끝

외 무 부 장 관 김 용 식

0196

13-7

제 19 차

한미간 주둔군지위협정 체결 실무자회의

보 고 서

1. 시 일 : 1963. 4. 11. 하오 2시부터 4시 20분 까지

2. 장 소 : 외무부장관 회의실

3. 참석자 : 한국측 : 황호을 (외무부 정무국장)

구충회 (외무부 미주과장)

이남구 (국방부 군무과장)

주문기 (법무부 법무과장)

박봉진 (재무부 관세과장)

이경훈 (외무부 2등서기관)

강석재 (외무부 3등서기관)

김윤택 (")

미국측 : 교섭대표단 전원

4. 토의사항:

(1) 군사우편, 관세업무 그리고 토지 및 시설문제를 순차적으로 토의함.

(2) 군사우편 조항에 있어서 미국측은 미국군대 구성원, 군속 및 그들의 가족의 사용을위하여 미국이 그의 군사우편국을 한국내 미국군사 우편국간 및 이러한 군사우편국과 기타 미국 우편국 간의 우편물의 송달을위하여 미국군대가 사용하고있는 시설 및 토지내에 설치하고 운영할수 있다 라는 규정을 제1항에서 제시 하고 있는데 이규정은 우리측안에서 한국 이라는 용어대신에 대한민국 이라는 용어를 사용하고 있는것을 제외하고는 우리측 안과 꼭같으므로 우리측은 "한국"이라는 용어보다 "대한민국" 이라는 용어를 사용함이 더좋을것이라고 주장하자 미국측은 이를 받아드려 본항은 한미간에 합의에 도달하였음. 63-1-70

0197

13-2

63-1-1

외신 89-7(4)

0198

(3) 군사우편 조항중 미국측이 제시한 제2항의 규정 즉, "미국군사우편국을 통상 해외에서 그러한 특권이 부여되고있는 미국정부의 기타 관리 및 직원과 그들의 가족에 의하여 사용될수 있다" 라는 추가적 항에대하여 우리측은 이러한 규정은 군사우편사용허여에대한 예외적 규정이므로 조약원문에 규정하는것보다 합의의사록에 규정함이 타당할것이라고 제의하자 미국측은 이를 수락하였음. 그런데 이추가적 조항은 상금 미해결로 되어있은 관세업무 조항 특히 관세검사 규정과 밀접한 관련이 있으므로 우리측은 본 군사우편 조항의 추가적 항에대한 완전한 합의는 관계관세 조항이 한미간에 합의될때까지 보류하자고 제의하자 미국측은 이에 동의하였음.

(4) 관세업무 조항에 있어서 공용 수입품의 관세면제 대상에관한 미국측 초안 제2항에 관하여 우리측은 미국측이 제시한 수정안보다 원안을 수락할것을 주장하자 미국측은 이에 동의하였고 또한 미국측안에서 공용 수입품의 관세면제 대상은 미국군대로부터 병참지원을 받는 주한기타 군대의 사용을위하여 미국군대가 수입하는 물품에도 적용된다라는 규정에대하여 우리측은 "통합군사령부하의" 주한 기타 군대로하자고 주장하자 미국측은 이것도 또한 수락하였음.

(5) 차량 및 부속품의 도입에관하여 우리측은 미국군대 구성원 및 군속이 그들자신 또는 그들의 가족의 사용을위하여 도입하는 차량에대하여 그들이 한국에 도착후 6개월내에 도입할것에 한하여 면세특권을 부여토록 하자고 주장한데 대하여 미국측은 이러한 시간제한을 부칠필요가 없다고하여 이문제는 다음에 다시 토의키로 함.

(6) 세관검사 면제 대상에관한 문제는 미국측에서 상금 새로운 안이 준비되어있지 않았으므로 다음에 다시 토의키로 함. 63-1-71

0199

13-3

63-1-11

외문 89-7

0200

(7) 한국관세 법규 위반방지를 위한 협조규정인 미국측 초안 제9항에 있어서 우리측은 미국측 안에 규정되어 있지않는 규정 즉, 미군당국은 세관검사의 목적을위하여 군이 관리하는 항구나 공항에 파견된 세관관리 들에게 모든 실질적 원조를 제공한다 라는 항을 미국측 초안에 삽입할것을 제시하자 미국측은 이를 수락하여 동 제9항은 한미간에 완전합의에 도달함.

(8) 관세업무 조항에 대한 합의의사록에 있어서 (가) 우리측은 개인용 수입품의 면세범위 규정에대한 세부 규정인 2항에 있어서 미국군대 구성원, 군속 및 그들의 가족이 수입하는 물품의 관세 면제를 "적절한 수량" 으로 제한하자고 제의한데 대하여 미국측은 이러한 제한은 불필요하다고 주장하여 이문제는 다음에 다시 토의키로 함. (나) 세관검사 규정으로서 군용품에 관한 정의 규정인 3 항에 있어서 미국측은 비세출기관에게 운송된 물자도 이에 포함시키자고 주장한데 대하여 우리측은 이를 제외하자고 주장하여 이문제는 다음에 다시 토의키로 함. (다) 미국군대가 제공할 모든 지원은 미국법령에서 허여된 범위내에서 적절하고 실질적인 조치이다라고 규정한 제 6 항에 대하여 우리측은 미국 법령에서 허여된 범위라는 구절을 삭제하자고 주장하자 미국측은 이를 수락하였음.

(9) 토지 및 시설문제에 관한 토의에 있어서 토지시설 개량에대한 보상의무 면제 문제와 가동설비 소유권 및 처분문제에 관하여 우리측은 미국측 수정안에 없었던 공급품 및 기타 물자까지도 토지시설 반환시 토지시설내에 잔류된것에 대하여는 보상하지 않을것이며 이와 관련하여미국측이 주장하는 가동설비 소유권 및 처분문제에 관한 규정에서 가동설비는 미국재산으로 남을것이다 라는 구절을 삭제하자고 주장하자 미측은 이에반대하여 이문제는 다음에 다시 토의키로 함.

63-1-72 0201

13-4

63-1-11

미분 89-7

0202

(10) 토지 및 시설에대한 보상문제에 관하여는 한국측은 그의 입장이 종전과 조금도 다름없다고 설명하자 미국측은 자국측으로서도 종전의 입장과 다름이 없다고하여 이문제는 다음에 다시 토의키로 함.

5. 기타사항 :

(1) 차기회의 일자 : 1963. 4. 24. 하오 2시

(2) 차기회의 의제 : 차기회의 까지 양측수석대표간에 합의된 사항

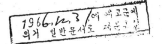

보통문서로 재분류(1966. 12. 31.)

63-1-73

1966.12.31에 예고문에 의거 일반문서로 재분류됨

0203

13-5

63-1-11(4)

明秘 89-7(4)

0204

CONFIDENTIAL

19th meeting

Military Post Offices

1. Mr. Whang opened the discussion by pointing out that there was no difference in the draft texts of paragraph 1 of the MPO Article, except for the reference in the Korean draft to the "Republic of Korea", whereas the U.S. draft referred only to "Korea". Mr. Habib stated that the U.S. side accepted the ROK wording in principle and suggested that editorial differences of this sort could be worked out at a later date.

2. Mr. Whang said the ROK side wished to place the text of paragraph 2 of the U.S. draft in an Agreed Minute rather than as paragraph 2 of the article, since this paragraph stipulated the exceptional provisions on the use of MPO's. He said the content of the paragraph was closely related to the Customs Article, which was still under discussion. He suggested, therefore, that discussion of paragraph 2 be suspended until agreement had been reached on the relevant portions of the Customs Article.Mr. Habib replied that the U.S. side ~~had tried~~ wished to limit the number of Agreed Minutes. For that reason, and for the sake of clarity, ~~this paragraph had been placed in the text~~ of the Agreement. The U.S. side believed it preferable to include it in the text rather than as an Agreed Minute. Therefore, it was hoped that the ROK side would reconsider the matter. However, if the ROK side insisted, the U.S. side would not object to making the paragraph an Agreed Minute.

3. Mr. Habib stated that the U.S. side had no fundamental objection to deferring further discussion of paragraph 2 until after the discussion of the Customs Article. ~~However, the U.S. side would prefer to obtain agreement in principle to as much of the draft agreement xxxquickly as possible, as quickly as possible.~~ He pointed out that the paragraph, by itself, had no more relevance to the customs article than did any other article of the SOFA. Mr. Whang replied that paragraph 2 was relevant to paragraphs 3 and 5 of the customs article. He said these latter paragraphs define the exemptions from customs duty and examination. He said it appeared that persons covered by paragraph 2 of the MPO article would not necessarily be entitled to the exemptions set forth in customs article. Therefore, the Korean side wished to defer

0205

CONFIDENTIAL

[redacted]

further discussion and final agreement on the substance of paragraph 2 until after the relevant paragraphs in the customs article had been agreed upon. However, the ROK side wished to reach agreement now [redacted] to convert paragraph 2 into an Agreed Minute. Mr. Habib expressed agreement.

Customs

4. Turning to the Customs Article, Mr. Whang reminded the negotiators that full agreement had previously been reached on the text of paragraph 1. He said that discussion of paragraph 2 had been held on the original U.S. draft rather than on the revised draft tabled by the U.S. side at the 7th meeting. Mr. Ford stated that the U.S. side was willing to continue to negotiate on the basis of the original U.S. draft of paragraph 2. The U.S. side wished to have the record show, however, that the U.S. side interprets this paragraph as providing exemption from customs duties and other such charges for articles imported by others than the U.S. Armed Forces, and/or forces logistically supported by the U.S. Armed forces, such as contractors, which articles are to be used exclusively by ~~the U.S. Armed~~ those Forces or are ultimately to be incorporated into articles or facilities to be used by such forces. Mr. Whang said that the Korean side would give its comments and views on Mr. Ford's remarks at the next meeting.

5. Mr. Whang noted that the ROK side had previously proposed the addition of the words "under the Unified Command" following the words "in Korea" in the final sentence of paragraph 2. Mr. Ford stated that the U.S. side agreed to this change.

6. Mr. Whang then recalled that there [redacted] was some question about the use of the word "organizations" or the [redacted] word "activities". Mr. Habib said the U.S. side had requested the ROK side to agree to [redacted] delete the word "organizations" and to insert in its place the word "activities" and further to place the phrase "including their authorized procurement agencies and their non-appropriated fund activities provided for in Article ___" in parentheses. He pointed out that these changes were desired in paragraph 2 (twice), paragraph 5 (c), and Agreed Minute #3.

7. Mr. Whang said the [redacted] side believed the word "activities" to be ambiguous

0206

and therefore preferred to stick to "organizations". He asked the U.S. side to give some examples of what was meant by "Activities". Mr. Habib replied that the word was a more practical definition of the entities to which it applied than was the word "organizations". He said that "activities" included organized sports [redacted] and officers clubs, to name but two, neither of which was an "organization" in the strict sense of the word. Nevertheless, the U.S. armed forces imported supplies for their use. Mr. Habib pointed out that the phrase "activities provided for in Article ___" obviously would include the activities covered by that article. Inasmuch as the U.S. armed forces import supplies for the use of these various activities, the use of the word "organizations" would be innacurate. Mr. Whang replied that the explanation given by the U.S. side would be of assistance to the ROK side in its [redacted] consideration of this question. He said the ROK side would [redacted] be prepared to discuss this point at a later meeting, after further [redacted] study.

8. Turning to paragraph 3, Mr. Whang reminded the negotiators that the introductory section and subparagraphs (a) and (c) had already been agreed upon. He recalled that the ROK side had proposed to introduce into subparagraph (b) a time limit of three months for the importation of vehicles and parts free from customs duties and charges. He asked if the Korean proposal was acceptable to the U.S. side. Mr. Ford replied that this point had already been thoroughly discussed and that the U.S. side had stated all of the reasons why it could not agree to a time limitation. Mr. Whang said that the ROK side realized that certain difficulties might arise from the imposition of a time limitation. However, the purpose of such a limitation was to limit the number of automobiles imported duty-free into the Republic of Korea in the future. He asked if the U.S. side had any alternative suggestions.

9. Mr. Ford reiterated the objections of the U.S. side to a time limitation. He cited the delays involved in ordering a new car from the factory, in shipment of the car from the factory to the port, the possibility of strikes, and the vagaries of the weather (during the past winter the port of Inchon harbor had completely frozen, as a

0207

부 전 지

수 신 19 . . .

제 목 (11) 조 vehicles 기존 a 계속.

요 약

Mr. Whang proposed a limitation of six months on the importation of duty free vehicles, no time limitation on the importation of spare parts as may be required for repair or replacement, and the establishment of procedures whereby a vehicle unserviceably demolished through accidents or collision while in Korea could be replaced without payment of customs duty.

관재부처

답 보 처

전화번호 주 부

발 신

양식 1—24 (1112-040-032-023) (130mm×190mm 32절지)

0208

result of which transportation schedules had been disrupted and incoming shipments delayed). He pointed out that many people might wish to wait until after their arrival in Korea to order a vehicle. He referred to the problem of obtaining replacement parts, required because of normal wear and tear or because of accident. If necessary parts could not be imported, the automobile would be useless. For many of the persons involved, he said, the personally owned automobile was their sole means of transportation to and from their places of employment. In short, he said, the possession of an automobile and the ability to maintain it in proper running condition was an important morale factor.

10. Mr. Habib added that the fundamental question at issue was not the entry of vehicles but their disposal. He said this was something which was well within the power of the ROK Government to control through its existing tax laws and regulations. This paragraph in the SOFA would not affect the ability of the ROK Government to protect itself against the indiscriminate importation of vehicles. The imposition or lack of imposition of a time limitation on importation would not affect this ability in any way.

11. Mr. Whang stated that the explanation given by the U.S. side showed the difficulties which would arise from the imposition of a time limitation. However, unlimited importation would also cause difficulties. He pointed out that Embassy personnel not included on the Diplomatic List were limited to a six-month period for duty-free importation of vehicles.

12. Mr. Habib said that there was also the problem of allowing for reasonable replacement, since many of the persons involved, particularly members of the civilian component, remained in the Republic of Korea for a relatively lengthy period. He again urged that this problem could be solved through use of the laws and regulations governing disposal of vehicles. He suggested that if the ROK side took the preceding discussion into account, it would understand why the U.S. side was reluctant to agree to a time limitation. Mr. Whang replied that the ROK side would take the explanation of the U.S. side under consideration.

13. Mr. Whang noted that the text of paragraph 4 had already been agreed upon. Mr. Habib then suggested that discussion of paragraph 5 be deferred until a later meeting, since the U.S. side was still considering certain portions. Mr. Whang pointed out that paragraph 5(b) was relevant to the second paragraph of the U.S. draft of the Military Post Offices Article. He asked whether the U.S. side was prepared to discuss paragraph 5(b). Mr. Habib replied that the U.S. side wished to reserve its position and postpone discussion of the entire paragraph.

14. Mr. Whang noted that paragraphs 6, 7, and 8 had already been agreed upon. He then recalled that the ROK side had proposed the insertion of paragraph 7(e) of the Korean draft immediately following paragraph 9(c) of the U.S. draft. Paragraph 7(e) would thus become paragraph 9(d) of the U.S. draft and the original paragraph 9(d) would become 9(e). Mr. Habib replied that the U.S. side had no objection to this change. The full text of paragraph 9 of the U.S. draft, as amended by the insertion of paragraph 7(e) of the Korean draft, was thereupon agreed upon.

15. Turning to the Agreed Minutes, Mr. Whang stated that the ROK side agreed to the text of Agreed Minute #1 of the U.S. draft. Mr. Habib pointed out that the U.S. side wished to substitute the word "activities" in place of the word "organizations", as previously pointed out with regard to paragraph 2. Mr. Whang said the ROK side would consider this proposed change on the basis of the foregoing discussion. When final agreement was reached with regard to the proposed change in paragraph 2, agreement on the wording of Agreed Minute #1 in conformity with the agreed wording for paragraph 2 would be automatic. The U.S. side agreed.

16. With regard to Agreed Minute #2, Mr. Whang recalled that the ROK side had previously suggested the insertion of the phrase "reasonable quantities of". If the U.S. side agreed to this addition, he said, complete agreement on the text of Agreed Minute #2 was possible. Mr. Ford replied that in the view of the U.S. side, this phrase would add nothing to the substance of the Minute and would have

no real meaning in this context. Mr. Habib pointed out that [redacted] the subject of the Minute was personal effects. He said there is no definition of what constitutes a [redacted] reasonable amount of personal effects. For that reason, this phrase does not appear in this context in any other Status of Forces Agreement. Mr. Ford added that one of the factors involved was the great variation in the type of quarters occupied by persons falling under this provision and [redacted] in the adequacy with which those quarters are furnished. Thus, what is a reasonable amount in one case might not be reasonable in another. Here again, Mr. Ford continued, the solution to the problem envisioned by the ROK side lay in the effective implementation of the ROK Government's disposal regulations.

17. Mr. Whang replied that the ROK side did not agree that the phrase had no meaning. He pointed out that the negotiators had already agreed on [redacted] the inclusion of this language in another paragraph of the article. He said the Korean side did not think it reasonable that one individual should be able to import 10 [redacted] television sets or 5 refrigerators, regardless of the size of his family. Mr. Habib replied that paragraph 3(c), to which Mr. Whang had alluded, deals with goods mailed through postal channels. The subject currently under discussion, however, was the personal effects of individuals; not articles ordered for initial delivery in the ROK. He reiterated that there is no definition of what constitutes a "reasonable" amount of household effects. Such a definition [redacted] could never be applied; therefore why insert it in this Minute? Mr. Whang assured the U.S. side that the Korean side did not intend to create difficulties or inconvenience. He suggested that both sides consider this question and be prepared for further discussion at a subsequent meeting. Mr. Habib agreed.

18. Turning to Agreed Minute #3, Mr. Whang said the ROK side proposed that the text be changed to read: "... including [redacted] their authorized procurement agencies, but excluding their non-appropriated fund organizations provided for in Article ___". Mr. Habib remarked that the U.S. side did not understand the desire of the Korean

0211

side to impose customs examination for goods imported for non-appropriated fund activities and not for goods imported for other purposes. He said this would be inconsistent with exemptions granted elsewhere in the customs article. He pointed out that in fact the non-appropriated fund activities are part of the U.S. armed forces and that they were referred to as a separate entity only for organizational reasons. He further pointed out that paragraph 2 of the article defined the scope of "military cargo", which includes goods imported by the U.S. armed forces and their non-appropriated fund activities. The U.S. draft of Agreed Minute #3, he continued, was consistent with that definition.

19. Mr. Whang said that Agreed Minute #3 was relevant to paragraph 5(c) of the article, on which agreement had not yet been reached. He suggested, therefore, that further discussion on Agreed Minute #3 be deferred until paragraph 5(c) had been discussed more fully. Mr. Habib agreed.

20. Mr. Habib recalled that Agreed Minutes #4 and #5 had already been agreed upon. He said the U.S. side agreed to the ROK side's previous proposal to delete from Agreed Minute #6 the phrase "authorized by United States law and service regulations." Complete agreement was then reached on the text of the U.S. draft of Agreed Minute #6, as amended.

Facilities and Areas

21. Turning to the Facilities and Areas articles, Mr. Habib recalled that at the previous meeting, the U.S. side had proposed alternate language to the text of paragraph 14 of the ROK draft. He asked if the Korean side had had a chance to consider the U.S. proposal. Mr. Whang replied that the Korean side had considered the U.S. proposal. ~~The ROK side agreed that~~ He continued that removable property brought into Korea by the U.S. armed forces remains the property of the United States and may be removed from Korea by the U.S. armed forces. However, ~~he continued,~~ the ROK side would like to ensure that no obligation is placed on the ROK Government to protect U.S.-owned

0212

[redacted]

supplies remaining on facilities which have been returned by the U.S. armed forces ~~to the~~ ROK Government. He suggested that the U.S. proposed language be revised by removing the word "or" before the word "structures", inserting commas before and after the word [redacted] "structures", and [redacted] inserting the phrase "supplies or any other materials" in front of the word "remaining". Mr. Whang said ~~suggested~~ that once ~~those supplies or materials remaining on~~ facilities were turned over to the ROK Government, ~~be moved to facilities still being used by the U.S. armed forces so that~~ no obligation would fall on the ROK Government [redacted] for ~~their~~ the protection of those supplies or materials left thereon.

22. Mr. Whang then suggested deletion from paragraph 2 of Article "C" of the U.S. draft of the phrase "will remain the property of the United States Government", taking into consideration the additional phrase "supplies or any other materials" proposed by the Korean side, and Mr. Habib replied that the U.S. side could not agreed to [redacted] the deletion of this phrase since the text of the Agreement must indicate U.S. ownership. With regard to the ROK side's proposal to amend the U.S. proposed [redacted] language (see preceding paragraph), Mr. Habib pointed out that there is in operation at the present time a [redacted] Surplus Property Disposal Agreement. Supplies and other materials which the U.S. armed forces did not wish to remove from Korea would be disposed of under the terms of that agreement or would be moved to facilities still in use by the U.S. armed forces. He said the ROK proposal would [redacted] merely delay the return of facilities to the ROK Government by the U.S. armed forces since those forces would not return a facility until all the movable supplies located thereon had been transferred to some other facility. Obviously, he continued, the supplies and materials which were not required by the U.S. armed forces would not be turned over to the ROK Government free of charge. If the supplies remained the property of the U.S. Government, the ROK Government would be under no obligation to protect them unless a special agreement to that effect were [redacted] made by the two governments. He pointed out that the ROK Government incurred no obligation to compensate the

0213

U.S. Government if such an obligation were not specifically mentioned in the SOFA. He expressed the opinion that the ROK side was creating a problem where none actually exists. Mr. ~~[illegible]~~ Whang stated that the ROK side would study the views expressed by the U.S. side and be prepared for further discussion of this question at a later date.

23. Mr. Whang pointed out that the agreement reached at the previous meeting on the text of paragraph 3 of the U.S. draft was conditional upon final agreement to the text of paragraphs 1 and ~~2.~~ of the U.S. draft and the text of paragraph 14 of the Korean draft. ~~Having proposed the deletion of the phrase "will remain the property of the United States Government" [illegible] from paragraph 2, the ROK side would give further study to the text of this paragraph.~~ Mr. Habib remarked that there was no clear relationship between the substance of paragraph 2 and that of paragraph 14 of the ROK draft.

24. Turning to article "D" of the U.S. draft, Mr. Whang stated that each side had fully discussed paragraphs 1 and 2. He said the ROK side was not prepared to discuss paragraphs 3 and 4, covering utilities and services, at that time. Mr. Habib agreed to defer discussion of utilities and services until the next meeting. Mr. Habib then expressed his confidence that, although paragraphs 1 and 2 had been thoroughly discussed with neither side changing its position, the negotiators would eventually be able to reach agreement. Mr. Whang expressed his personal opinion that since neither side had anything to add, some other method of discussing the substance of these two paragraphs would have to be found. Mr. Habib replied that although the U.S. side had nothing to add at the moment, he did not rule out the possibility of further discussion at a later date. ~~He reiterated the view of the U.S. side that the negotiators would eventually be able to reach agreement.~~

25. The closing minutes of the meeting were given over to expressions of appreciation for the splendid contribution to the negotiations which had been made by Colonel Solf, who was attending his last negotiating meeting.

26. It was agreed to hold the next meeting on April 24 at 2:00 p.m.

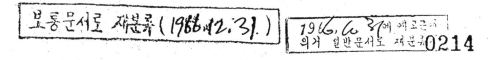

보통문서로 재분류(1966.12.31.)

1966.6.30에 예고문에 의거 일반문서로 재분류

0214

관리 933

JOINT SUMMARY RECORD OF THE 19TH SESSION
STATUS FORCES NEGOTIATIONS

April 11, 1963

I. Time and Place : 2:00 to 4:20 p.m. April 11, 1963 at the Foreign Minister's Conference Room

II. Attendants:

ROK Side:

Mr. Whang, Ho Eul	Director Bureau of Political Affairs Ministry of Foreign Affairs
Mr. Koo, Choong Whay	Chief, America Section Ministry of Foreign Affairs
Col. Lee, Nam Koo	Chief, Military Affairs Section Ministry of National Defense
Mr. Chu, Mun Ki	Chief, Legal Affairs Section Ministry of Justice
Mr. Park, Bong Jin	Chief of the Customs Section Ministry of Finance
Mr. Lee, Kyung Hoon	2nd Secretary Ministry of Foreign Affairs
Mr. Kang, Suk Jae	3rd Secretary Ministry of Foreign Affairs
Mr. Kim, Yoon Taik	3rd Secretary Ministry of Foreign Affairs

U.S. Side:

Mr. Philip C. Habib	Counselor of the Embassy for Political Affairs
Brig. Gen. J.D.Lawlor	Deputy Chief of Staff 8th Army
Mr. William J. Ford	First Secretary of the Embassy

기안	담 당	과 장	국 장	특별보좌관	차 관	장 관
양 그 재						

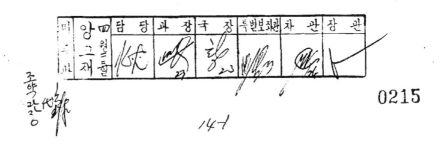

0215

147

Col. G.G. O'Connor	Deputy Chief of Staff 8th Army
Capt. R.M. Brownlie	Assistant Chief of Staff USN/K
Col. W.A. Solf	Staff Judge Advocate 8th Army
Mr. Benjamin A. Fleck (Rapporteur and Press Officer)	First Secretary of the Embassy
Mr. Robert A. Lewis	Second Secretary and Consul of the Embassy
Lt. Col. R.E. Miller	Staff Officer, JAG 8th Army
Lt. Col. W.A. Burt	J-5

Military Post Offices

1. Mr. Whang opened the discussion by pointing out that there was no difference in the draft texts of paragraph 1 of the MPO Article, except for the reference in the Korean draft to the "Republic of Korea", whereas the U.S. draft referred only to "Korea". Mr. Habib stated that the U.S. side accepted the ROK wording in principle and suggested that editorial differences of this sort could be worked out at a later date.

2. Mr. Whang said the ROK side wished to place the text of paragraph 2 of the U.S. draft in an Agreed Minute rather than as paragraph 2 of the article, since this paragraph stipulated the exceptional provisions on the use of MPO's. He said the content of the paragraph was closely related to the Customs Article, which was still under discussion. He suggested, therefore, that discussion of paragraph 2 be suspended until agreement had been reached on the relevant portions of the Customs Article.

0216

Mr. Habib replied that the U.S. side wished to limit the number of Agreed Minutes. For that reason, and for the sake of clarity, the U.S. side believed it preferable to include it in the text of the Agreement rather than as an Agreed Minute. Therefore, it was hoped that the ROK side would reconsider the matter. However, if the ROK side insisted, the U.S. side would not object to making the paragraph an Agreed Minute.

3. Mr. Habib stated that the U.S. side had no fundamental objection to deferring further discussion of paragraph 2 until after the discussion of the Customs Article. He pointed out that the paragraph, by itself, had no more relevance to the customs article than did any other article of the SOFA. Mr. Whang replied that paragraph 2 was relevant to paragraphs 3 and 5 of the customs article. He said these latter paragraphs define the exemptions from customs duty and examination. He said it appeared that persons covered by paragraph 2 of the MPO article would not necessarily be entitled to the exemptions set forth in customs article. Therefore, the Korean side wished to defer further discussion and final agreement on the substance of paragraph 2 until after the relevant paragraphs in the customs article had been agreed upon. However, the ROK side wished to reach agreement now to convert paragraph 2 into an Agreed Minute. Mr. Habib expressed agreement.

<u>Customs</u>

4. Turning to the Customs Article, Mr. Whang reminded the negotiators that full agreement had previously been

reached on the text of paragraph 1. He said that discussion of paragraph 2 had been held on the original U.S. draft rather than on the revised draft tabled by the U.S. side at the 7th meeting. Mr. Ford stated that the U.S. side was willing to continue to negotiate on the basis of the original U.S. draft of paragraph 2. The U.S. side wished to have the record show, however, that the U.S. side interprets this paragraph as providing exemption from customs duties and other such charges for articles imported by others than the U.S. Armed Forces and/or forces logistically supported by the U.S. Armed Forces, such as contractors, which articles are to be used exclusively by those Forces or are ultimately to be incorporated into articles or facilities to be used by such forces. Mr. Whang said that the Korean side would give its ~~be~~ comments and views on Mr. Ford's remarks at the next meeting.

5. Mr. Whang noted that the ROK side had previously proposed the addition of the words "under the Unified Command" following the words "in Korea" in the final sentence of paragraph 2. Mr. Ford stated that the U.S. side agreed to this change.

6. Mr. Whang then recalled that there was some question about the use of the word "organizations" or the word "activities". Mr. Habib said the U.S. side had requested the ROK side to agree to delete the word "organizations" and to insert in its place the word "activities" and further to place the phrase "including their authorized procurement agencies and their non-

appropriated fund activities provided for in Article ____" in parentheses. He pointed out that these changes were desired in paragraph 2 (twice), paragraph 5 (c), and Agreed Minute #3.

7. Mr. Whang said the ROK side believed the word "activities" to be ambiguous and therefore preferred to stick to "organizations". He asked the U.S. side to give some examples of what was meant by "activities". Mr. Habib replied that the word was a more practical definition of the entities to which it applied than was the word "organizations". He said that "activities" included organized sports and officers clubs, to name but two, neither of which was an "organization" in the strict sense of the word. Nevertheless, the U.S. armed forces imported supplies for their use. Mr. Habib pointed out that the phrase "activities provided for in Article ____" obviously would include the activities covered by that article. Inasmuch as the U.S. armed forces import supplies for the use of these various activities, the use of the word "organizations" would be innacurate. Mr. Whang replied that the explanation given by the U.S. side would be of assistance to the ROK side in its consideration of this question. He said the ROK would be prepared to discuss this point at a later meeting, after further study.

8. Turning to paragraph 3, Mr. Whang reminded the negotiators that the introductory section and subparagraphs (a) and (c) had already been agreed upon.

He recalled that the ROK side had proposed to introduce into subparagraph (b) a time limit of three months for the importation of vehicles and parts free from customs duties and charges. He asked if the Korean proposal was acceptable to the U.S. side. Mr. Ford replied that this point had already been thoroughly discussed and that the U.S. side had stated all of the reasons why it could not agree to a time limitation. Mr. Whang said that the ROK side realized that certain difficulties might arise from the imposition of a time limitation. However, the purpose of such a limitation was to limit the number of automobiles imported duty free into the Republic of Korea in the furture. He asked if the U.S. side had any alternative suggestions.

9. Mr. Ford reiterated the objections of the U.S. side to a time limitation. He cited the delays involved in ordering a new car from the factory, in shipment of the car from the factory to the port, the possibility of strikes, and the vagaries of the weather (during the past winter Inchon harbor had completely frozen, as a result of which transportation schedules had been disrupted and incoming shipments delayed). He pointed out that many people might wish to wait until after their arrival in Korea to order a vehicle. He referred to the problem of obtaining replacement parts, required because of normal wear and tear or because of accident. If necessary parts could not be imported, the automobile would be useless. For many of the persons involved, he said, the personally owned automobile was their sole

means of transportation to and from their places of employment. In short, he said, the possession of an automobile and the ability to maintain it in proper running condition was an important morale factor.

10. Mr. Habib added that the fundamental question at issue was not the entry of vehicles but their disposal. He said this was something which was well within the power of the ROK Government to control through its existing tax laws and regulations. This paragraph in the SOFA would not affect the ability of the ROK Government to protect itself against the indiscriminate importation of vehicles. The imposition or lack of imposition of a time limitation on importation would not affect this ability in any way.

11. Mr. Whang stated that the explanation given by the U.S. side showed the difficulties which would arise from the imposition of a time limitation. However, unlimited importation would also cause difficulties. He pointed out that Embassy personnel not included on the Diplomatic List were limited to a six-month period for duty-free importation of vehicles. Mr. Whang proposed a limitation of six months on the importation of duty free vehicles, no time limitation on the importation of spare parts as may be required for repair or replacement, and the establishment of procedures whereby a vehicle unserviceably demolished through accidents or collision while in Korea could be replaced without payment of customs duty.

12. Mr. Habib said that there was also the problem of allowing for reasonable replacement, since many of the persons involved, particularly members of the civilian component, remained in the Republic of Korea for a relatively lengthy period. He again urged that this problem could be solved through use of the laws and regulations governing disposal of vehicles. He suggested that if the ROK side took the preceding discussion into account, it would understand why the U.S. side was reluctant to agree to a time limitation. Mr. Whang replied that the ROK side would take the explanation of the U.S. side under consideration.

13. Mr. Whang noted that the text of paragraph 4 had already been agreed upon. Mr. Habib then suggested that discussion of paragraph 5 be deferred until a later meeting, since the U.S. side was still considering certain portions. Mr. Whang pointed out that paragraph 5(b) was relevant to the second paragraph of the U.S. draft of the Military Post Offices Article. He asked whether the U.S. side was prepared to discuss paragraph 5(b). Mr. Habib replied that the U.S. side wished to reserve its position and postpone discussion of the entire paragraph.

14. Mr. Whang noted that paragraphs 6,7, and 8 had already been agreed upon. He then recalled that the ROK side had proposed the insertion of paragraph 7(e) of the Korean draft immediately following paragraph 9(c) of the U.S. draft. Paragraph 7(e) would thus

become paragraph 9(d) of the U.S. draft and the original paragraph 9(d) would become 9(e). Mr. Habib replied that the U.S. side had no objection to this change. The full text of paragraph 9 of the U.S. draft, as amended by the insertion of paragraph 7(e) of the Korean draft, was thereupon agreed upon.

15. Turning to the Agreed Minutes, Mr. Whang stated that the ROK side agreed to the text of Agreed Minute #1 of the U.S. draft. Mr. Habib pointed out that the U.S. side wished to substitute the word "activities" in place of the word "organizations", as previously pointed out with regard to paragraph 2. Mr. Whang said the ROK side would consider this proposed change on the basis of the foregoing discussion. When final agreement was reached with regard to the proposed change in paragraph 2, agreement on the wording of Agreed Minute #1 in conformity with the agreed wording for paragraph 2 would be automatic. The U.S. side agreed.

16. With regard to Agreed Minute #2, Mr. Whang recalled that the ROK side had previously suggested the insertion of the phrase "reasonable quantities of". If the U.S. side agreed to this addition, he said, complete agreement on the text of Agreed Minute #2 was possible. Mr. Ford replied that in the view of the U.S. side, this phrase would add nothing to the sub-stance of the Minute and would have no real meaning in this context. Mr. Habib pointed out that the subject of the Minute was personal effects. He said there is

0223

14-9

no definition of what constitutes a reasonable amount of personal effects. For that reason, this phrase does not appear in this context in any other Status of Forces Agreement. Mr. Ford added that one of the factors involved was the great variation in the type of quarters occupied by persons falling under this provision and in the adequacy with which those quarters are furnished. Thus, what is a reasonable amount in one case might not be reasonable in another. Here again, Mr. Ford continued, the solution to the problem envisioned by the ROK side lay in the effective implementation of the ROK Government's disposal regulations.

17. Mr. Whang replied that the ROK side did not agree that the phrase had no meaning. He pointed out that the negotiators had already agreed on the inclusion of this language in another paragraph of the article. He said the Korean side did not think it reasonable that one individual should be able to import 10 television sets or 5 refrigerators, regardless of the size of his family. Mr. Habib replied that paragraph 3(c), to which Mr. Whang had alluded, deals with goods mailed through postal channels. The subject currently under discussion, however, was the personal effects of individuals; not articles ordered for initial delivery in the ROK. He reiterated that there is no definition of what constitutes a "reasonable" amount of household effects. Such a definition could never be applied; therefore why insert it in this Minute? Mr. Whang assured the U.S. side that the Korean side did not

0224

16-10

intend to create difficulties or inconvenience. He suggested that both sides consider this question and be prepared for further discussion at a subsequent meeting. Mr. Habib agreed.

18. Turning to Agreed Minute #3, Mr. Whang said the ROK side proposed that the text be changed to read: ".... including their authorized procurement agencies, but excluding their non-appriated fund organizations provided for in Article _____". Mr. Habib remarked that the U.S. side did not understand the desire of the Korean side to impose customs examination for goods imported for non-appropriated fund activities and not for goods imported for other purposes. He said this would be inconsistent with exemptions granted elsewhere in the customs article. He pointed out that in fact the non-appropriated fund activities are part of the U.S. armed forces and that they were referred to as a separate entity only for organizational reasons. He further pointed out that paragraph 2 of the article defined the scope of "military cargo", which includes goods imported by the U.S. armed forces and their non-appropriated fund activities. The U.S. draft of Agreed Minute #3, he continued, was consistent with that definition.

19. Mr. Whang said that Agreed Minute #3 was relevant to paragraph 5(c) of the article, on which agreement had not yet been reached. He suggested, therefore, that further discussion on Agreed Minute #3 be deferred until paragraph 5(c) had been discussed more fully. Mr. Habib agreed.

0225

14-11

20. Mr. Habib recalled that Agreed Minutes #4 and #5 had already been agreed upon. He said the U.S. side agreed to the ROK side's previous proposal to delete from Agreed Minute #6 the phrase "authorized by United States law and service regulations". Complete agreement was then reached on the text of the U.S. draft of Agreed Minute #6, as amended.

Facilities and Areas

21. Turning to the Facilities and Areas articles, Mr. Habib recalled that at the previous meeting, the U.S. side had proposed alternate language to the text of paragraph 14 of the ROK draft. He asked if the Korean side had a chance to consider the U.S. proposal. Mr. Whang replied that the Korean side had considered the U.S. proposal. He continued that removable property brought into Korea by the U.S. armed forces remains the property of the United States and may be removed from Korea by the U.S. armed forces. However the ROK side would like to ensure that no obligation is placed on the ROK Government to protect U.S. -owned supplies remaining on facilities which have been returned by the U.S. armed forces to the ROK Government. He suggested that the U.S. proposed language be revised by removing the word "or" before the word "structures", inserting commas before and after the word "structures", and inserting the phrase "supplies or any other materials" in front of the word "remaining". Mr. Whang said that

0226

12-12

once facilities were turned over to the ROK Government, no obligation would fall on the ROK Government for the protection of those supplies or materials left thereon.

22. Mr. Whang then suggested deletion from paragraph 2 of Article "C" of the U.S. draft of the phrase "will remain the property of the United States Government" and, taking into consideration the additional phrase "supplies or any other materials proposed by the Korean side. Mr. Habib replied that the U.S. side could not agreed to the deletion of this phrase since the text of the Agreement must indicate U.S. ownership. With regard to the ROK side's proposal to amend the U.S. proposed language (see prededing paragraph), Mr. Habib pointed out that there is in operation at the present time a Surplus Property Disposal Agreement. Supplies and other materials which the U.S. armed forces did not wish to remove from Korea would be disposed of under the terms of that agreement or would be moved to facilities still in use by the U.S. armed forces. He said the ROK proposal would merely delay the return of facilities to the ROK Government by the U.S. armed forces since those forces would not return a facility until all the movable supplies located thereon had been transferred to some other facility. Obviously, he continued, the supplies and materials which were not required by the U.S. armed forces would not be turned over to the ROK Government free of charge. If the supplies remained the property of the U.S. Government, the ROK Government would be under no obligation to protect them unless a

special agreement to that effect were made by the two governments. He pointed out that the ROK Government incurred no obligation to compensate the U.S. Government if such an obligation were not specifically mentioned in the SOFA. He expressed the opinion that the ROK side was creating a problem where none actually exists. Mr. Whang stated that the ROK side would study the views expressed by the U.S. side and be prepared for further discussion of this question at a later date.

23. Mr. Whang pointed out that the agreement reached at the previous meeting on the text of paragraph 3 of the U.S. draft was conditional upon final agreement to the text of paragraphs 1 and 2 of the U.S. draft and the text of paragraph 14 of the Korean draft. Mr. Habib remarked that there was no clear relationship between the substance of paragraph 2 and that of paragraph 14 of the ROK draft.

24. Turning to article "D" of the U.S. draft, Mr. Whang stated that each side had fully discussed paragraphs 1 and 2. He said the ROK side was not prepared to discuss paragraphs 3 and 4, covering utilities and services, at that time. Mr. Habib agreed to defer discussion of utilities and services until the next meeting. Mr. Habib then expressed his confidence that, although paragraphs 1 and 2 had been thoroughly disucssed with neither side changing its position, the negotiators would eventually be able to reach agreement.
Mr. Whang expressed his personal opinion that since neighter side had anything to add, some other method

0228

14-14

of discussing the substance of these two paragraphs would have to be found. Mr. Habib replied that although the U.S. side had nothing to add at the moment, he did not rule out the possibility of further discussion at a later date.

25. The closing minutes of the meeting were given over to expressions of appreciation for the splendid contribution to the negotiations which had been made by Colonel Solf, who was attending his last negotiating meeting.

26. It was agreed to hold the next meeting on April 24 at 2:00 p.m.

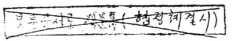

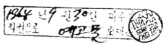

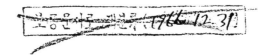

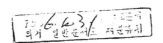

6. 제20차 회의, 4.24

0230

~~번호 936~~

기 안 용 지

자체 통제		기안처	미주과 이경훈	전화번호	근거서류접수일자
	과장	국장	보좌관	차관	장관
	4/23	23			
관계관 서명	조약과장		기획조정관		
기안 년월일	63. 4. 23	시행 년월일		보존 년한	정서기장
분류 기호		전체 통제		종결	
경유 수신 참조	건 의		발신		
제목	제20차 주둔군지위협정 체결교섭회의에 임할 우리측 입장				

4월 24일에 개최될 제20차 주둔군지위협정 체결 한미간 교섭 회의에서는 공익물 및 용역, 기상업무, 군계약자 그리고 비세출기관 문제에 관하여 토의될 예정이온바 이에관련하여 우리측 교섭실무자는 4월 22일 회합을 갖고 제20차 회의에서 취할 우리측 태도를 별첨과 같이 결정하였아오니 재가하여 주시기 바랍니다.

유첨 : 제20차 주둔군지위협정 체결 교섭 회의에임할 우리측태도.

끝

예고문에 의한 일반문서로 재분류(1966. 12. 31.)

~~보통문서로 재분류(협정체결시)~~ 1964 년 9 월 30 직권으로 예고문

1966.12.31.에 예고문에 의거 일반문서로 재분류됨

19-1

승인양식 1-1-3 (1112—040—016—018) (190mm×260mm16절지)

0231

1. 공익물 및 용역

(1) 공익물 및 용역의 사용허여를 규정한 미국측초안 3 (a) 항의 첫째문장 (이는 우리측 초안 1 항의 첫째문장에 해당함)에 있어서 "whether publicly or privately owned" 라는 구절은 "controlled or regulated by the Government of the Republic of Korea" 라는 구절과 중복된 것인바 우리측안에서 규정하고 있는바와 같이 "belonging to or controlled or regulated by the Government of the Republic of Korea " 라는 구절을 미측이 받아드리도록 주장한다.
"Political subdivisions thereof" 라는 구절에 대하여는 미국측이 기여코 삽입을 원한다면 합의의사록에 규정하자고 계속 주장한다.

(2) 공익물 및 용역의 정의에관한 미국측 초안 3 (a)항의 둘째문장 (이는 우리측 초안 1 항 둘째문장에 해당함)에 있어서 본규정은 공익물 및 용역 그자체의 정의에관한 것이니 만큼 "however produced" 라는 구절은 불필요하니 이의 삭제를 주장한다.

(3) 공익물 및 용역의 운영관리에 관한 미국측 초안 3 (a)항의 셋째문장에 대하여 우리측은 지난회의에서 이에대한 대안을 제시한바 있는데 우리측은 우리측의 대안을 받아주도록 미국측에 요구한다.

(4) 공익물 및 용역의 사용 우선순위에 관한 미국측 초안 3 (b) 항의 첫째문장 (이는 우리측 초안 1 항 셋째문장에 해당함) 에 있어서 "any other user, governmental or private" 라는 구절대신에 우리측 규정과같은 "the ministries and agencies of the Government of the Republic of Korea" 라는 용어로 대치토록 계속 주장한다.

0232

19-2

(5) 무차별 대우 보증에관한 미국측 초안 3 (b)항의 둘째문장 및 비상시의 운영에관한 미국측 초안 3 (b)항의셋째 문장은 우리측 초안에는 없는것으로 이에대하여 우리측은 이러한 규정은 우선 순위에관한 동항 첫째 문장의 규정에 비추어보아 불필요하니 삭제하자고 주장한다.

(6) 세부 규정으로서 협약의 유효성에 관한 미국측초안 4 항 (이는 우리측 초안 2(a)항에 해당함) 은 우리측안과 실질적인 큰차이는 없으나 우리측안이 보다 상세하고 광범하므로 우리측 초안을 받아드리도록 주장한다.

(7) 미국측이 제시한 합의의사록에 있어서 (가) 순위 및 사용율의 증가 변경에대한 합동위원회에서의 사전협의에 관한 미국측 초안의 1 항은 불필요한것이니 이의 삭제를 요구하고 (나) 기존협정의 유효성에 관한 2항은 우리측 초안 2 (b)항에 해당하는 것으로 우리측 초안과 실질적 큰차이는 없으나 우리측 초안이 보다며 광범하므로 우리측안을 받아드리도록 주장한후 에서 규정하고 있는 "Utilities and Claims Settlement Agreement of December 18, 1958"을 포함한다는구절은 우리초안에삽입토록 주장한다 ~~미국측이 그의안을 고집할때에는 미국측안을 수락하기로 한다.~~

2. 기상 업무

(1) 기상업무에 관한 양측 초안은 사실상 실질적 차이가 없으므로 미국측안을 수락하기로 한다.

3. 군계약자

(1) 우리측은 군계약자의 한국법에 대한 복속원칙, 계약자의 지정 및 지정철회, 계약자가 향유할 이익, 계약자가 소지할 여권, 조세의 면제,그리고 군계약자에 대한 재판관할권 등을 규정한 별첨 (1)과같은 안을 제시키로 한다.

(2) 미국측이 제시하는 안이 우리측안과 비등할때에는 우리측안을 수락하도록 주장 한다.

19-3 0233

4. <u>비세출 기관</u>

(1) 우리측은 피.엑스. 식당, 사교크럽, 극장등 미군의 비세출 기관의 설치허여, 조세면제, 이러한 기관에 의한 판매처분, 수량의 제한, 그리고 자료의 제공등을 내용으로하는 별첨 (2) 와같은 안을 제시키로 한다.

(2) 미국측이 제시하는 안이 우리측안과 비등할때에는 우리측 안을 수락하~~기로~~도록주장 한다.

12-4

0234

ARTICLE

1. Persons, including corporations organized under the laws of the United States, and their employees who are ordinarily resident in the United States and whose presence in the Republic of Korea is solely for the purpose of executing contracts with the United States for the benefit of the United States armed forces, and who are designated by the Government of the United States in accordance with the provisions of the paragraph 2 below, shall, except as provided in this Article, be subject to the laws and regulations of the Republic of Korea.

2. The designation referred to in paragraph 1 above shall be made upon consultation with the Government of the Republic of Korea and shall be restricted to cases where open competitive bidding is not practicable due to security considerations, to the technical qualifications of the contracts involved, or to the unavailability of materials or services required by United States standards, or to the limitations of United States law.

The designation shall be withdrawn by the Government of the United States.

18-5

0235

(a) upon completion of contracts with the United States for the United States armed forces;

(b) upon proof that such persons are engaged in business activities in the Republic of Korea other than those pertaining to the United States armed forces; or

(c) when such persons are engaged in practices illegal in the Republic of Korea.

3. Upon certification by the appropriate authorities of the United States as to their identity, such persons and their employees shall be accorded the following benefits of this Agreement:

(a) Entry into the Republic of Korea in accordance with the provisions of Article ____;

(b) The exemption from customs duties, and other such charges provided for in Article ____, paragraph 3 for members of the United States forces, the civilian component, and their dependents;

(c) If authorized by the Government of the United States, the right to use the services of the organizations provided for in Article ____;

(d) Those provided for in Article ____, paragraph 2, for members of the United States armed forces, the civilian component, and their dependents;

0236

19-6

(e) If authorized by the Government of the United States, the right to use military payment certificates, as provided for in Article ____;

(f) The use of postal facilities provided for in Article _____;

(g) Exemption from the laws and regulations of the Republic of Korea with respect to terms and conditions of employment.

4. Such persons and their employees shall be subject to the Korean passport and visa regulations and shall possess passports with their status described therein. Their arrival, departure and their residence while in the Republic of Korea shall be notified by the United States to the Government of the Republic of Korea.

5. Upon certification by an authorized officer of the United States armed forces, such contractors and their employees shall be exempt from taxation in the Republic of Korea on the holding, use, transfer by death, or transfer to persons or agencies entitled to tax exemption under this Agreement, of any movable property, the presence of which in the Republic of Korea is due solely to the temporary presence of these persons

in the Republic of Korea, provided that such exemption shall not apply to property held for the purpose of investment or the conduct of other business than those executing contracts as described in paragraph 1 of this Article in the Republic of Korea.

6. The persons and their employees referred to in paragraph 1 shall not be liable to pay income tax to the Government of the Republic of Korea or to any other taxing agency in the Republic of Korea on any income derived under a contract made in the United States with the Government of the United States in connection with the construction, maintenance or operation of any of the facilities or areas covered by this Agreement. The provisions of this paragraph do not exempt such persons from payment of income or corporation taxes on income derived from other engagement than those mentioned in this paragraph.

7. The Korean authorities shall have the primary right to exercise jurisdiction over the contractors and their employees referred to in paragraph 1 of this Article in relation to offences committed in the Republic of Korea and punishable by the law of the Republic of Korea. In those cases in which the Korean authorities decide not to exercise such jurisdiction they shall

notify the military authorities of the United States as soon as possible. Upon such notification the military authorities of the United States shall have the right to exercise such jurisdiction over the persons referred to as is conferred on them by the law of the United States.

17-9

0239

ARTICLE

1. (a) Navy exchanges, post exchanges, messes, commissaries, social clubs, theaters and other non-appropriated fund organizations authorized and regulated by the authorities of the United States forces may be established within the facilities and areas in use by the United States armed forces for the exclusive use of the members of such forces, the civilian component, and their dependents. Except as otherwise provided in this Agreement, such organizations shall not be subject to Korean regulations, license, fees, taxes or similar controls.

(b) When a newspaper authorized and regulated by the authorities of the United States armed forces is sold to the general public, it shall be subject to Korean regulations, license, fees, taxes or similar controls so far as such circulation is concorned.

2. No Korean tax shall be imposed on sales of merchandise and services by such organizations, except as provided in paragraph 1 (b) but purchase within the Republic of Korea of merchandise and supplies by such organizations shall be subject to Korean taxes unless otherwise agreed between the two Governments.

17-10

0240

3. Goods which are sold by such organizations shall not be disposed of in the Republic of Korea to persons not authorized to make perchases from such organizations. Administrative measures shall be taken by the authorities of the United States to prevent such disposition.

4. The quantity of goods imported by such organizations for use of the members of the United States armed forces, the civilian component, and their dependents shall be limited to the extent reasonably required for such use.

5. The organizations referred to in this Article shall provide such information to the authorities of the Republic of Korea as is required by Korean legislations.

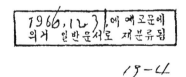

19-4

관리 번호 991

기 안 용 지

자체 통제		기안처	미주과 이 경 훈	전화번호	근거서류접수일자

	과장	국장	보좌관	차관	장관
	25	26		26	

관계관 서명	조약과장 기획조정관
기안 년월일	63. 4. 24.
시행 년월일	
보존 년한	
정서	
기장	
분류 기호	외정미 722.2
전체 통제	
종결	
경수참 유신조	국가재건최고회의 의장 (참조 : 외무국방위원장) 내각수반
발신	장 관
제목	주둔군지위협정 체결을위한 제20차 교섭회의 보고

1963. 4. 24. 하오 2시부터 동 3시 40분까지 외무부장관 회의실에서 개최된 제20차 주둔군지위협정 체결 교섭회의에서 토의된 내용을 별첨과같이 보고합니다.

유첨 : 제20차 교섭회의 보고서 부. 끝

발송 1963. 4. 26 외무부

보통문서로 재분류(1966. 12. 31.)

~~파 기 하 라(불필요시)~~

1964년 9월 30일 직권으로 예고문 로 재분류

1966. 6. 3. 의 예고문에 의거 일반문서로 재분류됨

0242

승인양식 1—1—3 (1112—040—016—018) (190mm×260mm16절지)

0044

외 무 부

외정미 722.2 1963. 4. 26.

수 신 국가재건최고회의 의장

참 조 외무국방위원장

제 목 주둔군지위협정 체결을위한 제20차 교섭회의 보고

1963. 4. 24. 하오 2시부터 동 3시 40분 까지 외무부장관 회의실에서 개최된 제20차 주둔군지위협정 체결 교섭회의에서 토의된 내용을 별첨과같이 보고합니다.

유첨 : 제20차 교섭회의 보고서 2부. 끝

63-1-86

외 무 부 장 관 김 용 식

0243

15-14

63-1-12 미원 89-6

0244

의 무 부

외정미 722.2 1963. 4. 26.

수 신 내각수반

제 목 주둔군지위협정 체결을위한 제20차 교섭회의 보고

1963. 4. 24. 하오 2시부터 동 3시 40분까지 외무부 장관 회의실에서 개최된 제20차 주둔군지위협정 체결 교섭회의에서 토의된 내용을 별첨과같이 보고합니다.

유첨 : 제20차 교섭회의 보고서 1부. 끝

63-1-87

외 무 부 장 관 김 용 식

0245

15-15

63-1-12 (14) 89-6 (14)

0246

제 20 차

한미간 주둔군지위협정 체결 실무자회의

보 고 서

1. 시 일 : 1963. 4. 24. 하오 2시부터 3시 40분까지

2. 장 소 : 외무부장관 회의실

3. 참석자 : 한국측 : 황 호 을 (외무부 정무국장)

신 관 섭 (재무부 세관국장)

윤 하 정 (외무부 1등서기관)

구 충 회 (외무부 미주과장)

이 남 구 (국방부 군무과장)

주 문 기 (법무부 법무과장)

이 경 훈 (외무부 2등서기관)

조 광 제 (")

김 윤 택 (외무부 3등서기관)

미국측 : 교섭대표단 전원 ("루이스" 대표 제외)

4. 토의사항 :

(1) 공익물 및 용역문제와 기상업무 문제를 순차적으로 토의하고 군계약자 및 비세출 기관에 관한 양측 초안을 교환함.

(2) 공익물 및 용역문제의 토의에 있어서 공익물 및 용역의 사용허여 규정에 관하여 미국측은 그의 초안에서 규정한 "공유이건 사유이건" 이라는 구절을 우리측 요청에 응하여 삭제하고 "대한민국 정부 또는 그의 정치상의 예하 기관에 의하여 관리되거나 규제되고 있는" 이라는 구절을 "대한민국 정부 또는 그의 지방행정 기관에 의하여 소유되거나 관리되거나 제약되고 있는" 이라는 용어로 대치할것을 제의하자 우리측은 원칙적으로만 이에합의하고 다음에 이문제를 다시 토의키로 함. 63-1-14

15-2 0247

63-1-12(14)

외정미 89-6(14)

0248

(3) 공익물 및 용역의 정의에관한 규정에 있어서 우리측은 이규정은 공익물 및 용역 그자체의 정의에관한 것이니만큼 "어떻게 생산 되든지" 라는 생산방식에 관한 수식어는 불필요하다고 주장한데 대하여 미국측은 해석상의 오해를 없애기위하여 이것이 필요하다고 주장하여 이문제는 다음에 다시 토의키로 함.

(4) 공익물 및용역의 운영관리에 관한 규정에 있어서 우리측은 "미국군대에 의한 군용운수, 통신, 전력 그리고 기타 공익물
운영은 미국군대의 운영에 필요한 정도와 이러한 공익물 및 용역의
및 용역의 대한민국에 의한 운영과 상치하지 않는 정도이어야 한다" 라는 수정안을 제시한바 있는데 이에대하여 미국측은 다시 이와 유사한 재수정안을 제시하여 왔기 우리측은 이 재수정안에 대하여 원칙적으로만 합의를 하고 다음에 다시 토의키로 함.

(5) 공익물 및 용역의 사용우선 순위 및 무차별대우 보증에관한 규정에 있어서 미국측은 정부이건 개인이건 간에 어떠한 사용자에게 부여하는것과 같은 대우를하여 줄것을 주장한 구절에 있어서 "정부이건 개인이건" 이라는 어구를 삭제하고 이어 계속하여 무차별대우 보증에관한 구절도 삭제하겠다고 제의하여 왔기 이문제는 다음에 다시 토의키로 함.

(6) 비상시의 조치 규정에관하여 우리측은 동규정은 불필요한 것이니 삭제하자고 주장한데 대하여 미국측은 이를 남겨 두자고 계속 주장하여 이문제는 다음에 다시 토의키로 함.

(7) 공익물 및 용역사용에 대한 사용료 지불에관한 협약의 유효성 규정에 있어서 우리측은 우리측안이 보다 상세하고 광범하므로 우리측안의 수락을 주장한데 대하여 미국측은 같은 이유로 자국측 안의 수락을 주장하여 이문제는 다음에 다시 토의키로 함.

63-1-75

15-3

0249

63-1-12　　　　　　　　　　　　　　미문 89-6

0250

(8) 공의물 및 용역조항에 대한 합의의사록에 있어서 (가) 기존 협정의 유효성에 관한 규정은 양측이 좀더 검토한후 다음에 다시 토의키로 하였고 (나) 우선 순위 변경에대한 합동위원회에서의 사전협의 규정에 관하여 미국측은 "우선순위의 여하한 변경 또는 공익물이나 용역율의 증가" 라는 구절을 "우선순위 또는 율의 여하한 변경" 이라는 용어로 대치할것을 제시하여 왔기 이문제는 검토후 다음에 다시 토의키로 함.

(9) 기상업무 조항에 있어서 미국측이 제시한 안은 우리측의 안과 실질적 차이가 없으므로 우리측은 미국측안을 수락하여 이문제는 완전합의에 도달함.

(10) 한미 양측은 군계약자 및 비세출기관에 관한 양측초안을 각각 교환함.

5. 중요합의사항 :

기상업무 문제에 관한 조항에 완전합의 함. ✓

6. 기타 사항 :

(1) 차기회의 일자 : 1963. 5. 3. 하오 2 시

(2) 차기회의 의제 : 차기회의가지 양측수석 대표간에 합의된 사항

7. 참고자료 : 미국측이 제의한 수정안 (공의물 및 용역) 및 미국측이 제의한 조문초안 (군계약자 및 비세출기관) 별첨 참조

63-1-76

보통문서로 재분류 (1966. 12. 31.)

1966, 12. 31. 에 예고문에 의거 일반문서로 재분류됨

0251

15-4

63-1-12

미문 89-6

[illegible]

0252

UTILITIES AND SERVICES

Proposed new third and fourth sentences, paragraph 3 (a)

Article "D"

The use of utilities and services as provided herein shall not prejudice the right of the United States to operate military transportation, communication, power and such other utilities and services deemed necessary for the operations of the United States armed forces. This right shall not be exercised in a manner inconsistent with the operation by the Government of the Republic of Korea of its utilities and services.

63-1-77

0253

15-5

63-1-12

비문 89-6

0254

ARTICLE _____

CONTRACTORS

1. Persons, including corporations, their employees, and the dependents of such persons, present in Korea solely for the purpose of executing contracts with the United States for the benefit of the United States armed forces or other armed forces in Korea under the Unified Command receiving logistical support from the United States armed forces, who are designated by the Government of the United States in accordance with the provisions of paragraph 2 below, shall, except as provided in this Article, be subject to the laws and regulations of Korea.

2. The designation referred to in paragraph 1 above shall be made upon consultation with the Government of Korea and shall be restricted to cases where open competitive bidding is not practicable due to security considerations, to the technical qualifications of the contractors involved, to the unavailability of materials or services required by United States standards, or to limitations of United States law. The designation shall be withdrawn by the Government of the United States:

63-1-78

15-6 0255

63-1-12

미문 89-6

0256

(a) Upon completion of contracts with the United States for the United States armed forces or other armed forces in Korea under the Unified Command receiving logistical support from the United States armed forces;

(b) Upon proof that such persons are engaged in business activities in Korea other than those pertaining to the United States armed forces or other armed forces in Korea under the Unified Command receiving logistical support from the United States armed forces;

(c) Upon proof that such persons are engaged in practices illegal in Korea.

3. Upon certification by appropriate United States authorities as to their identify, such persons shall be accorded the following benefits of this Agreement:

(a) Rights of accession and movement, as provided for in Article , paragraph 2;

(b) Entry into Korea in accordance with the provisions of Article ; 63-1-9P

(c) The exemption from customs duties, and other such charges provided for in Article ,

0257

4-7

63-1-12

미문 89-6

0258

paragraph 3, for members of the United States armed forces, the civilian component, and their dependents;

(d) If authorized by the Government of the United States, the right to use the services of the activities provided for in Article ;

(e) Those rights provided in Article , paragraph 2, for members of the United States armed forces, the civilian component, and their dependents;

(f) If authorized by the Government of the United States, the right to use military payment certificates, as provided for in Article ;

(g) The use of postal facilities provided for in Article ;

(h) Those rights accorded the United States armed forces by Article , paragraph 3, relating to utilities and services; 63-1-80

(i) Those rights provided to members of the United States armed forces the civilian component, and their dependents by Article , relating to driving permits and registration of vehicles;

0259

15-8

63-1-12

비문 89-6

0260

(j) Exemption from the laws and regulations of Korea with respect to terms and conditions of employment, and licensing and registration of businesses and corporations.

4. The arrival, departure, and place of residence in Korea of such persons shall from time to time be notified by the United States armed forces to the Korean authorities.

5. Upon certification by an authorized representative of the United States armed forces, depreciable assets, except houses, held, used or transferred by sucy persons exclusively for the execution of contracts referred to in paragraph 1 shall not be subject to taxes or similar charges of Korea.

6. Upon certification by an authorized representative of the United States armed forces, such persons shall be exempt from taxation in Korea on the holding, use, transfer by death, or transfer to persons or agencies entitled to tax exemption under this Agreement, of movable property, tangible or intangible, the presence of which in Korea is due solely to the temporary presence of these persons in Korea, provided that such exemption shall not apply to property held for the

63-1-81

0261

5-9

63-1-12

미문 89-6

0262

purpose of investment or the conduct of other business in Korea or to any intangible property registered in Korea.

7. The persons referred to in paragraph 1 shall not be liable to pay income or corporation taxes to the Government of Korea or to any other taxing agency in Korea on any income derived under a contract with the Government of the United States in connection with the construction, maintenance or operation of any of the facilities or areas covered by this Agreement. Persons in Korea in connection with the execution of such a contract with the United States shall not be liable to pay any Korean taxes to the Government of Korea or to any taxing agency in Korea on income derived from sources outside of Korea, nor shall periods during which such persons are in Korea be considered periods of residence or domicile in Korea for the purposes of Korean taxation. The provisions of this paragraph do not exempt such persons from payment of income or corporation taxes on income derived from Korean sources, other than those sources referred to in the first sentence of this paragraph, nor do they exempt such persons who claim Korean residence for United States income tax purposes from payment of Korean taxes on income.

63-1-8

15-10 0263

63-1-12

미문 89-6

0264

8.

Agreed Minute:

1. The execution of contracts with the United States in addition to those specified in paragraph 1 of Article_____ shall not exclude the persons provided for in Article_____ from the application of that Article.

63-1-83

0265

15-11

63-1-12

비문 89-6

0266

ARTICLE

Non-Appropriated Fund Activities

1. Military exchanges, messes, social clubs, theaters, newspapers and other non-appropriated fund activities authorized and regulated by the United States military authorities may be established by the United States armed forces for the use of members of such forces, the civilian component, and their dependents. Except as otherwise provided in this Agreement, such activities shall not be subject to Korean regulations, licenses, fees, taxes, or similar controls.

2. No Korean tax shall be imposed on sales of merchandise or services by such activities. Purchases within Korea of merchandise and supplies by such activities shall be subject to the Korean taxes to which other purchasers of such merchandise and supplies are subject and at rates no less favorable than those imposed on other purchasers. 63-1-84

3. Except as such disposal may be permitted by the United States and Korean authorities in accordance with mutually agreed conditions, goods which are sold by such activities shall not be disposed of in Korea

0267

63-1-12

비문 89-6

0268

to persons not authorized to make purchases from such activities.

4. The activities referred to in this Article shall, after consultation between the representatives of the two governments in the Joint Committee, provide such information to the Republic of Korea tax authorities as is required by Korean tax legislation.

5. The activities referred to in paragraph 1 may be used by other officers or personnel of the United States Government ordinarily accorded such privileges, by non-Korean persons whose presence in Korea is solely for the purpose of providing contract services financed by the United States Government, by the dependents of the foregoing, by organizations which are present in the Republic of Korea primarily for the benefit and service of the United States armed forces personnel, such as the American Red Cross and the United Service Organizations, and by the non-Korean personnel of such organizations and their dependents.

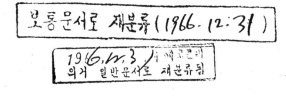

63-1-85

보통문서로 재분류(1966. 12. 31)

1966.12.31 에 예고문에 의거 일반문서로 재분류됨

0269

15-13

63-1-12

미문 89-6

0270

1. Mr. Whang opened the meeting by ~~introducing~~ First Secretary Yoon Ha-Jong, Assistant Director of the Bureau of Economic Affairs in the Foreign Ministry and Second Secretary Cho Kwang-je, of the same Bureau. Mr. Whang also announced that Mr. Kim [redacted] Yoon-Taik would act as interpreter for the Korean side at this meeting in place of Mr. Kang, who was on his honeymoon. Mr. Habib welcomed Mr. Yoon and Mr. Cho and then introduced Colonel Lawrence J. Fuller, Staff Judge Advocate of the United Nations Command, who assumed Colonel Solf's place on the U.S. negotiating team. Mr. Whang welcomed Colonel Fuller.

Utilities and Services

2. Mr. Whang began discussion of the utilities and services drafts by referring to the desire of the U.S. side to incorporate these provisions into the facilities and areas article. (He said) The Korean side~~, however,~~ believed that it would be better to have a separate utilities and services article in view of the great length of the facilities and areas article. He recalled that in the initial discussion of the scope of the SOFA, a list of 28 articles to be included in the Agreement had been drawn up and ~~but~~ utilities and services had ~~not~~ been included on the list.

3. Mr. Habib replied that the U.S. side had no objection in principle to placing utilities and services in a separate article, subject, of course, to the approval of U.S. Government authorities in Washington. He pointed out that the list of 28 subjects was not intended to be an all-inclusive list. The U.S. side had included utilities and services in its facilities and areas drafts. He suggested that the negotiators proceed on the [redacted] basis that utilities and services would [redacted] constitute a separate article, with final disposition and arrangement within the SOFA to be decided upon at a later date. Mr. Whang agreed and it was decided to proceed with discussion of the utilities and services drafts on a paragraph by paragraph basis.

4. Mr. Whang recalled that at the 14th meeting, the Korean side had proposed the deletion from the first sentence of paragraph 3(a) of the U.S. draft of the

0271

phrase "whether publicly or privately owned". Mr. Habib stated that the U.S. side had considered that proposal and was willing to agree to deletion of the phrase, provided that Korean side would agree to the insertion of "owned," following the words "which are". He said the U.S. side also wished to substitute the words "local administrative subdivisions" in place of the words "political subdivisions" in the latter portion of the same sentence. Mr. Whang said that he had no objection in principle to the insertion of "owned," but it would be necessary to obtain the concurrance of other Ministries. Therefore, the Korean side would reply to this proposal at a later date.

5. With regard to the suggested insertion of "local administrative subdivisions", Mr. Whang remarked that such subdivisions are included in the Government of the Republic of Korea and there is, therefore, no need to spell out the term. However, if the U.S. side believed it important, he suggested that this phraseology be placed in an Agreed Minute. Mr. Habib replied that the U.S. side did not want to proliferate Agreed Minutes. Indeed, both sides had consistently been trying to hold the number of Agreed Minutes to a minimum. He said it was clear that certain utilities are owned, controlled, or regulated by such subdivisions and not by the Government of the Republic of Korea. Mr. Whang stated that the Korean side would consider this point.

6. Mr. Whang then referred to the proposal of the Korean side that the phrase "however produced" be deleted from the second sentence of paragraph 3(a) of the U.S. draft. Mr. Habib stated that retention of the phrase does not complicate the sentence and is consistent with the ~~provisions of~~ language of the Utilities and Claims Settlement Agreement, which will remain in effect after the SOFA becomes effective. He said the phrase was a clarifying phrase and reminded the Korean side that the phrase had appeared in the original Korean draft as well as the U.S. draft.

7. Mr. Whang stated that the purpose of this paragraph was to enumerate the types of utilities and services to be furnished and that no reference should be made

0272

to the means of production. Mr. Habib pointed out that utilities and services can be produced by various means. The purpose of the paragraph is to clearly state that the U.S. armed forces shall have the use of certain types of utilities and services, regardless of how they are produced. He pointed out that if this clarifying phrase is not included, disagreement might later occur over the availability of utilities or services produced by certain means. The purpose of the article is to provide for the provision of utilities and services to the U.S. armed forces; it should not be subject to later misinterpretation over the furnishing of specific utilities or services. He suggested, therefore, that the Korean side reconsider its position. Pointing out that the phrase imposes no obligation on the Korean authorities ~~which the Korean side~~ [redacted] not already agreed to by the Korean side, he asked what was the specific objection of the Korean side to this phrase.

8. Mr. Whang replied that if the qualification "however produced" were included, then similar qualifications such as [redacted] "by whomsoever produced" or "whenever produced" should also be added. He said there was no need to include any of these phrases. The purpose of the presence of the U.S. forces in the Republic of Korea was to contribute to the common defense of the Free World. The Government of the [redacted] Republic of Korea, [redacted] therefore, considered the U.S. forces to be guests and treated them accordingly. The U.S. side should rest assured, he continued, that the ROK Government would furnish utilities and services to the U.S. forces.

9. Mr. Habib replied that the U.S. side was not worried about the provision of utilities and services by the ROK Government to the U.S. armed forces. He reiterated that if the phrase were not included, arguments could arise later [redacted] over the provision of utilities and services produced in certain ways. He pointed out that one of the arguments being advanced by the Korean side was the fact that the manner of production was irrelevant to the provisions of this article. He said this was precisely why the U.S. side wished to include the phrase, which made the irrelevancy clear. Otherwise, the question of means of production would be left unclear.

0273

Mr. Whang suggested that inclusion of the phrase was made unnecessary by the presence in the sentence of the phrase "shall include, but not be limited to". He also suggested that if any misunderstanding arose in the future concerning the meaning of the sentence, the negotiating record would clearly indicate the positions of the negotiators on this point. Mr. Habib suggested that both sides consider this matter further and stated that the U.S. side would study the arguments put forward by the Korean side.

10. Mr. Whang then requested an explanation of the third sentence in the U.S. draft and asked whether the U.S. side wished to comment on the alternative language suggested by the Korean side at the 14th meeting. Mr. Habib replied that the U.S. side was prepared to agree in principle to the Korean side's proposal but wished to suggest new language. The U.S. side thereupon tabled the following suggested new third and fourth sentences of paragraph 3(a):

> "The use of utilities and services as provided herein shall not prejudice the right of the United States to operate military transportation, communication, power and such other utilities and services deemed necessary for the operations of the United States armed forces. This right shall not be exercised in a manner inconsistent with the operation by the Government of the Republic of Korea of its utilities and services."

Mr. Habib stated that the use of the words "not .... inconsistent" means that the U.S. armed forces, in operating such facilities as military trains on the Korean railway system and military bus lines, will do so in conformance with existing Korean laws and regulations. Mr. Whang stated that he, personally, had no objection to the proposed language. He said the Korean side would consider the U.S. proposal and give its response at a later date.

11. Turning to subparagraph (b) of paragraph 3 of the U.S. draft, Mr. Whang stated that the most favorable rates are those which are provided to agencies of the ROK Government. Mr. Habib said that if that is the case, the Korean side should have no objection to the first sentence of the U.S. draft, with the phrase "governmental or private" deleted. He said this deletion would be

acceptable to the U.S. side and should satisfy the Korean side. He pointed out that this deletion did not constitute any substantive change in the intent of the subparagraph but was a word change designed to satisfy the desires of the Korean side. He assured the Korean side that all the U.S. side desired was the assurance that the U.S. armed forces would be charged rates no less favorable than those accorded any other user.

12. Mr. Whang replied that the term "any other user" requires specification. He said the language of the third sentence of paragraph 1 of the Korean draft was more appropriate. Mr. Habib stated that the purpose of this subparagraph was not to identify the various users of utilities and services but to establish the principle that the U.S. armed forces will not be charged discriminatory rates. He said the U.S. side was prepared to agree to deletion of the second sentence of paragraph 3(b) of the U.S. draft, to which the Korean side had previously objected, ~~but~~ only provided that the Korean side was willing to accept the ~~second~~ first sentence ~~(including the deletion mentioned in paragraph 11 above)~~ with the deletion of the phrase "governmental or private". He suggested that placing a period after the word "user" in the first sentence and deleting the second sentence would be the simplest way of meeting the desires of both sides. Mr. Whang replied that the Korean side would consider this proposal.

13. Regarding the third sentence of paragraph 3(b) of the U.S. draft, Mr. Habib recalled that the Korean side had previously indicated that it had under consideration a separate article dealing with emergency situations. He said the U.S. side was prepared to defer discussion of the third sentence until it had heard the views of the Korean side on possible alternatives. ~~Mr. Whang stated that the previous chief negotiator of the Korean side had proposed that this sentence be incorporated into a separate article.~~ He said the Korean side agreed to defer discussion of this sentence until it reached a decision on this matter.

14. Turning to the next paragraph, Mr. Whang stated that para-

0275

graph 2(a) of the Korean draft was more appropriate to the intent of the article than was paragraph 4 of the U.S. draft. Mr. Habib replied that the U.S. side could not accept paragraph 2(a) and (b) of the Korean draft because the language was too broad and indefinite. He said paragraph 4 was intended to cover one factor only, i.e. accounting arrangements, whereas paragraph 2(a) refers to arrangements regarding use of utilities and services. He pointed out that paragraph 3(a) of the U.S. draft states that "the United States armed forces shall have the use of all utilities and services". He said the U.S. side saw no reason to expand paragraph 4, which refers only to accounting procedures, into a paragraph which is indecisive and ill-defined. He added that the substance of paragraph 2(b) of the Korean draft was covered in Agreed Minute #2 of the U.S. draft.

15. ~~Mr. Whang stated that the views of the Korean side were contrary to those of the U.S. side. He~~ Mr. Whang said that paragraph 2(a) of the Korean draft provides for the concrete use of utilities and also arrangements necessary for payment for such use. Mr. Habib replied that payment is provided for in paragraph 3(b) of the U.S. draft, which states that "the use of utilities and services by the United States shall be in accordance with priorities, conditions, and rates or tariffs no less favorable than those accorded any other user". Arrangements for payment are provided for in paragraph 4 of the U.S. draft. He pointed out that the language of the entire U.S. draft article, including the Agreed Minutes, covers everything that the Korean side has in mind. Mr. Whang replied that the Korean side would give further consideration to this matter.

16. Turning to the Agreed Minutes of the U.S. draft, Mr. Whang remarked that they corresponded with paragraph 2(b) of the Korean draft. He then proposed that paragraph 2(b) be reworded as follows:

> "The existing arrangements (including the Utilities and Claims Settlement Agreement of December 18, 1958) concerning the use of such public utilities and services by the United States armed forces and the payment therefor ~~at~~ the effective date of this Agreement may ~~be regarded~~ be regarded as the arrangements referred to in the ~~foregoing~~ paragraph."

0276

17. Mr. Habib asked the Korean side to identify the "existing arrangements" referred to. He said if the Korean side was referring to the ordinary day-to-day arrangements entered into by various units, these should not be involved. So far as the U.S. side was concerned, he continued, the existing arrangements are those existing under the Utilities and Claims Settlement Agreement. The U.S. side wished to make it clear that this Agreement will continue in full force after the SOFA goes into effect. For this purpose, he stated, the language of the U.S. draft is clearer. Mr. Whang replied that "existing arrangements" include ~~those under~~ the Utilities and Claims Settlement Agreement and other arrangements entered into between the U.S. armed forces and the authorities operating various utilities and services.

18. Mr. Habib replied that day-to-day arrangements will always exist. He said any existing arrangement presumably would continue unless specificially modified or exempted from modification by the SOFA, as in the case of the Utilities and Claims Settlement Agreement. He said the U.S. draft meets the needs of the Korean side. He remarked that there was no need to change the language of paragraph 2(b) and suggested that the Korean side give further study to the U.S. draft paragraph 4 and Agreed Minute #2.

19. With regard to Agreed Minute #1, Mr. Habib recalled that at the 14th meeting, the Korean side indicated reluctance to accept a specific stipplation in the Minute,providing for changes in rates. He said the U.S. side had considered the Korean side's objections and was now prepared to agree to deletion of the phrase "increase in utility or service" from Agreed Minute #1. He pointed out that the U.S. side was trying to protect the U.S. armed forces from discriminatory or unwarranted changes in rates or priorities. Unless some other means of protection could be found, he said, the U.S. side was not prepared to drop the requirement for prior consultation.

20. Reverting to paragraph of the U.S. draft, Mr. Whang asked for an

0277

explanation of the word "accounting". Mr. Habib replied that the purpose of the paragraph was to provide for the establishment of systematic methods for keeping the accounts of payments made for the use of utilities and services by the U.S. armed forces. He stated that at the next session devoted to this article, the U.S. side would give a brief description of the current procedures.

Meteorological Services

21. Turning to the meteorological services article, Mr. Whang stated that the Korean side had studied the U.S. draft. He stated that at present, the ROK meteorological organizations were providing data to the U.S. meteorological services. He said that in view of the close cooperation which has existed between them in the past and which the Korean side is confident will continue to exist in the future, the Korean side accepted the U.S. draft of this article, provided the words "Government of Korea" were changed to read "Government of the Republic of Korea". Mr. Habib agreed to the change and complete agreement was reached on the text of this article.

Contractors & Non-Appropriated Fund Activities

22. Drafts of the articles regarding contractors and non-appropriated fund activities were then exchanged and it was agreed [to defer] discussion of them ~~be deferred~~ until the negotiators had had a chance to study them.

23. It was agreed to hold the next meeting on May 3 at 2:00 p.m.

Mr. Whang reminded the negotiators that the previous chief negotiator had said that a separate article, to be discussed later, would define steps to be taken in the event of the most serious emergency which could arise, and that even if it were not spelled out in this article, the treatment accorded to the U.S. armed forces in the event of emergency would be equivalent to that accorded to the ROK armed forces in such event.

보통문서로 재분류(1966. 12. 31.)

1966, 12, 31 에 예고문에 의거 일반문서로 재분류됨

0279

관리 992

JOINT SUMMARY RECORD OF THE 20TH SESSION
STATUS FORCES NEGOTIATIONS

April 24, 1963

I. Time and Place : 2:00 to 3:40 p.m. April 24, 1963 at the Foreign Minister's Conference Room

II. Attendants:

ROK Side:

Mr. Whang, Ho Eul	Director Bureau of Political Affairs Ministry of Foreign Affairs
Mr. Shin, Kwan Sup	Director Bureau of Costums Duty Ministry of Finance
Mr. Yoon, Ha Jong	1st Secretary Ministry of Foreign Affairs
Mr. Koo, Choong Whay	Chief, America Section Ministry of Foreign Affairs
Mr. Lee, Nam Koo	Chief, Military Affairs Section Ministry of National Defense
Mr. Chu, Mun Ki	Chief, Legal Affairs Section Ministry of Justice
Mr. Lee, Kyung Hoon	2nd Secretary Ministry of Foreign Affairs
Mr. Cho, Kwang Je	2nd Secretary Ministry of Foreign Affairs
Mr. Kim, Yoon Taik	3rd Secretary Ministry of Foreign Affairs

U.S. Side:

Mr. Philip C, Habib	Counselor of the Embassy for Political Affairs
Brig. Gen. J.D. Lawlor	Deputy Chief of Staff 8th Army
Mr. William J. Ford	First Secretary of the Embassy

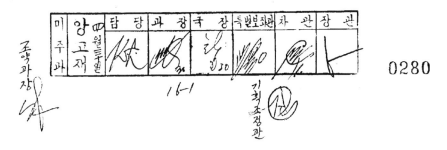

미주과	양고재	담당	과장	국장	특별보좌관	차관	장관

조약과장

16-1

기획조정관

0280

Col. G.G. O'Connor	Deputy Chief of Staff 8th Army
Capt. R.M. Brownlie	Assistant Chief of Staff USN/K
Mr. L.J. Fuller	Staff Judge Advocate United Nations Command
Mr. Benjamin A. Fleck (Rapporteur and Press Officer)	First Secretary of the Embassy
Lt. Col. R.E. Miller	Staff Officer, JAG 8th Army
Lt. Col. W.A. Burt	J-5
Kenneth Campen	Interpreter

1. Mr. Whang opened the meeting by introducing First Secretary Yoon Ha Jong, Assistant Director of the Bureau of Economic Affairs in the Foreign Ministry and Second Secretary Cho Kwang Je, of the same Bureau. Mr. Whang also announced that Mr. Kim Yoon Taik would act as interpreter for the Korean side at this meeting in place of Mr. Kang, who was on his honeymoon. Mr. Habib welcomed Mr. Yoon and Mr. Cho and then introduced Colonel Lawrence J. Fuller, Staff Judge Advocate of the United Nations Command, who assumed Colonel Solf's place on the U.S. negotiating team. Mr. Whang welcomed Colonel Fuller.

Utilities and Services

2. Mr. Whang began discussion of the utilities and services drafts by referring to the desire of the U.S. side to incorporate these provisions into the facilities and areas article. He said the Korean side believed

0281

16-2

that it would be better to have a separate utilities and services article in view of the great length of the facilities and areas article. He recalled that in the initial discussion of the scope of the SOFA, a list of 28 articles to be included in the Agreement had been drawn up and utilities and services had been included on the list.

3. Mr. Habib replied that the U.S. side had no objection in principle to placing utilities and services in a separate article, subject, of course, to the approval of U.S. Government authorities in Washington. He pointed out that the list of 28 subjects was not intended to be an all-inclusive list. The U.S. side had included utilities and services in its facilities and areas drafts. He suggested that the negotiators proceed on the basis that utilities and services would constitute a separate article, with final disposition and arrangement within the SOFA to be decided upon at a later date. Mr. Whang agreed and it was decided to proceed with discussion of the utilities and services drafts on a paragraph by paragraph basis.

4. Mr. Whang recalled that at the 14th meeting, the Korean side had proposed the deletion from the first sentence of paragraph 3(a) of the U.S. draft of the phrase "whether publicly or privately owned". Mr. Habib stated that the U.S. side had considered that proposal and was willing to agree to deletion of the phrase, provided that Korean side would agree to the insertion

0282

of "owned," following the words "which are". He said the U.S. side also wished to substitute the words "local administrative subdivisions" in place of the words "political subdivisions" in the latter portion of the same sentence. Mr. Whang said that he had no objection in principle to the insertion of "owned", but it would be necessary to obtain the concurrence of other Ministries. Therefore, the Korean side would reply to this proposal at a later date.

5. With regard to the suggested insertion of "local administrative subdivisions", Mr. Whang remarked that such subdivisions are included in the Government of the Republic of Korea and there is, therefore, no need to spell out the term. However, if the U.S. side believed it important, he suggested that this phraseology be placed in an Agreed Minute. Mr. Habib replied that the U.S. side did not want to proliferate Agreed Minutes. Indeed, both sides had consistently been trying to hold the number of Agreed Minutes to a minimum. He said it was clear that certain utilities are owned, controlled, or regulated by such subdivisions and not by the Government of the Republic of Korea. Mr. Whang stated that the Korean side would consider this point.

6. Mr. Whang then referred to the proposal of the Korean side that the phrase "however produced" be deleted from the second sentence of paragraph 3(a) of the U.S. draft. Mr. Habib stated that retention of the phrase does not complicate the sentence and is consistent with the language of the Utilities and Claims Settlement

0283

16-4

Agreement, which will remain in effect after the SOFA becomes effective. He said the phrase was a clarifying phrase and reminded the Korean side that the phrase had appeared in the original Korean draft as well as the U.S. draft.

7. Mr. Whang stated that the purpose of this paragraph was to enumerate the types of utilities and services to be furnished and that no reference should be made to the means of production. Mr. Habib pointed out that utilities and services can be produced by various means. The purpose of the paragraph is to clearly state that the U.S. armed forces shall have the use of certain types of utilities and services, regardless of how they are produced. He pointed out that if this clarifying phrase is not included, disagreement might later occur over the availability of utilities or services produced by certain means. The purpose of the article is to provide for the provision of utilities and services to the U.S. armed forces; it should not be subject to later misinterpretation over the furnishing of specific utilities or services. He suggested, therefore, that the Korean side reconsider its position. Pointing out that the phrase imposes no obligation on the Korean authorities not already agreed to by the Korean side, he asked what was the specific objection of the Korean side to this phrase.

8. Mr. Whang replied that if the qualification "however produced" were included, then similar qualifications such as "by whomsoever produced" or "whenever

produced" should also be added. He said there was no need to include any of these phrases. The purpose of the presence of the U.S. forces in the Republic of Korea was to contribute to the common defense of the Free World. The Government of the Republic of Korea, therefore, considered the U.S. forces to be guests and treated them accordingly. The U.S. side should rest assured, he continued, that the ROK Government would furnish utilities and services to the U.S. forces.

9. Mr. Habib replied that the U.S. side was not worried about the provision of utilities and services by the ROK Government to the U.S. armed forces. He reiterated that if the phrase were not included, arguments could arise later over the provision of utilities and services produced in certain ways. He pointed out that one of the arguments being advanced by the Korean side was the fact that the manner of production was irrelevant to the provisions of this article. He said this was precisely why the U.S. side wished to include the phrase, which made the irrelevancy clear. Otherwise, the question of means of production would be left unclear. Mr. Whang suggested that inclusion of the phrase was made unnecessary by the presence in the sentence of the phrase "shall include, but not be limited to". He also suggested that if any misunderstanding arose in the future concerning the meaning of the sentence, the negotiating record would clearly indicate the positions of the negotiators on this point. Mr. Habib suggested that both sides consider this matter further and stated that the U.S. side would study the arguments put forward by the Korean side.

0285

, 6-6

10. Mr. Whang then requested an explantion of the third sentence in the U.S. draft and asked whether the U.S. side wished to comment on the alternative language suggested by the Korean side at the 14th meeting. Mr. Habib replied that the U.S. side was prepared to agree in principle to the Korean side's proposal but wished to suggest new language. The U.S. side thereupon tabled the following suggested new third and fourth sentence of paragraph 3(a):

> "The use of utilities and services as provided herein shall not prejudice the right of the United States to operate military transportation, commun-cation, power and such other utilities and services deemed necessary for the operations of the United States armed forces. This right shall not be exercised in a manner inconsistent with the operation by the Government of the Republic of Korea of its utilities and services."

Mr. Habib stated that the use of the words "not .... inconsistent" means that the U.S. armed forces, in operating such facilities as military trains on the Korean railway system and military bus lines, will do so in conformance with existing Korean laws and regulations. Mr. Whang stated that he, personally, had no objection to the proposed language. He said the Korean side would consider the U,S. proposal and give its response at a later date.

11. Turning to subparagraph (b) of paragraph 3 of the U.S. draft, Mr. Whang stated that the most favor-able rates are those which are provided to agencies of the ROK Government. Mr. Habib said that if that is the case, the Korean side should have no objection to the

16-7 0286

first sentence of the U.S. draft, with the phrase "governmental or private" deleted. He said this deletion would be acceptable to the U.S. side and should satisfy the Korean side. He pointed out that this deletion did not constitute any substantive change in the intent of the subparagraph but was a word change designed to satisfy the desires of the Korean side. He assured the Korean side that all the U.S. side desired was the assurance that the U.S. armed forces would be charged rates no less favorable than those accorded any other user.

12. Mr. Whang replied that the term "any other user" requires specification. He said the language of the third sentence of paragraph 1 of the Korean draft was more appropriate. Mr. Habib stated that the purpose of this subparagraph was not to identify the various users of utilities and services but to establish the principle that the U.S. armed forces will not be charged discriminatory rates. He said the U.S. side was prepared to agree to deletion of the second sentence of paragraph 3(b) of the U.S. draft, to which the Korean side had previously objected, provided that the Korean side was willing to accept the first sentence with the deletion of the phrase "governmental or private". He suggested that placing a period after the word "user" in the first Sentence and deleting the second sentence would be the simplest way of meeting the desires of both sides. Mr. Whang replied that the Korean side would consider this proposal.

0287

/1-8

13. Regarding the third sentence of paragraph 3(b) of the U.S. draft, Mr. Habib recalled that the Korean side had previously indicated that it had under consideration a separate article dealing with emergency situations. He said the U.S. side was prepared to defer discussion of the third sentence until it had heard the views of the Korean side on possible alternatives. Mr. Whang reminded the negotiators that the previous chief negotiator had said that a separate article, to be discussed later, would define steps to be taken in the event of the most serious emergency which could arise, and that even if it were not spelled out in this article, the treatment accorded to the U.S. armed forces in the event of emergency would be equivalent to that accorded to the ROK armed forces in such event. He said the Korean side agreed to defer discussion of this sentence until it reached a decision on this matter.

14. Turning to the next paragraph, Mr. Whang stated that paragraph 2(a) of the Korean draft was more appropriate to the intent of the article than was paragraph 4 of the U,S. draft. Mr. Habib replied that the U.S. side could not accept paragraph 2(a) and (b) of the Korean draft because the language was too braod and indefinite. He said paragraph 4 was intended to cover one factor only, i.e. accounting arrangements, whereas paragraph 2(a) refers to arrangements regarding use of utilities and services. He pointed out that paragraph 3(a) of the U.S. draft states that "the United States armed forces shall have the use of all utilities and services".

16-8

0288

He said the U.S. side saw no reason to expand paragraph 4, which refers only to accounting procedures, into a paragraph which is indecisive and ill-defined. He added that the substance of paragraph 2(b) of the Korean draft was covered in Agreed Minute #2 of the U.S. draft.

15. Mr. Whang said that paragraph 2(a) of the Korean draft provides for the concrete use of utilities and also arrangements necessary for payment for such use. Mr. Habib replied that payment is provided for in paragraph 3(b) of the U.S. draft, which states that "the use of utilities and services by the United States shall be in accordance with priorities, conditions, and rates or tariffs no less favorable than those accorded any other user". Arrangements for payment are provided for in paragraph 4 of the U.S. draft. He pointed out that the language of the entire U.S. draft article, including the Agreed Minutes, covers everything that the Korean side has in mind. Mr. Whang replied that the Korean side would give further consideration to this matter.

16. Turning to the Agreed Minutes of the U.S. draft, Mr. Whang remarked that they corresponded with paragraph 2(b) of the Korean draft. He then proposed that paragraph 2(b) be reworded as follows:

> "The existing arrangements (including the utilities and Claims Settlement Agreement of December 18, 1958) concerning the use of such public utilities and services by the United States armed forces and the payment therefor at the effective date of this Agreement may be regarded as the arrangements referred to in the foregoing paragraph ".

0289

16-10

17. Mr. Habib asked the Korean side to identify the "existing arrangements" referred to. He said if the Korean side was referring to the ordinary day-to-day arrangements entered into by various units, these should not be involved. So far as the U.S. side was concerned, he continued, the existing arrangements are those existing under the Utilities and Claims Settlement Agreement. The U.S. side wished to make it clear that this Agreement will continue in full force after the SOFA goes into effect. For this purpose, he stated, the language of the U.S. draft is clearer. Mr. Whang replied that "existing arrangements" include the Utilities and Claims Settlement Agreement and other arrangements entered into between the U.S. armed forces and the authorities operating various utilities and services.

18. Mr. Habib replied that day-to-day arrangements will always exist. He said any existing arrangement presumably would continue unless specificially modified or exempted from modification by the SOFA, as in the case of the Utilities and Claims Settlement Agreement. He said the U.S. draft meets the needs of the Korean side. He remarked that there was no need to change the language of paragraph 2(b) and suggested that the Korean side give further study to the U.S. draft paragraph 4 and Agreed Minute #2.

19. With regard to Agreed Minute #1, Mr. Habib recalled that at the 14th meeting, the Korean side indicated reluctance to accept a specific stipulation in the Minute, providing for changes in rates. He said

0290

16-11

the U.S. side had considered the Korean side's objections and was now prepared to agree to deletion of the phrase "increase in utility or service" from Agreed Minute #1. He pointed out that the U.S. side was trying to protect the U.S. armed forces from discriminatory or unwarranted changes in rates or priorities. Unless some other means of protection could be found, he said, the U.S. side was not prepared to drop the requirement for prior consultation.

20. Reverting to paragraph 4 of the U.S. draft, Mr. Whang asked for an explanation of the word "accounting". Mr. Habib replied that the purpose of the paragraph was to provide for the establishment of systematic methods for keeping the accounts of payments made for the use of utilities and services by the U.S. armed forces. He stated that at the next session devoted to this article, the U.S. side would give a brief description of the current procedures.

Meteorological Services

21. Turning to the meteorological services article, Mr. Whang stated that the Korean side had studied the U.S. draft. He stated that at present, the ROK meteorological organizations were providing data to the U.S. meteorological services. He said that in view of the close cooperation which has existed between them in the past and which the Korean side is confident will continue to exist in the future, the Korean side accepted the U.S. draft of this article, provided the words

16-12

0291

"Government of Korea" were changed to read "Government of the Republic of Korea". Mr. Habib agreed to the changed and complete agreement was reached on the text of this article.

Contractors & Non-Appropriated Fund Activities

22. Drafts of the articles regarding contractors and non-appropriated fund activities were then exchanged and it was agreed to defer discussion of them until the negotiators had a chance to study them.

23. It was agreed to hold the next meeting on May 3 at 2:00 p.m.

주한미국군대 지위에관한 협[redacted] 제1차 한미간 실무자교섭회의는 1962년 9월 20일에 개최되었으며 1963년 4월 24일까지 20차에걸친회의가 개최됨.

1. 완전합의된 조항의 주요내용

(1) 서문

미국군대가 한국에 주둔하게된 근거가 국제연합 안전보장 이사회의 결의와 한미 상호방위조약 제4조에 있다는것.

(2) 용어의 정의

미국군대 구성원, 군속 및 그들의 가족에대한 정의를 규정하고 있음.

(3) 합동위원회

합동위원회의 기능 및 구성등을 규정하고 있음.

(4) 출입국 관리

미국군대 구성원, 군속 및 그들의 가족에대한 한국 영역의 출입에 있어서 소요되는 제증명서, 여권 및 사증과 등록문제 등을 규정하고 있음.

(5) 선박 및 항공기의 기착

미국소유 또는 미국의 관리하에 운영되는 외국선박 및 항공기의 한국항구 및 공항 출입에관한 사항을 규정하고 있음.

(6) 예비병의 소집 및 훈련

미국은 대한민국에 현존하는 해당 미국시민을 한국에서 미국의 예비군대에 소집하고 훈련시킬수 있다는 규정을 하고있음.

(7) 기상업무

기상업무에 관련된 제반자료의 제공에관한 규정을 하고있음.

2. 부분적으로 합의된 조항의 주요 문제점

(1) 토지 및 시설

우리측은 미군이 사용하고 있는 사유재산에 대하여 미군측이 보상을 지불할것을 요구하고 있는데 대하여 미국측은 이를 한국정부가 책임질것을 주장하고 있음.

2

17-2

0293

(2) 항공통제 및 항해보조 시설

보조시설 설치여부 문제에 대하여 쌍방간에 약간의 견해차이고 있을뿐임.

(3) 관세업무

우리측은 비세출 기관이 도입하는 물자에 대하여는 세관검사를 하자는데 대하여 미국측은 이를 거부하는 등 주로 세관검사에 관한 규정에 있어서 쌍방간의 견해에 차이가 계속되고 있음.

(4) 군표

인가되지 않은자의 군표 사용에 대하여 재정적인 의무 부담문제에 관하여 한미간에 견해의 차이를 보이고있음.

(5) 군사 우편

미국군대 구성원, 군속 및 그들의가족 이외의 미국정부 관리 및 직원의 군표사용 문제는 세관검사 조항과 관련이 있으므로 이들 미국정부 관리 및 직원의 군표사용문제에 대하여는 관세조항이 합의될때까지 토의를 보류하고 있음.

(6) 화폐 통제

미국군사 은행 시설에게 적용될 환율에 관한 용어 문제에 있어서 쌍방간에 아직도 다소간의 견해 차이를 보이고 있음.

(7) 접수국법의 존중

미국군대 구성원, 군속 및 그들의 가족 이외에 군계약자로 한국법을 존중할 의무가 있다는 점에 있어서 군계약자에 관한 조항이 합의될때까지 보류되고 있음.

1723 0294

3. 주요난점 및 전망

(1) 토지 및 시설

현재까지 토의된 조항중에서 가장 큰난점은 토지시설 조항에 있어서의 보상문제인바 우리측은 양국간의 우호관계 증진을 고려해서 미국군대가 사용중인 토지 및 시설중 사유재산에 대하여는 미국측이 보상해줄것을 요구하고 있는데 대하여 미국측은 이를 한국측이 부담하도록 주장하고 있을뿐만 아니라 미국이 사용하는 토지시설에 관련하여 제3자 (민간인)에 의하여 야기된지도 모르는 청구권으로부터 해를 받지않도록 한국정부가 책임질것을 주장하므로서 보상문제에 관한 양국측이 근본적인 견해의 대립을 보이고 있음.

(2) 형사 및 민사재판 관할권

아직 취급되지 않은 문제로서 큰난점으로 생각되는 조항은 형사 및 민사재판권에 관한 문제로 사료되는바 특히 형사재판 관할권 문제에 있어서는 미국 군인이 한국 법정에서 재판을 받게될 경우 한국법원에서의 재판이 미국의 수준과 비등하여야 할것이다 라고 미국측이 그의 종전의 주장을 되풀이할것으로 예상되어 이문제는 행정협정 교섭회담 최종단계까지 토의될 것으로 보임.

(3) 전망

되도록 조속히 실무자회의를 끝마치도록 노력할것임. 그런데 이에관련하여 1962년 9월 6일자로 발표된 미주둔군 지위협정 교섭재개에관한 한미간 공동성명서에서는 "한국에 불원간 있을 헌법개정에 감하여 주둔군지위협정의 체결은 민정 이양을 기다려 이루어지게 될것으로 이해하는바이다" 라고 선언한 점을 참고로 첨기함.

0295

(1966. 12. 31.)

17-4

1966.12.31. 에 예고문에 의거 일반문서로 재분류됨.

한미 행정협정에 있어서의 우리의 태도

(토지 및 시설, 형사 및 민사재판관활권)

외 무 부 정 무 국

17-5

0296

외교문서 비밀해제: 주한미군지위협정(SOFA) 5
주한미군지위협정(SOFA) 서명 및 발효 5

초판인쇄 2024년 03월 15일
초판발행 2024년 03월 15일

지은이 한국학술정보(주)
펴낸이 채종준
펴낸곳 한국학술정보(주)
주 소 경기도 파주시 회동길 230(문발동)
전 화 031-908-3181(대표)
팩 스 031-908-3189
홈페이지 http://ebook.kstudy.com
E-mail 출판사업부 publish@kstudy.com
등 록 제일산-115호(2000. 6. 19)

ISBN 979-11-7217-016-5 94340
979-11-7217-011-0 94340 (set)